# LEGAL FRONTIERS IN EDUCATION: COMPLEX LAW ISSUES FOR LEADERS, POLICYMAKERS AND POLICY IMPLEMENTERS

# ADVANCES IN EDUCATIONAL ADMINISTRATION

Series Editor: Anthony H. Normore

Recent Volumes:

Volume 15: The Management and Leadership of Educational Marketing: Research, Practice and Applications – Edited by Izhar Oplatka and Jane Hemsley-Brown

Volume 16: Transforming Learning Environments: Strategies to Shape the Next Generation – Edited by Fayneese S. Miller

Volume 17: Successful School Leadership Preparation and Development – Edited by Karen Sanzo, Steve Myran and Anthony H. Normore

Volume 18: Identifying Leaders for Urban Charter, Autonomous and Independent Schools: Above and Beyond the Standards – Edited by Kimberly B. Hughes and Sara A. M. Silva

Volume 19: Understanding the Principalship: An International Guide to Principal Preparation – Edited by Charles L. Slater and Sarah W. Nelson

Volume 20: Collective Efficacy: Interdisciplinary Perspectives on International Leadership – Edited by Anthony H. Normore and Nancy Erbe

Volume 21: Pathways to Excellence: Developing and Cultivating Leaders for the Classroom and Beyond – Edited by Antonia Issa Lahera, Kamal Hamdan, and Anthony H. Normore

Volume 22: Leading Small and Mid-Sized Urban School Districts – Edited by Ian E. Sutherland, Karen L. Sanzo and Jay Paredes Scribner

Volume 23: Living the Work: Promoting Social Justice and Equity Work in Schools around the World – Edited by Christa Boske and Azadeh F. Osanloo

ADVANCES IN EDUCATIONAL ADMINISTRATION
VOLUME 24

# LEGAL FRONTIERS IN EDUCATION: COMPLEX LAW ISSUES FOR LEADERS, POLICYMAKERS AND POLICY IMPLEMENTERS

EDITED BY

**ANTHONY H. NORMORE**
*California State University Dominguez Hills and International Academy of Public Safety, Carson – Los Angeles, CA, USA*

**PATRICIA A. L. EHRENSAL**
*The College of New Jersey, Ewing, NJ, USA*

**PATRICIA F. FIRST**
*Clemson University, Clemson, SC, USA*

**MARIO S. TORRES, JR.**
*Texas A&M University, College Station, TX, USA*

Emerald

United Kingdom – North America – Japan
India – Malaysia – China

Emerald Group Publishing Limited
Howard House, Wagon Lane, Bingley BD16 1WA, UK

First edition 2015





**British Library Cataloguing in Publication Data**
A catalogue record for this book is available from the British Library

ISBN: 978-1-78560-577-2
ISSN: 1479-3660 (Series)

**Printed and bound by CPI Group (UK) Ltd, Croydon, CR0 4YY**

# CONTENTS

# LIST OF CONTRIBUTORS


| | |
|---|---|
| *Susan C. Bon* | University of South Carolina, Los Angeles, CA, USA |
| *Darius Bone* | Los Angeles Police Department, Los Angeles, CA, USA |
| *Kevin P. Brady* | University of Arkansas, Fayetteville, AR, USA |
| *Jeffrey Burke* | Texas A&M University, College Station, TX, USA; Georgetown Independent School District, Georgetown, TX, USA |
| *Kathleen Conn* | Education Law group of King, Spry, Herman, Freund & Faul, Bethlehem, PA, USA |
| *Janet R. Decker* | Indiana University, Bloomington, IN, USA |
| *Cynthia A. Dieterich* | Cleveland State University, Cleveland, OH, USA |
| *Suzanne E. Eckes* | Indiana University, Bloomington, IN, USA |
| *Patricia A. L. Ehrensal* | The College of New Jersey, Ewing Township, NJ, USA |
| *Chinasa A. Elue* | Kent State University, Kent, OH, USA |
| *Patricia F. First* | Clemson University, Clemson, SC, USA |
| *Delaney Jones* | Los Angeles Police Department, Los Angeles, CA, USA |
| *Hollie J. Mackey* | University of Oklahoma, Norman, OK, USA |
| *Caron Mellblom-Nishioka* | California State University Dominguez Hills, Carson, CA, USA |

| | |
|---|---|
| *Anthony H. Normore* | California State University Dominguez Hills, Carson, CA, USA; International Academy of Public Safety, Holly Springs, NC, USA |
| *Mark Paige* | University of Massachusetts-Dartmouth, Dartmouth, MA, USA |
| *Delia E. Racines* | University of Southern California, Los Angeles, CA, USA |
| *Nicole D. Snyder* | Esq., Latsha Davis & McKenna, P.C., Exton, PA, USA |
| *Stacy Spell* | Los Angeles Police Department, Los Angeles, CA, USA |
| *Jacqueline A. Stefkovich* | Pennsylvania State University, State College, PA, USA |
| *Lori L. Taylor* | Texas A&M University, College Station, TX, USA |
| *Mario S. Torres, Jr.* | Texas A&M University, College Station, TX, USA |
| *James Vines* | Bloomsburg University, Bloomsburg, PA, USA |

# INTRODUCTION

This book examines complex law issues in education and its implications for leaders, policy makers, and policy implementers. As professors of educational law, the four of us discussed the need for a book that focuses on laws and policies in education. It began at the 2014 annual Educational Law Association (ELA) conference in San Diego, CA, where professors, administrators, and attorneys gathered to discuss current policy making and policy implementation issues in the discipline. As a result of various presentations and a discussion with the presenters at ELA, a potential book was born. A follow-up dialogue resulted two weeks later at the 2014 annual Convention of University Council for Educational Administration (UCEA) in Chicago, IL. It was at UCEA where the four of us met as co-editors and agreed to spearhead the project. Several presenters at the ELA conference were willing to contribute to the book. A common theme that resonated with us focused on the various dynamics and complexities of law making process; how laws are negotiated into policy; how these same laws are implemented; and, the impact of these laws on education and educational leaders.

Making new laws is usually a very slow process involving a number of layers and stages where key issues are debated and negotiated before being finalized as official government policy, or before being passed as a law. Based on the Education and Training Guide (2015), the policy and law making process is described as follows:

> It is the responsibility of the legislative branch (Parliament) of government to approve policies and pass new laws to give legal effect to the policies. But this is a long and slow process during which the policy or law proposed by the ruling party is debated and negotiated with various stakeholders, such as opposition parties, the public, non-government organizations, and so forth … . It can take a few years before a proposed law or policy is implemented and before its impact is felt on the ground.
>
> A policy outlines what a government ministry hopes to achieve and the methods and principles it will use to achieve them. A policy document is not a law but it will often identify new laws needed to achieve its goals. Laws set out standards, procedures and principles that must be followed. Policy sets out the goals and planned activities of a ministry and department but it may be necessary to pass a law to enable government to put in place the necessary institutional and legal frameworks to achieve their aims …. Laws must be guided by current government policy. (para. 1–6)

It is with this in mind authors in this volume examine topics such as First Amendment, Fourth Amendment, search and seizure, immigration, cyberbullying, anti-bullying, English academic language development, English language learners, law enforcement, equity in resource allocation, homelessness, collective bargaining, and special education – to name a few. The book is organized into 14 chapters with an epilogue at the end that summarizes the current state of educational law.

In Chapter 1, James Vines examines selected state laws regarding cyberbullying. The online bullying has left school leaders in a legal dilemma as to how and when to address an incident that occurs off school grounds. The findings in recent research reveal that some state bullying laws define specific terms such as electronic communication, and intimidation, and harassment. The varying school cyberbullying laws and policies mean that leaders across the United States do not have a unified way to handle issues originating off-campus. Vines includes a critical examination of current laws in the states and a review of proposed federal legislations presently stalled in the U.S. Congress. In Chapter 2, Janet R. Decker and Suzanne E. Eckes focus on the complexities involving special education law and bullying. Recent litigation illustrates how plaintiffs have alleged violations under the Individuals with Disabilities Education Act, Section 504 of the Rehabilitation Act of 1973 and/or the Americans with Disabilities Act when students with disabilities are bullied in schools. The authors examine several illustrative recent cases and the 2014 Guidance to highlight the relevant issues for school leaders. Chapter 3 focuses on the First Amendment in public school with specific focus on cyberbullying and harassing forms of communication. Kathleen Conn reviews the jurisprudence pertaining to the First Amendment as applied to the school setting. Conn emphasizes legislative, judicial, and societal responses to cyberbullying and cyber harassment in the school setting, from the elementary level to higher education. She offers recommendations for policies and procedures for dealing with cyberbullying and cyber harassment in schools.

In Chapter 4, Chinasa A. Elue and Patricia F. First review the rights to education of immigrant children as it stands amidst confusion in the absence of meaningful immigration reform by the U.S. Congress and the puzzle of the states arbitrarily denying rights flowing from the Fifth and Fourteenth Amendments of the U.S. Constitution. Chapter 5 is presented by Caron Mellblom-Nishioka who articulates the barriers for success for multilingual language learners. She examines the literature related to language development and second language learning and the laws and mandates that drive our classroom practice. Delia Racines presents Chapter 6.

Racines examines two established legal policy research methodologies, specifically the four-step method of analysis and the quantitative method of "simple box scoring," to systematically analyze case law outcomes and identify seven litigation trends from cases over the past 40 years. Her research bridges the gap of critical knowledge needed to help educators, attorneys, and professors who prepare school leaders and teachers to meet legal requirements for ELs, each of whom are entitled by law to access mainstream curriculum. In Chapter 7, Kevin P. Brady and Cynthia A. Dieterich provide a detailed legal/policy update of the leading legal considerations and concerns involving K-12 students with autism. These authors conclude with a detailed discussion of how today's school officials can become more legally literate and better serve the legal needs of students with autism in their schools. Chapter 8 is presented by Jeffrey Burke and Mario S. Torres, Jr.. These authors examine the relationship between community educational attainment and Fourth Amendment legal principles being implemented in public schools. Their findings suggest community educational attainment has little to no predictive influence on aspects related to student searches examined in the study, which include the intrusiveness level of the search and the number of searches occurring during a single search event.

In Chapter 9 Hollie J. Mackey explores the foundations of the inclusion of native languages into current federal policy and argues that the placement might be better suited as stand-alone legislation in order to more effectively promote community development and self-determination for Native American peoples. Susan C. Bon and Nicole D. Snyder discuss the McKinney-Vento Act in Chapter 10 and how the Act relates to educational access and opportunity. These authors provide analysis regarding the legal rights of homeless youth, including an overview of significant cases and federal policy updates, and concludes with several recommendations for school leaders to establish clear guidelines and implement procedures to address the educational needs of homeless students. In Chapter 11, the authors Anthony H. Normore, Darius Bone, Delaney Jones, and Stacy Spell provide a historical context of School Resource Officers' programs in the United States and highlight concerns and challenges of school communities. These authors briefly present the case of SRO in Los Angeles, and its implications for educational leadership.

In Chapter 12, Patricia A. L. Ehrensal explores the underlying values in schools that rejected the speech of Fraser while accepting the speech act of cheerleaders' dance routines. She examines how the interpretation of these speech acts by school officials contributes to gender reproduction, with all the inequalities imposed. Chapter 13 focuses on allocation of educational resources. Author Lori L. Taylor compares and contrasts the various strategies states use to make geographic cost adjustments to their school funding formula, describes the implications of geographic adjustment for interstate and intrastate measures of school finance equity (and corresponding litigation), and discusses the impact that such adjustments could have on the distribution of federal aid for economically disadvantaged students under Title 1 of the Elementary and Secondary Education Act. Chapter 14 is the final chapter. Author Mark Paige discusses the historical and legal framework of collective bargaining in public education. He identifies significant changes to collective bargaining statutes that have occurred or have been proposed, and suggests recommendations to policymakers and leaders that will assist them in understanding both the potential and limits of collective bargaining in improving schools. Concluding the book is an epilogue by Jacqueline Stefkovich. Stefkovich provides an in-depth summary of the book's content, its significance, how the fields of law and education work together, and why school leaders must have a greater understanding of the law.

Anthony H. Normore
Patricia A. L. Ehrensal
Patricia F. First
Mario S. Torres, Jr.
*Editors*

## REFERENCE

Education and Training Guide. (2015). *Policy and law making process*. Retrieved from http://www.etu.org.za/toolbox/docs/govern/policy.html

# CHAPTER 1

# INCONSISTENCIES ACROSS THE STATES: AN EXAMINATION OF ANTI-BULLYING LAWS

James Vines

## ABSTRACT

*The purpose of this chapter is to examine selected state laws regarding cyberbullying. The advances in technology have allowed bullying to take an online form, where bullies can remain anonymous and access their targets 24 hours a day. The online bullying has left school leaders in a legal dilemma as to how and when to address an incident that occurs off school grounds. The laws which guide school leaders are found at the state level. The major inconsistencies between state laws are illustrated in this chapter. The findings in recent research reveal that some state bullying laws define specific terms such as electronic communication, and intimidation, and harassment. Some state laws provide a detailed protocol for how teachers and administrators should report and handle online bullying that has an impact on the school environment. However, some states leave developing a protocol up to individual school districts. The varying school cyberbullying laws and policies mean that leaders across the United States do not have a unified way to handle issues originating off-campus. However, school leaders should have a comprehensive policy which helps*

**Legal Frontiers in Education: Complex Law Issues for Leaders, Policymakers and Policy Implementers**
**Advances in Educational Administration, Volume 24, 1–18**

**ISSN: 1479-3660/doi:10.1108/S1479-366020150000024027**

*to address cyberbullying issues. This chapter includes a critical examination of current laws in the states and a review of proposed federal statutes presently stalled in the U.S. Congress.*

## INTRODUCTION

The purpose of this chapter is to examine selected state laws regarding cyberbullying. The advances in technology have allowed bullying to take an online form, where bullies can remain anonymous and access their targets 24 hours a day. The online bullying has left school leaders in a legal dilemma as to how and when to address an incident that occurs off school grounds. The laws, which guide school leaders, are found at the state level, but there are major inconsistencies. State laws vary in defining specific terms such as electronic communication, intimidation, and harassment. Some state laws provide a detailed protocol for how teachers and administrators should report, and handle online bullying that has an impact on the school environment. Meanwhile, some states leave developing a protocol up to individual school districts. Inconsistencies in school cyberbullying laws and policies mean that school leaders across the United States do not have a unified way to handle issues originating off-campus. School leaders should have a comprehensive policy, which helps to address cyberbullying issues. The chapter includes a discussion of proposed federal legislation that could guide state laws in the future.

## BRIEF OVERVIEW OF CYBERBULLYING

The definition of cyberbullying varies depending on if you ask researchers, schoolteachers, policy-makers, or students. This chapter is guided by Hinduja and Patchin's definition of cyberbullying. Cyberbullying is defined as willful and repeated harm inflicted through the use of computers, cell phones, and other electronic devices (Hinduja & Patchin, 2015, p. 13).

Cyberbullying has become a major concern for students, school officials, parents, and policy-makers. Patchin and Hinduja (2010) postulated there is a need to examine cyberbullying because "as technology evolves, so do many of the problems faced by those who have access to it" (p. 615). The advances in technology have provided a new venue for bullying behavior to occur. Kowalski and Limber (2007) found that bullying occurred in chat rooms, through email and instant messages. Although taking place online, cyberbullying can be just as damaging as traditional face-to-face bullying.

Willard (2006) noted that cyberbullying may produce consequences ranging from low self-esteem, anxiety, anger, depression, school absenteeism, poor grades, an increased tendency to be violent against others, and suicide. Many, who experience cyberbullying, also face traditional face-to-face bullying. Hinduja and Patchin (2009) found that 42% of victims of cyberbullying were also victims of traditional face-to-face bullying. Cyberbullying victims often felt frustrated, sad, angry, scared and embarrassed. Given the impact of cyberbullying many states have adopted anti-bullying laws and policies.

## SELECTED STATE LAWS

The following provides a detailed description of five state cyberbullying laws. The description includes language from the laws, which identifies the varying ways each state addresses cyberbullying issues. Following the description, Table 1 provides a condensed and compact overview of the selected state laws. This table is meant to further highlight the inconsistencies. The states were selected to represent different regions within the United States. Arizona, the District of Columbia, Florida, Idaho, and Texas policies on cyberbullying differ in regard to addressing a cyberbullying incident.

Some states include electronic communication in their definition of bullying. Certain state policies include language that would make cyberbullying a criminal offense. The variances in the five selected state laws serve to illustrate the inconsistencies, which exists in current state laws across the country. There are not consistent guidelines for teachers, and school administrators to follow when cyberbullying concerns arise.

## ARIZONA

Arizona has two laws regarding bullying. H.B. 2368 was enacted in 2005. Under H.B. 2368 school district develop procedures for addressing intimidating, bullying, and harassing other students (H.B. 2368, 2005).

*Table 1.* Overview of Selected State Bullying Laws.

| | Defining Bullying | Electronic Communication Definition | Protocol for Addressing Bullying | Criminal Charges Component |
|---|---|---|---|---|
| Arizona | Leaves it up to schools to create their own definition | Includes electronic communication which occurs through school computers, networks, forums or mailing lists | Implement a procedure for students, parents, and school district employees to confidentially report incidents of harassment intimidation, or bullying | No criminal sanctions for bullying |
| District of Columbia | Any severe, pervasive, or persistent act or conduct, whether physical, electronic, or verbal | Communication transmitted by means of an electronic device, including a telephone, cellular phone, computer, tablet pager, or video or audio recording | The Mayor must establish a bullying prevention task force | No criminal sanctions for bullying |
| Florida | Bullying includes cyberbullying and means systematically and chronically inflicting physical hurt or psychological distress on one or more students | Includes online communication, e-mails. webpages, and facsimile communication | School district need to involve students, parents, teachers, administrators, school staff, school volunteers, community representatives, and local law enforcement agencies in the process of adopting an anti-bullying policy | No criminal sanctions for bullying, but misdemeanor crime for cyberstalking and cyberstalking |

**Table 1.** *(Continued)*

| | Defining Bullying | Electronic Communication Definition | Protocol for Addressing Bullying | Criminal Charges Component |
|---|---|---|---|---|
| Idaho | Harassment, intimidation, or bullying is defined as any intentional gesture, or any intentional written, verbal or physical act or threat by a student | The law acknowledges that acts of bullying can be carried out through the use of cell phones and computers | The Board of Trustees develop protocol for addressing harassment, intimidation, and bullying | Any student who commits or conspires to commit an act of harassment, intimidation or bullying shall be guilty of a misdemeanor |
| Texas | Engaging in written or verbal expression, expression through electronic means, or physical conduct that occurs on school property, at a school-sponsored or school-related activity | Electronic means is included in the definition of harassment | The board of trustees of each school district is responsible for developing policies to address bullying | No criminal sanctions for bullying |

Harassment, bullying and intimidation of other students is prohibited not only on school grounds, but on school buses, school bus stops and at school-sponsored events and activities (H.B. 2368, 2005).

In Arizona schools, there is a confidential procedure, which allows for reporting incidents of harassment, intimidation or bullying to school officials. School employees, students, parents are allowed to submit written reports concerning harassment, intimidation or bullying. All reports are properly documented and investigated. Any student who is found to violation of harassment, intimidation or bullying is subject to school discipline (H.B. 2368, 2005).

On April 9, 2011, Governor Jan Brewer signed into law the H.B. 2415, the Punishment Guidelines for Bullying in Schools (H.B. 2415, 2011). The bill addresses harassment, intimidation, and bullying through electronic means (H.B. 2415, 2011). The bill prohibits students from harassing others on school grounds, bus stops, at school-sponsored events, and through the use of electronic technology or electronic communication on school computers, networks, forums, and mailing lists. Schools are required implement proper protocol for confidentially reporting incidents of harassment, intimidation, or bullying (H.B. 2415, 2011). Each school provides forms which allows parents, students, and employees to submit an anonymous a written report (H.B. 2415, 2011). Once the reports are submitted, school officials must investigate to determine the validity of the report.

The passage of the two bills comes at a time when teachers and law enforcements are looking for answers on how to effectively address cyberbullying incidents. Bullying laws in the United States have yet to catch up to the rapidly growing technology. This means that school leaders and law enforcement are left on their own to figure out how to properly handling online bullying issues.

Law enforcement in Arizona have publically spoken out in regards to anti-bullying laws. Officer Delia Marquez, who is a member of Tucson Police Department stated that the "laws need to be more technical, spelling out specific terms when it comes to social media, and how cyberbullying is defined and enforced in schools and by police" (Cavazos, 2012, p. 2). Marquez argued that a law specifically defines cyberbullying and provides a detailed way to address the issue. Avoiding vague terms, and enacting comprehensive anti-bullying legislation would mean teachers and law enforcement would have a more effective legal tool to use when dealing with bullying incidents (Cavazos, 2012).

## DISTRICT OF COLUMBIA

On June 22, 2012, Mayor Vincent Gray signed into law the Youth Bullying Prevention Act (Youth Bullying Prevention Act, 2012). The bill protect against bullying, intimation and harassment based on or perceived sexual orientation, gender identity, and expression (Whelan, 2012). The act included electronic communication in the definition of bullying. The Youth Bullying Prevention Act defined bullying as any severe, pervasive, or persistent act or conduct, whether physical, electronic, or verbal. Electronic communication is defined as communication transmitted by means of an electronic device, including a telephone, cellular phone, computer, tablet, pager, or video or audio recording (Youth Bullying Prevention Act, 2012).

Enacting the Youth Bullying Prevention Act meant that schools as well as youth serving agencies will have the guidance needed to address bullying issues. Micki Freeny, who is the coordinator of youth services for the District of Columbia Public Library, thought that the passage of the Youth Bullying Prevention Act was a major step in the right direction (Whelan, 2012, p. 1). Freeny stated, "we hope it will do something to empower youth to speak up if bullied and to speak up if witnessing bullying." Freeny hopes "the model policy will help librarians better identify and handle these situations. A cyberbullying component will be crucial because libraries need clear guidance on whether they have jurisdiction over online harassment" (Whelan, 2012, p. 1).

## FLORIDA

The Florida House of Representative enacted H.B. 609 titled Bullying in the Public School System (H.B. 609, 2013). Both bullying and cyberbullying are defined in the bill. Bullying included cyberbullying and is defined as systematically and chronically inflicting physical hurt or psychological distress on one or more students. The bullying is shown is the form of teasing, social exclusion, threats, intimidation, stalking, physical violence, theft, sexual, religious, or racial harassment, public or private humiliation, or destruction of property Florida (H.B. 609, 2013).

In the Florida bill, cyberbullying is defined as bullying through the use of technology or any electronic communication, which includes, but is not limited to, any transfer of signs, signals, writing, images, sounds, data, or intelligence of any nature transmitted in whole or in part by a wire, radio, electromagnetic system, photo-electronic system, or photo-optical system, including, but not limited to, electronic mail, Internet communications, instant messages, or facsimile communications (H.B. 609, 2013).

The Florida H.B. 609 included and defined cyber-harassment and cyber-stalking. Cyberstalking is use of electronic means to threatening or stalk another person or groups of people. The threats can come in the form of online messages as well as through e-mails. Creating a malicious webpage to torment a person or group of people falls under cyber-harassment (H.B. 609, 2013). A person or group of people found in violation of cyberstalking or cyber-harassment can be charged with a misdemeanor crime (H.B. 609, 2013).

In Florida, harassment or bullying of a student or school employee through computer related activities is prohibited. The Florida bill required each school district to adopt a policy prohibiting harassment and bullying. The school district bullying and harassment policy states that all students have equal protection under this law. The school districts are required to involve students, parents, teachers, administrators, school staff, school volunteers, community representatives, and local law enforcement agencies in the process of adopting the policy (H.B. 609, 2013).

According to H.B. 609 the school district policies included two main components. The first component is that school district policy needed to include a process to investigate whether a reported act of bullying or harassment is within the scope of the district school system and, if not, a process for referral of such an act to the appropriate jurisdiction (H.B. 609, 2013). The second component required a procedure for providing instruction to students, parents, teachers, school administrators, counseling staff, and school volunteers on identifying, preventing, and responding to bullying or harassment, including instruction on recognizing behaviors that leads to bullying and harassment and taking appropriate preventive action based on those observations (H.B. 609, 2013).

The state of Florida also passed H.B. 699 titled the Jeffrey Johnston Stand Up for All Students Act in 2008 (H.B. 699, 2008). Jeffrey Johnston was a 15-year-old honor roll student in Florida. Jeffrey was the target of verbal attacks, being called "faggot," "ugly," and "fat." Jeffrey also was the target for online harassment as well. The torment became too much, and in 2005 Jeffrey took his own life by hanging himself in his closet (Brochu, 2011). Jeffrey's mother, his family, the community, and legislators all worked together toward the development and passage of H.B. 699 (Brochu, 2011).

H.B. 699 required each school district in Florida to adopt a policy prohibiting bullying and harassment of a student or employee of a public K-12 educational institution. Each school district's policy is aligned with the Department of Education's model policy. The school district bullying and harassment policy affords all students the same protection regardless of their status under the law. Each school district is required to involve students, parents, teachers, administrators, school staff, school volunteers, community representatives, and local law enforcement agencies in the process of adopting the policy (H.B. 699, 2008). The school district policy is implemented in a manner that is ongoing throughout the school year and integrated with the school's curriculum, a school's discipline policy, as well as other violence prevention efforts (H.B. 699, 2008). The H.B. 699 law required all school districts to provide guidelines on what steps to take to report a bullying incident, and investigating allegations of bullying. Finally, all school districts are required to specially outline the consequences for students and school employees who violate the policy (Brochu, 2011).

## IDAHO

In 2006 Idaho passed H.B. 750, also known as Jared's law, addressed harassment, intimidation, and bullying (H.B. 750, 2006). The bill is named after Jared High, who at 12 years old took his own life. Jared experienced bullying and physical assaults. Due to the bullying, Jared displayed emotional outbursts, had trouble sleeping, and suffered from depression (Jaredstory, 2015). On September 29, 1998, Jared shot himself due to the damages of bullying he experienced. After his death, Brenda, Jared's mother worked toward passing anti-bullying laws (Jaredstory, 2015).

Idaho's H.B. 750 included two major components. Jared's law outlined that both superintendents, and principals may temporarily suspend pupils for student harassment, intimidation or bullying. The guidelines for suspension were to be developed by the Board of Trustees for each school district. The Jared's law prohibits student on student harassment, intimidation, or bullying. Any student who commits or conspires to commit an act of harassment, intimidation or bullying is guilty of a misdemeanor crime (H.B. 750, 2006). The misdemeanor element of the H.B. 750 law makes Idaho stand out from other states. The criminalization component is not seen in many state laws.

## TEXAS

In 2011, Texas passed its anti-bullying law H.B. 1942. The bill required schools to adopt a bullying prevention policy (H.B. 1942, 2011). The bill included any behavior, which occurs off school ground. H.B. 1942 defined bullying as engaging in written or verbal expression, expression through electronic means, or physical conduct that occurs on school property, at a school-sponsored or school-related activity, or in a vehicle operated by the district (H.B. 1942, 2011). H.B. 1942 defined to bullying conduct as an imbalance of power between the student perpetrator and the student victim through written or verbal expression or physical conduct. The verbal expression and physical conduct refers to actions that makes an individual feel intimidated, afraid or threatened.

Students are found in violation of H.B 1942 if their actions cause mental, or physical harm or potential harm to a student or the student's property. The Texas law H.B. 1942 a students' action has to be sufficiently severe, persistent, and pervasive enough that the action or threat creates an intimidating, threatening, or abusive educational environment (H.B. 1942, 2011).

Table 1 provides a condensed overview of the selected state laws. Highlighting specific characteristics of each of the state laws, the table provides a visual layout to compare and contrast the varying definitions and protocols for addressing bullying issues. The table plainly shows the ways each state goes about addressing bullying varies greatly.

In the District of Columbia, a citywide bullying prevention task force was created. In Arizona a system was put in place to allow parents, students, and school employees to confidentially submit reports of harassment and bullying. In Florida, each individual school district is responsible for developing an anti-bullying policy. In Idaho, the Board of Trustees was charged with developing local school policies on how to address issues of harassment, intimidation and bullying. Texas, also utilizes the Board of Trustees within each school district to develop an anti-bullying policy.

Two of the selected anti-bullying laws outline criminal sanctions for individuals or groups of people who are found in violation of the law. In Florida, being charged with cyber-harassment and cyberstalking is a misdemeanor charge. In Idaho charges of harassment, intimidation, or bullying is a misdemeanor charge. Only two of the five states outlined criminal offenses further highlights the inconsistencies in state anti-bullying laws. School leaders are faced with the challenge of handling bullying incidents, albeit the ways to address an incident varies from state to state. The states have been left to develop these laws in our rapidly changing technological world without guidance of federal legislation to address these issues. This partially accounts for the different approaches in state laws. However, there are two federally proposed statues that seek to address bullying issues.

## PROPOSED FEDERAL STATUTES

This section provides a brief background of the stories of Megan Meier and Tyler Clementi. Both were two young people who were involved in an online situation which lead to them committing suicide. Although Megan and Tyler's life ended in a tragic way, each of their stories gain national attention, and resulted two proposed federal legislations. The legislations seek to address issues of bullying, and harassment. The proposed Megan Meier statute would allow criminal sanctions to be imposed on an individual who coerce, intimidate, harass, or cause substantial emotional distress to another person, using electronic means to support severe, repeated, and hostile behavior (H.R. 6123, 2008). The proposed Tyler Clementi Anti-Harassment Higher Education Act would give institutions of higher education the opportunity to apply for federally funding to implement anti-bullying programs on their campus (H.R. 6425, 2010).

The two proposed statutes while different, has the potential to impact schools leaders if enacted. The earlier discussion of the state laws found that many states are left to draft their own state bullying policy, with little to no guidance and lack of funding and resources. Federal laws like the proposed Megan Meier statute could provide clarify on the legal limits of schools leaders. If the proposed Tyler Clementi statute is passed and federal funding is made available to institutions of higher education, an argument could be make for funding to be available for school leaders at the K-12 level. The two proposed statutes serve as an example of how federal laws can have an impact on anti-bullying laws at the state level.

### *Megan Meier*

The Megan Meier Cyberbullying Prevention Act was named after Megan Meier. Megan took her own life in 2006 after an online message exchanges through MySpace. Megan thought she was engaging in conversation with a teenage boy named Josh Evans, when in fact she was talking to her neighbor Lori Drew. Lori Drew lived in the same neighborhood as Megan. Lori Drew became concerned after she felt Megan had started rumors about her daughter Sarah. In an attempt to get the truth, Lori Drew, Sarah, and Drew's co-worker, Ashley Grills, worked together in order to create a fake Myspace account under the name Josh Evans. On October 16, 2006 Josh told Megan, that the world would be better without her. On that same day Tina Meier, Megan's mother, reported that her daughter hung herself from her bedroom closet (EFF, 2008). Megan's story sparked national attention on youth suicide and cyberbullying. Her suicide gained attention of Congress and lead to the proposed Megan Meier Cyberbullying Prevention Act (H.R. 6123). The Megan Meier Cyberbullying Prevention Act (H.R. 6123) was introduced in the U.S. House of Representatives on May 22, 2008 by Representative Linda T. Sánchez. The goal of the bill is was to amend Title 18, United States Code with respect to cyberbullying (H.R. 6123, 2008).

Title 18 addresses crime and criminal procedures. The bill would seek to amend the federal criminal code to impose criminal penalties on anyone who transmits in interstate or foreign commerce a communication intended to coerce, intimidate, harass, or cause substantial emotional distress to another person, using electronic means to support severe, repeated, and hostile behavior (H.R. 6123, 2008). Communication is defined as the electronic transmission, between or among points specified by the user, of information of the user's choosing, without change in the form or content of the information as sent and received. In addition, electronic means refers to any equipment dependent on electrical power to access an information service, including email, instant messaging, blogs, websites, telephones, and text messages (H.R. 6123, 2008). Currently, the bill has not been passed, and is current stalled in congressional committee. The bill has gained momentum, but many people continue to feel that bullying is not a big deal, and it is a part of growing up. If this bill hopes to move pass it will take changes in attitude not only in Congress but in our society as well.

### *Tyler Clementi*

The second proposed statute is named after Tyler Clementi, who was a freshman at Rutgers University. While at Rutgers Clementi his roommate, Dharvi Ravi, broadcast on a live webcam. The webcam showed the encounters between Clementi and another man. Ravi used his webcam, to live tweet a link for anyone to watch what was occurring with Clementi. Ravi went to room of Molly Wei, a fellow student at Rutgers, while Clementi had the room to himself. Ravi utilized Wei's computer, to connect to his computer's iChat. Ravi turned on the webcam, which revealed that Clementi was kissing another man. Clementi learned of the incident and felt his privacy has been violated (Huffingtonpost, 2012). On September 22, 2010, Tyler Clementi left the campus of Rutgers University, where he was a freshmen, took a bus to New York City. Clementi took his own life by jumping of the George Washington Bridge (Huffingtonpost, 2012). The story of Clementi brought national attention on cyberbullying, anti-bullying laws, and rights of LGBT youth. A federal statute was proposed in his name to help combat bullying issues in higher education.

Representative Rush Holt proposed the Tyler Clementi Anti-Harassment statute was first proposed on November 18, 2010, by New Jersey (H.R. 6425). The goal of the bill is to have institutions of higher education within the United States to develop a Disclosure of Campus Security and Harassment Policy and Campus Crime Statistics. Institutions of higher education would have to publish the report, and provide a statement of policy regarding harassment. The bill includes the following four procedures, which institutions of higher education must adhere to (a) procedures for timely institutional action in cases of alleged harassment, which procedures shall include a clear statement that the accuser and the accused shall be informed of the outcome of any disciplinary proceedings in response to an allegation of harassment; (b) possible sanctions to be imposed following the final determination of an institutional disciplinary procedure regarding harassment; (c) notification of existing counseling, mental health, or student services for victims or perpetrators of harassment, both on campus and in the community; and (d) identification of a designated employee or office at the institution that will be responsible for receiving and tracking each report of harassment by a student, faculty, or staff member (H.R. 6425, 2010). Through the Tyler Clementi Act, institutions of higher education would be able to apply for a grant to implement anti-bullying programming.

The grant could be awarded for up to three years and potentially could be rewarded for up to two years. An institution could use the grant in an effort to initiate, improve, or expand programs: (1) to prevent the harassment of students at institutions of higher education; (2) to provide counseling or redress services to students who have suffered such harassment or students who have been accused of subjecting other students to such harassment; or (3) that educate or train students, faculty, or staff of institutions of higher education about ways to prevent harassment or ways to address such harassment if it occurs (H.R. 6425, 2010). The Tyler Clementi statute has not been passed, but was recently re-introduced in March 2015. The bill has yet to make it to a committee hearing. The bill is in reference to an incident involving gay youth. When issues involving members of the LGBT community, there continues to be a divide between LGBT support and religious beliefs against homosexuality. The proposed Tyler Clementi Anti-Harassment statute would have to face and overcome those who hold strong religious beliefs if it hopes to get enacted.

The proposed Megan Meier and Tyler Clementi statute seek to provide a consistence way to address, and report bullying issues. The Megan Meier act, if passed, would provide criminal sanctions for those found in violation of harassment or intimidation through electronic means. The Tyler Clementi Act, if passed, would provide a comprehensive way for institutions of higher education to monitor and report bullying incidents.

## CONCLUSION AND IMPLICATIONS

Bullying continues to be a concern both inside and outside the school grounds. Technology, particularly the uses of computers and cell phones have provided a venue for people to attack others, and remain anonymous. Patchin and Hinduja (2010) were right when they stated that there is a need to study cyberbullying as technology increases so do the problems.

The lack of consistency means that each state and school districts are left to interpret the law. Passable of a federal legislation would provide a strong legislation which has passed constitutional muster, and would be able to be enforced and upheld not only at the federal level but at the state level as well. A strong federal anti-bullying policy would give school leaders the legal backing they need in order to properly address bullying issues whether they occur on or off school grounds. Furthermore, cyberbullying is a unique form of bullying where the target is accessible 24 hours a day, and the impact of the bullying goes from the electronic world to the school environment. A comprehensive federal law would serve as a guideline to assist school leaders in properly dealing with bullying which occur online.

Due to an exchange of online messages, and webcam broadcasting, there have been two young people who took their own life. The humiliation and harassment became too much to bear, and their stories drew more attention and discussion on the issue of bullying. Although occurring online, the impact of these incidents leads to suicide. The consequences of cyberbullying can have the same impact as traditional face-to-face bullying. Willard (2006) reinforced this concept earlier, by noting that cyberbullying may produce consequences including violent against others, and suicide.

The impact of bullying which occurs through online communication is just as harmful as traditional face-to-face bullying. Jeffrey Johnson from Idaho, Jared High from Florida, Megan Meier from Missouri and Tyler Clementi from New Jersey are examples of where young people have been deeply impacted by online bullying. Cases like these highlight the need for more consistent anti-bullying laws not only at the federal, but the state level as well. All of these young people have had legislation named after them. The legislation serve as an example of efforts made in order to turn the tragic death of young people into something positive.

Earlier in this chapter, the anti-bullying laws for Arizona, District of Columbia, Florida, Idaho, and Texas. All five had different approaches to addressing bullying issues. The states had an anti-bullying plan, or created a task force to address bullying. In regards to developing anti-bullying laws, many states left it up to the individual school district to make their own plan. Florida and Idaho were the only two states that had a clause outlining criminal sanctions for misdemeanor charges.

The lack of a consistent plan for all states, means that school leaders are left to figure out what are their legal boundaries when it comes to addressing bullying incidents. The inconsistencies are an important aspect to examining anti-bullying laws. If school districts are left to develop their own policies, which means within a state there would be varying rules and a regulation depending on which school a child is attending. School leaders are charged with ensuring students are safe, and feel supported. School leaders wear many hats each school day, and have to be prepared to handle many situations. However, school leaders should not have to be lawyers, and try to figure out when and where does my obligation start and stop in regards to addressing bullying concerns. If the goal is to safeguard students, and ensure school leaders have the necessary tools and resources to address bullying issues, then clear policies need to be in place to achieve this goal.

## IMPLICATIONS FOR SCHOOL LEADERS

Educators who find themselves confused or requiring more resources need to advocate for themselves through local, state, and federal teacher organizations. Affiliations with educational organizations, like the National

Association of State Boards of Education, and the National Education Association ensure that school leaders get up-to-date information on issues relating to schools and students. Being a member of an organization can help you connect with other individuals who share your beliefs.

School leaders play a central role in handling and addressing bullying. Every day, schools work closely with the students. School leaders have the ability to build and maintain a positive school climate where students feel safe and supported. There are ways for school leaders to be involved in developing anti-bullying policies both inside and outside the school ground. Experienced school leaders can share their expertise of best practices. In addition, school leaders can use their share their experience with schools boards in order to help develop future anti-bullying policies. School leaders can take an active role by serving as an advocate, and a voice for policy-makers. School leaders can bring their experience to the table to help shape and develop future anti-bullying policies in order to provide more consistency in the way bullying issues are addressed in schools.

## IMPLICATIONS FOR POLICY-MAKERS

Policy-makers at the federal level are in a position of power to introduce and vote to pass anti-bullying laws. These laws not only can protect students but also can give school leaders proper guidance and resources to address bully issues whether they occur on- or off-campus. Policy-makers should be thoughtful when drafting, and passing anti-bullying legislation, and ensure that representatives from school leaders, bullying researchers, parents and counselors are involved in the conversation when drafting a new legislation. Policy-makers need to focus on meaningful language that clearly defines and addresses bullying. When developing a new policy, think of how this can be implemented in varies school districts. Policy-makers need to avoid simply developing a policy that proclaims how bad it is to bullying others online, yet leaves school leaders the daunting task of making their own meaning of the policy.

## FINAL THOUGHTS ON LAWS AND CYBERBULLYING

This chapter has illustrated the importance of a federal anti-bullying law to provide more clear guidance for school leaders. A federal legislation needs to be carefully crafted and read through to ensure the language has substance. A well-developed federal policy can help to strengthen anti-bullying laws at the state level. The federal policy should include both depth and breadth when addressing anti-bullying concerns. We need laws that can concurrently catch up with the advances in technology.

Policies alone will not stop bullying whether online or in person. It will take a collaborative effort national school leadership, federal statutes, state statutes, policy-makers, students, and parents to help create a positive school environment. Students need to be educated about proper online activity, and about not being afraid to tell someone if they receive harassing messages. The tragic stories of Megan Meier and Tyler Clementi and other young people who have committed suicide due to issues of harassment and bullying serve as indicators that this is an issue we cannot ignore, or mildly address. Bullying whether online or in person is a societal issue that we all must address in a comprehensive and consistent way.

## REFERENCES


Brochu, N. (2011). Mother turns tragedy into triumph with anti-bullying law. *Sun-Sentinel*, September 18. Retrieved from http://articles.sun-sentinel.com/2011-09-18/health/fl-nbcol-bullying-jeff-johnston-column-20110918_1_anti-bullying-jeffrey-johnston-mother

Cavazos, V. (2012). Cyberbullying: What AZ laws are on the books to combat the problem? *Kgun9 News*, February 9. Retrieved from http://www.jrn.com/kgun9/news/139059269.html

DCGov. (2012). *Youth bullying prevention act of 2012, D.C.* Act §19-384. Retrieved from http://www.dcregs.dc.gov/Gateway/NoticeHome.aspx?noticeid=2692737

Electronic Frontier Foundation (EFF). (2008). *United States v. Lori Drew case brief.* Retrieved from http://www.eff.org/files/filenode/US_v_Drew/Drew_Amicus.pdf

H.B. 609. (2013). *Bullying in public schools system.* Florida legislature. Retrieved from http://www.myfloridahouse.gov/Sections/Bills/billsdetail.aspx?BillId=49796

H.B. 699§ 1006.147. (2008). *Jeffrey Johnston stand up for all Florida Statutes.* Florida legislature. Students Act. Retrieved from http://www.leg.state.fl.us/statutes/index.cfm?App_mode=Display_Statute&URL=1000-1099/1006/Sections/1006.147.html

H.B. 1942. (2011). *Relating to bullying in schools.* Texas legislature online (82nd legislature). Retrieved from http://www.legis.state.tx.us/tlodocs/82R/billtext/pdf/HB01942F.pdf

H.B. 2368. (2005). *Arizona revised statutes: Relating to school district governing boards.* 47th legislature. Retrieved from http://www.azleg.state.az.us/legtext/47leg/1r/bills/hb2368s.pdf

H.B. 2415. (2011). *Arizona revised statutes: Punishment guidelines for bullying in schools.* 50th legislature. Retrieved from http://www.azleg.gov/legtext/50leg/1r/bills/hb2415h.pdf

Hinduja, S., & Patchin, J. W. (2009). *Bullying beyond the schoolyard: Preventing and responding to cyberbullying.* Thousand Oaks, CA: Corwin Press.

Hinduja, S., & Patchin, J. W. (2015). *Bullying beyond the schoolyard: Preventing and responding to cyberbullying* (2nd ed.). Thousand Oaks, CA: Corwin Press.

H.R. 6123. (2008). *Megan Meier Cyberbullying Prevention Action of 2008*. 110th congress. Retrieved from http://thomas.loc.gov/cgi-bin/query/z?c110:H.R.6123

H.R. 6425. (2010). *Tyler Clementi Higher Education Anti Harassment Act of* 2010. 111th congress. Retrieved from http://www.congress.gov/111/bills/hr6425/BILLS111hr6425ih.xml

Huffingtonpost. (2012). *Dharun Ravi and Tyler Clementi Timeline: Former Rutgers roommate in dorm room spying trial*. Retrieved from http://www.huffingtonpost.com/2012/02/24/dharun-ravi-tyler-clementi-timeline_n_1297056.html

Idaho Legislature. (2006). *H.B. 750*. Retrieved from http://legislature.idaho.gov/legislation/2006/H0750.html

JaredStory.com. (2015). *Jared's story*. Retrieved from http://www.jaredstory.com/blh.html

Kowalski, R. M., & Limber, S. P. (2007). Electronic bullying among middle school students. *Journal of Adolescent Health*, *41*(6), S22–S30.

Patchin, J. W., & Hinduja, S. (2010). Cyberbullying and self-esteem. *Jal of School Health*, *80*(12), 614–621.

Whelan, D. L. (2012, June 27). DC mayor signs law requiring youth anti-bullying policies in libraries, other city agencies. *School Library Journal*. Retrieved from http://www.slj.com/2012/06/schools/dc-mayor-signs-law-requiring-youth-anti-bullying-policies-in-libraries-other-city-agencies/#_

Willard, N. (2006). Flame retardant. *School Library Journal*, *52*(4), 55–56.

# CHAPTER 2

# RECENT LITIGATION AND GUIDANCE INVOLVING BULLYING OF STUDENTS WITH DISABILITIES

Janet R. Decker and Suzanne E. Eckes

## ABSTRACT

*While there are myriad legal issues confronting school leaders, the focus on the complexities involving special education law and bullying has increased recently. The U.S. Department of Education wrote in a 2014 "Dear Colleague Letter" (Guidance) that its office "has received an ever-increasing number of complaints concerning the bullying of students with disabilities and the effects of that bullying on their education, including on the special education and related services to which they are entitled" (p. 1). The Guidance as well as recent litigation illustrates how plaintiffs have alleged violations under the Individuals with Disabilities Education Act, Section 504 of the Rehabilitation Act of 1973 and/or the Americans with Disabilities Act when students with disabilities are bullied in schools. In this chapter, after discussing the related literature and the legal context, we examine several illustrative recent cases and the 2014 Guidance to highlight the relevant issues for school leaders. We*

**Legal Frontiers in Education: Complex Law Issues for Leaders, Policymakers and Policy Implementers**
**Advances in Educational Administration, Volume 24, 19–34**

**ISSN: 1479-3660/doi:10.1108/S1479-366020150000024028**

*conclude with recommendations and emphasize that school leaders must become knowledgeable about this emerging legal topic. Specifically, with a greater understanding of how they can prevent and respond to the bullying of students with disabilities, school leaders have the power to make great social change within schools.*

L.K., a 12-year-old girl with a learning disability, was repeatedly bullied by classmates over the course of a school year. Despite being accompanied by a one-to-one aide, L.K.'s peers intentionally tripped her, physically backed away to avoid her, drew disparaging pictures of her, and ridiculed her. L. K.'s aide testified that teachers usually ignored the bullying but reprimanded L.K. for causing a scene when classmates tripped her (*T.K. v. N.Y. C. Dep't of Educ.*, 2011, pp. 296–297).

L.K.'s parents attempted to address the problem with the principal on multiple occasions. They tried to discuss the bullying at L.K.'s annual special education meeting, but the principal told them it was not the appropriate time. The parents again attempted to communicate with the principal by sending several letters and calling the school; however, the principal never replied. On one occasion, the parents brought L.K. to the principal's office to discuss the bullying, but the principal responded that it was not an appropriate topic to discuss in front of L.K. and told them that she would call security if they did not leave. The school had no records documenting that L.K. had been bullied or that her parents had complained; the school did, however, have several reports alleging L.K. as the aggressor. The principal testified that she could "not recall" if she ever investigated any of the multiple reports of bullying made by parents or aides (p. 297).

Believing that the principal "stonewalled" their efforts to help their daughter, L.K.'s parents enrolled her in a private school (p. 294). The parents then filed a lawsuit against the school district seeking reimbursement for the private school tuition. The parents claimed the district violated federal disability law, the Individuals with Disabilities Education Act (IDEA), because district employees failed to respond to the bullying, which resulted in a hostile learning environment where L.K. could not receive an educational benefit (*T.K. v. N.Y.C. Dep't of Educ.*, 2011). Both decision-makers in the two tiers of administrative review of the case found in favor of the school district, reasoning that the school's failure to address the bullying was irrelevant to whether L.K. was receiving IDEA's guarantee of a Free Appropriate Public Education (FAPE). Ultimately, however, a New York federal district court denied the school district's motion for summary judgment to dismiss the case. It reasoned that evidence existed that a fact-finder could determine that (1) L.K. had been harassed based on her disability; (2) school officials knew about the harassment; (3) the school had failed to take reasonable measures to address the harassment; and; (4) the harassment led to L.K. being deprived an educational benefit in violation of IDEA (p. 318). The court cited research finding that "students with disabilities are less popular, have fewer friends, and struggle more with loneliness and peer rejection, increasing the likelihood they will become the victim of bullying" (p. 303). The court also concluded:

> No one gains from ignoring school bullying – not even the bullies themselves. The students who are bullied may suffer lasting scars in the form of an inferior education, emotional damage, and decreased self-confidence; the bullies are left to continue on a path that may lead to future violence. (p. 293)

While there are myriad legal issues confronting school leaders, the focus on the complexities involving special education law and bullying have increased recently.

In 2014, the U.S. Department of Education (USDoE) wrote in a "Dear Colleague Letter" (Guidance) that its office "has received an ever-increasing number of complaints concerning the bullying of students with disabilities and the effects of that bullying on their education, including on the special education and related services to which they are entitled" (p. 1). The Guidance, as well as recent litigation, illustrates how plaintiffs have alleged violations under IDEA, Section 504 of the Rehabilitation Act (Section 504), and/or Title II of the Americans with Disabilities Act (ADA) when students with disabilities are bullied in schools.

In this chapter, we begin by explaining the historical and current context surrounding this issue. Next, we describe the legal avenues that victims of disability-based harassment could pursue to claim that school districts are liable for the harassment. Then, we examine several illustrative recent cases and the USDoE Guidance to highlight the relevant issues for school leaders. We conclude with recommendations emphasizing that school leaders must become knowledgeable about this emerging legal topic. Specifically, with a greater understanding how they can prevent and respond to the bullying of students with disabilities, school leaders have the power to make great social change within schools.

## HISTORICAL AND CURRENT CONTEXT

Historically, students with disabilities have been excluded from public schools. In fact, as recently as the 1970s, many were not only excluded but were also forced to live in dismal, restrictive, filthy, and sometimes, abusive environments (Blatt, 1970; Hehir, 2005). Within the past century, many students with disabilities were warehoused at institutions built to protect society from the perceived negative influences of disability (Pazey & Yates, 2012). Many institutions only provided shelter, with minimal food and clothing. Before federal disability laws were enacted that prohibited discrimination and guaranteed a FAPE, more attention was placed on providing basic care to students with disabilities rather than providing education and rehabilitation (USDoE, 2010b). In fact, prior to the 1975 passage of the Education for All Handicapped Children's Act—IDEA's precursor—some state legislation explicitly forbid schools from enrolling students with intellectual disabilities (Hehir & Gamm, 1999). Therefore, parents and disability-rights advocates have overcome incredible obstacles to ensure that students with disabilities now have legal entitlements and protections.

Regardless of these impressive strides for students with disabilities, the vestiges of past exclusion remain. To illustrate, the U.S. Department of Education's Office for Civil Rights (OCR) reported in 2014 that students with disabilities represent only 12% of the student population; yet, nearly 60% of students placed in seclusion and 75% of those physically restrained at school are students with disabilities (USDoE, 2014b). Suspension rates are more than twice as high (13%) for students with disabilities than for their nondisabled peers (6%) (USDoE, 2014b). Another example of the current discrimination facing students with disabilities is bullying and harassment (Hartley, Bauman, Nixon, & Davis, 2015).

Part of the problem is that educators have focused on improving instruction to ensure the needs of students with disabilities are being met in general education classrooms, but corresponding efforts have not been devoted to teaching them how to interact socially with their peers, which leaves students with disabilities as targets for bullying (Carter & Spencer, 2006, p. 11). By enacting IDEA, Congress sought to improve the inclusion of students with disabilities in public schools—that is, whenever possible, students with disabilities are to be taught in general education settings with nondisabled students (Yell, 2012). IDEA requires that each individual student with a disability is educated in the least restrictive environment (LRE) to the maximum extent appropriate. In spite of the law, school districts are often still accused of violating LRE, and the debate persists about the extent to which students with disabilities should be included in general education classrooms.

Therefore, *all* students with disabilities are *not* truly *integrated* in schools today. As we described earlier, L.K. was taught alongside her nondisabled peers; however, she was subjected to a hostile environment. Eventually, her parents transferred her to a private school that taught students with learning disabilities in a segregated setting (*T.K. v. N.Y.C. Dep't of Educ.*, 2011, p. 295). L.K.'s case illustrates that while students with disabilities may be physically present in general education classrooms, presence alone does not guarantee that they are socially accepted or treated fairly in many cases. In situations like L.K.'s, where students have been harassed based on physical or mental differences, courts may or may not find the school district liable. Thus, all educators, including school leaders, must be keenly aware of this type of harassment and understand when schools can be held legally liable for it. It is the responsibility of teacher and leadership preparation programs and school districts to ensure this type of training occurs.

## LEGAL CLAIMS

There are several legal avenues parents may pursue when a student with a disability is harassed or bullied and the parents believe the school should be held liable. These lawsuits are different from claims where parents believe the student(s) responsible for the bullying should be held liable. First, parents could allege a constitutional violation by bringing a Section 1983 claim alleging that the school district violated the Equal Protection and/or Due Process clauses of the Fourteenth Amendment of the U.S. Constitution, but these claims are relatively uncommon (Weber, 2002) and unsuccessful (Conn, 2013). Another avenue would be to allege the school district and its employees violated their obligations under state tort statutes such as negligence or intentional infliction of emotional distress. Yet, claims that school employees were negligent for failing to protect students with disabilities from bullying are typically unsuccessful because it is difficult to prove the harm caused by the bullying was foreseeable (Conn, 2013; *Gaudino v. Stroudsburg Area Sch. Dist.*, 2013). Most recently, parents have more commonly and more successfully alleged violations under federal disability law including IDEA, Section 504 of the Rehabilitation Act

(Section 504), and/or Title II of the Americans with Disabilities Act (ADA).

Many parents have brought claims under IDEA. IDEA requires students with disabilities receive a FAPE in the LRE. What constitutes as a FAPE is decided on a case-by-case basis as outlined in the Individualized Education Program (IEP). Each student's IEP must be developed by a team of educational professionals in collaboration with the parents/guardians (the IEP team). Although bullying and harassment are not discussed in IDEA, courts have begun to outline how schools' failure to adequately address disability-based harassment could result in the denial of a FAPE in violation of IDEA. Successful claims have involved persistent bullying related to a student's disability where the student's IEP lacked sufficient instructional supports to minimize bullying or where the IEP was not designed to help the student develop appropriate peer relationships (Ferster, 2008).

Yet many other parents pursue claims under Section 504 and/or ADA. ADA and Section 504 are federal civil rights laws enacted to provide comprehensive protection for disabled individuals against discrimination based on disability (*Theriault v. Flynn*, 1998). Section 504 applies to federally funded programs, whereas ADA extends Section 504's protection because ADA applies to both private and public institutions. In practical terms, the two laws mirror one another. Students who meet the definition of disability under Section 504, but who are ineligible under IDEA, typically have a Section 504 Plan. These 504 plans are similar to IEPs and require that these students also receive a FAPE (Yell, 2012).

The majority of federal courts analyzing harassment claims under ADA, Section 504, and IDEA have relied on the U.S. Supreme Court *Davis v. Monroe* (1999) decision. Courts commonly apply *Davis* to determine whether school districts are liable for student-to-student sexual harassment in violation of Title IX of the Education Amendments of 1972. In *Davis*, the Court held that school districts could be liable if school officials knew about the harassment, were deliberately indifferent toward the harassment, and the harassment was so severe, pervasive, and objectively offensive that it deprived the student of an educational benefit. The last criteria evaluating the severity of the harassment differentiates claims of bullying that may involve less severe and pervasive behavior from harassment that is considered so severe that schools can be held liable for failing to respond appropriately to it.

Some courts analyzing claims of disability-based harassment under IDEA, Section 504, and ADA have borrowed the factors enumerated in

*Davis*. Specifically, parents must first prove that the student has a disability and was harassed because of the disability. Second, parents must demonstrate that the harassment was so severe or pervasive that it had a negative impact on the student's learning, and that school officials were aware of the harassment but acted with deliberate indifference toward the harassment (see *Long v. Murray Cnty. Sch. Dist.*, 2012). In some earlier Section 504 and/or ADA cases, the courts did not applied *Davis* at all, but instead required the student plaintiff to demonstrate that school officials acted in "bad faith" or engaged in "gross misjudgment" when responding to students with disabilities who have been harassed (see *M.P. v. Indep. Sch. Dist. No. 721*, 2006; *R.P. ex rel. K.P. v. Springdale Sch. Dist.*, 2007; *Scruggs v. Meriden Bd. of Educ.*, 2007).

Weber (2002) posits that under Section 504 and ADA, students might also be able to make a claim for relief by showing a "hostile environment" and this language is included in multiple disability harassment cases (e.g., *T.K. v. N.Y.C. Dep't of Educ.*, 2011). The USDoE also seems to have adopted the approach reflected in some of the litigation in this area. In 2014, the USDoE stated that the Office for Civil Rights (OCR) would find a disability-based harassment violation under Section 504 and ADA when: (1) a student is bullied based on a disability; (2) the bullying is sufficiently serious to create a hostile environment; (3) school officials know or should know about the bullying; and, (4) the school does not respond appropriately" (USDoE, 2014a, 2014b). The requirement that school officials "know or should know" about the bullying is consistent with earlier USDoE Guidance and would subject more districts to potential liability than would the *Davis* requirement of "actual knowledge." It should be noted though, that this standard only applies to OCR's administrative enforcement. Specifically, Dear Colleague Letters are not binding as precedent in court cases.

Multiple scholars have suggested that the current standard used in disability harassment cases needs to be clarified and amended (see, e.g., Bentley, 2014; Burris, 2014; Weissinger, 2012). Needless to say, the legal standard for peer harassment of students with disabilities is still evolving, but most courts have adopted some hybrid of the *Davis* standard. Also of interest is that many of the more recent cases were filed under Section 504 and ADA rather than under IDEA, perhaps because IDEA requires plaintiffs to exhaust administrative remedies first. Specifically, IDEA requires that administrative remedies must be pursued before the case can be heard in state or federal court; thus, plaintiffs may opt to file under Section 504 and ADA as a quicker route. Parents may also be reluctant to file under IDEA because only educational relief is available (i.e., paying for a student to attend another school), while Section 504 and ADA allow courts to decide that parents are entitled to compensatory or punitive damages (i.e., monetary damages are only available in Section 504 and ADA litigation) (Conn, 2013, 2009).

## ILLUSTRATIVE CASES

There are several recent cases involving the harassment of students with disabilities. We have selected a few illustrative cases in order to examine the issues alleged by parents and the courts' rulings. We specifically included the most recent court decisions addressing bullying or harassment and tried to include decisions from a variety of federal district and circuit courts. Within this discussion, we also highlighted court decisions that involved students with disabilities who committed suicide.

### *Recent Illustrative Cases*

In Idaho, parents argued that their son, M.A., who was diagnosed with Asperger's Syndrome, experienced relentless bullying while he was a student at his public high school (*D.A. v. Meridian Joint Sch. Dist.*, 2014). The bullying included, but was not limited to, stealing M.A.'s gym clothes, physical assaults, constant name calling, and other emotional attacks. M.A.'s parents alleged that they reported the bullying to school officials and that nothing was done in response. As a result, they sued under Section 504, claiming a denial of a FAPE in the LRE. The school district filed a motion for summary judgment. The court examined whether under Section 504, the school district denied M.A. a FAPE when school officials allegedly did very little to investigate known acts of harassment.

A federal district court found that the parents identified materials in the record demonstrating a genuine dispute regarding the facts of this case. For example, the court concluded that a reasonable juror could find that M.A. was subjected to severe and pervasive disability-based harassment by his classmates, that school officials were aware of the harassment, and that the harassment altered the conditions of M.A.'s educational experience by denying him a FAPE. The school district's motion for summary judgment was therefore denied.

Likewise, in New York, A.P., a student who also had Asperger's Syndrome, was allegedly bullied by his classmates while in his high school electronics course (*Preston v. Hilton Cent. Sch. Dist.*, 2012). The students in this class often referred to him as a "fucking retard," "asshole," "faggot," and "bitch," and made other highly inappropriate commentary related to his disability. The parents informed school personnel, and the electronics course teacher apologized to A.P. and his parents. Additionally, school officials made sure that A.P.'s one-on-one aide attended this particular class. Unfortunately, A.P. did not believe that the aide had any impact on reducing the bullying, and the aide eventually stopped attending the electronics class. The parents spoke about the continued harassment and bullying with school personnel and the electronics teacher but felt that no meaningful action was taken to address the problem.

After the electronics course ended, A.P. claimed that the harassment worsened when he enrolled in a construction course. The school district responded by arranging for the aide to be present again. Once more, the aide was purportedly ineffective at curbing the bullying and eventually stopped accompanying A.P. to class. In addition to repeated egregious comments, students allegedly threw pencils and other objects at A.P. After the parents complained to the construction teacher and others, they were told that "teens will be teens" (p. 5). Although school officials promised to take action, the parents contended that nothing was done and that the harassment worsened. As a result of the harassment, A.P. became emotionally unstable and his grades in two courses dropped by 40%. His parents eventually filed a lawsuit under the ADA and Section 504, among other claims.

The federal district court examined whether school officials violated ADA and Section 504 when they allegedly failed to address the bullying directed at A.P. The school district posited that this lawsuit should have been filed under IDEA and that the parents did not comply with IDEA's exhaustion requirements. The court disagreed with the school district and noted ADA and Section 504 were appropriate avenues for relief. Furthermore, the court found that the parents' allegations – that they repeatedly called and emailed school officials about the problems discussed above and that A.P.'s grades dropped by 40% in two courses as a result of the bullying – were sufficiently stated. The court held that plaintiffs sufficiently stated a claim that school officials were deliberately indifferent in responding to the harassment directed at A.P. by his classmates because of his disability and that he was denied access to educational opportunities. Thus, the school district's motion to dismiss the ADA and Section 504 claims was denied.

These cases, along with L.K.'s case discussed above, demonstrate schools that ignore parent's requests or take no meaningful steps toward intervening have not fared well. The plaintiffs in these cases also were able to demonstrate to the court that the harassment was based on disability. In cases where this connection is not specifically established, parents have been less successful (see, e.g., *J.W. v. Johnston Cnty. Bd. of Educ.*, 2014; *S. S. v. District of Columbia*, 2014; *Thomas v. Springfield Sch. Comm.*, 2014).

### *Student Suicide*

A few recent cases have involved students with disabilities who committed suicide. The parents in these cases claimed the suicides were a result of the bullying and harassment that took place in school. To illustrate, in Georgia, Tyler, was allegedly harassed for several years in school before he ultimately committed suicide (*Long v. Murray*, 2013). His parents contended that school officials failed to intervene, investigate, or train their staff, and that those failures were a substantial contributing cause in Tyler's suicide. After his death several students reported that Tyler, who was diagnosed with Asperger's Syndrome, was harassed in school. They reported Tyler was called "gay," "stupid," and was often cussed at in the school. Kids knocked books out of his hands in the hallway, pushed him into desks, and spit on his food, but sometimes the harassment was not reported to teachers. Tyler's parents wrote emails to school officials about the harassment and in many cases school officials addressed the harassment.

The Eleventh Circuit affirmed the district court's decision to grant the school district's motion for summary judgment. The court applied the *Davis* standard under Section 504 because the parties "effectively agreed that the deliberate indifference" standard with applied (p. 577, n. 1, 2013). According to the court, while school officials could have taken more action to address the disability harassment, the plaintiffs failed to meet the high bar of deliberate indifference, and the defendant's response was not completely unreasonable. Additionally, the court reasoned that a jury could reasonably conclude that school officials did not know that their actions were ineffective in addressing the harassment.

In another case involving a student with a disability who also committed suicide after he experienced harassment in school, the Fifth Circuit found that school officials in Texas actively responded to incidents involving harassment against the student (see *Estate of Lance v. Lewisville Indep. Sch. Dist.*, 2014). The parents alleged violations of Section 504 among other claims, but the circuit court affirmed the grant of summary judgment to the school district for the federal disability harassment claim. The school district's response was not clearly unreasonable under *Davis*. The court found that there was a pattern of school leaders effectively responding to the harassment incidents involving the student and that school officials tried to assist the student by promoting friendships with other students.

A similar case from an Alabama federal district court also granted the school district's motion for summary judgment. In this case school officials with authority to act did not have actual knowledge of the harassment (*Moore v. Chilton Cnty. Bd. of Educ.*, 2014). Courts addressing this issue have consistently held that a school official, with authority to act, must have actual knowledge about the harassment before being is expected to address the harassment. Courts have examined who is an "appropriate person" employed by the board when determining who has authority to act in these situations. In this case, the court highlighted that prior precedent in this circuit suggests that an "appropriate person" with authority to act is a fact-based inquiry because school officials' roles vary among school districts (p. 15–16). The court ultimately decided that the plaintiffs wrongly assumed that *any* district employee is an appropriate person with authority to act. Further, even if they had the appropriate authority to act, it was not evident that they had actual knowledge about the harassment. Thus, they could not act with deliberate indifference when responding to known acts of harassment against a student with disability who eventually committed suicide (see *Moore v. Chilton Cnty. Bd. of Educ.*, 2014).

In another case involving a student with a disability who committed suicide, a Maryland federal district court granted the school district's motion to dismiss. The student's parents alleged school officials did not do enough to address the harassment. For example, school officials failed to change the seating arrangements to separate the victim from the perpetrator in class. Although the court acknowledged some poor judgment on the part of school officials, it did not result in a finding of deliberate indifference (*Wright v. Carroll Cnty. Bd. of Educ.*, 2013).

These cases taken as a whole stress the need for school officials to act when they are aware that a student with a disability is being harassed or bullied in school. The courts held in favor of the school districts in the four cases involving suicide which suggests that when school officials' responses to the harassment are not clearly unreasonable, liability will be difficult to prove. However, school districts' ability to escape legal liability does not change the devastating reality that students with disabilities have committed suicide after being harassed in schools and school leaders have a legal and ethical responsibility to respond to and prevent harassment from occurring. The Guidance from the USDoE highlights these points as well.

## GUIDANCE FROM U.S. DEPARTMENT OF EDUCATION

Since 2000, the USDoE has issued four letters providing guidance about the law surrounding disability-based harassment. This guidance is found in "Dear Colleague Letters" that the USDoE issued in 2000, 2010, 2013, and 2014. In the most recent Dear Colleague Letter, the USDoE explained that the guidance is a continuation of previous assistance from the Office for Civil Rights (OCR) and the Office of Special Education and Rehabilitative Services (OSERS). The OCR enforces both Section 504 and Title II of the ADA and OSERS administers IDEA. When the OCR is enforcing Section 504 and ADA rights, they are also enforcing the rights of IDEA-eligible students.

In 2000, the OCR and the OSERS issued a joint guidance informing school leaders of their legal responsibilities under Section 504 and ADA as they relate to disability harassment. It also addressed ensuring that students receive a FAPE under Section 504 and IDEA. In 2010, the OCR issued another Dear Colleague Letter reminding school personnel that inappropriate responses to bullying or harassment of a student based on disability constitutes disability-based harassment under Section 504 or ADA. OSERS released a third Dear Colleague Letter in 2013 highlighting that when a student with a disability is bullied on any basis, even if the student's disability is not the focus, it can result in a denial of a FAPE under IDEA.

The 2014 Guidance began by discussing how students with disabilities are disproportionately affected by bullying in schools. The USDoE clarified that the bullying of a student "on any basis" can result in a denial of a FAPE under Section 504 and that school personnel must be proactive to ensure the bullying is addressed. For example, if a student with a peanut allergy who has a Section 504 Plan is bullied by other students with peanut candy bars at school (e.g., "ha, ha I am eating peanut candy – do you want a bite so you can die"), it could result in a disability-based harassment violation and a denial of a FAPE if the bullying is not promptly addressed by school officials. This Guidance offered several other scenarios to help illustrate what types of conduct might constitute both a disability-based harassment violation and a FAPE violation, a FAPE violation, or neither. If a student who is eligible under Section 504 or IDEA experiences bullying constituting disability-based harassment, the Guidance suggests that there is a strong likelihood that the student has been denied a FAPE.

The Guidance also provided some helpful suggestions for school leaders who need to respond to instances of bullying in the event that disability-based harassment is found, including, but not limited to, counseling for the student and creating school-wide prevention strategies. Interestingly, the Guidance used the terms bullying and harassment interchangeably. It noted that the label being used to describe the conduct—whether bullying or harassment—does not determine how school officials are obligated to respond. Instead, such determination should be made by examining whether the negative conduct involved any civil rights implications.

## RECOMMENDATIONS

Despite the evolution of legal protections and entitlements under IDEA, Section 504 and ADA, disability-based discrimination persists including the bullying and harassment of students with disabilities. To combat the myriad of negative effects of disability-based harassment in schools, educational leaders must be aware of their legal and ethical responsibilities. Most leaders may be aware of—and more likely to act upon—their legal responsibilities. Therefore, it is especially crucial that leadership training focuses on ethics. Leadership training should include a variety of ethical dilemmas so that leaders can identify what they will do when their ethical and legal responsibilities are in conflict with one another. School leaders must understand how to apply past court decisions and the USDoE's Guidance to situations they encounter in their schools. The following recommendations are intended to highlight a few key steps that educational preparation programs, leaders, and policymakers can undertake to address this significant issue.

1. Increase awareness of the problem of disability-based harassment by publicizing the research suggesting that students with disabilities are bullied in higher numbers than their nondisabled peers (e.g., Rose, Espelage, & Monda-Amaya, 2009) and by discussing current events documenting that disability-based harassment is a significant problem in schools today (e.g., Cornwell, 2015).
2. Train teachers and other school personnel about how to respond to student-to-student harassment in schools with particular emphasis on more vulnerable populations such as students with disabilities. This training should occur across settings (i.e., in pre-service teacher and leadership preparation programs, as well as through the district's professional development sessions).

3. Develop student-centered programming to explain that harassment and bullying will not be tolerated. Be sure students are provided with multiple examples of disability-based harassment (see USDoE, 2014a, 2014b).
4. Ensure that school leaders are trained not only about school liability for harassment under Title IX, but also liability for disability-based harassment under Section 504, ADA and/or IDEA.
5. Provide special supports to students with disabilities (e.g., counseling, social skills training) (Rose, Monda-Amaya, & Espelage, 2011). Although these supports may add another expense for financially strapped school systems, the districts will likely save legal fees by offering special supports. More importantly, preventative measures like these will help to reduce the harassment of students with disabilities.
6. Clarify to school leaders that courts have not always been consistent with what analysis is used in disability discrimination cases. While some courts apply a standard related to the U.S. Supreme Court *Davis v. Monroe* decision, other courts have used different standards. For example sometimes the analysis will turn on whether the school district acted in "bad faith" or "gross misjudgment." Additionally, the USDoE's 2014 Guidance confirms its earlier Guidance that OCR may become involved in situations where schools "should know" about harassment as opposed to the stricter "actual knowledge" standard enumerated in *Davis*.
7. Train school officials to respond appropriately when a student is harassed by another student in school. When school officials fail to respond, they may be considered "deliberately indifferent." Deliberately indifferent has been defined by some courts as clearly unreasonable in light of the known circumstances.
8. Explain that school officials are afforded some flexibility in responding to unacceptable student conduct and may tailor their responses to the circumstances. For example, a student who repeatedly kicks and slams a student with a disability into a locker should face more serious repercussions than those imposed for calling that same student "ugly" at recess.

Educational preparation programs, leaders, and policymakers should build upon these recommendations in order to truly diminish disability-based harassment in schools today. As evidenced by the historical and current context, the bullying and harassment of students with disabilities is a significant issue in need of greater attention. When students with disabilities are bullied and harassed, parents can pursue a variety of legal avenues to hold schools liable. In recent years, plaintiffs have had the most success filing claims under IDEA, Section 504, and ADA. The court decisions that have resulted from this litigation and the USDoE Guidance provide school leaders with some clarification about how courts may analyze future claims filed against school districts; however, the legal parameters surrounding this issue are still evolving. Instead of waiting for clearer legal guidance about what they must do as a matter of legal obligation, educational leaders should proactively seek ways to prevent students with disabilities from bullying and harassment.

## REFERENCES

Bentley, B. C. L. D. (2014). A novel IDEA: Protecting students with disabilities from school bullies. *Clearinghouse Review*, *48*, 23–45.

Blatt, B. (1970). *Exodus from pandemonium*. Boston, MA: Allyn & Bacon.

Carter, B. B., & Spencer, V. G. (2006). The fear factor: Bullying and students with disabilities. *International Journal of Special Education*, *21*(1), 11–23.

Conn, K. (2009). Bullying and harassment: Can IDEA protect special students? *West Education Law Reporter*, *239*(3), 789–800.

Conn, K. (2013). Guidance on bullying of students with disabilities. *Education Law Reporter*, *297*(1), 1–11.

Cornwell, P. (2015). 5 Juanita high students charged with rape of classmate. *The Seattle Times*, February 6. Retrieved from http://blogs.seattletimes.com/today/2015/02/5-juanita-high-students-charged-with-attempted-rape-of-classmate/

D.A. v. Meridian Joint School District No. 2 (2014) U.S. Dist. LEXIS 1699 (D. Idaho 2014).

Davis v. Monroe County Board of Education, 526 U.S. 629 (1999).

Estate of Lance v. Lewisville Independent School District. 743 F.3d 982 (5th Cir. 2014).

Ferster, D. E. (2008). Deliberately different: Bullying as a denial of a free appropriate public education under the individuals with disabilities education act. *Georgia Law Review*, *43*(1), 191–228.

Gaudino v. Stroudsburg Area School District, 2013 U.S. Dist. LEXIS 102382 (M.D. Pa. 2013).

Hartley, M. T., Bauman, S., Nixon, C. L., & Davis, S. (2015). Comparative study of bullying victimization among students in general and special education. *Exceptional Children*, *81*(2), 176–193.

Hehir, T. (2005). *New directions in special education: Eliminating ableism in policy and practice*. Cambridge, MA: Harvard Education Press.

Hehir, T., & Gamm, S. (1999). Special education: From legalism to collaboration. In J. Heubert (Ed.), *Law and school reform* (pp. 205–227). New Haven, CT: Yale University Press.

J.W. v. Johnston County Board of Education, 2014 U.S. LEXIS 134342 (E.D.N.C. 2014).

Long v. Murray County School District, 2012 U.S. Dist. LEXIS 86155 (N.D. Ga. 2012).

Long v. Murray County School District, 522 Fed. Appx. 576 (11th Cir. 2013).

Moore v. Chilton County Board of Education, 1 F. Supp. 3d 1281 (M.D. Ala. 2014).

Office of Special Education and Rehabilitative Services (OSERS). (2013). *Dear colleague letter on bullying of students with disabilities*. Retrieved from http://www.ed.gov/policy/speced/guid/idea/memosdcltrs/bullyingdcl-8-20-13.doc

Pazey, B. L., & Yates, J. R. (2012). Conceptual and historical foundations of special education administration. In J. Crockett, B. Billingsley, & M. L. Boscardin (Eds.), *Handbook of leadership in special education* (pp. 17–36). London: Routledge.

Preston v. Hilton Central School District. 876 F.Supp.2d 235 (W.D.N.Y. 2012).

R.P. ex rel. K.P. v. Springdale Sch. Dist., 2007 U.S. Dist. LEXIS 12073 (W.D. Ark. Feb. 21, 2007).

Rose, C. A., Espelage, D. L., & Monda-Amaya, L. E. (2009). Bullying and victimization rates among students in general and special education: A comparative analysis. *Educational Psychology*, *29*(7), 761–776.

Rose, C. A., Monda-Amaya, L. E., & Espelage, D. L. (2011). Bullying perpetration and victimization in special education: A review of the literature. *Remedial and Special Education*, *32*, 114–130.

S.S. v. District of Columbia, 2014 U.S. Dist. LEXIS 131327 (D.D.C. 2014).

Scruggs v. Meriden Board of Education, 2007 U.S. Dist. LEXIS 58517 (D. Conn. 2007).

T.K. v. N.Y.C. Dep't of Educ., 779 F. Supp. 2d 289 (E.D.N.Y. 2011).

Theriault v. Flynn, 162 F.3d 46 (1st Cir. 1998).

Thomas v. Springfield School Community, 2014 U.S. Dist. LEXIS 161970 (D. Mass. 2014).

U.S. Department of Education. (2000). *Dear colleague letter*. Retrieved from www.ed.gov/about/offices/list/ocr/docs/disabharassltr.html

U.S. Department of Education. (2010a). *Dear colleague letter*. Retrieved from http://www2.ed.gov/about/offices/list/ocr/letters/colleague-201010.html

U.S. Department of Education. (2010b). Thirty-five years of progress in educating children with disabilities through IDEA. Washington, DC. Retrieved from http://www2.ed.gov/%20about/offices/list/osers/idea35/history/index.html

U.S. Department of Education. (2013). *Dear colleague letter*. Retrieved from http://www.ed.gov/policy/speced/guid/idea/memosdcltrs/bullyingdcl-8-20-13.doc

U.S. Department of Education. (2014a). *Dear colleague letter*. Retrieved from http://www2.ed.gov/about/offices/list/ocr/letters/colleague-bullying-201410.pdf

U.S. Department of Education. (2014b). *Civil rights data collection: Data snapshot (school discipline)*. Retrieved from http://www2.ed.gov/about/offices/list/ocr/docs/crdc-discipline-snapshot.pdf

Weber, M. (2002). Disability harassment in the public schools. *William and Mary Law Review*, *43*(3), 1079–1158.

Weissinger, K. (2012). Bullying that results in a denial of a free appropriate public education: Staking the claim under the IDEA. *Children's Legal Rights Journal*, *32*, 52–66.

Wright v. Carroll County Board of Education, 2013 U.S. Dist. LEXIS 120892 (D. Md. 2013).

Yell, M. L. (2012). *Law and special education* (3rd ed.). Upper Saddle River, NJ: Pearson.

# CHAPTER 3

# FROM STUDENT ARMBANDS TO CYBERBULLYING: THE FIRST AMENDMENT IN PUBLIC SCHOOLS

Kathleen Conn

## ABSTRACT

*The American public greatly esteems their First Amendment right to freedom of speech, but generally understands poorly its true ambit. Unfortunately, this defect in understanding permeates American educational institutions, from the lowest grades to higher education and even professional schools. Students' pervasive ability to engage in technological speech and expression further complicates the issue, especially when inappropriate or offensive speech originating outside school crosses the geographic boundary and enters school. School administrators at all levels, challenged with maintaining atmospheres of safety and security conducive to learning, are being asked to respond to such student speech, but they fear to exceed the limits of their authority. Cyberbullying and harassing communications continue to distract victims and educators and detract from the quality of education at all institutions. The legal system and judiciary provide little guidance, and what guidance there is suffers from lack of consistent definitions and conflicting analyses. This chapter will review the jurisprudence pertaining to the First Amendment as*

**Legal Frontiers in Education: Complex Law Issues for Leaders, Policymakers and Policy Implementers**
**Advances in Educational Administration, Volume 24, 35–58**

**ISSN: 1479-3660/doi:10.1108/S1479-366020150000024029**

*applied to the school setting. The emphasis will be on legislative, judicial, and societal responses to cyberbullying and cyber harassment in the school setting, from the elementary level to higher education. Finally, recommendations for policies and procedures for dealing with cyberbullying and cyber harassment in schools will be presented.*

## BULLYING

Bullying is pervasive in American educational institutions (Banks, 2013), and efforts to curb its spread have had only modest success. Perhaps because bullying appears to peak in middle school (Ackerman, Kramer, & Bruno, 2014), and continues at only slightly less-elevated levels throughout high school, most of the attention on bullying and bullying prevention efforts have focused on bullying in grades 6 through 12 in American public schools. Estimates of the prevalence of bullying at these school levels report 25–30% of students involved in bullying on a regular basis, as either victim, bully, or bully-victim, with up to 85% of bullying incidents largely unaddressed by either teachers or school administrators (Bullying Statistics, n.d.a). However, bullying begins in pre-school (Evans, 2011) and persists throughout college, university, and professional schools (Chappell et al., 2006; Krasselt, 2014; Major, 2014).

### *Federal Definition of Bullying*

In 2014, The Centers for Disease Control and Prevention (CDC) and the U.S. Department of Education (U.S. DOE) released the first uniform federal definition of bullying (Gladden, Vivolo-Kantor, Hamburger, & Lumpkin, 2014). The core elements identified were unwanted aggressive behavior, observed or perceived power imbalance, and repetition of behaviors or a high likelihood of repetition. The researchers divided bullying into two modes, direct and indirect, and within those modes, four types of behaviors were identified: physical, verbal, relational (efforts to harm the reputation or relationship of the victim), and damage to property.

Technology-facilitated bullying or cyberbullying is largely verbal or relational, although it can include damage to property if the bully hacks into and destroys the victim's electronically stored messages (Gladden et al., 2014). Bullying can escalate to criminal behavior, as in harassment, hazing, or assault.

### *Effects of Bullying*

Bullying has serious and lasting negative effects on the mental health and overall well-being of a child or young adult. Bullying can lead to or exacerbate feelings of isolation, inferiority, rejection, despair, and, in most serious cases, acute depression and suicide. The actual number of bullied students who commit suicide is relatively small, but for students with multiple risk factors, suicide may be seen as a "way out." Students who self-identify as, or are perceived as, lesbian, gay, bisexual, transgender, or questioning (LGBTQ) are disproportionally bullied; up to 84.6% of LGBTQ students nationally report being verbally victimized, and 40.1% report being physically assaulted because of their gender orientation (Espelage, 2011). Any involvement with bullying, as victim, bully, or witness/bystander, may be the stressor that leads to suicide. However, LGBTQ students are at significantly greater risk of suicide completion than heterosexual youth (Espelage, 2011).

## CYBERBULLYING

### *Bullying Morphs into Cyberbullying*

As students move from elementary school into middle school, face-to-face bullying behaviors often transform into electronically-mediated bullying, or cyberbullying (Olson, 2014). Cyberbullying is even more insidious than face-to-face bullying because of the anonymity of the bully or bullies and the pervasive and persistent nature of cyberbullying. A cyberbully may be a student's worst enemy or someone pretending to be his or her friend in school. And cyberbullying is "on" 24/7; its menacing messages never completely disappear from hyperspace. The audience for a cyberbullying message is potentially limitless.

With technology, cyberbullying has challenged the core element of repetitive behavior defining bullying. A single posting, email, text or tweet can be re-sent repeatedly, or forwarded once to unlimited recipients. The repetition may be accomplished by the bully or by anyone copying or even editing the original communication to make it more vicious, lascivious, or threatening. Cyberbullying also removes the necessity of power imbalance in the bullying equation (Bullying Statistics, n.d.b). The cyberbully does not need to be capable of intimidation to instill fear; with anonymity comes the ability of a victim to become the bully. In fact, the "get-even" mentality inspires many cyberbullies who could never retaliate in person; they retaliate against school administrators who disciplined them, teachers whom they perceive as too strict or unfair, and classmates who are more powerful or more popular.

### *Teenagers' Technology Access and Use*

According the November 2011 Pew Research Center Report, 95% of all teenagers ages 12–17 had online access at the time of the study, and 80% of those teens used social media, defined as social networking sites (SNS) or Twitter (Lenhart et al., 2011). One out of every five teen SNS-users reported that online users are "mostly unkind" to each other. What was especially concerning was that 62% of SNS-using teens said they set their primary profiles to private, suggesting that individuals to whom they had granted access to their sites as "friends" either initiated or participated in the unkind communications. The Pew researchers also investigated teens' text messaging habits and found that texts are also used to cyberbully (Lenhart et al., 2011). Almost one-tenth, or 9%, of the teens surveyed reported that they had been cyberbullied via text messages in the 12 months prior to the survey.

A 2013 Pew report, *Teens, Social Media, and Privacy*, indicated that American teens are intensely interested in communicating about their daily activities with peers using social media (Madden et al., 2013). A companion Pew survey, *Teens and Technology 2013*, found that, at the time of the study's conclusion, 78% of teens had mobile phones, and of these, 47% had smart phones with which they could access the internet. One in four teens reported that they were "cell-mostly" internet users, meaning that their preferred access to social media was through their mobile phones (Madden, Lenhart, Duggan, Cortesi, & Gasser, 2013). Among middle school students, instant chatting and bullying by cell phone were the most prevalent forms of cyberbullying (Ackerman et al., 2014).

### *The Prevalence of Cyberbullying*

Attempts to accurately document the prevalence of cyberbullying have been hampered by different sample sizes in different populations of study, non-uniformity of definitions of cyberbullying or time period during which students experienced cyberbullying (e.g., last year, last 30 days), and phrasing of questions about the content of the unwanted communications themselves (e.g., unwanted, upsetting, threatening communications) (Bauman, 2013; Kowalski, Limber, & Agatson, 2012; Shariff, 2008). In Pew's 2007 report, *Cyberbullying*, Amanda Lenhart found that 32% of teenagers who use the internet for any reason said that they had been targets of annoying or potentially threatening communications online, having rumors spread about them, private messages forwarded without their permission, or having embarrassing photos of them posted (Lenhart, 2007). Most teens who responded to the 2007 survey thought that bullying happened more frequently offline than online.

Cross-sectional national telephone surveys of youth ages 10 through 17 showed a growing number of teens experienced online harassment between 2000 and 2010, with 6% of teens reporting online harassment in 2000, 9% in 2005, and 11% in 2009 (Jones, Mitchell, & Finkelhor, 2012). More recently, Justin Patchin, University of Wisconsin-Eau Claire researcher, found in a survey of 1,500 U.S. middle and high school students that 24% of teens reported that they had experienced cyberbullying at some point, with 8% reporting they had experienced cyberbullying in the last 30 days (Patchin, 2013).

### *Effects of Cyberbullying*

One in every five students who report that they are cyberbullied also report that they are also bullied face-to-face (Hoff & Mitchell, 2009). These authors also found that cyberbullying most commonly emerges from relationship issues like break-ups, envy, intolerance, or mobbing, that is, ganging-up on a victim. They hypothesized that this relational link was responsible for the peaking of cyberbullying among 14–15-year-olds, the age at which hormonal forces propel the primacy of romantic relationships.

Spanish researchers interviewed 1,755 adolescent students in Cordoba, Spain to compare the effects of face-to-face bullying and cyberbullying, and found that victims of both types of bullying reported negative effects that the researchers categorized into five groups: "not bothered," fear, anger, depression, and shame (Ortega, Elipe, Mora-Merchan, Camaestra, & Vega, 2009). Approximately 35–44% of students in the study reported that they were not bothered by mobile phone or internet cyberbullying, but females were significantly less able to brush off cyberbullying than males. For example, 28.6% of females reported not being bothered by cyberbullying via mobile phone, contrasted with 55.6% of males who reported not being bothered; 30.6% of females reported being worried by mobile phone cyberbullying contrasted with only 5.6% of males (Ortega et al., 2009). Only 2% of Spanish males reported being stressed by internet cyberbullying, but 13.7% of females reported being stressed by the same kind of communications. However, over twice as many females reported being angry over such internet communications as males (37% of females contrasted with 18% of males) (Ortega et al., 2009).

American researchers agree that cyberbullying victimization causes psychological, emotional, and physical stress, and that depression is a major negative effect of cyberbullying victimization (Tokunaga, 2009). In addition, researchers have found a measurable link between cyberbullying victimization and suicidal ideation (Hinduja & Patchin, 2010). Studying 2,000 students 10- to 16-year-olds in 30 American schools, Hinduja and Patchin (2010) found that cyberbullying victims were 1.9 times more likely to have attempted suicide than student who had not experienced cyberbullying. However, perpetrators of cyberbullying were also 1.5 times more likely to have attempted suicide.

While the researchers agree that it is unlikely that cyberbullying by itself causes adolescent suicides, Hinduja and Patchin (2010) contend that cyberbullying victimization exacerbates the instability and helpless feelings in adolescents already affected by other stressful life circumstances or underlying mental health problems. The rise in internet use, mobile phone accessibility and use, and social networking use by American teenagers (Eddy, 2013) correlates with the rise in teenagers' suicidal ideation and suicide attempts by American teenagers from 2009-2013 [Centers for Disease Control (CDC), 2014]. The National Youth Risk Behavior Survey (YRBS) *Trends in the Prevalence of Suicide-Related Behavior* indicates that the percentages of high school students who reported having seriously considered attempting suicide during the 12 months before the survey increased from 13.8% in 2009 to 17% in 2013. Similarly, the percentages of students who reported having actually attempted suicide in during that time period had increased from 6.3% in 2009 to 8.0% in 2013, with a concomitant rise in the number of students who required treatment by a doctor or nurse after the suicide attempts, from 1.9% in 2009 to 2.7% in 2013.

### *The Geographic Origin of Cyberbullying*

One of the more difficult issues with cyberbullying is that cyberbullying occurs more outside school than in school (Smith et al., 2008). Because cyberbullying often translates into in-school problems and school avoidance for victims, parents increasingly look to school administrators to discipline the cyberbullies (Hoffman, 2010). However, because of the non-school origin of cyberbullying, many school administrators do not know how to deal with the issue. Administrators who do discipline the cyberbullies often find themselves in court, sued by the parents of the cyberbullies for disciplining their children's expressive behaviors occurring outside school. School administrators and school districts often see their authority crumble under the force of legal precedents that have limited relevance in an online world.

## THE FIRST AMENDMENT IN AMERICAN PUBLIC SCHOOLS

The First Amendment of the U.S. Constitution is the bedrock for Americans' freedom of speech and expression. The First Amendment states, among other guarantees, "Congress shall make no law ... abridging the freedom of speech" (U.S. CONST. amend. I). The Fourteenth Amendment extended the guarantee to prohibit infringement of speech and expression by the states, and by attribution, to those considered to be acting for state governments, "state actors," that is, federal and state employees, including public school administrators. However, the First Amendment does not protect all categories of speech; defamatory speech, threats, speech inciting to riot, and hate speech are among the categories of speech unprotected by the First Amendment (Haynes, Chaltain, Ferguson, Hudson, & Thomas, 2003).

The U.S. Supreme Court qualifiedly affirmed the right of students in public schools to be free from infringement of their speech and expression by state actors in the seminal student speech decision *Tinker v. Des Moines Independent Community Schools* (1969). Students in the *Tinker* case wore black armbands to school to protest America's involvement in the Vietnam War. School administrators sent the students home and suspended them from school until they would return to school without the armbands. In the *Tinker* decision, the majority stated that

> First Amendment rights, applied in the light of the special characteristics of the school environment, are available to teachers and students. It can hardly be argued that either students or teachers shed their constitutional rights to freedom of speech or expression at the schoolhouse gate. (p. 506)

The Court continued

> In order for the State in the person of school officials to justify prohibition of a particular expression of opinion, [the state] must be able to show that its action was caused by something more than a mere desire to avoid the discomfort and unpleasantness that always accompany an unpopular viewpoint. *Certainly where there is no finding and no showing that engaging in the forbidden conduct would 'materially and substantially interfere with the requirements of the public discipline and the operation of the school,' the prohibition cannot be sustained* [italics added]. (p. 509, quoting *Burnside v. Byars*, 363 F.2d 744, 749 (1966))

These quotations from *Tinker* appear almost universally in court decisions involving student speech and expression, in student speech controversies K-16 and even beyond, in litigation concerning speech and expression in professional schools (Conn, 2013). The "*Tinker* standard" has come to mean that state actors cannot infringe the speech and expression of students in the school environment or in school-sponsored activities unless that speech or expression materially and substantially disrupts school operations, or that state actors have a reasonable fear that the speech or expression will cause such disruption. However, the *Tinker* Court also stated a much less-often quoted phrase, what has been dubbed "the second prong" of the *Tinker* standard, that school officials may regulate student speech or expression that causes "the invasion of the rights of others" in the educational environment (Tinker, 1969, p. 513). Unfortunately, this second prong has received almost no consideration or application in court decisions on student speech issues at any level (McCarthy, 2009).

After the *Tinker* decision, the Supreme Court decided three additional student speech cases sporadically over the next 40 years. Each decision limited the expansive student speech rights conferred by the *Tinker* decision. In *Bethel School District No. 403 v. Fraser* (1986), the Court affirmed the right of public school officials to regulate lewd and offensive student speech spoken in front of a captive audience of fellow students. In *Hazelwood School District v. Kuhlmeier* (1988), the Court upheld the right of school officials to censor a school newspaper produced in journalism class because the newspaper would appear to the public to bear the *imprimatur* of the school. Finally, in *Morse v. Frederick* (2007), the "Bong Hits 4 Jesus" decision, the Court upheld the right of school officials to prohibit student speech that advocated illegal drug use.

Analysis of these four seminal student speech decisions by the Supreme Court reveals a critical similarity, that the Court considered the student speech in each controversy to be "in-school" speech or speech at a sanctioned school activity. In fact, in *Morse*, the Court cautioned that, "There is some uncertainty at the outer boundaries as to when courts should apply school speech precedents" (p. 401). By the time of the *Morse* decision, it was clear that the "outer boundaries" to which the Court referred were the controversies arising from student speech and expression originating outside the confines of schools, cyberbullying communications that were percolating through the lower courts with conflicting results.

## LITIGATION INVOLVING STUDENTS' CYBERBULLYING COMMUNICATIONS

### *The Early Cyberbullying Controversies*

The early litigation concerning online communications related to K-12 schools, and still the most frequently litigated issue in recent years, involved students' offensive, lewd, and denigrating online postings directed toward school staff and school administrators. If, as the new federal definition of bullying asserts, the core elements of bullying are unwanted aggressive behavior, observed or perceived power imbalance, and repetition of behaviors or a high likelihood of repetition; and if cyberbullying reverses the power imbalance necessary for face-to-face bullying and changes the repetitive behavior element so that a unique online posting potentially repeated to a unlimited audience still constitutes bullying, then the online postings of students denigrating their school administrators fits the definition of cyberbullying.

The communications of the late1990s/early 2000s in the form of student-created web pages criticizing school personnel were simply regarded as violations of school policies or disrespect to school staff members by technology savvy middle and high school males. The true pervasive and destructive nature of cyberbullying was yet to emerge. Most legal controversies surrounding the early offensive and disrespectful postings were decided in favor of the students and their parents who sued the school districts for disciplining their students for their internet postings (*Beussink v. Woodland R-IV School District*, 1998; *Emmett v. Kent School District*, 2000; *Killion v. Franklin Regional School District*, 2001).

One of the only court decisions during that time period that upheld the authority of the school district to discipline a student for off-campus, school-related expression despite multiple parental challenges in lower courts was the decision of the Pennsylvania Supreme Court in *J.S. v. Bethlehem Area School District* (2002) Academic Press (2002). In *J.S.*, middle school student Justin Swidler posted a series of web pages that he created on his home computer, showing his algebra teacher Kathleen Fulmer with her face morphed into Adolf Hitler, and on another page, with her head cut off and blood dripping from her neck. He criticized the teacher as an incompetent math teacher, and requested that anyone who saw the web pages should give him $20.00 to help pay for a "hitman" to get rid of her. He also alleged that his principal Thomas Kartsotis was having a sexual affair with the female principal of a neighboring school.

When the lawsuit finally arrived at the Pennsylvania Supreme Court, the majority noted the "special characteristics of the school environment" pronouncement in *Tinker*, and, while agreeing that young Swidler created his web pages at home, ruled that the web pages were in-school speech because the web pages were accessed in school. The court held that Justin's web pages caused material and substantial disruption of school operations, interpreting the *Tinker* standard by stating that "while there must be more than some mild distraction or curiosity created by the speech [citations omitted], complete chaos is not required" (J.S., 2002, p. 673). The disruption of school operations specifically noted by the majority included: (a) Kathleen Fulmer's trauma which caused her to miss teaching her classes for twenty days at the end of one school year and the entire next school year, making it necessary for the district to hire substitute teachers to teach her classes, (b) anxiety among the students, many of whom sought counseling in school, (c) parental concerns about the safety of their students, the quality of instruction provided by the substitute teachers, and the negative impact on their students' education, and (d) the feelings of helplessness and low morale caused by the whole affair among students, staff, and parents.

While the Bethlehem Area School District defendants were able to successfully enunciate a totality of effects of J.S.'s web postings sufficient to constitute "material and substantial disruption," the question has remained, "To what level does disruption have to rise to be enough to negate the First Amendment protection of students' online speech?" (Wenkart, 2008). Even more problematic is the question of deciding when the fear of impending disruption is reasonable enough to satisfy the *Tinker* standard. Public school administrators have little to no reliable guidance, with lower courts in different, and even in the same, jurisdictions handing down different and conflicting rulings.

## *Cyberbullying of K-12 School Administrators: The* Layshock *and (Female)* J.S. *Decisions*

### *The* Layshock *Decision*

Two contemporaneous decisions which are illustrative of conflicting outcomes in neighboring jurisdictions where courts applied the same *Tinker* standard to resolve student speech controversies with similar fact patterns are the *Layshock v. Hermitage School District* (2007) and the *J.S. v. Blue Mountain School District* (2008) decisions. Both high school student Justin Layshock and a female middle school student, known to the court only as J.S., created imposter profiles of their school principals on MySpace. The imposter profile Layshock created purported to be the MySpace profile of his high school principal Eric Trosch, with a "big keg" behind his desk, getting "hard-ons" when he saw attractive female students, and being "too drunk" to remember his birthday." The imposter profile J.S. and a friend created was much more sexual, vulgar and demeaning of her middle school principal James McGonigle, representing him as a married, bisexual man who "hit on" students and parents and f***-ed them in the school office. J.S. also added sexual comments relating to McGonigle's wife, a counselor in the middle school. Both Layshock and J.S. copied their principals' photographs from their district websites and posted them in the profiles. The profiles circulated in their respective schools, viewed by approximately 20 students in each case.

The Hermitage School District took harsh disciplinary action against Layshock, suspending him and removing him to an alternative curricular program, as well as imposing other social and academic penalties. Layshock's parents went to district court and sought both a temporary restraining order and a preliminary injunction, both of which the court initially refused. However, shortly afterward, the presiding judge reversed his initial decision, stating that the more fully developed record showed that, although students had accessed the principal's imposter profile at school, no substantial disruption of school operations had occurred (Layshock, 2007). The school district appealed to the Third Circuit Court of Appeals, which affirmed that the Hermitage Area School District lacked the authority to discipline a student for expressive conduct that originated outside the school "when that conduct did not disturb the school environment and was not related to any school-sponsored event" (Layshock, 2010, p. 251). The Third Circuit also found unpersuasive the district's argument that Layshock's appropriation of the principal's photograph from the district website created a *nexus* to the school.

### *The* J.S. *Decision*

On the other hand, the outcome following J.S.'s postings was quite different. When the profile was discovered, J.S.'s principal suspended her for 10 days. Like the Layshocks, J.S.'s parents sought to overturn the disciplinary action in court, but the district court denied relief. When J.S.'s parents sued to have the school district's action declared unconstitutional, the court ruled that J.S.'s off-campus expression had an on-campus effect that caused a "buzz" among students. The court upheld the constitutionality of all Blue Mountain School District student speech and computer policies (J.S., 2008). J.S.'s parents then appealed to the Third Circuit Court of Appeals. The Third Circuit ruled that because of J.S.'s posting, the school authorities could have reasonably forecast a substantial disruption or material interference with school operations (J.S., 2010). The Third Circuit noted the extent of disruption after the profile circulated in school, (a) two teachers had to quiet their classes, (b) a guidance counselor had to change her schedule to accommodate an administrator who had to meet with J.S. and her parents, and (c) students decorated J.S.'s locker when she returned to school after her suspension, and other students congregated around the locker. The principal testified to a "deterioration in discipline" at the school after the profile circulated, and he alleged that he suffered stress-related health problems as a result of the profile (J.S., 2008, pp. 293–294).

### *The* En Banc *Decisions*

Both decisions of the Third Circuit were eventually reheard on the same day, June 3, 2010, by the Third Circuit sitting *en banc*, that is, all 13 judges hearing the arguments and deliberating together. The *en banc* court reviewed the *Layshock* decision in the morning, and the same *en banc* panel reviewed the *J.S.* decision later that afternoon. Separate opinions were filed on June 13, 2011. Both decisions were rulings in favor of the students, with the court upholding the First Amendment rights of the students to freedom of speech originating out of school, and denying the disciplinary authority of school administrators over out-of-school speech that did not rise, in the court's opinion, to material and substantial disruption of school operations (Conn, 2011).

## *Cyberbullying of Peers in K-12 Schools: The* J.C. *and* Kowalski *Decisions*

### *The* J.C. *Decision*

Courts have also reached conflicting decisions with regard to school administrators' authority to discipline students for peer cyberbullying, even if the cyberbullying reaches the school and parents seek the help of school administrators. In *J.C. v. Beverly Hills Unified School District* (2010), the California District Court specifically acknowledged that school administrators had the authority to discipline a student for cyberbullying that originated entirely outside school if it were reasonably foreseeable that the cyberbullying communications would reach the school, and cause material and substantial disruption or a reasonable forecast of such disruption there.

J.C. was a female high school student who met friends at a diner after school one day, and, while urging her friends to insult and criticize a classmate named C.C., video recorded their nasty comments. The friends called C.C. a "slut," the "ugliest piece of s***" they had ever seen, and "spoiled," and laced the video with profanity (J.C., 2010, p. 1098). That evening J.C. uploaded the video to YouTube and called C.C. to tell her to watch the video. J.C. also invited five to 10 other students to watch the video on YouTube, and later estimated that about 15 people had seen the video that night. J.C. even overheard 10 students discussing the video in school the next day.

C.C.'s mother brought a copy of the video to school the next day, to make school administrators aware of the video. C.C. spent time crying in the counselor's office, and school administrators investigated the making of the video. Both parties to the lawsuit agreed that it was unlikely that any students accessed the video at school because school computers blocked access to YouTube, and, although some students may have been able to access the site through cell phones, cell phone use in school was prohibited. The only time the video was viewed at school was during the school administrators' investigation. However, J.C. was suspended for two days.

The California court reviewed the *Tinker* standard and the other Supreme Court decisions limiting the First Amendment rights of students, as well as a number of lower court decisions from different jurisdictions, before deciding that the geographic origin of J.C.'s video was immaterial; the court stated that *Tinker* applied to both in-school and out-of-school student speech. However, the court ultimately found no substantial disruption, nor reasonable forecast of disruption, at school as a result of the video.

Stating that, "The substantial disruption inquiry is highly fact-intensive," and for that reason, "existing case law has not provided clear guidelines as to when a substantial disruption is reasonably foreseeable" (J.C., 2010, p. 1111), the *J.C.* majority reviewed decisions from sister courts to determine what those courts had considered as sufficient evidence of material and substantial disruption, or reasonable forecast of the same: violent or threatening speech, negative impact on the delivery of instruction, the pulling away of school administrators from their regular duties, or evidence of past disruption arising from similar speech. However, the record in *J.C.* merely showed that school personnel had to calm an upset student and her parent and conduct an investigation of allegations of cyberbullying. The court merely noted, "That is what school administrators do" (J.C., 2010, p. 1118), and ruled that J.C.'s video was protected speech. The majority stated:

> The Court cannot uphold school discipline of student speech simply because young persons are unpredictable or immature, or because, in general, teenagers are emotionally fragile and may often fight over hurtful comments. (J.C., 2010, p. 1122)

As a result of the court's decision, the school district was forced to pay J. C.'s attorneys' fees and court costs, $107,150.80 (Hoffman, 2010).

### *The* Kowalski *Decision*

Despite the *J.C.* court's strong language limiting the authority of school administrators to discipline one student for mean-spirited comments to or about a fellow student, without evidence that the speech caused material and substantial disruption of school operations, the *Kowalski* court appeared to completely disagree. Kara Kowalski, a high school student from West Virginia, was suspended from school for 5 days and put on "social suspension" for 90 days, prohibiting her participation in school and extracurricular activities, for creating a MySpace site set up to ridicule a female classmate, Shay N. (*Kowalski v. Berkeley County Schools*, 2011). Kowalski claimed the site, called S.A.S.H., stood for "Students Against Sluts Herpes" (Kowalski, 2011, p. 567), but the web pages were actually created to give Kowalski and other students an online site where they could post pictures and vulgar insults directed at Shay.

The facts in the *Kowalski* case were parallel to those in the *J.C.* decision. Like J.C., Kara Kowalski used her home computer to set up the site and she invited fellow students to join in, about two dozen of whom did. Kowalski never accessed the MySpace site at school. Shay and her parents brought a printout of the site to the school principal, just as C.C.'s parents did. School administrators investigated and concluded that Kowalski had created a "hate website" (Kowalski, 2011, p. 568), in violation of school policy against harassment and bullying.

School officials contended that it was foreseeable that Kowalski's off-campus speech would reach the campus and cause a disruption, but the court record noted no details at all of any disruption of school operations caused by Kowalski's website. In fact, Kowalski had even tried to remove the postings after she found out that Shay's father had discovered them. The court quoted extensively from *Tinker*, distilling from the *Tinker* opinion and from *Morse* that, "Just as schools have a responsibility to provide a safe environment for students free from messages advocating illegal drug use, schools have a duty to protect their students from harassment and bullying in the school environment [citations omitted]" (Kowalski, 2011, p. 572). "We are confident," the court continued, "that Kowalski's speech caused the interference and disruption described in Tinker as being immune from First Amendment protection," but the only substantiating fact provided by the court was that Shay and her parents brought the MySpace site to the attention of school administrators, thereby transforming Kowalski's speech to in-school harassment. Like C.C., Shay was upset. However, unlike J.C., whose discipline was reversed by the court, Kowalski's discipline was upheld.

Attorneys in the *Kowalski* decision, as well as the attorneys in the *Layshock v. Hermitage School District* and *J.S. v. Blue Mountain School District* decisions, petitioned the U.S. Supreme Court to grant certiorari, to re-hear and perhaps reconcile the decisions. The Supreme Court refused on January 17, 2012, signaling that they would provide no guidance to school administrators wrestling with uncertainty about disciplining students for off-campus technology-facilitated speech.

### *Cyberbullying in Post-Secondary Educational Institutions*

Cyberbullying is not only the province of students in K-12 schools. Darby Dickerson, then-Vice-President and Dean of Stetson University College of Law, writing in the *University of Toledo Law Review* in 2005, may have been the first to warn the higher education community to be alert to the dangers from a "sinister e-culprit" (Dickerson, 2005), the cyberbully, whose high-tech incivility today dogs both professors and students. Today the higher education community has seen the worst effects of such incivilities: the suicides of Tyler Clementi, former Rutgers University student who jumped to his death from the George Washington Bridge after his roommate released a secret video recording he had made of Tyler having homosexual relations in his dorm room (Pilkington, 2010); and University of Wisconsin student Alyssa Funke who committed suicide after being mercilessly cyberbullied for starring in a porn flick (Kuruvilla, 2014). Colleges and universities must annually report certain so-called "Clery crimes," but cyberbullying is not a reportable crime unless it escalates into cyberstalking. Suicides are also not reportable Clery crimes, so colleges and universities are not obligated to report student suicides precipitated by cyberbullying (Conn, 2014).

*The Prevalence of Cyberbullying in Post-Secondary Educational Institutions*
Determining the extent of cyberbullying in colleges and universities is fraught with the same difficulties that accompany studies of cyberbully prevalence in K-12 institutions: varied definitions of cyberbullying, differences in sample sizes and nature of participants, and different study methodologies. In addition, many institutions of higher education are reluctant to survey students, for fear of negative publicity from the findings. Cyberbullying is especially dangerous for college and university students who are in new, often stressful situations, largely devoid of their traditional supports (Conn, 2014). The surveys that have been conducted on college and university campuses indicate that from approximately 10–22% of students are targets of cyberbullies (Sturgis, 2014). Many students who were cyberbullied in high school go on to be the victims of cyberbullies in college and university. Zalaquett and Chatters (2014) surveyed 613 college students. Of these, 19% reported that they were cyberbullied in college; 35% of these individuals had been cyberbullied in high school.

Minor, Smith, and Brashen (2013) emphasize that cyberbullying, while it occurs student-to-student, also occurs student-to-instructor. However, many instructors are reluctant to report cyberbullying for fear of losing their jobs. Instructors of online courses are especially vulnerable. The researchers surveyed 346 online instructors from the undergraduate, graduate, and doctoral programs at a large online university. Nearly 34% of instructors in the survey reported that they had been cyberbullied by students, and over 60% reported that no resources were available to help them, or that they did not know of any resources available.

Cyberbullying in higher education occurs via gossip sites like JuicyCampus, College Anonymous Confessions Board, or College Wall of Shame; revenge porn sites, where former lovers post photos of ex-girlfriends; emails and text messages, spreading of rumors, and creating false profiles (Sturgis, 2014). Mahal and Kulothungan (2014) stress the problems attendant upon students' over-sharing of personal information via social networking websites; such information can make the individual vulnerable to attacks by cyberbullies.

*Effects of Cyberbullying in Higher Education*

Two Yale University Law School students, Heide Iravani and Brittan Heller, cyberbullied on a gossip site AutoAdmit, found out that cyberbullying by older students is just as upsetting, just as nasty, as the K-12 versions. However, with age often come cyberbullies' more sophisticated methods of safeguarding anonymity. Anonymous speech is protected by the First Amendment, and Iravani and Heller were forced to navigate a tortuous path through the courts to finally unmask at least some of the anonymous defamers who posted sexually demeaning charges against the duo, along with lascivious descriptions and photographs of the females' breasts (*Does I and II v. Individuals*, 2008). Their journey finally unmasked male harassers from as far away from Yale as Texas, and they settled with some of them, but the settlements followed a long and protracted legal battle (Seager, 2009).

*Litigation of Cyberbullying Controversies in Higher Education*

Cyberbullying of students in higher education and professional schools reaches the courts much less frequently than cyberbullying at lower levels of education. No Supreme Court case as of 2015 has dealt with post-secondary school student speech, so it falls to lower courts to apply the K-12 precedents in adjudicating cyberbullying communications in colleges and universities. The precedent overwhelmingly used is the *Tinker* decision. The application of this standard has led to conflicting results in adjudicating higher education cyberbullying controversies, just as it has in K-12 cases.

Several court decisions are illustrative of the conflicts. In the first, Maciej Murakowski, a 19-year-old sophomore at the University of Delaware, used the university's server to create a personal website where he posted about 80 essays, approximately eight of which were graphic essays about his desires to engage in sexual violence or sexual abuse (*Murakowski v. University of Delaware*, 2008). One was purported to be a sex guide that described how to kidnap, rape, and torture women. Several female students became aware of his postings and reported Murakowski to campus police. Several complained that they felt uneasy and fearful, and one woman so feared for her personal safety that she requested to audit a course. The university ultimately sanctioned Murakowski and barred him from his dorm. However, Murakowski continued to enter his dorm. He was ultimately suspended and totally barred from campus.

Murakowski sued the university. The court applied a litany of student speech decisions from lower courts, but ultimately relied on the *Tinker* standard, ruling that, although some women were upset by Murakowski's writings, others were not. The court described the writings as "racist, sexist, homophobic, insensitive, degrading," and said the essays "contained graphic descriptions of violent behavior and promoted such behavior," but they did not constitute true threats nor did they rise to material and substantial disruption of university operations. Therefore, the court refused to grant the university summary judgment on the issue of disciplining Murakowski for his online expression. Murakowski's Linked In pages now indicate that he is a programmer at Flipkey in Cambridge, Massachusetts (Murakowski, 2014).

In a student-on-professor cyberbullying case, *Osei v. Temple University* (2011), the application of the *Tinker* standard resulted in the court dismissing the student's claim of denial in due process in his disciplinary hearing for emails he sent to a professor. Michael Osei was a Ghanian student who was dissatisfied with his grade of "C" in his Fall 2009 graduate Organic Chemistry class. He contacted his professor, Dr. Grant Krow, by email in mid-December, and requested details of his grade calculation and a copy of his examination paper. Feeling that Krow's response was inadequate, Osei sent a total of three subsequent mass emails to all students in Krow's Organic Chemistry course. Osei also sent two additional emails to Dr. Krow, saying in one, "If my grade was not a genuine or fair grade .... It will be a curse against your life and family forever. I am serious!" (Osei, 2011, p. 2). In another, Osei said, "Your game is over! Mine begins. You played with the wrong person this time," and "Mark my words. The year 2010 will not start well for you" (Osei, 2011, p. 3).

Dr. Krow reported Osei's emails to his Department Chair and to campus police. Osei was charged with violating the Temple University Student Code of Conduct by sending what were believed to be threatening emails to Dr. Krow. After several hearings at which Osei apologized for his flawed English, Osei was suspended from Temple, and when his appeal was unsuccessful, Osei began legal action. Osei claimed violations of due process, infringement of his First Amendment right to freedom of speech, retaliation, discrimination, and other claims. The court quoted *Tinker*, affirming Osei's right to freedom of speech, but also quoted extensively from the *Murakowski* decision to establish that "true threats," such as the troublesome language in Osei's emails to Dr. Krow, were not protected by the First Amendment. Ultimately, the Third Circuit Court of Appeals affirmed (Osei, 2013). Osei's federal claims were dismissed with prejudice, and the court declined to exercise supplemental jurisdiction on any remaining state claims.

Amber Tatro, a female student in the University of Minnesota's Mortuary Science Program, ran afoul of university's program rules by posting messages on Facebook referring to her finishing the required dissection of a cadaver as part of her course, a cadaver that she had facetiously named "Bernie" (Tatro, 2011). She referred to her taking out her aggressions by using her trocar, a long hollow needle used to aspirate fluids, on Bernie. In another post she wrote about wanting to use a trocar on another individual, a man she later revealed she had dated but who had broken up with her. A fellow student saw the postings; she admitted she had set her Facebook pages to be viewed by friends and friends of friends, opening them to a wide audience. The university accused Tatro of threatening conduct in violation of the university rules and the disclosure form she had been required to sign when being assigned her cadaver, and brought Tatro before a hearing with the student conduct committee. The committee issued a written decision imposing sanctions on Tatro, including failing the cadaver course, mandatory enrollment in a clinical ethics course, and being put on probation for the remainder of her program.

Tatro appealed, but the provost's appeals committee affirmed the decision. Tatro then filed suit in state court, alleging that the university violated her First Amendment freedom of speech for what was off-campus speech and satire. The court cited *Tinker* and *Fraser* for the propositions that the rights of students in schools must be applied in light of the special circumstances of the educational environment, which, of course, in *Tinker* and *Fraser* referred to the K-12 environment. The court did note that "what constitutes a substantial disruption in a primary school may look very different in a university" (Tatro, 2011, p. 821), but did not elaborate. The court noted that there was a fear of substantial disruption as a result of Tatro's postings, and upheld the university's disciplinary actions.

## ANALYSIS, CONCLUSIONS, AND RECOMMENDATIONS

As the court decisions show, educators at all levels are facing challenges from cyberbullying. State legislatures have responded by enacting laws requiring schools to develop anti-cyberbullying policies, but these policies often go far beyond what is constitutionally permissible regulation of speech. For example, the New York Court of Appeals ruled in July 2014 that the local law prohibiting cyberbullying "against any minor or person" was overbroad and, therefore, void (*People v. Marquan*, 2014). However, K-12 administrators are under great pressure from parents whose students are being cyberbullied; parents want school administrators to be the police who investigate and punish cyberbullies. This puts school administrators in the firing line of judges who apply inconsistent standards to determine whether "material and substantial disruption" in school operations justified the administrative discipline. And school administrators themselves are being maligned on websites, social networking sites, and in an increasing variety of other electronic communication modalities.

Until the Supreme Court steps in and clarifies the rights and responsibilities of K-12 school administrators to discipline students for cyberbullying speech, speech that originates outside the school environment, administrators must resist parental pressures. If the alleged cyberbullying speech is a threat or hate speech, that speech is not protected by the First Amendment and may be criminal. Law enforcement is the proper channel through which to address such speech, and administrators should avail themselves of memoranda of understanding to seek the help of law enforcement. Parents should be advised to proceed with a complaint to police.

Likewise, if the alleged cyberbullying is defamatory speech, that speech also is not protected by the First Amendment. Parents need to work out conflicts on a parent-to-parent level. In the most egregious cases, parents can seek redress in the court system, not in the school principal's office. School administrators have educational leadership and management responsibilities, and parents who burden them with the responsibility of investigating and adjudicating students' petty interpersonal disputes that occur outside school detract from the overall educational process for all students.

However, when cyberbullying becomes in-school bullying, administrators need to act. Anti-bullying policies need to be clear, with progressive discipline for the in-school bully, redress for the victim, and education for both bully and victim about the serious consequences of bullying for both victim and bully. If these policies were adopted and uniformly implemented, the court system would be spared the flood of litigation now pressing their dockets in cyberbullying cases, and administrators would be spared the conflicting decisions like the *Layshock*, *J.S.*, *J.C.*, and *Kowalski* decisions. School administrators would not be placed in the Solomonic position of deciding whether school disruption caused by out-of-school speech was "material and substantial" enough to merit disciplining the speaker.

Court decisions in higher education cases that rely on the precedent set by the *Tinker* decision also underscore the tension inherent in the First Amendment's guarantee of freedom of speech on college and university campuses. In the *Murakowski* decision, despite the fact that the student used the university server to create and post to the website containing essays about kidnap, rape, and torture of females, which several females regarded as personal threats to their safety, the Delaware court ruled that the university appropriately disciplined the student for accessing campus without permission, but declined to uphold the authority of the university to discipline him for what several female students regarded as threatening speech. And yet, the Minnesota court upheld Amanda Tatro's ambiguous Facebook postings as posing a reasonable forecast of substantial disruption at the university, which disruption the court declined to explain or elaborate. In the case of Michael Osei's email messages, the court ruled that Osei's email communications to his chemistry professor were threatening without allowing for language and cultural differences that may have been relevant in a Ghanian/American exchange of communications, whether face-to-face or via email.

College administrators must not bury their collective heads in the sand. Awareness assemblies, training for faculty, staff, and students to recognize the dangers of cyberbullying, and mechanisms for reporting it to campus police must be undertaken. Fear of negative publicity cannot be an excuse for failing to find out if cyberbullying is taking place on campus. Cyberbullies do not take time off during college and university years. However, here, too, college administrators need to rely on their memoranda of understanding with local law enforcement, and refer threats and hate speech to their jurisdiction. Instructors need not suffer defamatory communications from students in silence. Clearly worded campus "netiquette" policies should govern all online communications at the post-secondary level. Instructors who receive defamatory communications or who find such communications occurring between and among students in online coursework need to report such communications to campus police who are trained to recognize unlawful behavior.

The First Amendment protections for speech in America are among the strongest in the countries of the world (Haynes et al., 2003). Technology has created opportunities for miscreants to abuse those protections. However, the American court system is not the solution for all abuses. "Law can only establish a bottom line" (Zwemer, 2008; "Candor and Civility," para. 29). Individuals in a free society must assume personal responsibility, taking advantages of all that is available in that society to maintain freedom for legitimate expression.

# REFERENCES

Ackerman, M. S., Kramer, C., & Bruno, M. (2014). From the school yard to cyber space: A pilot study of bullying behaviors among middle school students. *Research in Middle Level Education*, *37*(6), 1–18. Retrieved from http://www.eric.ed.gov/?q=bullying+peaks+in+middle+school&ft+on&id=%20EJ1032363

Associated Press (2002). Pennsylvania high court upholds student's expulsion over web site. *Associated Press*, September 27. Retrieved from http://www.firstamendmentcenter.org/pennsylvania-high-court-upholds-students-expulsion-over-web-site

Banks, R. (2013). *Bullying in schools*. Retrieved from http://www.education.com/reference/article/Ref_Bullying_Schools

Bethel Sch. Dist. No. 403 v. Fraser. 478 U.S. 675 (1986).

Bauman, S. (2013). *Principles of cyberbullying research: Definitions, measures, and methodology*. New York, NY: Routledge.

Bullying Statistics (n.d.a). *School bullying statistics*. Retrieved from http://www.bullyingstatistics.org/content/school-bullying-statistics.html

Bullying Statistics (n.d.b). *School bullying statistics*. Retrieved from http://www.bullyingstatistics.org/content/cyber-bullying.html

Centers for Disease Control [CDC]. (2014). National youth risk behavior survey: 1991–2013. *Trends in the Prevalence of Suicide-Related Behavior*. Retrieved from www.cdc.gov/healthyyouth/yrbs/factsheets/inex.htm?s_cid+cs739

Chappell, M. S., Hasselman, S. L., Kitchin, T., Lomon, S. N., MacIver, K. W., & Sarullo, P. L. (2006). Bullying in elementary school, high school, and college. *Adolescence*, *41*(164), 633–648.

Conn, K. (2011). The third circuit en banc decisions on out-of-school student speech: Analysis and recommendations. *West's Education Law Reporter*, *270*, 389–407.

Conn, K. (2013). Cyberbullying in American higher education: Litigation challenges and recommendations. *International Journal of Law and Education*, *18*(1), 21–38.

Conn, K. (2014). It's not just kid stuff: Peer-peer cyberbullying in colleges and universities. Collegiate Comment. Retrieved from http://www.kingspry.com/peer-to-peer-cyberbullying-continues-in-colleges/

Dickerson, D. (2005). Cyberbullies on campus. *University of Toledo Law Review*, *37*(1), 51–74.

Eddy, N. (2013). Smartphone use among American teens grows: Pew Research. eWeek. Retrieved from http://eweek.com/mobile/smartphone-usage-among-american-teens-grows-pew-research

Espelage, D. L. (2011). *Bullying & the lesbian, gay, bisexual, transgender, questioning (LGBTQ) community*. In White House, White House 2011 Conference on Bullying Prevention (pp. 65–72). Retrieved from http://www.stopbullying.gov/resources-files/white-house-conference-2011-materials.pdf

Evans, B. (2011). Bullying: Can it begin in preschool? *HighScope Extensions*, *25*(3), 1–6. Retrieved from http://www.highscope.org/file/NewsandInformation/Extensions/ExtVol25No3_low.pdf

Gladden, R. M., Vivolo-Kantor, A. M., Hamburger, M. E., & Lumpkin, C. D. (2014). *Bullying surveillance among youths: Uniform definitions for public health and recommended data elements. Version 1.0.* Atlanta, GA: National Center for Injury Prevention and Control, Centers for Disease Control and Prevention and U.S. Department of Education.

Haynes, C. C., Chaltain, S., Ferguson, J. E., Hudson, D. L., & Thomas, O. (2003). *The First Amendment in schools.* Alexandria, VA: Association for Supervision and Curriculum Development.

Hazelwood Sch. Dist. v. Kuhlmeier. 484 U.S. 260 (1988).

Hinduja, S. & Patchin, J. W. (2010). Bullying, cyberbullying, and suicide. *Archives of Suicide Research, 14*, 206–212. In J. Sveticic, A. Milner, & D. DeLeo (Eds.), *Suicide Research: Selected Readings* (Vol. 4, pp. 31–32). Retrieved from www.griffith.edu.au/_data/assets/pdf_0020/518105/Suicide-Research-Text-Vol4.pdf%20(Original%20work%20published%202010)

Hoff, D. L. & Mitchell, S. N. (2009). Cyberbullying: Causes, effects, and remedies. *Journal of Educational Administration, 47*(5), 652–665. Retrieved from http://www.emeraldinsight.com/doi/abs/10.1108/09578230910981107

Hoffman, J. (2010, June 27). Online bullies pull schools into the fray. *The New York Times.* Retrieved from http://www.nytimes.com/2010/06/28/style/28bully.html?pagewanted+all&_r=0

Jones, L. M., Mitchell, K. J., & Finkelhor, D. (2012). Trends in youth internet victimization: Findings from three youth internet safety surveys, 2000–2010. *Journal of Adolescent Health, 50*(2), 179–186. Retrieved from http://www.nchi.nlm.nih.gov/pubmed/22265114. doi:10.1016/j.jadohealth2011.09.015

Kowalski, R. M., Limber, S. P., & Agatson, P. W. (2012). *Cyberbullying: Bullying in the digital age* (2nd ed.). Hoboken, NJ: Wiley.

Krasselt, K. (2014). *1.2K shares.* Retrieved from http://college.usatoday.com/2014/10/21/bullying-not-a-thing-of-the-past-for-college-students/

Kuruvilla, C. (2014, May 24). Alyssa Funke's suicide: Mom speaks out about bullying, chilling last texts. *N.Y. Daily News.* Retrieved from http://www.nydailynews.com/news/national/alyssa-funke-story-teen-committed-suicide-porn-flick-bullied-life-mom-article-1.1804216

Layshock v. Hermitage Sch. Dist. 496 F. Supp. 2d 587 (W.D. Pa. 2007).

Layshock v. Hermitage Sch. Dist. *rev'd* 593 F.3d 249 (3d Cir. 2010).

Layshock v. Hermitage Sch. Dist. *aff'd* 650 F.3d 205 (3d Cir. 2011) (*en banc*).

Layshock v. Hermitage Sch. Dist. *cert. denied*, 132 S. Ct. 1095 (2012).

Lenhart, A. (2007). *Cyberbullying.* Retrieved from http://www.pewinternet.org/2007/06/27/cyberbullying/

Lenhart, A., Madden, M., Smith, A., Purcell, K., Zickuhr, K., & Rainie, L. (2011). *Teens, kindness and cruelty on social network sites.* Retrieved from http://www.pewinternet.org/2011/11/09/teens-kindness-and-cruelty-on-social-network-sites/

Madden, M., Lenhart, A., Cortesi, S., Gasser, U., Duggan, M., Smith, A., & Beaton, M. (2013). *Teens, social media, and privacy.* Retrieved from http://www.pewinternet.org/2013/05/21/teens-social-media-and-privacy/

Madden, M., Lenhart, A., Duggan, M. Cortesi, S., & Gasser, U. (2013). *Teens and technology 2013.* Retrieved from http://www.pewinternet.org/2013/03/13/teens-and-technology-2013/

Mahal, N., & Kulothungan, V. (2014). *Cyberbullying in higher education* [Web log message]. Retrieved from http://www.educause.edu/blogs/vvogel/cyberbullying-higher-education

Major, A. (2014). To bully and be bullied: Harassment and mistreatment in medical education. *Virtual Mentor*, *16*(3), 155–160.

McCarthy, M. (2009). Student expression that collides with the rights of others: Should the second prong of tinker stand alone? *West's Education Law Reporter*, *240*, 1–23.

Minor, M. A., Smith, G. S., & Brashen, H. (2013). Cyberbullying in higher education. *Journal of Educational Research and Practice*, *3*(1), 15–29.

Morse v. Frederick. 551 U.S. 393 (2007).

Murakowski, M. (2014). *LinkedIn*, March 15. Retrieved from https://www.linkedin.com/pub/maciej-murakowski/89/a19/888

Olson, S. (2014). *Bullying behavior transforms as students move from elementary to middle school: Cyberbullying takes over*. Retrieved from http://wwwmedicaldaily.com/bullying-behavior-transforms-students-move-elementary-middle-school-takes-303030

Ortega, R., Elipe, P., Mora-Merchan, J. A., Camaestra, J., &Vega, E. (2009). The emotional impact on victims of traditional bullying and cyberbullying: A study of Spanish adolescents. *Journal of Psychology*, *217*(4), 197–204.

Osei v. Temple Univ. 2011 WL 4549609 (E.D. Pa. Sept. 30, 2011). *aff'd*, 518 F. Appx. 86 (3d Cir. 2013) (Unpublished decision).

Patchin, J. W. (2013). *Cyberbullying research: 2013 update*. Retrieved from http://cyberbullying.us/cyberbullying-research-2013-update/

Pilkington, E. (2010). Tyler Clementi, student outed as gay on internet, jumps to his death. The Guardian, September 30. Retrieved from http://www.theguardian.com/world/2010/sep/30/tyler-clementi-gay-student-suicide

Seager, I. (2009). Law graduates settle suit. *Yale Daily News*, October 23. Retrieved from http://yaledailynews.com/blog/2009/10/23/law-graduates-settle-suit/

Shariff, S. (2008). *Cyberbullying: Issues and solutions for the school, the classroom and the home*. New York, NY: Routledge.

Smith, P. K., Mahdavi, J., Carvalho, M., Fisher, S., Russell, S., & Tippett, N. (2008). Cyberbullying: Its nature and impact in secondary school pupils. *Journal of Child Psychology and Psychiatry*, *49*(4), 376–385.

Sturgis, I. (2014). High-tech bullies. Chronicle of Higher Education, March 7. Retrieved from http://chronicle.texterity.com/chronicle/Convergence2014?pg=3#pg3

*Tatro v. Univ. of Minn.*, 800 N.W. 2d 811 (App. Ct. Minn. 2011).

Tokunaga, R. S. (2009). Following you home from school: A critical review and synthesis of research on cyberbullying victimization. *Computers in Human Behavior*, *26*, 277–287.

Wenkart, R. (2008). Disruptive student speech and the First Amendment: How disruptive does it have to be? *West's Education Law Reporter*, *236*, 551–574.

Zalaquett, C. P., & Chatters, S. J. (2014). Cyberbullying in college. *Sage Journals*, March 19. Retrieved from http://sgo.sagepub.com/content/4/1/2158244014526721

Zwemer, T. J. (2008). Candor and civility. *Liberty*, March–April. Retrieved from http://www.libertymagazine.org/article/candor-and-civility

# CHAPTER 4

# A PORTRAIT OF THE LEGAL BARRIERS TO THE EDUCATION OF IMMIGRANT CHILDREN: AN ANALYSIS OF STATE STATUTES AND NATIONAL INITIATIVES

Chinasa A. Elue and Patricia F. First

## ABSTRACT

*In the 1982, ruling of* Plyler v. Doe *the Supreme Court of the United States ruled that undocumented children cannot be denied a public education. Yet, as this chapter is being written in 2015, states across the United States have passed statutes preventing the education of these children and by practical extension documented children and their families. A package of Executive Actions by President Obama in November of 2014 modestly benefited and impacted the rights of undocumented immigrants, but did not challenge the state laws affecting school children and university students. In this chapter, we will review the rights to education of immigrant children. We will review the national scene as it stands amidst confusion in the absence of meaningful immigration reform by the U.S. Congress and the puzzle of the states arbitrarily denying rights*

**Legal Frontiers in Education: Complex Law Issues for Leaders, Policymakers and Policy Implementers**
**Advances in Educational Administration, Volume 24, 59–84**

**ISSN: 1479-3660/doi:10.1108/S1479-366020150000024030**

*flowing from the Fifth and Fourteenth Amendments of the United States Constitution, carefully articulated in* Plyler. *We intend to present a blunt portrait of rights denied and children left behind.*

As the United States seeks to compete in a more global economy, the necessity to address the educational needs of the nation's most marginalized student populations is a growing concern. Specifically, with the growing number of undocumented and documented immigrant children in American schools, educating all immigrant children and addressing their needs have become more and more complex. Immigration status is playing an increasingly significant role in the educational opportunities and outcomes of immigrant students in the United States. In this chapter, we discuss the educational impact of legislation for both documented and undocumented immigrant children, as several families may be comprised of children from either categorization. The legal battles for immigrant children have endured in order to access education in the United States and have been systematically documented for several decades. Despite *Plyler v. Doe* extending a free public K-12 education to all students regardless of immigration status, recent immigration legislation has negatively impacted the educational trajectories of all immigrant children. The decisions rendered from the U.S. Supreme Court have been pivotal in paving the way for immigrant children to access education in the K-12 system. Given that participation in education generates substantial private and public benefits, society as a whole is being negatively impacted.

Initial strides for immigrant children were made in *Lau v. Nichols*, the Supreme Court decision that addressed the educational needs for non-English speaking students. This 1974 U.S. Supreme Court ruling noted that a school district receiving federal aid must provide special instruction for non-English speaking students whose education is severely hampered by language barriers, at least when there are substantial numbers of such students within the district (*Lau v. Nichols*, 1974, 414 U.S. 563). The U.S. Supreme Court ruled that a failure to provide non-English speaking students with special instruction denied them a meaningful opportunity to participate in the public education program. The U.S. Supreme Court noted that "... there is no equality of treatment merely by providing students with the same facilities, textbooks, teachers, and curriculum; for students who do not understand English are effectively foreclosed from any meaningful education" (*Lau v. Nichols*, 1974, 414 U.S. 563 para 28).

Immigrant (specifically undocumented) children also benefitted from the 1982 U.S. Supreme court ruling in *Plyler v. Doe*. In *Plyler*, the U.S. Supreme Court ruled that a state statute that denies a free public education for undocumented children similar to that provided to other children violates the Equal Protection Clause (EPC) of the Fourteenth Amendment of the U.S. Constitution (Plyler v. Doe, 1982, 457 U.S. 202). The EPC, which provides that no state shall "deny to any person within its jurisdiction the equal protection of the laws," applies to all persons regardless of citizenship. According to the Court, "public education is not a 'right' granted to individuals by the Constitution. But neither is it merely some governmental 'benefit' indistinguishable from other forms of social welfare legislation. Both the importance of education in maintaining our basic institutions, and the lasting impact of its deprivation on the life of the child mark the distinction" (*Plyler v. Doe*, 1982). The right to a K-12 education is a right granted to all children regardless of legal status in this country.

The purpose of this chapter is to paint a portrait of the legal barriers to education all immigrant children encounter. First, we will discuss important demographic characteristics of immigrant children and their families. We then present the theoretical framework used to guide this work. An overview of national initiatives and state statutes that are impacting the education of these children is presented along with proposed comprehensive immigration reform plans. Next, we discuss the impact of these initiatives in the states followed by a discussion on the need to break down educational barriers for immigrant children. Finally, we present the implications for educational leaders and offer some perspectives to consider as these realities are developing for the future of all immigrant children.

## IMMIGRANT CHILDREN AND THEIR FAMILIES

Despite citizenship or residency status, immigrant families face countless challenges, complexities, uncertainties, and contradictions (Passel, 2006; Suarez-Orozco & Suarez-Orozco, 2009). Although immigration to the United States is generally conceived as an opportunity for better economic and social conditions, immigrant families and their children consistently fall into the low-income bracket. According to Jiang, Ekono, and Skinner (2015), in 2013 "55% of children of immigrant parents – 9.7 million – live [d] in low-income families" (p. 4). In addition to immigrant children's socioeconomic status, language proficiency issues (Dinan, 2006; Paez, 2008) pose greater challenges, specifically in their pursuit of American education.

The increase in immigration has led to an increase in the number of English language learners and limited English proficient students in schools (Dinan, 2006). Approximately 9.1 percent or 4.4 million English language learners attended U.S. public schools in 2011–2012 (National Center for Education Statistics, 2015). That number rose slightly in the 2012–2013 school year to 9.2 percent (National Center for Education Statistics, 2015). As previously stated, today one in nine students enrolled in grades K-12 is an English language learner (Nieto, 2010). The ability to speak English is essential for both academic and future financial success (Laanan, 2000; Verdugo & Flores, 2007); however, the needs of English language learners, most of whom were born in the United States (Dinan, 2006), are not being properly met (Reeves, 2004).

The variety of compositions of immigrant families is yet another challenge faced by this group. Passel (2006) estimated a total of 6.6 million "unauthorized families" in the United States. However, although families are referred to as unauthorized, not all members of the family may have illegal statuses (Passel, 2006; Suarez-Orozco & Suarez-Orozco, 2009). These families have "mixed status" (Passel, 2006, p. 8) and live in "mixed-status legal limbo" (Suarez-Orozco & Suarez-Orozco, 2009, p. 328). For example, only one spouse or parent may be unauthorized. Similarly, not all the children in the family may be unauthorized. Generally, in such instances, the older child or children are undocumented (The Urban Institute, 2006). In 2005, 460,000 families had both US citizen and non-citizen children, 725,000 families had only non-citizen children, and 1.5 million families had children where all were U.S. citizens (Passel, 2006).

Mixed statuses create difficult situations for immigrant families. For example, families may choose to forego benefits to which some members may be entitled. As noted by The Urban Institute (2006) "children who are citizens are entitled to public benefits, but their unauthorized parents may be reluctant to approach public institutions for services because they fear deportation" (p. 2). Recent legislation, such as Alabama's controversial HB 56, makes the complexities faced by immigrant families more pronounced. An important consequence of this statute is that after the enactment of this legislation, which called for K-12 schools to check the immigration status of incoming students, record numbers of children were pulled out of school (Valdes, 2011). Although some children were perhaps authorized/documented, their parents' or siblings' statuses may have compounded the situation. Thus, for the purposes of this chapter, we define immigrant children as children who are classified by the government as being either lawfully[1]/unlawfully present and/or having parents or guardians born outside of the United States and migrated to the country.

This chapter takes a glance at the issues impacting the efforts to educate one of the nation's most marginalized groups, immigrant children. The problems that need to be addressed have led to the exploration of these questions: How will federal and state legislation and initiatives impact educational access for immigrant student populations? What are the implications of federal and state legislation on educational equity and justice for all immigrant children, both documented and undocumented? How or to what extent can the outcomes from state legislation inform and shape the national dialogue on federal comprehensive immigration reform? In the next section, we present the theoretical lens that will guide the analysis of the national initiatives and state statutes impacting immigrant children.

## THEORETICAL FRAMEWORK: LEGAL REALISM

Although there are several theoretical frameworks that can be used to study legal matters such as legal positivism, legal realism, and critical legal studies, this chapter will use the lens of legal realism. Legal realism provides a critical lens for analyzing the effects of these statutes on the education of immigrant children. We selected legal realism because it is a philosophy of law positioned between the traditional legal approach and the more extreme view of critical legal studies. Legal realism has set the stage for the emergence of modern jurisprudence (Minda, 1995). In this vein, laws are created to rectify certain situations and social conditions, as well as show how laws are implemented to allow society to "gain a life of their own and develop into abstractions that [were] out of touch with social circumstances" (de Been, 2008, p. 128). Thus, legal realism is the belief that law is more than a body of rules, principles, and precedents used by judges to decide cases. Legal realism examines the defects, constraints, and openness of the law as it actually affects society (Tamanaha, 2009).

"Legal realism has shaped modern legal thought by developing and exploiting strand[s] of pragmatic instrumentalism" (Minda, 1995, p. 25). Though today's legal realists would not agree with the belief of critical legal theorists that an inherently unjust societal structure is designed to protect the positions of the elite, contemporary realists do believe there is no way to escape the essentially political nature of the law (Altman, 2001). The law, according to legal realists, is ultimately what legal actors and policy makers actually carry out in the world. Thus, social, psychological, and economic forces are used to determine the results of the law (Feldman, 2010). From contemporary times, legal realism views the law as a reflection of personal and cultural biases that are constantly adjusting to match the realities of a changing world (Bravin, 2009). What is actually happening under the law is what matters. Thus, what is actually happening or could happen to the education for immigrant children under state immigration statutes and national initiatives is a serious concern. In the next section, we offer an overview of federal initiatives and executive actions that are critical to the discussion on educational access for immigrant children.

## OVERVIEW OF FEDERAL INITIATIVES

As the United States has become more and more diverse, legislation and policies have evolved to address several issues in society. To date, there has been a move in legislation that has significantly impacted the lives of those who live in the margins. Specifically, immigrant children and their families have been greatly impacted by past and present legislation. As education is one of the most driving forces for coming to the United States, immigrant children and their families have faced several hurdles. Thus, it is important to explore national initiatives and legislation that can improve the educational outcomes for all of our students. In the following section, a brief snapshot of federal initiatives is presented to highlight the importance, and these initiatives have on the lives of immigrant children.

### *The DREAM Act*

There have been several attempts to provide a pathway for comprehensive immigration reform in the United States. One of these efforts has been the Development, Relief, and Education Alien Minors (DREAM) Act. First introduced by Congress in 2001, the DREAM Act was intended to provide a means to allow undocumented students to apply for legal permanent resident status (Gonzales, 2007). This proposed federal legislation would have also allowed undocumented students an opportunity to receive in-state tuition while applying to become a legal resident in the United States (Garcia & Tierney, 2011). The law would have impacted more than 360,000 unauthorized high school graduates between the ages 18 and 24

(Garcia &Tierney, 2011). In addition to these components, undocumented high school students would have the chance to work legally, finish high school, and have the option to attend college (Gonzales, 2007). Essentially, the legislation would have allowed them to overcome two major barriers: the opportunity to enter into higher education while applying for financial aid and have the chance to work on legalizing their tenure here in the United States. Unfortunately, in 2010, this legislation was not passed, thus thwarting the hopes of several undocumented students. Approval of the DREAM Act would have been an important move for the federal government to establish support for the education and economic mobility of undocumented students beyond high school (Rodriguez & Cruz, 2009).

### *Executive Action*

President Obama has used his executive powers to mandate extensive action to support the complex needs of immigrant children. In 2012, President Obama announced an executive order that would begin to help undocumented immigrant children access resources that had once been barred from them through the Deferred Action for Childhood Arrivals (DACA) program. This program allowed eligible undocumented students to receive temporary deferment on deportation and have the opportunity to apply for a work permit as long as they met specific outlined criteria. Under the DACA program, undocumented immigrant children would have access to these benefits if they meet the following requirements (UCIS, 2015):

- Were under the age of 31 as of June 15, 2012
- Came to the United States before reaching their 16th birthday
- Have continuously resided in the United States since June 15, 2007 to present
- Were physically present in the United States on June 15, 2012, and at the time of making the request for consideration of deferred action with United States Citizenship and Immigration Services (USCIS)
- Had no lawful status on June 15, 2012
- Were currently in, graduated from, or have received a certificate of completion from their high school. If they had obtained a general education development certificate or were an honorably discharged veteran of the Coast Guard or Armed Forces of the United States would also fulfill this requirement.

- Have not been convicted of a felony, significant misdemeanor, or three or more other misdemeanors, and did not otherwise pose a threat to national security or public safety.

Since the program's inception in 2012, over 553,000 have been approved for participation in the program as of March 2014 (Gonzales & Bautista-Chavez, 2014). Although this program does not provide a pathway to legalization, it has offered these students a chance to become active and viable participants in society. For DACA participants who have been able to obtain a college education, they have been able to increase their economic and social mobility profoundly (Gonzales & Bautista-Chavez, 2014). However, despite the positive outcomes of this program, there is still the need to address financial aid access for these students as well as providing them with the opportunities to work experiences and internships that will support their educational credentials.

Similar to the DACA program, President Obama passed an executive order that would support the needs of unauthorized parents of U.S. citizen children through the Deferred Action for Parental Accountability (DAPA) program. Under this program, parents would receive temporary relief from deportation and have the opportunity to work lawfully if they fulfilled the following requirements (USCIS, 2015):

- Have lived in the United States continuously since January 1, 2010
- Have a son or daughter who are a U.S. citizen or lawful permanent resident as of November 20, 2014
- Are not an enforcement priority for removal from the United States

Through this program, families in "mixed family limbo" would be able to confidently participate in their children's schooling as well as other public institutions without the increased fear of deportation. According to the Migration Policy Institute (2014), more than 3.7 million parents are impacted by DAPA. The implementation of both the DACA and DAPA programs has changed the lives over 5 million immigrant children and their families. These programs have provided an avenue for parents to take a more active role in the education of their children, while affording also the children the opportunity to increase their educational opportunities beyond the confines of *Plyler*. Table 1 summarizes the programmatic impact of DAPA.

Table 1 shows that this program will impact millions of immigrant families, especially as the program continues to expand and more and more families are able to join in the educational processes of their children.

***Table 1.*** Anticipated and Under Anticipated New Immigrant Populations.

| Populations Potentially Eligible to Apply for Anticipated New Deferred Action Program | Estimate |
|---|---|
| Parents of U.S. citizens with 5+ years of U.S. residence | 3.53 million |
| Parents of legal permanent residents with 5+ years of U.S. residence | 180,000 |
| *Subtotal for anticipated new deferred action program* | 3.71 million |
| New Populations Potentially Eligible under Anticipated DACA Program Expansions | Estimate |
| Eliminating the age cutoff (currently applicants must be under age 31) | 205,000 |
| Advancing the U.S. residency requirement (from 2007 to 2010) | 85,000 |
| *Subtotal for populations newly eligible under anticipated expanded DACA program* | 290,000 |
| Immediately eligible for the current DACA program | 1.2 million |
| *Subtotal for revised DACA program with anticipated changes* | 1.5 million |
| **Total** | **5.2 million** |

*Source*: Migration Policy Institute (2014).
*Notes*: Because a certain number of individuals could appear in more than one category, these estimates highlight these overlaps. The estimates for the new deferred action program for parents 6 exclude individuals eligible for DACA.

## PROPOSED COMPREHENSIVE IMMIGRATION REFORM PLANS

To this date, a comprehensive federal immigration reform plan has not been passed despite the President's executive measures. Currently, there are two proposed plans for comprehensive immigration reform: one proposed by the President and another organized by a bipartisan group of senators. If one of these plans was passed, the impact for immigrant children and their families would be paramount.

### *The President's Proposed Plan*

In January 2013, President Obama presented his comprehensive immigration reform plan. This plan consists of four main principles (USCIS, 2015):

- Continuing to strengthen border security
- Cracking down on employers hiring undocumented workers
- The ability to earn citizenship
- Having a streamlined legal immigration process

The plan also discusses the process for improving the infrastructure at ports of entry, investing in foreign visitor processing, as well as using technology to secure the borders of the country. The plan is also dedicated to fighting transnational criminal activity such as human trafficking and visa and passport fraud.

In November 2014, President Obama announced another series of executive actions aimed at ending illegal immigration at the country's border, prioritization for deporting felons not families, and requiring certain undocumented immigrants to pass a criminal background check and pay taxes in order to temporarily stay in the United States (The White House, 2014).

These proposed new initiatives would:

- Expand the population eligible for the DACA program to persons of any current age who entered the United States before the age of 16 and lived in the United States continuously since January 1, 2010. This action would also extend the period of DACA and work authorization from two years to three years.
- Allow parents of U.S. citizens and lawful permanent residents to request deferred action and employment authorization for three years, in the Deferred Action for Parents of Americans and Lawful Permanent Residents (DAPA) program, provided they have lived in the United States continuously since January 1, 2010, and have passed required background checks.
- Expand the use of provisional waivers of unlawful presence to include the spouses and sons and daughters of lawful permanent residents and the sons and daughters of U.S. citizens.
- Improve and clarify immigrant and nonimmigrant visa programs to grow the economy and create jobs.
- Promote citizenship education and public awareness for lawful permanent residents and providing an option for naturalization applicants to use credit cards to pay the application fee.

The President has continued to use executive power to disrupt the social, economic, and educational barriers facing immigrant children and their families. These initiatives would open new doors for immigrant children and their families to actively contribute to the communities they live in. Parents would be able to legally work in the country and have the opportunity to pay taxes. From these taxes, immigrant families would be able to contribute to the financial resources used to support the schools their children attend. Ultimately, all children would be able to benefit from these initiatives.

### *The Senate's Proposed Plan*

The "Border Security, Economic Opportunity, and Immigration Modernization Act", also known as S. 744 (2013), is a bipartisan comprehensive immigration reform plan proposed by eight senators: Michael Bennet (D-CO), Dick Durbin (D-IL), Jeff Flake (R-AZ), Lindsey Graham (R-SC), John McCain (R-AZ), Robert Menendez (D-NJ), Marco Rubio (R-FL), and Charles Schumer (D-NY) (Immigration Policy Center, 2015). These senators joined together to pass a bipartisan plan that would change the face and scope of immigration in this country. This bill is comprised of five sections (Immigration Policy Center, 2013):

- Title I: Boarder Security – addresses problems facing oversight and security of the country's borders.
- Title II: Immigrant Visas – addresses issues with obtaining permanent legal status. This section also provides a pathway for undocumented youth and agricultural workers to register in a provisional immigrant program through merging versions of the DREAM Act and the AgJOBS Act (a proposed immigration legislation plan geared at providing a safe and stable work environment for agricultural workers).
- Title III: Interior Enforcement – supports the power given to the Department of Homeland Security to correct the procedural problems that plague the immigration system.
- Title IV: Reforms to Nonimmigrant Visa Programs – creates new programs for less skilled workers while reforming the nonimmigrant visa program for skilled workers.
- Title V: Jobs for Youth – establishes a Youth Jobs Fund that will be used in creating employment opportunities for low-income and underserved youth.

Similar to the President's proposed plan, this plan would allow immigrant families to remain intact while providing them with the opportunity to navigate through the legal barriers that have impeded them in the past. Senate Bill 744 successfully passed in the Senate, however, is still pending approval in the House. In order to not relegate immigrant children and their families to poverty, Congress' passage of this legislation is pivotal to making sure these children have a chance to pursue advanced educational opportunities as well as be able to work upon completion of their educational training. The tenets of each of these legislative plans set the stage for immigrant populations to become active and viable contributors to society.

## LEGISLATION IN THE STATES

With the absence of a federal immigration plan, states have been actively proposing and passing legislation that is impacting the lives of immigrant populations. According to a 2015 report from the National Conference of State Legislatures, enacted immigration-related legislation dropped by 7.5 percent in 2014 to 171 laws from 185 in 2013. In Fig. 1, 3 percent of enacted immigration-related legislation focused on education. Although this is a small percentage, several of the laws passed impact the potential educational trajectories of immigrant children.

Some of these laws have enabled immigrant children and their families access to public health care benefits, the ability to obtain driver's licenses, and provide translated school documents and forms into the native language of immigrant children and their families in the district. By extension of these laws, immigrant families need the provisions in these laws to be able to support their families. If families are negatively impacted by legislation, the children will ultimately experience the backlash of these

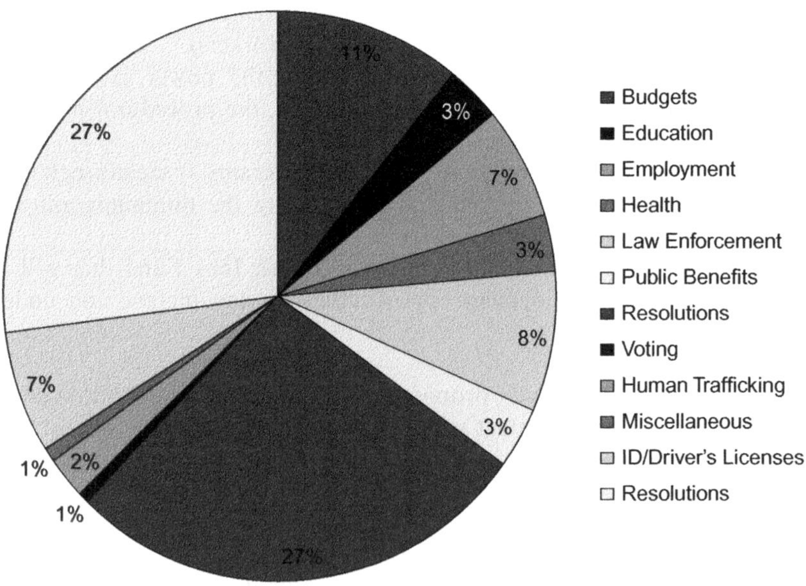


*Fig. 1.* Enacted Immigration-Related Laws by Subject during January–December 2014. *Source*: National Conference of State Legislatures from: http://www.ncsl.org/documents/immig/ImmigrationReport2014Final.pdf

consequences. If children are unable to receive health care because of legal restrictions or parents unable to go to work to support their families due to their inability to drive to their jobs, it is the children who will lack the proper care and economic support to thrive in their educational environments.

Fig. 2 provides an additional illustration of immigration-related laws passed in 2014. Specifically in 2014, 15 education-related laws were passed in nine states: California, Colorado, Florida, Idaho, Kentucky, Minnesota, Missouri, Tennessee, and Washington. These laws addressed topics from in-state tuition and financial aid, to increased learning opportunities for English language learners (National Conference of State Legislatures [NCSL], 2015). As highlighted in Fig. 1, Fig. 2 illustrates the frequency of the laws passed in each state. These immigration-related laws are greatly impacting the educational opportunities for immigrant children.

Fig. 2 shows that a majority of the states passed some type of legislation that will impact immigrant communities. In effort to discuss in detail the educational impact of these laws, we will present an analysis on selected states. The following section introduces the methodology we used to select states for analysis.

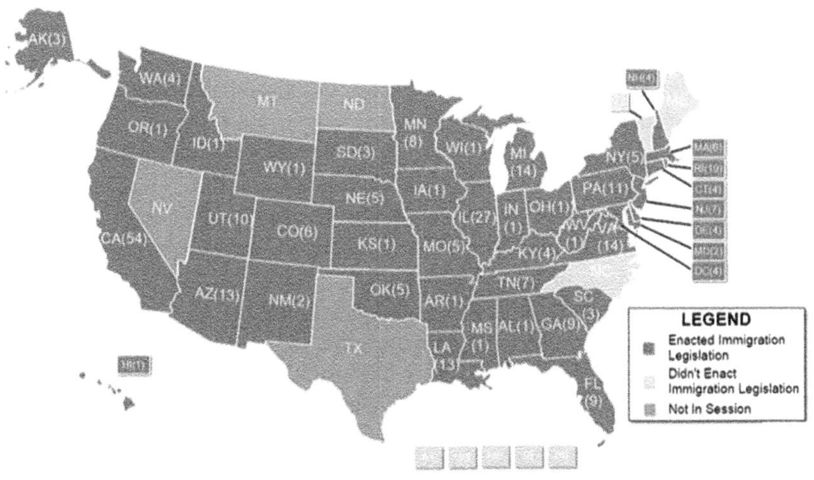


*Fig. 2.* Immigration-Related Laws in the States during January–December 2014. *Source*: National Conference of State Legislatures from: http://www.ncsl.org/documents/immig/ImmigrationReport2014Final.pdf

## POLITICAL CULTURE: THE SELECTION OF THE STATES

Since the federal government has been unable to pass a comprehensive immigration reform plan, states have now moved forward in passing legislation that is greatly affecting immigrant children and their families. In an effort to provide an overview of the legislation passed in the states, Elazar's (1966, 1970, 1984) concept of political culture was used to select states for analysis in this chapter. Elazar (1966) defines political culture as "the particular pattern of orientation to political action in which each political system is imbedded" (p. 84). Political culture provides a distinctive approach to understanding how values and beliefs of the populace are embedded in the legal and governmental process. The use of political culture:

> ... leads to the presumption that, although all states are responding to a broad national shift in expectations about the accountability of educational institutions, a state's interpretations of and assumptions about specific policies and practices to support accountability usually reflect their unique culture makeup and other historical circumstances. (Febey & Louis, 2008, p. 52)

Elazar's work also posits that politics in the states is greatly influenced by their respective political (sub) cultures: individualistic, moralistic, or traditionalistic (Elazar, 1966, 1984; Hero & Tolbert, 1996).

Individualistic political cultures describe the government's utilitarian perspective that it should be restricted to those areas, which encourage private initiative (Elazar, 1966, 1984). The individualistic political culture highlights the marketplace (Gray, 2008). There is a strong emphasis on the economic ties amongst political parties in the marketplace, while the government's participation is limited (Febey & Louis, 2008). The government has a restricted role, primarily to assist the marketplace with working correctly (Gray, 2008; Zimmerman, 2001). Individualistic states tend to experience more corruption in the government, as private matters dominate over public concerns (Elazar, 1970; Febey & Louis, 2008).

Moralistic political cultures describe the belief that views in society should be held in higher regard than individual views (Elazar, 1984). The government in these states has a strong role in regulating economic equality and common welfare amongst its citizens (Elazar, 1984; Febey & Louis, 2008). This strand of political culture also highlights the government's role in advancing the public's interest and the good of the commonwealth (Gray, 2008). Political leaders are prepared to undertake policy initiatives they think are in the best interest of the public and see politics as a means for handling issues and concerns of civil society (Zimmerman, 2001). Ultimately, politics revolve around issues of the people and government corruption is not tolerated (Elazar, 1984; Gray, 2008).

Traditionalistic political cultures describe social and familial ties as paramount in government decision-making (Elazar, 1966). Positioned in an ambivalent attitude toward the marketplace and a paternalistic and elitist conception of the commonwealth, "this largely Southern traditionalistic culture offers a different model for the role of government and democratic institutions" (Zimmerman, 2001, p. 164). Participation in the government is primarily from the elite. Traditionalistic political cultures "comparatively have less policy innovation, democratic political participation, and inter-party competition" (Febey & Louis, 2008, pp. 53–54). Ultimately, the government's role in these states is to secure the current social order and maintain economic hierarchy (Elazar, 1966). Fig. 3 shows the dominant political culture in each state. Fig. 3 highlights the majority of Southern states as being primarily traditionalistic, the Midwestern states as individualistic, and the Western states as moralistic.

Elazar attributes political processes and outcomes to both dominant or predominant cultural values and common normative tenets (Hero & Tolbert, 1996). These values are believed to derive from a state's dominant

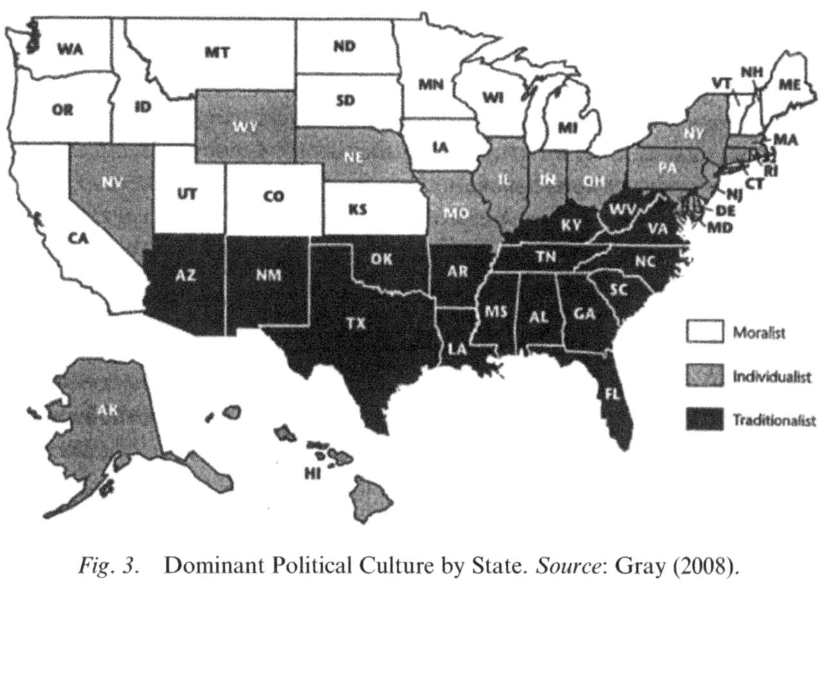


*Fig. 3.* Dominant Political Culture by State. *Source*: Gray (2008).

ethnic and religious groups. "Those without an assigned role in politics are not expected to be even minimally involved as citizens or even expected to vote" (Zimmerman, 2001, p. 164). Few states are solely examples of one subculture, however, there is a dominant culture that gives the state its particular political style (Gray, 2008). "The habits, perspectives, and attitudes that influence present day political life" (p. 20) can shape the political culture of a state (Gray, 2008). The use of political culture will provide a systematic process for selecting states to analyze. Political culture, which embodies the beliefs of attitudes held within a specific state, can also shed light on the types of legislation states are passing that are impacting the lives of immigrant children. It is important to note that the long-term impact of political culture may not be visible in all legislative session due to the fact that not all governments are entirely fluid; but the impact can become more overt as time progresses (Febey & Louis, 2008).

### *States Selected for Analysis*

Using Elazar's typology, the states selected for this analysis will be: Arizona (traditionalistic), Alabama (traditionalistic), California (moralistic), and New Jersey (individualistic). We opted to highlight two traditionalistic states in this analysis to provide examples of the extreme impact of the legislation being passed in these states on the education of immigrant children. The National Conference of State Legislatures' immigration database and policy reports from 2010 to 2015 were reviewed, as well as summaries of immigration-related statutes, excluding holiday observances and special dedications, were also accessed for these states. Although the states that were selected in this analysis are in the midst of extensive changes to their immigration laws and statutes, our analysis concluded with any information obtained prior to February 2015.

### *Arizona: A Traditionalistic View*

Arizona, a traditionalistic state, rose to the forefront of the national debate on illegal immigration when they enacted SB 1070. The passage of this law propelled Arizona to national headlines as several states began to follow suit with similar legislation. SB 1070, also known as the Support Our Law Enforcement and Safe Neighborhoods Act (2011), included but was not limited to expanding the role of police officers to check the immigration status of anyone detained in a traffic stop and allowed the detention of individuals suspected of being illegal immigrants.

Immigrant children and their families were gravely impacted by this legislation. "Many Latino-heavy school districts say the recession already has pushed many of their families out of state to look for work. The passage of [SB 1070] … has tipped the balance for some parents who tried to stick it out" (Kossan, 2010, para 3). For example, this law has been partially blamed for 2,000 students decline in enrollment in the Mesa Public School District (Parker, 2010). In a time of fiscal exigency in state budgets, a decline in per-student funding may result in an inability to pay for reading specialist, tutoring, and manageable class sizes (Kossan, 2010). Unfortunately, "for schools the impact could be loss of students and as a result, loss of state funding and parent support" (Kossan, 2010, para 4). Thus, as student enrollment decreases, the aftershock of their departure can eventually be seen in a decline in resources for all children in the schools.

### *Alabama: A Traditionalistic View*

Alabama, a traditionalistic state, has passed laws appearing to support the maintenance of the social and economic hierarchy amongst citizens within the state. With the passage of Alabama law, HB 56, a range of topics affecting immigrant populations, including but not limited to, law enforcement, public benefits, and education were impacted (Beason-Hammon Alabama Taxpayer and Citizen Protection Act 2011-535). Section 2 of HB 56 states that "the State of Alabama finds that illegal immigration is causing economic hardship and lawlessness in this state and that illegal immigration is encouraged when public agencies within this state provide benefits without verifying immigration status" (p. 4). The law forbids immigrants from entering into private contracts or conducting business with any state entities (Beason-Hammon Alabama Taxpayer and Citizen Protection Act 2011-535). The economic and societal impact for immigrant families has been devastating.

Immigrant children's educational opportunities have been stymied as a result. A record number of absences from immigrant student populations throughout the Alabama school system followed after the passage of the law (Gomez, 2012). In the weeks leading up to the enactment of the law, there were 1,120 Latino students absent from the schools. These children account for about 3.5 percent of the state's Latino student population

(Gomez, 2012). After the passage of the law, there were a noted 1,500 absences from Latino students daily throughout the state (Gomez, 2012). Due to Section 28 of the law calling for K-12 school officials to compile and report data on the citizenship status of a student at the time of their enrollment, we can attribute this as one of the causes of student departure in these districts. This law placed mixed status families in limbo as public school officials were required to gather data on the number of illegal immigrants present in their schools (Beason-Hammon Alabama Taxpayer and Citizen Protection Act 2011-535). HB 56 was used to intimidate and dissuade undocumented immigrant parents and their children from seeking a public education (Canupp, 2011). The federal court eventually blocked certain portions of the law, including the school checks; however, the unintended consequences of this legislation may have a ripple effect on the children and the state for several years to come.

### *California: A Moralistic View*

California, a moralistic state, has passed laws that have increased the educational opportunities for immigrant children and their families. California has made strides to grant access to postsecondary options for immigrant children. In 2011, California passed two education-related bills in support of undocumented students, the California DREAM Act. Comprised of bills AB 130 and AB 131, this legislation has opened financial aid access for undocumented students who wish to pursue higher education. Under Section 2 of AB 130, the bill states "increased access to financial aid for all students in California's universities and colleges increases the state's collective productivity and economic growth" (Assembly Bill 130: – California DREAM Act, 2011). Thus, the content in the legislation highlights the state's efforts to enhance its economic returns that result from having a more educated populace. Additionally, AB 131 allows undocumented students to participate in state student aid programs at California's public colleges and universities (Assembly Bill 131: California DREAM Act, 2011). Through these measures, undocumented students are being offered a viable option to gain access to higher education (Darolia & Potochnick, 2015).

Trends in immigration-related legislation portray California as being one of the most active in passing immigration laws, enacting 26 laws and 28 resolutions in 2014. An additional example of education-related immigration laws passed in California was the state's mandate that classes should be held to teach elementary and secondary basic skills for immigrant families. In addition, the law called for providing classes for immigrant populations in an effort to allocate instruction on federal, state, and local government initiatives as well as inform them of the importance of civic engagement (NCSL, 2015).

### *New Jersey: An Individualistic View*

New Jersey, an individualistic state, has also passed legislation to support increased educational opportunities for immigrant children. NJ A 718 (2012), passed in 2014, required the New Jersey Department of Education to issue a letter to each school district biannually to remind all districts of their duty to enroll immigrant children in schools regardless of the child's immigration status and in accordance with the rules and regulations of the State Board of Education (NCSL, 2014). An additional law, NJ S 2479 (2014), provided instates tuition benefits to children who attended high school for three years, graduated or received the equivalent of a high school diploma, and chose to attend a public college or university (NCSL, 2014). The law mandated that if a student did not have legal status prior to going to college, he or she must file an affidavit to legalize when they are eligible to do so (NCSL, 2014). In 2014, the New Jersey resolution, *NJ SR 61* (2014), commended the opportunities provided by the national DREAM US scholarship fund and encouraged Congress to move toward passing a comprehensive immigration reform plan (NCSL, 2015). Resolutions are commonly used to commend the efforts of citizens, immigrants, and organizations that serve immigrant populations on their efforts in recognizing the cultural heritage of immigrant populations within the state and by extension urge the President and Congress to take specific actions on issues such as immigration reform (NCSL, 2015).

## THE NEED TO BREAK DOWN LEGAL BARRIERS

The consequences for not having a comprehensive immigration reform plan are being played out in the lives of thousands of immigrant children and their educational trajectories in the respective states they live in. As poignantly noted by Suarez-Orozco and Suarez-Orozco (2009), "the lives of immigrant children are structured by deep contradictions that seriously compromise their future well-being" (p. 328). For immigrant children who are able to successfully overcome the barriers they encounter in the K-12 education system, they experience discontinued or limited opportunities in the higher education (Suarez-Orozco & Suarez-Orozco, 2009). Although *Plyler v. Doe* granted access to free public primary and secondary education for all students regardless of their immigration status, access does not extend to postsecondary education. Utilizing the lens of legal realism, we are able to clearly see the law in action in the states. This lens allows us to see both the intended and unintended consequences of the laws being passed and the delay in the passage of federal comprehensive immigration reform. As aforementioned, Alabama bill, HB 56, bans students who are classified as having an unlawful presence from attending any public college or university within the state. The realities of the educational opportunities for immigrant children are thwarted as a result of this law. Missouri also barred funding to higher education for unlawfully present students if the tuition presented was less than that offered to U.S. citizens that were not residents of the state. This law further prohibited immigrant children from receiving any type of financial or educational benefit in pursuing higher education within the state. On the other hand, since the executive action of DACA, some states have moved to pass legislation to support the educational endeavors of immigrant children. In 2014, Washington passed S 6523, the Real Hope Act, which allowed students who are in-state residents to apply for financial aid within the state regardless of their immigration status. The state also enacted House Bill 1817 to extend access to the State's need based grant programs as long as the students fulfilled DACA requirements and received a high school diploma from a Washington high school. The combined legal realities of federal and state legislative measures are significantly impacting the educational opportunities for immigrant children.

## IMPLICATIONS FOR EDUCATIONAL LEADERS

With the shifting demographics in schools, educational leaders have to be equipped with the leadership skills and expertise to support students from diverse backgrounds. The diverse composition of students in today's schools requires greater responsiveness to the services, practices, and policies needed to serve this evolving population. More attention is needed to support the social and cultural context of schools, that all students, but more specifically, immigrant children experience when they enter into U.S.

schools. In an era where closing the achievement gap or meeting national standards takes priority amongst teachers and educational leaders, students from marginalized populations often face isolation when their needs are often not considered in the race to meet these standards (Horsford, Grosland, & Gunn, 2011).

These implications for economic and social mobility for immigrant children and their families warrant the need to assess opportunities, experiences, and outcomes in American education for all students. According to Frum (2007):

> ... a high school diploma creates fewer opportunities for those entering the labor market. Arguably, the ticket to social and economic mobility has increasingly become a college degree, with college graduates' average annual earnings almost double those of high school graduates and nearly three times those of high school drop-outs. While in 1982 the Supreme Court sought to prevent the creation of an underclass of undocumented individuals by assuring access to free public K-12 education, the new educational "ticket to the middle class" may well be a college degree. By today's standards, then, not extending similar protections to undocumented students once they reach college age may create the very socio-economic chasms the Court had originally sought to avoid. (p. 83)

By providing these children with a good education, you are providing them with the chance to overcome barriers that keep them from better opportunities in life and from becoming active participants in society. It cannot be stressed enough that in society, a lack of education can and often does lead to poverty (Haskins & Tienda, 2011). Associated with failure to achieve, higher levels of education are lower unemployment and poverty rates (Baum & Ma, 2007). This statement reinforces the need to address the inequities faced by immigrant children and breakdown the legal barriers they face in education.

Given that immigrant students and their families contribute significantly to the economy of the United States, the new wave of immigration laws need to be revisited. Education ultimately translates into higher wages in the labor force, which leads to more tax revenue for federal, state, and local governing bodies (Ewing, 2012). "The U.S. Small Business Administration has estimated that small businesses have generated 64% of the net new jobs over the past 15 years and credits immigrant businesses with a significant recognition to this job growth" (Hohn, 2012, p. 5; Office of Advocacy, 2011). Additionally, "immigrant entrepreneurship ranges from creating businesses and local growth operations to technology and science innovations" (Hohn, 2012, p. 9). These significant contributions made by immigrant populations will not only increase jobs but also contribute to the tax base, which can be used for educational resources. Additionally, immigrant families also send money back home to relatives in their native countries to assist them financially. The money that is sent to these families members is seen as a significant contribution of aid to their countries in eradicating some of the poverty issues plaguing communities and is used to increase the national economy through more spending expenditure's from the funds received (Conger, 2006).

Immigration status is playing an increasingly significant role in educational opportunities and outcomes for immigrant students in the United States. Despite *Plyler v. Doe* (1982) extending a free public K-12 education to all students regardless of immigration status, recent anti-immigration legislation has restricted or entirely blocked undocumented immigrant students' educational pathways. Although undocumented immigrant children and their families are the primary group affected by statutes such as Arizona's SB 1070 and Alabama's HB 56, given that participation by immigrants in education generates substantial private and public benefits, society as a whole is being negatively impacted. According to Diaz-Strong, Gomez, Luna-Duarte, and Meiners (2011), "if current population trends continue and states do not improve the education of all ethnic, racial, and immigrant groups, the skills of the workforce and the income of the U.S. residents are projected to decline over the next two decades" (p. 115). This statement reinforces the need to address the educational inequities faced by immigrant children that are being exacerbated by immigration legislation.

The direct impact of these laws for educational leaders is paramount. Educational leaders have to exercise culturally responsive leadership practices in order to support the educational needs of immigrant children (Horsford et al., 2011). As schools become more racially, ethnically, and culturally diverse, educational leaders will need to be prepared to address the diverse needs and perspectives these children bring with them to school (Moll, 1992). More responsiveness is needed to provide for the services, practices, and policies that are used to serve and support the educational needs of immigrant children and their families. Educational leaders need to be prepared to engage in bridge leadership and bridge the disconnect to inequitable access to educational opportunities that immigration-related legislation has tried to bar these children and their families from receiving. By bridge leadership, we are referring to "a kind of epistemology in which the [school] leader[s] understands that the core of his or her work is rooted in traversing spaces between people" (Tooms & Boske, 2010, p. xviii). These spaces cut across a gamut of parameters that include equity, opportunity, and productivity. The premise behind bridge leadership calls for school leaders to connect themselves to others. Thus, school leaders must be able to create environments where parents with ethnic, language, racial, or academic backgrounds that differ from the dominant groups within their communities and school staff, to still feel respected, welcomed, and valued (Uline & Johnson, 2005). We cannot assume that school leaders who work with marginalized students know how to serve as bridges. There needs to be training both within leadership preparation programs and beyond in professional development opportunities in schools on how they can take make this critical connection amongst the communities they serve. Through making these strides, we can continue to break down the educational barriers immigrant children and their families encounter and move towards more positive educational change for years to come.

## NOTE

1. According to U.S. Department of Homeland Security (2012), an immigrant, also known as a permanent resident alien, is defined as "an alien admitted to the United States as a lawful permanent resident" (p. 1).

## REFERENCES

Altman, A. (2001). *Arguing about law*. Belmont, CA: Wadsworth/Thomson Learning.

Assembly Bill 130: California DREAM Act of 2011. (2011). *Legislative Counsel's Digest*. Retrieved from http://www.leginfo.ca.gov/pub/11-12/bill/asm/ab_0101-0150/ab_130_bill_20110725_chaptered.html

Assembly Bill 131: California DREAM Act of 2011. (2011). *Legislative Counsel's Digest*. Retrieved from http://www.csac.ca.gov/pubs/forms/grnt_frm/AB131.pdf

Baum, S., & Ma, J. (2007). *Education pays: The benefits of higher education for individuals and society*. New York, NY: The College Board.

Beason-Hammon Alabama Taxpayer and Citizen Protection Act. HB 56. (2011). *Ala. Laws Act 2011-535*. Retrieved from http://immigration.alabama.gov/docs/Immigration-AL-Law-2011-Highlighted.pdf

Bravin, J. (2009). Legal realism informs judge's views. *The Wall Street Journal*. Retrieved from http://online.wsj.com/article/SB124346735555660341.html

Canupp, D. (2011). *Immigration and the law: Will the new Alabama immigration law result in a loss of federal funding to Alabama schools?* Alabama School Boards. Retrieved from http://lanierford.com/images/NewsPDFs/immigration.pdf

Conger, L. (2006). *The Value of Remittances*. Retrieved from http://www.emergingmarkets.org/Article/1019803/The-Value-of-Remittances.html

Darolia, R., & Potochnick, S. (2015). Educational "when", "where", and "how" implications of in-state resident tuition policies for Latino undocumented immigrants. *The Review of Higher Education, 38*(4), 507–535.

de Been, W. (2008). *Legal realism regained.* Stanford, CA: Stanford University Press.

Department of Homeland Security. (2012). *Definition of Terms.* Retrieved from http://www.dhs.gov/definition-terms

Diaz-Strong, D., Gomez, C., Luna-Duarte, M., & Meiners, E. (2011). Purged: Undocumented students, financial aid policies, and access to higher education. *Journal of Hispanic Higher Education, 10*(2), 107–119.

Dinan, K. A. (2006). *Young children in immigrant families the role of philanthropy sharing knowledge, creating services, and building supportive policies.* National Center for Children in Poverty. Retrieved from http://www.aecf.org/~/media/Pubs/Topics/Special%20Interest%20Areas/Other/YoungChildreninImmigrantFamiliesTheRoleofPhil/NCCP%20Role%20of%20Philanthropy.pdf

Elazar, D. (1966). *American federalism: A view from the states.* New York, NY: Thomas Y. Crowell Company.

Elazar, D. (1970). *Cities of the prairie.* New York, NY: Basic.

Elazar, D. (1984). *American federalism: A view from the states.* New York, NY: Thomas Y. Crowell Company.

Ewing, W. (2012). *How the president's deferred action initiative will help save the U.S. economy.* American Immigration Council. Retrieved from http://immigrationimpact.com/2012/06/29/how-the-presidents-deferred-action-initiative-will-help-the-u-s-economy/

Febey, K. S., & Louis, K. S. (2008). Political cultures in education at the state and local level: Views from three states. In B. S. Copper, J. G. Cibulka, & L. D. Fusarelli (Eds.), *Handbook of education politics and policy.* New York, NY: Routledge.

Feldman, N. (2010). *Scorpions: The battle and triumphs of FDR's Great Supreme Court Justices.* New York, NY: Twelve.

Frum, J. (2007). Postsecondary educational access for undocumented students: Opportunities and constraints. *American Academic, 3*, 81–108.

Garcia, L., & Tierney, W. (2011). Undocumented immigrants in higher education: A preliminary analysis. *Teacher College Record, 113*(12), 1–28.

Gomez, A. (2012). In wake of immigration law, some migrants return to Alabama. *USA Today News.* Retrieved from http://www.usatoday.com/news/nation/story/2012-02-21/alabama-immigration-hispanic/53180746/1

Gonzales, R. (2007). Wasted talent and broken dreams: The lost potential of undocumented students. *Immigration Policy Center, 5*(13), 1–12.

Gonzales, R., & Bautista-Chavez, A. M. (2014). *Two Years and Counting: Assessing the Growing Power of DACA.* Retrieved from http://www.immigrationpolicy.org/sites/default/files/docs/two_years_and_counting_assessing_the_growing_power_of_daca_final.pdf

Gray, V. (2008). The socioeconomic and political context of states. In V. Gray & R. Hanson (Eds.), *Politics in the American states: A comparative analysis.* Washington, DC: CQ Press.

Haskins, R., & Tienda, M. (2011). The future of immigrant children. *Future of Children, 21*(1), 1–8.

Hero, R., & Tolbert, C. (1996). A racial/ethnic diversity interpretation of politics and policy in the states of the U.S. *American Journal of Political Science, 40*(3), 851–871.

Hohn, M. (2012). *Immigrant entrepreneurs: Creating jobs and strengthening the economy.* American Immigration Council. Retrieved from http://www.immigrationpolicy.org/sites/default/files/docs/Hohn_-_Immigrant_Entrepreneurs_012512.pdf

Horsford, S. D., Grosland, T., & Gunn, K. M. (2011). Pedagogy of the personal and professional: Toward a framework for culturally relevant leadership in education. *Journal of School Leadership*, *21*(4), 582–606.

Immigration Policy Center. (2013). *A Guide to S. 744: Understanding the 2013 Senate Immigration Bill.* Retrieved from http://www.immigrationpolicy.org/sites/default/files/docs/guide_to_s744_corker_hoeven_final_12-02-13.pdf

Immigration Policy Center. (2015). *A Guide to the Immigration Accountability Executive Action.* Retrieved from http://www.immigrationpolicy.org/special-reports/guide-immigration-accountability-executive-action

Jiang, Y., Ekono, M., & Skinner, C. (2015). *Basic facts about low-income children, 2013.* National Center for Children in Poverty. Retrieved from http://www.nccp.org/publications/pdf/text_1100.pdf

Kossan, P. (2010). *Schools: Immigrant Families Leaving Arizona Because of New Immigration Law.* Retrieved from http://www.azcentral.com/news/articles/2010/05/28/20100528arizona-immigration-law-schools.html

Laanan, F. S. (2000). Community college students' career and educational goals. *New Directions for Community Colleges*, *2000*(112), 19–33. doi:10.1002/cc.11202

*Lau v. Nichols*. 414 U.S. 563. (1974).

Migration Policy Institute. (2014). *Press Release.* Retrieved from http://migrationpolicy.org/news/mpi-many-37-million-unauthorized-immigrants-could-get-relief-deportation-under-anticipated-new

Minda, G. (1995). *Postmodern legal movements.* New York, NY: New York University Press.

Moll, L. (1992). Funds of knowledge for teaching: Using qualitative approach to connect homes and classrooms. *Theory into Practice*, *31*(1), 132–141.

National Center for Education Statistics. (2015). *English Language Learners.* Retrieved from https://nces.ed.gov/programs/coe/indicator_cgf.asp

National Conference of State Legislatures. (2014). *2013 Immigration Report.* Retrieved from http://www.ncsl.org/research/immigration/2013-immigration-report.aspx

National Conference of State Legislatures. (2015). *2014 Immigration Report.* Retrieved from http://www.ncsl.org/research/immigration/2014-immigration-report.aspx

Nieto, S. (2010). *The light in their eyes: Creating multicultural learning communities.* New York, NY: Teachers College Press.

NJ A 718. (2012). *Senate No. 718 State of New Jersey.* Retrieved from https://legiscan.com/NJ/text/S2123/2012

NJ S 2479. (2014). *Senate No. 2479 State of New Jersey.* Retrieved from https://legiscan.com/NJ/text/S2479/id/933652/New_Jersey-2012-S2479-Chaptered.html

NJ SR 61. (2014). *Senate No. 2123, State of New Jersey Senate Bill 61.* Retrieved from https://legiscan.com/NJ/text/SR61/2014

Office of Advocacy. (2011). *How important are small businesses to the U.S. economy?* Small Business Administration. Retrieved from https://advocacysba.sites.usa.gov/2011/10/17/how-important-are-small-businesses-to-the-u-s-economy/

Paez, M. (2008). English language proficiency and bilingual verbal ability among Chinese, Dominican, and Haitian immigrant students. *Equity & Excellence in Education*, *41*(3), 311–324.

Parker, R. (2010). *Mesa schools' enrollment continues to decline*. The AZ Central. Retrieved from http://www.azcentral.com/community/mesa/articles/2010/10/14/20101014mesa-schools-enrollment-dropping1009.html

Passel, J. (2006). *The size and characteristics of the unauthorized migrant population in the U.S.: Estimates based on the March 2005 current population survey*. Washington, DC: Pew Hispanic Center. Retrieved from http://www.pewhispanic.org/files/reports/61.pdf

*Plyler v. Doe*. 457 U.S. 202. (1982).

Reeves, J. (2004). Like everybody else: Equalizing opportunity for English language learners. *TESOL Quarterly*, *38*(1), 43–66.

Rodriguez, G., & Cruz, L. (2009). The transition to college of English learner and undocumented immigrant students: Resource and policy implications. *Teachers College Record*, *111*(10), 2385–2418.

Suarez-Orozco, C., & Suarez-Orozco, M. (2009). Educating Latino immigrant students in the twenty-first century: Principles for the Obama administration. *Harvard Educational Review*, *79*(2), 327–401.

Tamanaha, B. (2009). Understanding legal realism. *Texas Law Review*, *87*(4), 731–785.

The Border Security, Economic Opportunity, and Immigration Modernization Act – S. 744. (2013). Retrieved from http://www.gpo.gov/fdsys/pkg/BILLS-113s744pap/pdf/BILLS-113s744pap.pdf

The Support Our Law Enforcement and Safe Neighborhoods Act – S.B.-1070. (2011). Retrieved from http://www.azleg.gov/legtext/49leg/2r/bills/sb1070s.pdf

The Urban Institute (2006). *Children of immigrants: Facts and figures*. Washington, DC: Author.

The White House. (2014). *Immigration: Taking Action on Immigration*. Retrieved from https://www.whitehouse.gov/issues/immigration

Tooms, A. K. & Boske, C. (Eds.). (2010). *Bridge leadership: Connecting educational leadership and social justice to improve schools*. Greenwich, CT: Info Age.

UCIS. (2015). *Consideration of Deferred Action for Childhood Arrivals (DACA)*. Retrieved from http://www.uscis.gov/humanitarian/consideration-deferred-action-childhood-arrivals-daca

Uline, C., & Johnson, J. F. (2005). Closing achievement gaps: What will it take? *Theory into Practice*, *44*, 1.

USCIS. (2015). *Executive Actions on Immigration*. Retrieved from http://www.uscis.gov/immigrationaction#2

Valdes, G. (2011). Alabama's attorney general balks at giving feds school data. *Cable News Network*. Retrieved from http://www.cnn.com/2011/11/03/us/alabama-schools-feds/index.html

Verdugo, R., & Flores, B. (2007). English-language learners: Key issues. *Education and Urban Society*, *39*(2), 167–193.

Zimmerman, S. (2001). *Family policy: Constructed solutions to family problems*. Thousand Oaks, CA: Sage.

# CHAPTER 5

# ACADEMIC LANGUAGE DEVELOPMENT: BARRIERS TO SUCCESS FOR MULTILINGUAL LANGUAGE LEARNERS

Caron Mellblom-Nishioka

## ABSTRACT

*Language is a social and engaging process (Bloom & Lahey, 1978), which is not fully formed until a child is six or seven (Roseberry-McKibben, 2007). Language is developed through social experiences, modeling, observing, and experimenting. Yet our educational system operates on the premise that typically developing children enter kindergarten, at age five with a firm foundation in speaking and listening, and equivalent exposures to pre-literacy skills (Roseberry-McKibben, 2007). For many children who speak a first language other than English, this is not the case. Typically, their first language is not supported in school, and the expectation is that they will learn to speak, communicate, and use English in order to understand grade level core content. Thus, they begin their education at a disadvantage. For many children this expectation creates an initial learning knowledge gap that appears to widen annually. This chapter will examine the literature related to language*

**Legal Frontiers in Education: Complex Law Issues for Leaders, Policymakers and Policy Implementers**
**Advances in Educational Administration, Volume 24, 85–98**

**ISSN: 1479-3660/doi:10.1108/S1479-366020150000024031**

*development and second language learning and the laws and mandates that drive our classroom practice.*

The educational system in the United States operates on the premise that typically developing children enter kindergarten, at age five with a firm foundation in speaking and listening, and equivalent exposures to pre-literacy learning experiences (Roseberry-McKibben, 2007). For many children whose mother tongue is a language other than English this is not the case. Typically, their first language is not supported in school, and the expectation is that they will learn to speak, communicate, and use English in order to understand grade level core content. Thus, they begin their education at a disadvantage. Many children begin school without a firm foundation in the first language and thus experience an initial learning knowledge gap that appears to widen annually.

This chapter will examine the literature related to language development and the apparent disconnect between language development theory and teaching practices related to second language learners. Next, second language learning and the laws and mandates that drive our classroom practice will be explored. The third section provides a discussion of Culture and English Language Learners, followed by a section on Leading Evidence-Based Practices in the Education of English Language Learners and then Role of Educational Leaders is presented. The chapter concludes with, conclusion and implications.

## LANGUAGE DEVELOPMENT

Language is a social and engaging process, (Bloom & Lahey, 1978). According to McLaughlin (1998) typical children begin attending to speech sounds in their environment soon after they are born. Within a few months babies begin to experiment with sound production and are known to make all sorts of sounds with their articulators, (the tongue, teeth, cheeks, nasal cavity, and palate). It is also noted that between six and eight months of age, children begin to refine the sounds they produce during vocal play based on those sounds they hear and that are reinforced in their environment (McLaughlin, 1998). This is true for children who are exposed to one or more different languages (Paradis, Genesee, & Crago, 2011).

As children become aware that different sounds and words exist in different parts of their world, they begin to refine the use of these sounds and words to conform with their developing awareness and are often observed to switch between the languages depending on the situation. As children age, they begin to apply the rule systems of the languages that they are learning based on the situational context (McLaughlin, 1998). This process referred to as "code switching" allows the child to participate in communication in the various environments in which they live. The amount of exposure to each language appears to be directly related to the development of language proficiency (Paradis et al., 2011).

It is widely accepted that the foundations for language are not firmly set until a child reaches 6–7 years old (Roseberry-McKibben, 2007). Until this time children are gaining awareness of the rules and conventions of the language or languages they will come to use (Roseberry-McKibben, 2007). It is also widely acknowledged that while basic informal conversational skills (BICS) develop rather quickly and are based on contextual awareness, cognitive, academic language proficiency (CALP), and a deeper academic language understanding may take up to 10 years to develop. These theories coupled with the practice of English-only preschool and primary education is contradictory. The persistent practice in the United States is to immerse bilingual and multilingual children in an English-only classroom, with the expectation that they will somehow transfer meaning from the English they are learning, to the home language that has not yet fully developed.

Monolingual children enter school with a developing awareness of the rules of the dominant language system. In the early grades, they receive instruction that supports this growing understanding of the language of their community and academic environment. Their vocabulary expands as does their understanding of the syntactic rules that govern spoken and written language, as does the awareness of language cues related to semantics, (word choice) and pragmatics, (when certain conventions are appropriately used and the impact of our roles affect the syntax and semantics). According to Piagetian theory, as children are exposed to new curriculum content they attach this knowledge to their expanding language schemata (Wadsworth, 1989). So, what happens to children who are expected to simultaneously learn new content and a new language?

Multilingual children enter school with the same levels of developing awareness of the language of their homes and cultures, but have vastly different experiences than their monolingual peers. They are thrust into an environment where the developing language that they bring to the classroom is largely unsupported in the mainstream monolingual classrooms.

They are immersed in a new environment with different cultural expectations and a language that is unfamiliar. While it has been noted bilingual children reach some language developmental milestones similarly to monolingual children, they also may demonstrate delays in other aspects of language development, (Paradis et al., 2011) such as the use of and understanding of irregular plurals and verbs, figurative language, idioms, metaphors, and vocabulary expansion. As they learn to function in the academic classroom, the expectation of the educational community is that they will simultaneously learn the language of the classroom and the core standard curriculum for their grade level. Evidence from the literature indicates this is not the case (Baker, 2011; Cummins, 2000; Menken & Kleyn, 2010). Multilingual children appear to focus first on gaining access to the language of the classroom. For many this occurs in stages (Paradis et al., 2011) and as a result multilingual children often miss key curriculum. Educators who become familiar with the processes that multilingual children experience when immersed in an English-only academic setting, gain a deeper awareness of the challenges these student face when attempting to learn core academic content and English the language of the teaching simultaneously. The stages multilingual children typically experience (Paradis et al., 2011) are briefly described here.

The first stage refers to the language of the home and the community. Often stage two involves a silent phase in which the children appear to attend to the language of the school environment and rely on gestures and pantomime for expressive communication. In the third stage the bilingual child often begins to use the language of the classroom for expressive but continues to rely on gestures to support monosyllabic utterances. Eventually, in this stage they begin to use learned or rote sentences and phrases without variations of unique productions. Examples may be found in the social conventions of "chit-chat" such as, "Good Morning! How are you? I am fine. Today is Friday," etc. In these examples, the children may have memorized the appropriate time and place to use the phrases but are yet unable to converse at deeper levels, (Paradis et al., 2011). Cummins (2000) indicated that this is the stage in which Basic Informal Conversation Skills (BICS) begin emerge (Roseberry-McKibben, 2008). As children develop increased awareness of the vocabulary and use of the second language they enter Stage four.

At this point, the children begin to use the second language expressively but tend to substitute words from their home language to supplement their verbalizations. A child may demonstrate competent BICS and appear able to engage in idle comprehensible contextualized conversation but not have developed Comprehensive Academic Language Proficiency (CALP) (Roseberry-McKibben, 2007). The literature supports the notion that BICS develops much more rapidly for second language learners in 3–5 years and may mask the need for continued Specifically Designed Academic Instruction in English, (SDAIE) (Roseberry-McKibben, 2008). Evidence suggests that the development of CALP may take from five to seven and possibly even 10 years instruction and exposure to the second language (Roseberry-McKibben, 2007). This should have important implications for classroom teaching strategies for engaging multilingual children in successful learning and development.

## NO CHILD LEFT BEHIND LAW (NCLB): MANDATES FOR TEACHING AND LANGUAGE

A review of the laws and mandates affecting our schools reveal a connection between the No Child Left Behind act of 2001 and a decrease in programs to support bilingual language learning and education (Baker, 2011; Collins, 2014; García, Kleifgen, & Falchi, 2008; Krashen & McField, 2005; Menken & Kleyn, 2010; Menken & Solorza, 2014).

The No Child Left Behind (NCLB) act (U.S. Department of Education, 2002) was passed with overwhelming congressional support. It was hailed as a program of comprehensive educational reform. NCLB includes five primary goals. First, All students will demonstrate high academic achievement. Second, All teachers will be highly qualified. Third, Students will learn in safe drug free environments. Next, All English Language Learners will become proficient in English and finally, all students will graduate with a high school diploma, (Yell & Drasgow, 2009). The law requires individual schools, districts and state accountability and requires that they demonstrate student improvement and student success. The law emphasizes "closing the achievement gap," (Thu-Hoang, 2009; Yell & Drasgow, 2009). Accountability measures, annual state-wide academic performance testing, results are attached to financial incentives and disincentives. A further tenant of the NCLB mandate requires all children, regardless of their educational placement be assessed annually to determine learning progress. Under the NCLB guidelines, schools were no longer able to exclude special populations from the testing or the reporting of results due to their individual learning needs. The law did include provisions known as "Title III" to support the English Language learning of multilingual students and included the requirement for states to develop comprehensive support systems for second language learners. Title III further allows districts to exclude second language learners from the reported assessment results for the first year of their English language learning (U.S. Department of Education, 2005, cited in Thu-Hoang, 2009). It should also be noted that according to the congressional record, Report to Congressional Requesters 2006 (cited in Thu-Hoang, 2009) funding for programs to support English Language learners increased with the creation of Title III. This raises some questions including such as: where did the money go, and how is it being used?

Researchers have found that perhaps due to the restrictive nature of the way in which NCLB funds are allocated and the misconceptions that abound about the impact of bilingual programs and effective second language learning, bilingual education programs have decreased considerably in the years since the implementation of NCLB (Baker, 2011; Collins, 2014; García et al., 2008; Krashen & McField, 2005; Menken & Kleyn, 2010; Menken & Solorza, 2014; Collier & Thomas, 2004). If in fact funding has increased and Title III of NCLB instructs states to develop programs to support English language learners, why is this the case?

The findings are troubling. Menken and Solorza (2014) interviewed school administrators and found consistently that testing and the need to perform was linked to the elimination of bilingual education programs. When probed further, these authors found school administrators blamed the Bilingual programs for declining test scores and the believed that eliminating these programs would benefit the learning and development of English Language Learners. The data from multiple research studies provide evidence that Bilingual education programs promote student learning and are related to positive increases in student assessment scores (Collier & Thomas, 2004; Collins, 2014; García et al., 2008; Schwartz, 2014).

Menken and Solorza (2014) note further the decrease in the number of bilingual programs to support learning represents a disturbing trend to disregard evidence-based studies that demonstrate the benefits of providing bilingual instruction for English Language Learners. Prior to the 2001 passage and subsequent implementation of NCLB, states had passed restrictive laws limiting Bilingual Education. In California, voters passed proposition CA, 227 in 1998. This proposition included that language for English Language Learners must overwhelmingly be taught in English. In 2000, Arizona passed proposition 203 by a wide majority of voters. Similar to CA, 227 the use of languages other than English for teaching and learning was severely curtailed. Then in 2002, Massachusetts voters passed Question 2 which was also designed to make English the only language used for content teaching (Menken & Solorza, 2014). A similar measure to these three failed in Colorado. The restrictive policies such as Proposition CA, 227 have always been problematic, but appear senseless when one acknowledges the globalization and interconnectedness of the world in which communicating in more than one language is important and should be valued (Weisman & Hanson, 2002).

Discussions regarding immigration policy and employment issues are politically charged. It appears that Multilanguage learners, bilingual education, and the children we serve, have been caught in the crossfire of these issues (Gándara & Hopkins, 2010). Menken and Solorza (2014) indicated that the policies regarding language and education are influenced by and reflective of the greater attitudes surrounding issues facing the nation. Since immigration, culture and diversity have been so highly politicized so has the interpretation of evidence-based studies designed to evaluate the effectiveness of bilingual education.

## CULTURE AND ENGLISH LANGUAGE LEARNERS

One critical and controversial issue in American public education today is the lack of progress that Local Educational Agencies (LEA) demonstrate as a result of teaching millions of children throughout the country. Among these students, we find the "special group" English Language Learners (ELL). According to Abbot (2014), "There have been many definitions or labels given to these students: Limited English Proficient (LEP), non-native English speakers, language-minority students, and either bilingual students or emerging bilingual students" (Abbot, 2014, p. 1). This contentious change in definitions is testimony to the confusion among educators. We can say that an English Language Learner (ELL) is a student who speaks a language other than English and is in the process of learning English.

There are significant numbers of foreign-born individuals living in the United States. According to the American Community Survey (2010), there were approximately 40,000,000 foreign-born individuals living in the United States that year. 21,224,087 foreign-born individuals living in the United States claimed their place of birth from one Latin American country. Mexico was the country cited as place of birth for 11,711,103 foreign-born individuals making it the country from where most immigrants come.

China was second with a little more than 2,000,000 and India was third with nearly 2,000,000. Foreign-born individuals, whose primary language is not English (making them ELLs), are forming families and having children. Typically, their children, learn the language of their parents, prior to enrolling in school. Consequently, this would qualify the children as English Learners. ELL students from all over the world are present in every single state of the United States but there are several states that have a much larger concentration of ELLs with California as the leader. Schildkraut (2007) states, "English proficiency is a virtual requirement for full participation in US society .... Americans also view English language use as a key component of national identity" (p. 603). The charge then is to determine how best to provide the learning environment necessary for ELL students to develop English proficiency while maintaining their cultural identify and connections to their community.

## LEADING EVIDENCE-BASED PRACTICES IN THE EDUCATION OF ENGLISH LANGUAGE LEARNERS

While the size and number of bilingual education programs continues to decline, (Menken & Solorza, 2014), research to support the effectiveness of educating students in bilingual environments continues to grow (Baker, 2011; Collins, 2014; García et al., 2008; Krashen & McField, 2005; Schwartz, 2014).

Studies of bilingual preschool programs indicate that contrary to the belief that teaching children in the home language hinders learning and development of the language of the classroom, the practice actually enhances the development of the second language, (Schwartz, 2014). Collins (2014) noted that the language environment in school has a positive effect on the language development in the home. When children are able to freely interact with teachers and peers in both, the home language and the classroom language, improvement is noted in both languages (García et al., 2008). Barnett, Yarosz, Thomas, Jung, and Banco (2007) studied Spanish speaking preschool children in Bilingual preschools and found that the children made significant gains in both languages, while a control group of Spanish speaking preschoolers in English-only programs demonstrated gains in English-only. This is consistent with previous research demonstrating the benefits of bilingual education programs to the increased development of the home and classroom languages (Collier & Thomas, 2004, cited in Collins, 2014; García et al., 2008; Thomas and Collier, 2003).

Based on the recent work of Esparza Brown and Sanford (2011), this population of English Language Learners is statistically the fastest growing segment of the school-age population. They are also a very diverse group representing numerous ethnicities, nationalities, cultures, languages, educational level, and socioeconomic backgrounds. Many of the ELLs are first-generation citizens of the United States but they live with parents, grandparents, and extended family who speak a language other than English. Thus, ELL students face additional and in some cases different challenges than their monolingual peers. This has an adverse impact on their academic language development and academic progress. Other important factors such as poverty, transiency, legal status, war trauma, or life-threat concerns have additional influence on their academic progress. English Learner students are more likely to be in poor, overcrowded schools and in many places represent an added cost to already budget dilapidated school districts (August & Shanahan, 2006).

The confusion as to how to best teach this segment of the school population begins with the division over what program to choose. Bilingual programs generate heated debates led by those who favor English-only program. Border states like Arizona, California, New Mexico and Texas, and others like Florida, Nevada, and New York have the largest numbers of English Learners in their school-age populations and they do not have a unified philosophy or approach to language acquisition. In many states, English Learners are concentrated in low-income, urban schools with volatile administration and less experienced.

Esparza Brown and Sanford (2011) indicate that due to the changing classroom demographics teachers must address the issues of educational equity in their classrooms. High standards must be the expectation for all students. They state further that teachers must acknowledge the three unique individual cultural, linguistic and environmental factors that accompany each child in the learning environment. Finally, Esparza Brown and Sanford (2011) indicate that educators must plan for adaptive assessment and learning activities to reflect the individual backgrounds of the students in their classes.

Student centered small group learning strategies are favored over large group based lecture approaches. Such approaches include, "think-pair -share", with true peers, (Brown & Doolittle, 2008). True peers are defined as students with comparable cultural, linguistic and environmental background. Other recommended strategies include interactive small group tasks that involve the use of manipulatives, visual aids, graphic organizers, video streamed content, and actual objects that relate to the curriculum, (Echevarria & Vogt, 2011; Echevarria, Vogt, & Short, 2007).

Additionally, teachers must intentionally teach the vocabulary of activity directions and in some case reword the instructions to make the language more comprehensible to multilingual learners.

## ROLE OF EDUCATIONAL LEADERS

Educational leaders are faced with increased accountability demands. Ill-conceived expectations that one size fits all testing procedures will capture meaningful data regarding student achievement has become the doctrine of the No Child Left Behind federal mandates. Yet, by placing such high stakes on this type of testing many children are in fact being left behind. Teaching to the test does not support the unique needs of any learners especially and especially bilingual children.

However, as an apparent result of the NCLB mandates, administrators seek to foster uniform teaching practices among their teaching faculty. The apparent assumption is that this will promote increased scores on annual achievement tests that have become the basis for school accountability data. This assumption is not grounded in scientifically based evidence. In fact the opposite is the case. Multiple studies indicate that multilingual students educated in bilingual programs outperform multilingual students who learn in English-only programs, (Krashen & McField, 2005). Even so, the evidence indicates that students engaged in unique learning experiences designed to engage prior knowledge and home cultures tend to support learning in multiple contexts (Cook, Boals, & Lundberg, 2011; Krashen & McField, 2005; WIDA, 2013). According to Cummins et al. (2004), pre-existing knowledge is initially learned in the child's first language. Therefore, administrators must take bold steps to encourage classroom instructors to explicitly teach in ways that activate and support the transfer of experiences and understanding from the student's home language to the academic language of the classroom. The use of supported dual language instruction is recommended (Cummins et al., 2004). Allowing students to create identity texts is cited as beneficial for all students. For the multilingual student this allows the opportunity to explain who they are and from where they have come, while for the monolingual peers it allows them to become familiar with the cultures of others in their world (Krashen & McField, 2005). Additional studies by WIDA, (World-Class Instructional

Design and Assessment) support the idea that collaboration among content and language teachers is key to the success of the multilingual learner as, one would argue, it is for all learners. Cook et al. (2011), note that WIDA indicate that the development of Academic Language requires three elements: support, instruction, and enculturation. Also suggested is the use of multiple examples as well as visual, tactile, kinesthetic and various interactive supports. WIDA also recommends that educators acknowledge the many possible pathways in that language is developed within any given context.

## CONCLUSIONS AND IMPLICATIONS

The evidence conflicts with the practice. A marked decline in the number of Bilingual Programs has been noted in spite of conclusive data that support the effectiveness of Bilingual Education programs. Additionally, it is a widely accepted developmental language theory, that the foundations of language development are not firmly set until the age of six or seven (McLaughlin, 1998; Roseberry-McKibben, 2007). It is also widely accepted that while basic informal conversational skills develop rather quickly and are based on contextual awareness deeper academic language understanding may take up to 10 years to develop. These theories coupled with the practice of English-only preschool and primary education is contradictory – assuming we agree that the foundation for language is not fully formed when children enter school. The question we must ask is: how is it possible for children to learn content rich curriculum in monolingual learning environments that do not support their first language?

The evidence consistently supports the belief that offering learning opportunities in both the first and second language increases in the child's knowledge of both languages. The answer to these questions lies in dialogue sure to incite some, but that appears to be in the best interest of children. In this increasingly global economy, shouldn't schools in the United States offer all children the opportunity to learn in an environment that mirrors the adult world in which they will live? Perhaps all children should be educated in Bilingual Programs designed to support multilingual children and to teach additional languages to monolingual children. Short of that multilingual children must be afforded the opportunity to learn grade level content in their first language while be offered intensive second language instruction in the academic language of the classroom (Krashen,

1996, 2004) until such time as CALP has been firmly established and multi-faceted assessment evidence supports this claim.

The literature supports the notion that multilingual children develop best when they are given the opportunity to learn in a language rich and culturally inclusive environment that support both the language and culture of the home and of the classroom. The determination of a student's Cognitive Academic Language Proficiency (CALP) is dependent on many factors. Educators must strive to identify the unique and individual differences that all language learners bring to the classroom and acknowledge that there is no one size fits all strategy that will support the learning requirements of multilingual learners as they access the academic language of the curriculum. Also noted is the limited number of studies available to determine leading practices in supporting the language development and grade level learning of multilingual children and monolingual children in various dual/multi language emersion programs. Therefore, additional studies are necessary to demonstrate the efficacy of dual language emersion programs that support the ongoing development of the child's first language, the development of the academic language of the classroom and achievement in age appropriate content curriculum.

Finally, efforts must be made to modify the erroneous assumptions of educational leaders who in the quest for higher achievement scores tend to blame perceived failings in this area on the bilingual programs they offer and the children who learn in them.

## REFERENCES

Abbot, S. (2014, August 26). *Hidden curriculum: The glossary of education reform*. Retrieved from http://edglossary.org/hidden-curriculum

American Community Survey. (2011). Census bureau releases 2010 american community survey single year estimates. *Education Letter*, 41.

August, D., & Shanahan, T. (2006). *Executive summary: Developing literacy in second language learners*. Report of the national literacy panel on language-minority children and youth. Erlbaum, Mahwah, NJ.

Baker, C. (2011). *Foundations of bilingual education and bilingualism* (5th ed.). Bristol: Multilingual Matters.

Barnett, W. S., Yarosz, D. J., Thomas, J., Jung, K., & Banco, D. (2007). Two way and monolingual English immersion in preschool education: An experimental comparison. *Early Childhood Research Quarterly*, *22*(3), 277–293.

Bloom, L., & Lahey, M. (1978). *Language development and disorders in children*. Hoboken, NJ: Wiley.

Brown, J. E., & Doolittle, J. (2008). A cultural, linguistic and ecological framework for response to intervention with English language learners. *Teaching Exceptional Children*, *40*(5), 66–72.

Collier, V. P., & Thomas, W. P. (2004). The astounding effectiveness of dual language education for all. *NABE Journal of Research and Practice*, *2*(1), 1–20.

Collins, B. A. (2014). Dual language development of Latino children: Effect of instructional program type and the home and school language environment. *Early Childhood Research Quarterly*, *29*, 389–397.

Cook, H. G., Boals, T., & Lundberg, T. (2011). Academic achievement for English learners. What can we reasonably expect? *Kappan*, *93*(3), 66–69.

Cummins, J. (2000). *Language power and pedagogy: Bilingual children in the crossfire*. Clevedon: Multilingual Matters.

Cummins, J., Bismilla, V. B., Chow, P., Cohen, S., Giampapa, F., Leoni, L., ... Sastri, P. (2004). Affirming identity in multilingual classrooms. *Educational Leadership*, *63*(1), 38–43.

Echevarria, J., & Vogt, M. E. (2011). *Response to Intervention (RTI) and English learners: Making it happen*. Boston, MA: Pearson.

Echevarria, J., Vogt, M. E., & Short, D. J. (2007). *Making content comprehensible for English learners: The SIOP model* (3rd ed.). Boston, MA: Allyn & Bacon.

Esparza Brown, J., & Sanford, A. (2011). *RTI for English language learners: Appropriately using screening and progress monitoring tools to improve instructional outcomes*. Washington, DC: U.S. Department of Education, Office of Special Education Programs, National Center on Response to Intervention. Retrieved from http://www.rti4success.org/images/stories/pdfs/rtiforells.pdf

Gándara, P., & Hopkins, M. (2010). *Forbidden languages: English learners and restrictive language policies*. New York, NY: Teachers College Press.

García, O., Kleifgen, J. A., & Falchi, L. (2008). *From English language learners to emergent bilinguals*. New York, NY: Campaign for Educational Equity, Teachers College Columbia University.

Krashen, S. (1996). *Under attack: The case against bilingual education*. Culver City, CA: Language Education Associates.

Krashen, S., & McField, G. (2005). What works? Reviewing the latest evidence on bilingual education. *Language Learner*, *1*(2), 7–10, 34.

Krashen, S. D. (2004). False claims about literacy development. *Educational Leadership*, *61*(6), 18–21.

McLaughlin, S. (1998). *Introduction to language development*. San Diego, CA: Singular Publishing Group.

Menken, K., & Kleyn, T. (2010). The long-term impact of subtractive schooling in the educational experiences of secondary English language learners. *International Journal of Bilingual Education and Bilingualism*, *13*(February), 399–417.

Menken, K., & Solorza, C. (2014). No child left bilingual: Accountability and the elimination of bilingual education programs in New York city schools. *Educational Policy*, *28*(1), 96–125.

Paradis, J., Genesee, F., & Crago, M. B. (2011). *Dual language development and disorders*. Baltimore, MD: Paul H. Brookes.

Report to Congressional Requesters, United States Government Accountability Office. (2006). *No child left behind: Education's data improvement efforts could strengthen the basis for distributing title III funds*. GAO.

Roseberry-McKibben, C. (2007). *Language disorders in children: A multicultural and case perspective*. Boston, MA: Pearson.

Roseberry-McKibben, C. (2008). *Multicultural students with special language needs: Practical strategies for assessment and intervention* (3rd ed.). Oceanside, CA: Academic Communication Associates.

Schildkraut, D. (2007). Defining American identity in the twenty-first century: How much "there" is there? *The Journal of Politics*, *69*(3), 597–615.

Schwartz, M. (2014). The impact of the first language first model on vocabulary development among preschool bilingual children. *Reading and Writing*, *27*, 709–732.

Thomas, W. P., & Collier, V. P. (2003). *What we know about: Effective instructional approaches for language minority learners*. Arlington, VA: Educational Research Service.

Thu-Hoang, T. (2009). English language learners and the No Child Left Behind Act of 2001. ERIC.

U.S. Department of Education. (2002). *No child left behind: A desktop reference*. Washington, DC: Education Publications Center.

U.S. Department of Education. (2005). Biennial evaluation report to congress on the implementation of the State Formula Grant Program, Washington, DC.

Wadsworth, B. J. (1989). *Piaget's theory of cognitive and affective development* (4th ed.). New York, NY: Longman.

Weisman, E. M., & Hanson, D. Z. (2002). Teaching English language learners after Proposition 227: Reflections of bilingual teachers. *Issues in Teacher Education*, *11*, 53–68.

WIDA. (2013). *Amplification of the English language development standards for kindergarten–Grade 12*. Wisconsin Center for Educational Research 2012, Madison, WI.

Yell, M. L., & Drasgow, E. (2009). *No Child Left Behind: A guide for professionals* (2nd ed.). Boston, MA: Pearson Publishing.

CHAPTER 6

# A LITIGATION TREND ANALYSIS OF CASE LAW OUTCOMES PERTAINING TO THE EDUCATIONAL RIGHTS OF ENGLISH LEARNERS: A CIVIL RIGHTS ISSUE

Delia E. Racines


## ABSTRACT

*The current 5.4 million English Learners (ELs) make up the lowest performing academic group in the United States (US) today. A number of weaknesses and struggles in the field of EL education have been simmering below the surface for years, and while previously treated as an unspoken dysfunction in our education system, the inequitable treatment of ELs can no longer be ignored. There is an urgent need to ensure equitable, inclusive, high-quality educational opportunities and outcomes for ELs, including preparation for college and career readiness. This study relies on two established legal policy research methodologies, specifically the four-step method of analysis and the quantitative method of*


**Legal Frontiers in Education: Complex Law Issues for Leaders, Policymakers and Policy Implementers**
**Advances in Educational Administration, Volume 24, 99–118**

**ISSN: 1479-3660/doi:10.1108/S1479-366020150000024032**

*"simple-box scoring," to systematically analyze case law outcomes and identify seven litigation trends from cases over the past 40 years. This research can provide alternative proactive remedies other than costly litigation and demonstrates the need for a more effective coordination of mechanisms to unite institutions that service ELs. This study bridges the gap of critical knowledge needed to help educators, attorneys, and professors who prepare school leaders and teachers to meet legal requirements for ELs, each of whom are entitled by law to access mainstream curriculum. Further limitations and implications are presented.*

## ENGLISH LEARNERS, SCHOOLING, AND THE LAW

By 2025, it is estimated that one out of every four students will be an English Learner (EL) (Kihuen, 2009). The impact of these changing demographics is significant in education given the looming mandate to ensure that all students, including ELs, are prepared to graduate and attend college and/or begin a career. Over the last decade, the 2001 No Child Left Behind (NCLB) Act resulted in the most significant federal education reform package, pressuring states to implement its extensive requirements, to ensure that all schools are held accountable for the academic progress of every child, regardless of race, ethnicity, income level or zip code (Evans, 2005). It is because of NCLB that closing the achievement gap between Whites and Blacks, Hispanics, ELs, Students with Disabilities (SWD), and economically disadvantaged students became a national priority. Local education agencies (LEAs) and state education agencies (SEAs) have been forced to revisit and revise their practices as ELs have been pushed to, and have stayed in, the center of national education conversations. Ultimately, NCLB committed the federal government to a more central role in driving states and districts toward measureable improvement in student achievement, especially for ELs. Yet, while the Elementary and Secondary Education Act's (ESEA) mandates have required school districts to regularly evaluate ELs, the Department does not necessarily provide guidance or regulations on *how* such evaluations should be structured; only guidance on minimum expectations are outlined (Faulkner-Bond et al., 2012). NCLB is well-intended in supporting ELs, yet, with a heavy emphasis on instructional strategies to increase the achievement of ELs. There has been a failure to incorporate as equal an emphasis on legal parameters and examine federal policies that protect ELs' rights and establish school districts' responsibilities. As school districts across the country try to best serve the ever-increasing number of ELs, numerous questions remain unanswered, while some practices have yet to be questioned at all (Rossell, 2005). The purpose of this chapter is increase awareness and comprehension of legislation related to the educational rights of ELs to begin to improve ELs' equitable educational opportunities and outcomes.

The year 2010 ignited a renewed vigilance for policy and practice on the enforcement of ELs' civil rights (Faulkner-Bond & Forte, 2011). Nationwide data, collected from nearly 7,000 school districts by the US Department of Education's (DOE, 2010) Office of Civil Rights (OCR) not only revealed stark racial and ethnic disparities in student retentions but also sparked the official opening of 15 investigations (2011). These 15 investigations focused on whether ELs were being denied equal educational opportunities (Bartholomew & Llanos, 2010; Faulkner-Bond & Forte, 2011; Maxwell, 2011; Zehr, 2010). The OCR released the names of a few school districts, scattered from coast to coast, including Los Angeles Unified, California, Hazelton, Pennsylvania, DeQueen, Arkansas, New London, Connecticut, Tigard-Tualatin, Oregon, and Lake Washington, Washington. ELs have also been at the center of a continued dispute in Colorado where mandatory changes must be made to EL programs as investigations uncovered there were no programs being provided *at all* in charter schools for beginner ELs (Maxwell, 2013). Such investigative efforts with the help of the Civil Rights Data Collection (CRDC) have shed light on numerous ongoing weaknesses and trends of unmet educational services in the field of ELs that have been simmering below the surface for years. Four recurrent themes have been identified in this research that underlie the unmet educational services of ELs, including: (a) a general lack of understanding the legislation pertaining to the educational rights of ELs; (b) variability in the identification of ELs, in addition to the services and programs provided to ELs; (c) the lack of guidance for, and compliance of, various program requirements; and (d) the lack of monitoring and/or evaluating the effectiveness of such requirements (Faulkner-Bond & Forte, 2011, p. 14).

## [MIS]UNDERSTANDINGS IN EL LEGISLATION

The lack of a clear understanding of legislation pertaining to ELs' educational rights has resulted in the noticeable misalignment of enforcement systems with LEAs' responsibilities to provide adequate educational services for students (Faulkner-Bond & Forte, 2011). As the formal entities directly responsible for educating children, LEAs hold primary responsibility for ensuring that ELs, in particular, receive the services civil rights laws guarantee, yet, from district to district, civil rights investigations uncovered significant variation among service gaps, in addition to a variety of reasons for such gaps. ELs in the Seattle, WA district, for example, did not receive language services of *any* kind in the 2006–2007 school year, while in 2010, multiple LEA evaluation outcomes with similar results surfaced in Boston, Massachusetts, Buffalo, New York, and Portland, Oregon; all of which caused ELs to miss eligible services (Faulkner-Bond & Forte, 2011). Results from such Department of Justice (DOJ) investigations required LEAs to implement changes to their practices, as ELs were not receiving services entitled to them by law, mostly due to misunderstanding EL-related legislation.

Similarly, SEAs like Illinois and Arizona came under scrutiny for statewide practices that affected the education of ELs and faced DOJ investigations for misinterpreting EL-related policies (Zehr, 2010). Though Illinois denied the allegations, the DOJ found the Illinois State Board of Education was in violation of the EEOA due to a policy that allowed non-proficient ELs to exit out of transitional-bilingual programs after three years of instruction with no clear mandate that LEAs must continue support for ELs after they exit the program (Faulkner-Bond & Forte, 2011). The EEOA's main purpose is to ensure equal opportunities through reporting and monitoring activities designed to make certain that no state denies equal educational opportunities to an individual on account of his or her race, color, sex, or national origin or language barriers. Failure by an educational agency to take "appropriate action" to overcome language barriers may impede equal participation in its instructional programs (Berenyi, 2008; Depowski, 2008; Rios-Aguilar & Gándara, 2012). Much flexibility is granted to states to comply with EL-related policies, like the EEOA, to create their own language remedial programs, which explains the vast assortment of remedial Language Instruction Educational Program (LIEPs) for ELs across the country. However, the very lack of consistency and great variation in program content have become major concerns for the quality of education ELs receive nationwide (Wiley & Wright, 2004).

Parental waiver decisions have also contributed to confusion and violation of other EL-related policies, in particular Titles I and III. Multiple states and districts (Boston, Seattle, Portland, and Illinois) were under investigation for failure to provide language support to ELs who had opted out of language programs because their parents had requested their child not participate or because the child attended schools in a district that did not have formal LIEPs (Faulkner-Bond & Forte, 2011; Ragan & Lesaux, 2006; Rossell, 2005). The monitoring agencies believed the decision made by ELs' parents to opt-out of such programs waived the district or state's responsibility to help a student learn English (Faulkner-Bond & Forte, 2011). To the contrary, Titles I and III under NCLB grant parents of ELs the right to deny their child's participation in LIEPs, but do not necessarily waive the LEAs' civil rights obligations to overcome previously identified linguistic barriers (Berenyi, 2008; Faulkner-Bond & Forte, 2011). Both Title VI of the Civil Rights Act of 1964 and the EEOA require LEAs to take active steps to help *all* students attain sufficient proficiency, which essentially "trumps" the NCLB service refusal clause (Berenyi, 2008; Faulkner-Bond & Forte, 2011, p. 6; Ragan & Lesaux, 2006; Wright, 2005). This is another example of common noncompliance that stems more from misunderstanding laws, rather than deliberate disregard for ELs' educational rights (Faulkner-Bond & Forte, 2011). Once classified as an EL, schools must include the student in the EL subgroup, offer accommodations, and annually administer assessments to test English Language Proficiency (ELP).

## EXTENSIVE VARIABILITY IN EL IDENTIFICATION, RECLASSIFICATION, PROGRAMS, AND SERVICES IDENTIFICATION OF ELS: ENTRY AND EXIT CRITERIA

The identification of ELs for and actual duration of an EL program may have significant effects on ELs' academic achievement (Ragan & Lesaux, 2006). While states use the same ESEA definition of an EL, criteria used to make initial EL placement decisions vary widely across the United States, as does how to determine when an EL should no longer be designated as EL; referred to as both redesignation or reclassification (Klingner, 2010; Ragan & Lesaux, 2006). The major lack of standardization and clarity of entry, as well as exit criteria, for EL programs at the national, state, and or/district level effects all ELs. Similarly, tremendous inconsistencies also affect the validity, accuracy, and comparability of outcome data for EL subgroups (Klingner, 2010; The Working Group on ELL Policy, 2009).

A study conducted by Ragan and Lesaux (2006) examined federal laws, including published entry and exit criteria, for EL programs for 10 individual states and districts with the largest enrollment of ELs in the United States. These states, from largest to smallest, included: California, Texas, Florida, New York, Arizona, Illinois, Colorado, New Mexico, Georgia, and New Jersey (Ragan & Lesaux, 2006); EL enrollment in the aforementioned cities and states made up more than 80% of total EL enrollment in the 50 states, including the District of Columbia (Hoffman, 2003). With data gathered from the DOE's websites regarding entrance criteria, each of the 10 states studied, except GA and NJ, used a home language survey (HLS) to identify students for whom a language other than English is spoken at home. In six of the states (AZ, CA, CO, GA, NM, and NY), the identification process for EL programs involves two steps, an initial prescreening tool (a HLS or prescreening by a teacher) and one additional criterion, a test of English Language Proficiency (ELP), which, currently, Klingner (2010) emphasizes, is not peer-reviewed.

As for exit criteria, the majority of states studied use ELP tests to redesignate ELs to mainstream programs (Ragan & Lesaux, 2006). The lack of agreement between ELP tests is even greater at the point of redesignation with the problem of the tests being unable to differentiate between a student who does not know the answer and a student who does not know enough English to understand the question (Rossell, 2005). This problem becomes more apparent especially upon redesignation when ELP exams are more difficult (Rossell, 2005). Only three states, Colorado, Illinois, and New York, specify the amount of time ELs should be served in EL programs. In Colorado, after only two years in an EL program, ELs are no longer funded, whereas in New York, after three years an ELs' individual progress is reviewed, and in IL, ELs cannot be considered for redesignation before spending at least three years in language support programs (Ragan & Lesaux, 2006). Some districts could not provide any written documentation of district policies either online or via hard copy. Overall, findings from Ragan and Lesaux's (2006) study suggest that the entry and exit criteria for EL programs are overly broad and focus primarily on ELP without much consideration to the overall long-term academic achievement of ELs. There is a lack of consideration for the developmental nature of language acquisition in the entry and exit criteria used by states and districts; language does not vary as a function of grade level. Baker (2006) stresses how insensitive essentially all forms of standardized tests are to the qualitative aspect of language and to the great range of language competencies. Likewise, Baker suggests that NCLB subjects ELs to various types of testing without adequate preparation.

## REDESIGNATION/RECLASSIFICATION FROM EL TO FLUENT ENGLISH PROFICIENT

In addition to the identification of ELs, there is also great variation, and great tension, surrounding one of the most common milestones used for defining and measuring an ELs' progress - redesignation or reclassification from an EL to fluent English Proficient (FEP) (Linquanti, 2001). According to Linquanti, the concept of reclassification, as it is currently defined and implemented, may actually be contributing to educational inequity, lack of accountability, and student failure. Linquanti's policy report reviews the purposes and methods of identifying, classifying, and serving ELs and identifies specific problems with the current methods. These specific problems with the current methods include the complexity of what ELs have to demonstrate in order to be reclassified as FEP, the inadequate procedures which rely on standardized tests to "trigger" a review for reclassification, and ultimately, the distortion of EL progress due to how reclassification rates are calculated (Linquanti, 2001, p. 10).

A civil rights investigation, under a joint DOJ and ED civil rights offices investigation, cited AZ for violation of the identification instruments used with ELs and instructional programs and services provided to ELs under another EL-related policy, Title VI of the Civil Rights Act of 1964 (Faulkner-Bond & Forte, 2011). With regards to the identification instruments used, the psychometrician hired for AZ's investigation concluded that the state's placement test was an invalid measure of language skills and also ruled that the use of its *one-question* HLS, a survey given to parents for initial placement, was insufficient to identify all students who are eligible for and may need EL services (Faulkner-Bond & Forte, 2011; Zehr, 2010).

Overall, although well-intended, the identification of ELs and adoption of a variety of programs and services for ELs among public schools, although often a response to sanctions, reflect a lack of consistency and great variation in its content and quality across state programs (Wiley & Wright, 2004). As seen through various examples across the country, quantity has increased, yet, the quality of education has decreased; ELs, now, more than ever, are subjected to hours of rote test preparation without much consistency in the way ELs are identified, reclassified nor serviced (Linquanti, 2001; Ragan & Lesaux, 2006; Wiley & Wright, 2004).

## LACK OF COMPREHENSIVE GUIDANCE AND COMPLIANCE FOR EL SERVICE REQUIREMENTS

Currently, there is no one authoritative source of guidance or governing body dictating the full extent of EL service requirements. While NCLB is arguably one of the more influential federal initiatives in the United States today related to ELs, prior legislative initiatives are critical underpinnings necessary to examine in an effort to understand current efforts (Faulkner-Bond & Forte, 2011; Ragan & Lesaux, 2006). EL-related legislation outlines specific service requirements with guidelines for implementation that stem from multiple legal sources of authority and are governed by various entities under which all laws and requirements for each one must be met (Faulkner-Bond & Forte, 2011) (see Fig. 1).

Both advocates and parents of ELs have sought protection under Titles I and III under NCLB. Protection has also been sought under Title VI of the Civil Rights Act of 1964, including the *Lau* Memoranda and the *Castañeda* principles, the Equal Educational Opportunities Act (EEOA) of 1974, and the Fourteenth Amendment Equal Protection Clause (EPC) (Berenyi, 2008; Faulkner-Bond & Forte, 2011; Kihuen, 2009;

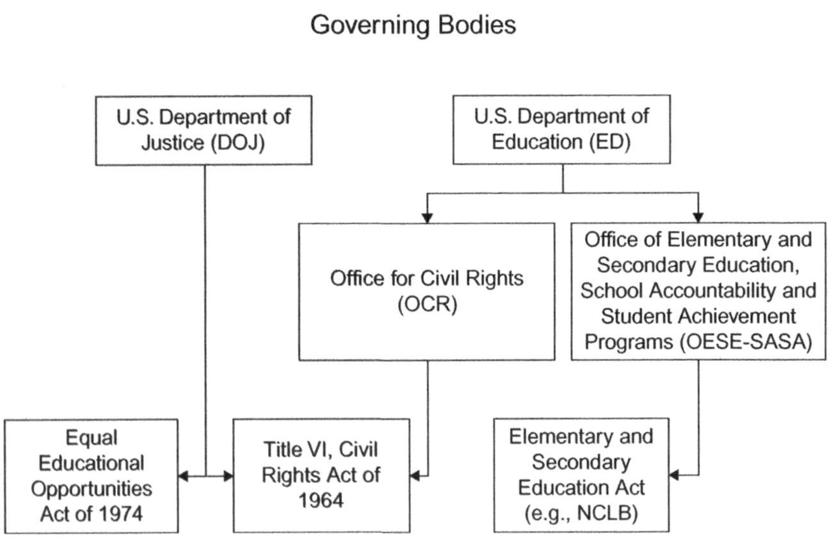


*Fig. 1.* A Flowchart of the Laws and Multiple Governing Bodies Overseeing EL-Related Legislation. *Source*: Faulkner-Bond and Forte (2011).

Ragan & Lesaux, 2006; Smith, 1990). The two main governing bodies overseeing EL-related legislation are the US DOJ and the US DOE (Faulkner-Bond & Forte, 2011).

Under the US DOJ are the EEOA and Title VI of the Civil Rights Act. Under the US DOE is the OCR, which also oversees Title VI of the Civil Rights Act as well as The Office of ESEA, School Accountability and Student Achievement Program (SASA), which ultimately oversees the NCLB Act. These offices watch for implementation errors and failures, yet only LEA administrators are held accountable for ensuring that each of these requirements are met (Faulkner-Bond & Forte, 2011). As for the EPC of the Fourteenth Amendment, this Clause forbids states from denying any person equal protection of the law. Similarly, the Fifth Amendment EPC applies to the federal government. Both the EPC and Due Process Clauses of the Fourteenth Amendment are significant sources of legal, and as some might argue, moral authority over educational rights (Bon, 2012).

Comprehensively, these federal laws, policies, and supporting documents reveal that it is up to individual states and districts to develop a system for identifying ELs who need language support programs. Additionally, states and districts must also develop EL services according to various language proficiencies and assess ELs with appropriate assessments. It is also up to states and districts to determine when ELs no longer need support as determined by their EL status (Ragan & Lesaux, 2006). The mere multiplicity of governing statutes have far-reaching implications for compliance; meeting program requirements for one of these laws does not exactly guarantee compliance with each across the gamut of legal protections since each initiative is governed by its own agency or combination of agencies that each serve a unique purpose. Exact details of the systems that must be used to ensure ELs progress academically and develop ELP to participate in the mainstream classroom are left to the discretion of each individual state and district without much guidance. Yet, services for ELs must be designed to satisfy criteria for each governing body of law which often become the product of practitioners' own initiatives (Faulkner-Bond & Forte, 2011; Ragan & Lesaux, 2006; Samson & Collins, 2012). While ED and OCR offer resources on how to interpret and implement NCLB and Title VI, such support is almost completely isolated and has to be retrieved separately. Not much support is offered to LEAs nor is there a way to ensure requirements have been met thoroughly or correctly until after the fact. The problem only trickles down to school districts, mandated by ESEA to evaluate ELs regularly and meet specific academic targets. Further, the

Department does not necessarily provide guidance on *how* such evaluations should be structured. Once again, only guidance on minimum expectations are mentioned (Faulkner-Bond et al., 2012; Samson & Collins, 2012).

## MONITORING AND EVALUATING EFFECTIVENESS OF EL REQUIREMENTS

Lastly, the OCR examined the academic opportunities and access of ELs in the two largest school systems in the nation, LAUSD and NYC DOE schools, to assess whether they were being denied equal educational opportunities. This investigation found that there was absolutely *no* centralized process for evaluating the effectiveness of EL services. Furthermore, there was no process for identifying how to improve EL services across schools. Essentially, both school systems acknowledged that they were not meeting the needs of hundreds of thousands of ELs (Maxwell, 2011, 2013). The probe also found that a vast majority of ELs in middle and high schools continued to struggle academically even after being deemed FEP.

Just as there is no one authoritative source of guidance or governing body dictating the full extent of EL service requirements, there is also no one effective comprehensive system of data collection to monitor and/or evaluate EL service requirements (The Working Group on ELL Policy, 2009). The Working Group on ELL Policy emphasizes just how important it is to track ELs longitudinally because each EL's designation and achievement levels in reading and mathematics changes their ELP improves. Disaggregating performance data by the number of years in the program or by classifications such as former ELs or ELs with interrupted schooling allows states and districts to determine the effectiveness of programs for ELs. However, only 22 states and DC have data systems that would allow them to track former ELs beyond the two years of monitoring which are required under Title III of ESEA. As of 2010, 22 states provided information to the ongoing National Evaluation of Title III, but only one state reported that it could directly identify ELs whose formal education was interrupted (Boyle, Taylor, Hurlburt, & Soga, 2012). The Working Group on ELL Policy (2009) ultimately recommends Title I and Title III to include reporting requirements for ELs across all language proficiency levels. This requirement would reflect ELP and academic content outcomes to be reported out as well as the long-term performance of students that have exited EL status and services. This stronger framework is needed to ensure that all educators are given clearer information and held accountable for an ELs' academic performance and ELP progress, simultaneously (The Working Group on ELL Policy).

The final lever for institutionalizing change in introducing educational reform has historically been through the courts (Samson & Collins, 2012). Courts have played a key role in the advocacy of educational rights and equity for ELs, as in the landmark 1974 case, *Lau v. Nichols*. Currently, it seems to be the only route to ensure the civil rights of ELs, including compliance of various EL services (Samson & Collins, 2012). In the face of numerous OCR investigations regarding the educational rights of ELs there is an incentive for practitioners to increase their knowledge regarding ELs services. There is an emphasis on alternative remedies rather than litigation to establish more effective coordination of mechanisms to bring together institutions that service ELs is of upmost importance. ELs and education systems will continue to face challenges because comprehensive resources and guidance regarding the educational rights of ELs are not readily available today (Faulkner-Bond & Forte, 2011; Samson & Collins, 2012; The Working Group on ELL Policy, 2009).

The aforementioned four recurrent themes underlying the unmet educational services of ELs highlight the importance of examining EL-related legislation that undergirds compliance (Kihuen, 2009). The remainder of this chapter presents a discussion of the results from a systematic analysis of case law outcomes and identification of litigation trends with the intention to contribute to the effort to understand EL-related legislation. The following discussion may also inform comprehensive policy decisions and contribute to the adoption of compliant EL practices and services.

## A LITIGATION TREND ANALYSIS OF EL-RELATED CASE LAW OUTCOMES

A legal trend analysis investigates not only whether a category of cases are increasing, but also examine *why* litigation in this area is increasing (Adler, 1996; Kihuen, 2009). Two of the primary legal policy research methodologies were adopted to achieve the identified purposes in this study (Baldwin & Ferron, 2006; Kunz, Schmedemann, Downs, & Bateson, 2008). Through the four-step method of analysis (Kunz et al., 2008) and Baldwin and Ferron's quantitative method of "simple-box scoring," this research study first identified what the law is and then answered the why and how questions relative to ELs' educational rights.

The following data set was composed of cases in which the following criteria were met. First, the cases occurred between 1974 and 2013. The starting point for cases was the 1974 landmark US Supreme Court case *Lau v. Nichols*, which significantly impacted the education of ELs, and the ending point was April of 2013, the latest lawsuit filed by the ACLU in CA. Second, the cases were published. Third, the cases were considered "good law" meaning that they had precedential value; cases were shepherdized using Lexis Nexis. Fourth, the cases involved at least one specific claim regarding the educational rights and/or assessment issues of ELs. Fifth, the cases were brought by a parental suit or advocacy group(s) on behalf of an EL, and sixth, at least one of the defendants listed in the suit was an educational institution serving public, PK-12 grade-range ELs. Exclusions were extended to higher education institutions. If the cases did not include substantive issues related to the education of ELs, they were considered irrelevant and were excluded from the data set. If a case was a lower court decision and its appeal was in the data set, this too was excluded based on its appeal.

After an initial search with the aforementioned Boolean key-words with a combination of EL acronyms, an initial 998 cases were collected from Lexis Nexis and Westlaw. After eliminating cases that were not published, eliminating cases that dealt with *only* immigration issues regarding ELs, and limiting cases to only federal and state cases, 106 cases were left. These 106 cases then were subjected to a subsequent review in order to eliminate cases that did not fit within the specified dates ranging from 1974 to 2013. Cases that did not meet such criteria were excluded and considered irrelevant to this data set. After accounting for duplicate cases and excluded/irrelevant cases on the aforementioned criteria, the final number for this sample totaled 25. Each of the final 25 cases was then entered into one document, organized with specific details in chronological order by year, and case law outcomes were coded. All data were transferred into a case analysis chart; a "simple-box scoring" spreadsheet that included a case number, case name, citation, date decided, state of origin, claim(s), outcome, relief sought, remedy awarded, findings and clarifying comments, case law outcome codes, and outcome code of prevailing party. Outcome codes used a one to seven Likert scale adapted from Lupini and Zirkel (2003). The range included one that signified a "complete win for parents/ELs/advocacy groups on behalf of ELs," a four signified a "split decision," and seven signified a "complete win for the school authorities."

Results gleaned from the data set are presented through the following four subcategories: (1) number and frequency of cases, (2) prevailing party,

(3) geographical distribution, and (4) [research question] litigation trends in case law outcomes.

## RESULTS

The 25 cases originated in 11 different states/federal districts. The highest number of cases ($n=8$) were litigated in California. Three states, Texas, Arizona, and New York tied for the second highest number of cases. Overall, 64% ($n=16$) of the 25 cases were decided in favor of parents of ELs and/or advocacy groups on behalf of ELs and 28% ($n=7$) of the cases were decided in favor of the school districts. One case resulted in an inconclusive win for the school district/authorities, while another case was decided largely for ELs' Parents/Advocacy Groups.

As for litigation trends of case law outcomes, after analyzing the 25 cases, a total of 95 codes emerged. These 95 outcomes were then examined to identify themes, which resulted in the documentation of the following seven litigation trends that have emerged over the past 40 years (from 1974 to 2013): (1) EL-related legislation, claims, and violations; (2) equal education opportunity violations; (3) inequitable educational programs for ELs; (4) inadequate EL programs and services; (5) EL program funding issues; (6) ineffective EL identification; and (7) assessment issues. These trends are consistent with the aforementioned four major themes recognized by the civil rights investigations that are ongoing around the United States and essentially triggered this study. These four themes identified by the OCR included (1) [mis]understandings in EL legislation, (2) extensive variability in EL identification, reclassification, programs, and services, (3) the lack of comprehensive guidance and compliance for EL service requirements, and (4) monitoring and evaluating the effectiveness of EL requirements (Faulkner-Bond & Forte, 2011).

One key trend, EL-related legislation claims/violations, included the following major federal statutes and constitutional guarantees. The extensive analysis of cases provided further clarification to understand to what extent each piece of legislation was more of a misunderstanding over the other. The four major pieces of legislation include the following, in order of highest violations: (1) the EEOA of 1974 ($n=15$), (2) Title VI of the Civil Rights Act of 1964, including the *Lau Memoranda* clarifying LEA responsibilities for ELs along with the *Castañeda* principles ($n=13$), (3) the Fourteenth Amendment's Equal Protection Clause ($n=8$), and (4) the NCLB Act of 2001 ($n=2$).

Additionally, while funding is not one of the major trends, this is an issue that is likely to emerge as a more prominent trend in future litigation. This trend includes seven case law outcomes related to issues and claims, such as the school district's failure to comply with federal funds, as well as the "arbitrary and capricious" funding levels provided for ELs' instructional needs. Each of these case law outcomes was a result of either: (1) too many students in a classroom; (2) not enough classrooms; (3) not enough qualified teachers; (4) not enough teacher aids; (5) inadequate tutoring programs; and (6) insufficient resources for teaching, and in these particular cases, were found to be a direct result of inadequate funding for ELs. The case law outcomes for this trend were generally determined in accordance with the EEOA requirements, which are imposed on school districts and mandate the use of funds to adequately prepare teachers, provide sufficient instructional materials, and establish appropriate English Language Development (ELD) programs and services.

## SCHOOL LEADERS, THE LAW, AND PROMOTING LEGALLY JUST PROCESSES IN SCHOOLS

Analyzing litigation trends and outcomes provides critical insight into the key pieces of EL-related legislation for school leaders, teachers, policymakers, researchers, and parents/advocates of ELs that are seemingly misunderstood and frequently overlooked. With a heavy emphasis on increasing test scores with specific instructional strategies for ELs, the rights of ELs have not received much attention. The final data set of cases reveals the untold stories of ELs and brings awareness to their inequitable educational experiences in public schools across the nation. Each of these cases reveals how US courts have interpreted various EL-related legislation and ultimately how the courts ruled in cases dealing with the educational rights of ELs; reflecting the continued efforts in an attempt to fulfill *Brown's* promise. The Equal Protection Clause prohibits states from denying any person equal protection of the law and is most notably referenced in the landmark desegregation case, *Brown v. Board* (1954). In short, the Supreme Court's decision in Brown established that the "separate but equal" doctrine, first endorsed by the court in Plessy v. Ferguson (1896), violated the Fourteenth Amendment Equal Protection Clause, making segregation in the educational setting unconstitutional. Unfortunately, the mere fact that these cases exist reflect that the legal requirements of educating ELs are still not being met. ELs are not adequately served in our nation's schools by current efforts.

The findings of this study are significant because they reveal litigation trends and patterns that could promote more effective compliance for ELs and provides alternative proactive remedies to avoid costly litigation. It also demonstrates the need for more effective coordination of mechanisms to bring together institutions that service ELs. Parents/advocates of ELs are empowered with a realization of better pathways of litigation for successful outcomes in the courts and have a better understanding of the trends of EL-related legislation violations from cases with the most successful claims. What must be kept in mind, however, is that during litigation, ELs continue to receive a poor education. Again, more proactive solutions are possible with a better understanding of EL-related legislation. Similarly, requirements identified in this study do not encourage EL services to be solely "triggered" by standardized test scores nor ELs "exited" from services based on standardized test scores alone either.

Overall, this research educates how to advocate with legal knowledge of the educational rights of ELs. It is equally important, however, to stress that the majority of the 7,000 civil rights complaints that have been filed with the OCR do not necessarily proceed to the courts and, therefore, do not and did not result in a case law outcome. Many of these investigations are settled outside of court. These 25 cases do not necessarily provide a true and complete picture of the challenges that ELs encounter (Faulkner-Bond & Forte, 2011).

The results are significant because they can provide alternative proactive remedies other than costly litigation. Furthermore, they demonstrate the need for more effective coordination of mechanisms to bring together institutions that service ELs. Without alternative options, however, parents and advocates of ELs are empowered with better pathways of litigation for successful outcomes in court with knowledge of *how* to be stronger advocates, with legal knowledge of the educational rights of ELs. These 25 cases and the plaintiffs' ongoing efforts to resolve their disputes with school districts in the courts reveal that there is an unmet need for ELs in the public school setting and that there is seemingly no other alternative for justice besides this contentious legal venue. However, while the final lever for institutionalizing change in introducing educational reform has historically been through the courts, the results of this study strongly encourage and demonstrate the need for a more proactive and less reactive approach (Samson & Collins, 2012). The Lawyers Committee for Civil Rights under Law. (2012) reminds educational leaders the following:

> More than fifty years ago, it took the persistent efforts of parents and students in cities and hamlets across the country to persuade the Supreme Court in *Brown v. Board of Education* to rule that all students should have access to an inclusive, high-quality education. Today, our nation is still struggling to fulfill *Brown's* promise. (Lawyers Committee for Civil Rights under Law, 2012, p. 14)

## RECOMMENDATIONS TO MEET CONTINUED EL-RELATED LEGAL CHALLENGES: SCHOOL LEADERSHIP PREPARATION AND PRACTICE

There are many additional implications for school personnel, leadership preparation, faculty members in teacher education, administrators, researchers, and most importantly for families/advocates of ELs. What has previously been treated as an unspoken dysfunction in our education system – the inequitable treatment of ELs as evident throughout these cases – is no longer an area that can be ignored. As the litigation trends and outcomes examined in this study reveal, the responsibility to educate and promote equity for ELs in all regions of the nation is presumed to fall upon educational agencies, yet, without much guidance and without comprehensive resources (Hopkins, Thompson, Linquanti, Hakuta, & August, 2013).

Guided by the US Constitution, state law and local regulations, school leaders are ultimately bound to deliver the educational services required by these federal and state laws (Militello, Schimmel, & Eberwein, 2009). The majority of principals, however, are generally uninformed or misinformed about school law issues with regards to the rights of students and teachers (Militello et al., 2009). The most frequent area of threatening lawsuits, that although filed were dismissed or settled against principals/schools, include student discipline and issues related to both special education and ELs (Militello et al., 2009). Very few states actually require training for either administrators or teachers in educational law, so it is by no surprise that there is such a large gap in legal knowledge. After discussing the number of legal challenges of being a school administrator, one principal concluded, "I should have gone to law school" (Militello et al., 2009, p. 40). Schools need legal updates and access to user-friendly resources regarding legislation to not only practice preventative law, but build a legally literate staff who can reduce the risks of lawsuits and spend more time equally educating ELs (Militello et al., 2009, p. 42). There is a significant need for additional preparation for all future teachers in school law related issues. This study begins to fill the critical gap in research and in legal knowledge regarding understanding the pieces of legislation related to the educational rights of ELs. It also demonstrates the urgent need for inclusion of legal research/educational law research in teacher education and leadership preparation programs nationwide.

While the purpose of the EEOA is to ensure equal opportunities, the verbiage is narrowly defined. The EEOA does not mention five different categories of ELs' claims including programming, grouping of students, management of programming, teaching training and hiring, and funding, all of which Berenyi (2008) proposes need be specified in the EEOA. It should also be noted that the EEOA only applies to the activities of SEAs and LEAs at the elementary and secondary levels; the EEOA does not impose any obligation on any state higher education systems. The courts have also not required teachers to possess language-specific credentials in order to deliver remediation programs consistent with the EEOA. Without specific language in the EEOA indicating improper training as a failure to comply with the statute, ELs may continue to be taught by unqualified teachers. Fewer than one sixth of teacher education institutions address EL content *or* policies in their preparation curricula, while currently, only five states (AZ, CA, FL, NY, and PA (as of 2011)) require mainstream teachers to complete any type of coursework focused on ELs, all of which are only related to instructional practices (Ballantyne, Sanderman, & Levy, 2008; Menken & Atunez, 2001). Teachers often enter and stay in the profession without a clear understanding of laws regarding ELs like the EEOA; any understanding of laws beyond the basics about the NCLB Act (Faulkner-Bond & Forte, 2011). If states do not commit resources to ELs, the EEOA should also indicate that such funding deficiencies equate to a violation of the statute and further clarify the standards necessary to state a claim under the EEOA.

The review of legal cases and legislative enactments relevant to ELs is limited in its predictive value. Therefore, while there is critical knowledge to be gained through this systematic review of cases decisions, legislative mandates, and policies, these data sources are only one aspect of the overall challenges facing ELs and do not reveal uncontroverted guidelines for educating ELs. The threat of lawsuits of educational inequities are not new, with advocates bringing up threats to file suit against school districts about every two years (Doughman, 2013). The court decisions that grew and continue to grow out of these lawsuits have and led to legislative changes that have helped shape the policy climate of today (Wright, 2010, p. 1). Rios-Aguilar and Gándara (2012), however, suggest that resolving educational policy through the courts may not be the most effective way to solve the educational inequities experienced by thousands of ELs.

In summary, this study highlighted numerous issues and exposes an urgent need to understand and ensure equitable, inclusive, high-quality educational opportunities and outcomes for all ELs. Furthermore, the complex tapestry of federal laws, regulations, and court ordered mandates, while challenging to navigate, guarantees an educational entitlement to ELs that educators and educational leaders are bound to protect.

## REFERENCES

Adler, L. (1996). *Qualitative research of legal issues*. In Research that makes a difference: Complementary methods for examining legal issues in Education. National Organization on Legal Problems in Education. No. 56 in the NOLPE Monograph Series 3-32.

Baker, C. (2006). *Foundations of bilingual education and bilingualism* (4th ed.), Clevedon: Multilingual Matters.

Baldwin, G., & Ferron, J. (2006). Quantitative research strategies. In S. Permuth & R. D. Mawdsley (Eds.), *Research methods for studying legal issues in education* (pp. 57–90). Dayton, OH: Education Law Association.

Ballantyne, K. G., Sanderman, A. R., & Levy, J. (2008). Educating *E*nglish language learners: Building teacher capacity. Roundtable Report Volume III State requirements for pre-service teachers of ELLs. Washington, DC: National Clearinghouse for English Language Acquisition. Retrieved from http://www.ncela.gwu.edu/files/uploads/3/EducatingELLsBuildingTeacherCapacityVol3.pdf

Bartholomew, D., & Llanos, C. (2010). Federal civil rights office to probe LAUSD's treatment of English-language learners. *The Daily Breeze*. Retrieved from http://www.dailybreeze.com/new/ci_14643701

Berenyi, J. R. (2008). Appropriate action, inappropriately defined: Amending the equal educational opportunities act of 1974. *Washington & Lee Law Review*, *65*, 639–657.

Bon, S. C. (2012). Examining the crossroads of law, ethics, and education leadership. *Journal of School Leadership*, *22*(2), 285–308.

Boyle, A., Taylor, J., Hurlburt, S., & Soga, K. (2012). Title III accountability behind the numbers: ESEA evaluation brief: The *E*nglish language acquisition, language enhancement, and academic achievement act (ED-04-CO-0025/0017). Washington, DC: American Institute for Research. Retrieved from http://www2.ed.gov/rschstat/eval/title-iii/behind-numbers.pdf

Brown v. Board of Education, 347 U.S. 483 (1954).

Depowski, K. L. (2008). Limited English proficiency students left behind. *Washington and Lee Journal of Civil Rights and Social Justice*, *14*, 331–355.

Doughman, A. (2013). Education advocates threaten lawsuit over funding public school. *Las Vegas Sun News*, May 1. Retrieved from http://www.lasvegassun.com/news/2013/may/01/education-advocates-threaten-lawsuit-over-public-s/

Evans, R. (2005). Reframing the achievement gap. *Phi Delta Kappan*, *86*, 582–589.

Faulkner-Bond, M., & Forte, E. (2011). *English learners and civil rights: Growing concern for a growing population*. Washington, DC: Thompson Publishing Group.

Faulkner-Bond, M., Waring, S., Forte, E., Crenshaw, R. L., Tindle, K., & Belknap, B. (2012). *Language instruction educational programs (LIEPs): A review of the foundational literature*. Office of Planning, Evaluation and Policy Development, US Department of Education. Retrieved from http://www2.ed.gov/rschstat/eval/title-iii/language-instruction-ed-programsreport.pdf

Hoffman, L. M. (2003). *Overview of public elementary and secondary school districts: school year2001–2002*. (NCES Publication No. 2003-411). Washington, DC: U.S. Department of Education.

Hopkins, M., Thompson, K. D., Linquanti, R., Hakuta, K., & August, D. (2013). Fully accounting for English learner performance: A key issue in ESEA reauthorization. *Educational Researcher*, *42*(2), 101–108.

Kihuen, M. (2009). Leaving no child behind: A civil right. *American University Journal of Gender Social Policy & Law*, *17*, 113–147.

Klingner, J. (2010). *Review of meeting the needs of English learners and other diverse learners*. Boulder, CO: National Education Policy Center. Retrieved from http://www2.ed.gov/policy/elsec/leg/blueprint/english-learners-diverse-learners.pdf

Kunz, C. L., Schmedemann, D. A., Bateson, A., Konar-Steenberg, M., & Downs, M. P. (2008). *The process of legal research* (7th ed.). New York, NY: Aspen Publishers, Inc.

Lawyers Committee for Civil Rights under Law. (2012). Civil rights framework for providing all students an opportunity to learn through reauthorization of the elementary and secondary education act. Cambridge, MA: National Opportunity to Learn Campaign. Retrieved from http://www.otlcampaign.org/resources/civil-rights-framework-providing-all-students-opportunity-learn-through-reauthorization-el

Linquanti, R. (2001). *The redesignation dilemma: Changes and choices in fostering meaningful accountability for English learners*. (Policy Rep. 2001-1). University of California Linguistic Minority Research Institute. San Francisco, CA: West Ed. Retrieved from http://www.wested.org/online_pubs/redesignation.pdf

Lupini, W. H., & Zirkel, P. A. (2003). An outcomes analysis of education litigation. *Educational Policy*, *17*(2), 257–279.

Maxwell, L. A. (2011, October 25). ELL programs get overhaul in New York and Los Angeles. *Education Week*. Retrieved from http://www.edweek.org/ew/articles/2011/10/26/09ell_ep.h31.html

Maxwell, L. A. (2013, February 1). English language learners at center of dispute in Denver. *Education Week – Learning the Language*. Retrieved from http://blogs.edweek.org/edweek/learning-the-language/2013/02/english-language_learners_at_c.html?cmp=SOC-SHR-FB

Menken, K., & Atunez, B. (2001). *An overview of the preparation and certification of teachers working with limited English proficient (LEP) students*. Washington, DC: National Clearinghouse for Bilingual Education. Retrieved from http://www.usc.edu/dept/education/CMMR/FullText/teacherprep.pdf

Militello, M., Schimmel, D., & Eberwein, H. J. (2009). If they knew, they would change: How legal knowledge impacts principals' practice. National Association of Secondary School Principals. NASSP Bulletin, *93*(1), 27–52.

Plessy v. Ferguson, 163 U.S. 537 (1896).

Ragan, A., & Lesaux, N. (2006). Federal, state, and district level English language learner program entry and exit requirements: Effects on the education of language minority learners. *Education Policy Analysis Archives*, *14*(20), 1–29.

Rios-Aguilar, C., & Gándara, P. (2012). Horne v. Flores and the future of language policy. *Teachers College Record*, *114*(9), 1–13.

Rossell, C. H. (2005). The flawed requirements for limited English proficient children of the no child left behind act. *Journal of Education*, *186*(3), 29–40.

Samson, J. F., & Collins, B. A. (2012). *Preparing all teachers to meet the needs of English language learners*. Retrieved from http://www.americanprogress.org/issues/education/report/2012/04/30/11372/preparing-all-teachers-to-meet-the-needs-of-english-language-learners/

Smith, W. L. (1990). *Policy regarding the treatment of national original minority students who are limited English proficient*. Washington, DC: US Department of Education. Retrieved from http://www2.ed.gov/about/offices/list/ocr/docs/lau1990_and_1985.html

The Working Group on ELL Policy (2009). *The American recovery and reinvestment act: Recommendations for addressing the needs of English language learners*. Palo Alto, CA: Author. Retrieved from http://www.stanford.edu/~hakuta/ARRA/ELL%20Stimulus%20Executive%20Summary.pdf

United States (US) Department of Education (DOE). (2010). *US education department announces civil rights review of English learner students in Los Angeles* [Press release]. Retrieved from http://www2.ed.gov/news/pressreleases/2010/03/03102010.html

Wiley, T. G., & Wright, W. E. (2004). Against the undertow: Language-minority education policy and politics in the "Age of accountability. *Educational Policy*, *18*(1), 142–168.

Wright, W. E. (2005). *Evolution of federal policy and implications of No child left behind for language minority students*. Tempe, AZ: Education Policy Studies Laboratory, EPSL–0501–101–LPRU. Retrieved from http://epsl.asu.edu/epru/documents/EPSL-0501-101-LPRU.pdf

Wright, W. E. (2010). Landmark court rulings regarding English language learners: ELL topics from A-Z. *Colorín Colorado*. Retrieved from http://www.colorincolorado.org/article/49704/

Zehr, M. A. (2010). Boston settles with federal officials in ELL investigation. *Education Week*, *30*(7), 10.

# CHAPTER 7

# NAVIGATING THE CURRENT LEGAL LANDSCAPE OF THE IDENTIFICATION AND ELIGIBILITY OF CHILDREN WITH AUTISM SPECTRUM DISORDER

Kevin P. Brady and Cynthia A. Dieterich

## ABSTRACT

*According to the Centers for Disease Control and Prevention (CDC), the number of children diagnosed with autism has increased dramatically, especially over the past decade. Most recently, the CDC estimates that an average of one in 88 children have an autism spectrum disorder (ASD). In terms of numbers, this translates into approximately 730,000 people between the ages of 0 and 21 who have ASD. While the primary cause(s) of increases in the identification of autistic students continue to generate debate school officials across the nation need to be prepared for the changing legal landscape associated with children diagnosed with ASD. The primary purpose of this chapter is to provide a detailed legal/policy update of the leading legal considerations and concerns involving K-12 students with autism. The chapter will discuss four specific legal*

**Legal Frontiers in Education: Complex Law Issues for Leaders, Policymakers and Policy Implementers**
**Advances in Educational Administration, Volume 24, 119–145**

**ISSN: 1479-3660/doi:10.1108/S1479-366020150000024033**

*topics involving the identification and eligibility of K-12 students with autism. These four legal topics include: Changes in the New DSM-5 Diagnostic Manuel and its Impact on Legal Definitions of Autism; Insurance Reform and Autism Coverage: A Comparison of the States; Developing Legally Compliant Individualized Education Plans (IEPs) for High-Functioning Students with Autism, and; Recent Legal Developments in Case Law Involving K-12 students who are autistic. The chapter will conclude with a detailed discussion of how today's school officials can become more legally literate and better serve the legal needs of students with autism in their schools.*

## INTRODUCTION

It is undisputable that the diagnosis of ASD among school-aged children nationwide has reached epidemic proportions. The Centers for Disease Control and Prevention (CDC) estimate that 1 in 68 children in the United States have been identified with ASD. This most recent estimate is approximately 30 percent higher than earlier reported in 2012, which was 1 in 88 children (Centers for Disease Control and Prevention [CDC], 2014). A 2005 report by the U.S. General Accounting Office (GAO) estimated that the number of children diagnosed with autism covered by the Individuals with Disabilities Education Improvement Act (IDIEA)[1] had risen 500 percent in the last decade. Along with the recent and dramatic increases in the identification of children with ASD (Steurnagel, 2005), autism-related litigation has also increased dramatically. For instance, in the years 1965 through 1985, the number of reported court decisions involving "education-oriented" autism was 214; in the years between 1985 and 2004, the number of reported "education-oriented" autism cases in the federal courts skyrocketed to 1,483 (Mayerson, 2014; Slater & Norlin, 2012; Unumb & Unumb, 2011).

While the incidence of childhood autism has been increasing for decades, the recognition of ASD as an important legal and policy issue has emerged much more gradually (Mandlawitz, 2002; Steurnagel, 2005; Zirkel, 2011a, 2011b, 2012). For example, the IDEA has only included autism as one of its current thirteen eligibility classifications starting in 1990. Prior to 1990, a child with autism could only qualify for special education and related services under the IDEA under one of the other "traditional" eligibility classifications, such as Other Health Impairment (OHI) (Fogt, Miller, & Zirkel, 2003).

The purpose of this chapter is to provide both context and insight to leading legal issues related to children with ASD. We will explore these leading legal issues involving school-aged children with ASD and its implications on today's school communities, namely school leaders. More specifically, the authors will discuss four leading legal and policy topics relating to the education of students with autism. These topics include

- the changing diagnostic definition of autism under the new Diagnostic and Statistical Manual of Mental Disorders (DSM-5) and its legal implications involving eligibility of students with ASD;
- the current legal status among states involving autism insurance reform;
- emerging litigation trends involving students with ASD and schools; and
- legal and concerns involving the bullying and harassment of students with ASD.

## HISTORICAL ORIGINS OF AUTISM LITIGATION

Before discussing the leading, contemporary legal and policy issues involving students with ASD, it is necessary to provide historical context to the emergence of autism as a viable legal issue debated in the nation's courts. Kanner (1943), an Austrian physician and psychiatrist, who later immigrated to the United States, published the first clinical description of the "autistic disturbances of affective conduct." Kanner's seminal research initiated the modern study of autism spectrum disorder or ASD. Debate among scientists regarding the appropriate clinical definition as well as the presumed biological and genetic causes of autism soon developed. Several decades after Kanner's initial article detailing a clinical discussion of autism, Bettelheim (1967) published his controversial and influential book, *The Empty Fortress*, arguing that a child's autism diagnosis was the result of distant mothers, referred to as "refrigerator mothers." The impact of Bettelheim's "blame the parents" theory was significant and resulted in many children with autism being separated from their families and being institutionalized for the rest of their lives (Mayerson, 2014).

In contrast to Bettelheim (1967) theory maintaining that autism was largely a result of bad parenting, a growing number of physicians and scientists challenged this assumption arguing that autism was a neurodevelopmental disorder (Rutter, 1968). During this same period, the federal government introduced sweeping legislation addressing students with disabilities in the nation's schools, namely the Education for All Handicapped

Children Act, the predecessor to today's Individuals with Disabilities Education Act (IDEA).

In 1977, Sloan and Schopler designed a treatment program known as TEACHH (Treatment and Education of Autistic and related Communications-Handicapped Children) for children with autism based on a theoretical model that emphasized parents as cotherapists. Greenspan (1979) also encouraged the active participation of parents in an approach derived from a developmental individual-difference relationship-based model (DIR) that builds on the strengths and abilities of the child through purposeful play. Another method that emerged was developed by Lovaas (1987) to teach children with autism how to learn and become successful in inclusive educational settings using Applied Behavior Analysis (ABA). In the aftermath of these approaches, an increasing number of parents of children with autism questioned existing autism-related intervention and special education programs provided by schools. Consequently, many parents of children with autism demanded that Congress enact and expand eligibility under the federal Individuals with Disabilities Education Improvement Act (IDEIA) to explicitly include autism.

## DEFINING AUTISM AND THE NEW DSM-5: LEGAL IMPLICATIONS FOR SCHOOL LEADERS

The prevailing diagnostic and legal definitions of autism are far from identical. Despite these definitional differences, the categorically-based legal definition of autism formulated and included in the 1990 amendments of the IDEA combined with the *Diagnostic and Statistical Manual of Mental Disorders*, the primary psychiatric diagnostic manual for mental health professionals in the United States have had the greatest impact on the assessment and classification of school-aged children with ASD in the United States (Kamphaus, Reynolds, & Imperato-McCammon, 1999). A new Diagnostic and Statistical Manual of Mental Disorders (DSM-5) (2013) substantially revised its criteria for diagnosing and defining autism. According to Ne'eman and Kapp (2012), the three major changes in the DSM-5 clinical definition of autism include

- the combination of three major autism spectrum diagnoses into a single diagnoses, called Autism Spectrum Disorder;

- a change in some individuals receiving or who would have received a diagnoses of PDD-NOS under the DSM-IV to Social Communication Disorder diagnoses, a non-autism diagnoses; and
- a shift in some individuals currently receiving or who would have received a diagnoses of Asperger's Syndrome off the autism spectrum.

Compared to the previous DSM-IV, which provided multiple subcategories of autism, including Asperger's Syndrome and pervasive developmental disorders (PDD-NOS), the new DSM-5 defines ASD as a single diagnostic category (Jeste, Lieberman, Schully, & Kupfer, 2012). The DSM-5 will now encompass all previous ASD disorders, including Asperger's Syndrome, Pervasive Development Disorder Not Otherwise Specified (PDD-NOS), Childhood Disintegrative Disorder, and Rett's Disorder. The new DSM-5 specifically states, "[i]ndividuals with a well-established DSM-IV-TR diagnosis of autistic disorder, Asperger's disorder, or pervasive development disorder not otherwise specified should be given the diagnosis of autism spectrum disorder" (CDC, 2015). Under the new DSM-5, Social (Pragmatic) Communication Disorder is a new diagnosis defined as "individuals who have marked deficits in social communication, but whose symptoms do not otherwise meet criteria for autism spectrum disorder, should be evaluated for social (pragmatic) communication disorder" (CDC, 2015).

While the DSM was originally meant to serve exclusively as a clinical tool, insurance companies are increasingly relying on the DSM-5 as a primary benchmark of whether someone receives benefits or not for a particular disability, including autism. Thus far, however, the new DSM-5 definition does not impact the definition of autism found in the Individuals with Disabilities Education Act (IDEA). IDEA's definition of autism states:

> Autism means a developmental disability significantly affecting verbal and nonverbal communication and social interaction, generally evident before age three that adversely affects a child's educational performance. Other characteristics often associated with autism are engagement in repetitive activities and stereotyped movements, resistance to environmental change or change in daily routines, and unusual response to sensory experiences. (Individuals with Disabilities Education Act (IDEA), 34 C.F.R. Section 300.8(c)(1)(i))

While a recent revision in the DSM-5 does change how children with ASD are currently diagnosed, it is important to distinguish that a DSM-5 diagnosis is a medical diagnosis compared to legal eligibility under the IDEA, which is an educational determination and based on the disability's impact on the child's ability to learn. The IDEA was never intended as a diagnostic tool for determining childhood disabilities. However, the legal definitions of autism are critical for determining a particular student's eligibility for special education and related services under existing federal legislation (Kamphaus & Frick, 1996).

The DSM-5's significant changes to the clinical definition of ASD has substantial implications for disability service accommodations and supports for school-aged children with ASD. The current DSM-5 is neither a legal or educational rationale for changing a child's special education or related services under the IDEA. Nevertheless, it is critical that educators and parents understand the difference between the DSM-5 medical diagnostic definition of autism compared to the legal definition of ASD found in federal and state statutes, such as the IDEA governing the provision of special education and related services to eligible students. The legal requirement to provide special education and related services under the IDEA is not determined by medical diagnosis, but rather by a child's individualized educational need(s) (Freedman, 2013).

There are several legal cases illustrating the point that a child diagnosed under the DSM-5 with ASD may be ineligible for special education and related services under the existing legal definition of ASD under the IDEA. For example, in *A.L. by C.J. v. Board of Education of East Islip Union Free School District* (2010), a US District Court in New York held that a student with Asperger's Syndrome was ineligible for special education and related services. The court maintained that the student's academic success in school demonstrated that his disability did not have a negative impact on his educational performance in the classroom. In a second case, *La Mesa-Spring Valley School District* (2009), a child diagnosed with ASD was also determined ineligible under the IDEA's legal definition of ASD eligibility for special education and related services. In this case, a five-year-old boy with ASD exhibited numerous behavioral problems, including temper tantrums as well as noise sensitivity while at home. However, teachers indicated that the young student did not display any of these behavioral issues while in school and engaged in appropriate social interactions with both the teachers and other children. The court agreed with school officials that the child was ineligible for IDEA special education and related services based on insufficient evidence that his behavioral issues occurred at school and interfered with his educational performance.

Notwithstanding, recent changes in the diagnostic definition of autism under the DSM-5 does raise valid legal and policy concerns, especially for children with high functioning autism, including Asperger's Syndrome, who do not meet stricter DSM-5 medical diagnostic criteria of autism and could result in fewer children being identified as autistic and receiving necessary benefits and services (Wang, 2012). Additionally, there is uncertainty regarding how state and local educational agencies as well as leading insurance companies will incorporate these new changes in clinically defining ASD under the DSM-5.

## AUTISM INSURANCE REFORM: A COMPARISON OF THE STATES

Imagine the frustration of having a child with autism, knowing there is significant, early intervention treatment available but being unable to provide it – because it costs over $70,000 a year and is not covered by insurance (Stuart, 2011). A 2006 study by the Harvard School of Public Health estimates that it costs nearly $3.2 million to properly care for a person with autism over their lifetime and nearly $35 billion to care for everyone with autism (Ganz, 2007). While some states legally require insurers to provide coverage for the treatment of autism, other states maintain that it is the responsibility of parents or the school systems to pay for these services. Interestingly, states that presently have autism insurance mandates are not legally required to offer comparable autism benefits through The Patient Protection and Affordable Care Act (PPAC, 2010) (42 U.S.C. § 18001), commonly referred to as the Affordable Care Act, or "Obamacare."

As of May 2015, 41 states and the District of Columbia require insurance companies to provide some level of coverage for the treatment of autism (see the Appendix). These 41 states (and the District of Columbia) include: Alaska, Arizona, Arkansas, California, Colorado, Connecticut, Delaware, District of Columbia, Florida, Georgia, Hawaii, Illinois, Indiana, Iowa, Kansas, Kentucky, Louisiana, Maine, Massachusetts, Michigan, Minnesota, Mississippi, Missouri, Montana, Nebraska, Nevada, New Hampshire, New Jersey, New Mexico, New York, Ohio, Oregon, Pennsylvania, Rhode Island, South Carolina, South Dakota, Texas, Utah, Vermont, Virginia, West Virginia, and Wisconsin. Only a handful of states currently do not have any insurance coverage for the treatment of autism. These states include: Alabama, Idaho, North Dakota, Oklahoma, and Wyoming. Over the last several years, considerable debate has resulted among state legislatures over autism and the level of insurance support that should be provided.

While the specifics of autism insurance mandates vary by state, all of the states currently with autism insurance require health insurers to provide the behavioral therapy, Applied Behavior Analysis to young children with ASD. Some states, however, have set age limits on autism benefits. For instance, Maine requires insurers to provide the behavioral therapy, Applied Behavior Analysis only until the age of 10 (Me. Rev. Stat. Ann. Tit. 24-A § 2768, 2010 Me. Laws, Chap. 635 (SB 446 of 2010).

Historically, health insurance providers have avoided covering treatments for children with autism and this has resulted in non-cost-effective or timely methods to secure treatment of children with ASD Stuart, (2011). While controversial, comprehensive ASD insurance reform is currently the best way to ensure treatment for individuals, especially school-aged children with ASD. It is critical that today's school leaders familiarize themselves with the autism insurance initiatives and policies in their respective states.

## EMERGING LITIGATION TRENDS OF STUDENTS WITH ASD

Hill and Hill (2012) conducted a study reviewing 62 legal cases that involved students with ASD ranging in ages from 3 to 21. An analysis of IDEA procedural and substantive violations revealed five of the most common procedural legal violations including the following:

1. Individualized Education Program (IEP) issues involving students with ASD
2. Student placement in the least restrictive environment (LRE)
3. Parental participation
4. Evaluation issues
5. Unqualified school personnel.

In terms of the substantive legal violations under the IDEA, the seven most common reported violations were the following:

1. Failure to provide appropriate special education and related services
2. Student with ASD behavioral issues
3. Extended school year services
4. Failure to use Applied Behavior Analysis (ABA)

5. Failure to provide appropriate functional behavioral assessments (FBA's) and behavior intervention plans (BIP's)
6. Failure to provide appropriate student transition services
7. Special education and related services that provide no progress for the student.

More recently, Bon and Osborne (2014), provided a comprehensive review of legal cases involving students with disabilities and highlighted an influential federal case decided by the Ninth Circuit, *Doug C. ex rel. Spencer C. v. Hawaii Department of Education* (2013). In this case, the Ninth Circuit held that an IEP team denied a free and appropriate education (FAPE) to a high school student with ASD by creating a new IEP for the student without the father's input. The legal significance of this case was that a legally compliant IEP must include parental participation and school officials' failure to prioritize parental participation resulted in a violation of the IDEA.

### *Legal and Policy Concerns Involving the Bullying and Harassment of Students with ASD*

An IEP that includes positive behavioral supports and interventions can be used to provide an FAPE when students with ASD are harassed, bullied, and/or the perpetrator. (Dieterich, Snyder, & Villani, 2015). For example, in the case of *T.B. v. Waynesboro Area School* (2011), a high-school-aged student, A.B., was identified with Asperger's Syndrome and experienced difficulty with peer relationships. His parents alleged that because of his inability to successfully communicate with his peers, he became the target of bullying; he responded negatively; and in turn became the perpetrator. In response, the district designed the IEP with positive supports that included the following:

> visual and verbal cues and prompts; role-playing situations; positive reinforcement; peers to provide good models; monitoring use of appropriate social skills such as using non-threatening words and good problem solving strategies; being concrete and specific, providing information about change in routine; and talking him through stressful situations or allowing him time in a stress-free environment. Location and the frequency of each service were also identified on the IEP. (Dieterich et al., 2015, p. 117)

Following an altercation with another student, A.B. threatened to harm himself. His parent's maintained that the district failed to recognize the severity of the bullying and this denied their son an FAPE. In the District Court ruling it was found that the comprehensive program the school designed did not deny their child an FAPE; that his IEP was appropriate; and that he was making positive progress under his IEP. Although the altercation was unfortunate, the court further stated that it did not negate the appropriateness of his educational program.

A similar outcome was found in *J.E. v. Boyertown Area School District* (2011) in which, J.E., a student with Autism Spectrum Disorder experienced harassment by classmates. His parents sought a private placement because J.E. had a history of being bullied and his parents were concerned that due to J.E.'s difficulty in social situations he was at high risk of being bullied in the future. In ruling for the school district, the court stated that educators are required to provide individualized instruction that meets the unique needs of the child, but "a fair appropriate public education does not require that the District be able to prove that a student will not face future bullying at a placement, as this is impossible" (*J.E v. Boyertown*, 2011, p. 177). It is not the responsibility of the school district to guarantee that the child will always have close friends or be free of any negative social situations. "It would be an onerous task for districts to prove that a child would never experience bullying even under the most ideal circumstances" (Dieterich et al., 2015, p. 115).

However, in cases when students with autism are harassed to the extent that the district acted in bad faith and with gross misjudgment courts rule with a heavy hand against the school. In *Galloway v. Chesapeake Union Exempted Village School Board of Education* (2012) the parents filed suit against the school district when their child, Joseph who was identified with Asperger's Disorder, ADHD, seizure disorder, and specific learning disability was a victim of disability-based harassment. On 15 different occasions, Joseph's parents brought to the school employees attention the almost daily bullying that he experienced. Dieterich et al. (2015) provide excerpts of these incidents in the following:

> [O]ne teacher repeatedly questioned Joseph about his seizures in front of the entire class and questioned whether he really had seizures; students threw water on their pants to mock the fact that during seizures Joseph could become incontinent; students would call Joseph 'seizure boy,' with the knowledge and approval of the teacher; ... students would ... hide his belongings, shove him, threaten to break his computer, steal his backpack ... a student punched Joseph in the back; students encouraged Joseph to commit suicide; and the bullying culminated in several sexual assaults, in which students would come up behind Joseph in a locker room and grind their penises into Joseph's back. (p. 118)

In Judge Black's decision he noted that the incidents were not simple acts of teasing; that "the school district knew about the incidents; and the school district did nothing to remedy the problem which constitutes knowing acquiescence" (Dieterich et al., 2015, p. 119). Joseph's parents prevailed in proving that the school district "was aware of the bullying and that he was discriminated against due to his disability" (*Galloway v. Chesapeake*, 2012, p. 25).

Outcomes of these cases suggest that school districts need to establish policies that not only respond to harassment and reprimand the bullies, but teach student's with autism functional social skills to respond to bullies in a meaningful way. Students with autism are less likely to pick up on social cues and know when it is necessary to walk away from a harassing incident or when to report an incident to the appropriate authorities. "Students may need to have changes in an IEP that reflect their need to develop appropriate social skills to avoid bullying [or] life skills that give them methods to either avoid bullying or limit the negative effect of possible bullying in the future" (Dieterich et al., 2015, p. 128).

To determine the extent a student identified with ASD requires direct instruction to develop skills to successfully manage their response to bullying it is the responsibility of educators to conduct a Functional Behavioral Assessment (FBA) and implement a Behavior Intervention Plan (BIP). By evaluating the student's responses to bulling with an FBA, the educational team can garner information to determine the extent bullying is interfering with the child's education (Dieterich & Villani, 2000; Dieterich, Villani, & Bennett, 2003). Within the BIP framework educators can then "teach appropriate and/or replacement behaviors to students with an emphasis on research-based strategies ... to teach skills that encourage students to manage emotions appropriately whereby avoiding bullying or minimizing the effects" (Dieterich et al., 2015).

## CONCLUSIONS AND IMPLICATIONS FOR SCHOOL LEADERS: THE SIGNIFICANCE OF SPECIAL EDUCATION LEGAL LITERACY

The general public's awareness of autism has grown as the number of children identified with autism continues to exponentially increase. Today's school officials face challenging legal and policy concerns ranging from autism insurance reform to changing definitions of autism (Freedman, 2013).

"School district administrators are in the business of managing a school, [yet] also are in the business of leading educators to provide programs that meet the needs of their students. They must therefore consider solutions to minimize litigation" (Dieterich et al., 2015, p. 126). A sound plan to address student needs and limit litigation is providing education leaders with a foundation in legal literacy particularly since despite nearly four decades of documented increased legal protections for students with disabilities, legal illiteracy of special education laws and policies persist because many of today's school leaders have been woefully underprepared to apply the principles of special education law to their daily practices (Militello, Schimmel, & Eberwein, 2009; Umpstead, Decker, Brady, Schimmel, & Militello, 2015). While over half of the nation's students with disabilities are presently educated in general education classrooms, most educators, including those enrolled in educational leadership preparation programs are not required to complete any coursework in special education, especially a course focusing on legal issues involving students with disabilities (Institute of Education Sciences, 2010). Based on widespread special education legal illiteracy, many of today's school leaders expose both themselves and their schools to liability and legal non-compliance issues violating the legal rights of students with disabilities (Katsiyannis, Losinski, & Prince, 2012).

In conclusion, below are pragmatic suggestions based on existing legislation and case law that today's school leaders can implement to develop a systematic plan that maximizes efficiency and uses minimal resources when providing appropriate services to students with ASD.

1. Conduct a FBA and implement a BIP for all students identified as autistic particularly since social skill deficits is a defining feature of the disability. In a BIP framework the student with autism is taught replacement skills to manage emotions and responses appropriately whereby increasing positive peer social interactions and minimize the effects of difficult social situations.
2. Recognize that the IEP not only provides academic, but social goals and supports as a means to minimize the potential for the student to be bullied or the bullying perpetrator.
3. Identify intervention strategies that are research-based to meet the student's needs, yet are not so restrictive that only one staff member is qualified to provide the service.
4. Provide evidenced-based instruction that are delivered by educators who are qualified to implement strategies with fidelity.

5. Recognize that students with ASD prepare for a variety of post-secondary opportunities (e.g., college, employment, independent living, etc.) and create transition plans that represent the option that is appropriate for the student based on their strengths, preferences, and interests.
6. Provide professional development for general educators to become familiar with the ASD and dispel any myths particularly since placement in the general education classroom is a viable option for students across the ASD.
7. Use the RTI model to provide high-quality instruction and gather data to monitor student progress even before a student is formally identified as autistic as a means to provide early intervention services.
8. Be familiar with state specific requirements for providing services to the child with autism and the degree a school district, parent, or insurance provider is liable for payment of services.
9. Design a system-wide professional development plan that informs and maintains the legal literacy of all faculty, staff, and administrators as a strategy to meet individual student needs and minimize litigation.

It is clear that the diagnoses of autism among students in on the rise. Equally important is that today's school leaders must have the proper knowledge of special education law to make informed and legally compliant decisions in the "best interest of the student."

## NOTE

1. Although it was reenacted in 2004 as IDEIA it is more commonly referred to as IDEA (hereafter it will be referred to as IDEA).

## REFERENCES

*A.L. by C.J. v. Board of Education of East Islip Union Free School District*. 679 F.Supp. 2d 299 (E.D.N.Y. 2010).

Autism Speaks. (2015). *State autism insurance reform laws*. Retrieved from https://www.autismspeaks.org/advocacy/insurance/faqs-state-autism-insurance-reform-laws

Bettelheim, B. (1967). *The empty fortress: Infantile autism and the birth of the self*. New York, NY: Free Press.

Bon, S. C., & Osborne, A. G. (2014). Students with disabilities. In C. J. Russo (Ed.), *The yearbook of education law 2014*. Cleveland, OH: Education Law Association.

Centers for Disease Control and Prevention. (2014). *CDC estimates 1 in 68 children has been identified with autism spectrum disorder*. Retrieved from http://www.cdc.gov/media/releases/2014/p0327-autism-spectrum-disorder.html

Centers for Disease Control and Prevention. (2015). *Diagnostic criteria for 299.00 autism spectrum disorder*. Retrieved from http://www.cdc.gov/ncbddd/autism/hcp-dsm.html

Dieterich, C. A., Snyder, N. D., & Villani, C. (2015). Bullying issues impacting students with disabilities: Highlights of section 1983, title IX, section 504, ADA, and IDEA cases. *Brigham Young University Education and Law Journal*, *1*, 103–130.

Dieterich, C. A., & Villani, C. J. (2000). Functional behavioral assessment: Process without procedure. *Brigham Young University Education and Law Journal*, *2*, 209–219.

Dieterich, C. A., Villani, C. J., & Bennett, P. T. (2003). Functional behavioral assessments: Beyond student behavior. *Journal of Law and Education*, *34*, 357–368.

*Doug C. ex rel. Spencer C. v. Hawaii Department of Education*. 720 F.3d1038 (9th Cir. 2013).

Fogt, J., Miller, D., & Zirkel, P. (2003). Defining autism: Professional best practices and published case law. *Journal of School Psychology*, *41*, 201–216.

Freedman, A. J. (2013, April). The changing face of autism: Legal issues surrounding the identification and education of autistic students. National Schools Boards Association (NSBA) Council of School Attorneys.

Galloway v. Chesapeake Union Exempted Village School Board of Education. U.S. Dist. LEXIS 152080 (S.D. of OH 2012).

Ganz, M. L. (2007). The lifetime distribution of the incremental societal costs of autism. *Archives of Pediatrics and Adolescent Medicine*, *161*, 343.

Government Accounting Office [GAO]. (2005, January). *Special education: Children with autism*. Report No. GA-05-2200. Retrieved from http://www.gao.gov/new.items/d05220.pdf

Greenspan, S. I. (1979). Intelligence and adaptation: An integration of psychoanalytic and Piagetian developmental psychology [monograph]. *Psychological Issues*, *12*, 1–408.

Hill, D. A., & Hill, S. J. (2012). Autism spectrum disorder, individuals with disabilities education act, and case law: Who really wins? *Preventing School Failure*, *56*(3), 157–164.

Institute of Education Sciences. (2010, July). *Do states have certification requirements for preparing general education teachers to teach students with disabilities*? Experience in the Northeast and Islands Region. Institute for Educational Sciences, No. 090. Retrieved from http://ies.ed.gov/ncee/edlabs/projects/project.asp?ProjectID=238

J.E. v. Boyertown Area Sch. Dist. 452 F. App'x 172 (3d Cir. 2011).

Jeste, D. V., Lieberman, J. A., Schully, J. H., & Kupfer, D. (2012). DSM crosses the finish line. *Psychiatric News*, *47*, 4–23.

Kamphaus, R. W., & Frick, J. P. (1996). *Clinical assessment of child and adolescent personality and behavior*. Needham Heights, MA: Allyn and Bacon.

Kamphaus, R. W., Reynolds, C. R., & Imperato-McCammon, C. (1999). In C. R. Reynolds & T. B. Gutkin (Eds.), *The handbook of school psychology* (3rd ed., pp. 292–306). New York, NY: Wiley.

Kanner, L. (1943). Autistic disturbances of affective contact. *Nervous Child*, *2*, 217–250.

Katsiyannis, A., Losinski, M., & Prince, A. (2012). Litigation and students with disabilities: A persistent concern. *NASSP Bulletin*, *96*(1), 23–43.

*La Mesa-Spring Valley School District*. 109 LRP 54643 (SEA Colo. August 20, 2009).

Lovaas, O. I. (1987). Behavioral treatment and normal educational and intellectual functioning in young autistic children. *Journal of Consulting and Clinical Psychology*, *55*, 3–9.

Mandlawitz, M. (2002). The impact of the legal system on the educational programming for young children with autism spectrum disorder. *Journal of Autism and Developmental Disorders*, *32*, 495–508.
Mayerson, G. S. (2014). Autism in the courtroom. In F. R. Volkmar, S. J. Rodgers, R. Paul, & K. A. Pelphrey (Eds.), *Handbook of autism and pervasive developmental disorders* (4th ed., pp. 1036–1050). New York, NY: Wiley.
Militello, M., Schimmel, D., & Eberwein, H. J. (2009). If they know they would change: How legal knowledge impacts principals' practice. *NASSP Bulletin*, *93*(1), 27–52.
Ne'eman, A., & Kapp, S. (2012, June). *What are the stakes? An analysis of the impact of the DSM-5 draft autism criteria on law, policy and service provision*. Autistic Self Advocacy Network Policy Brief. Retrieved from http://autisticadvocacy.org/wp-content/uploads/2012/06/DSM-5_Policy_Brief_ASAN_final.pdf
Patient Protection and Affordable Care Act. 42 U.S.C. § 18001 (2010).
Rutter, M. (1968). Concepts of autism: A review of research. *Journal of Child Psychology and Psychiatry*, *9*(1), 1–25.
Slater, A. E., & Norlin, J. W. (2012). *Autism case law: A desktop reference to key decisions*. Palm Beach Gardens, FL: LRP Publications.
Sloan, J. L., & Schopler, E. (1977). Some thoughts about developing programs for autistic adolescents. *Journal of Pediatric Psychology*, *2*, 187–190.
Steurnagel, T. (2005). Increases in identified cases of autism spectrum disorders. *Journal of Disability Policy Studies*, *16*, 138–146.
Stuart, M. (2011). Autism insurance reform: A comparison of state initiatives. *Indiana Health Law Review*, *82*, 498–538.
T.B. v. Waynesboro Area School District. U.S. Dist. LEXIS 23534 (M.D. of PA 2011).
Umpstead, R., Decker, J., Brady, K. P., Schimmel, D., & Militello, M. (2015). *How to prevent special education litigation: Eight legal lessons*. NY: Teachers College Press.
Unumb, L. S., & Unumb, D. R. (2011). *Autism and the law: Cases, statutes, and materials*. Durham: NC: Carolina Academic Press.
Wang, S. S. (2012). Study damps fear of autism change. *The Wall Street Journal*, May 7. Retrieved from http://online.wsj.com
Zirkel, P. (2011a). Autism litigation under the IDEA: A new meaning of "disproportionality"? *Journal of Special Education Leadership*, *24*(2), 92–103.
Zirkel, P. (2011b). The case law for students with autism: An update. West's Education Law Reporter, p. 262.
Zirkel, P. (2012). Autism spectrum disorder: A legal update. Principal, May–June, pp. 50–51.

# APPENDIX

Current States Requiring Insurance Companies to Provide Insurance for Persons with Autism.

*Source*: Adapted from Autism Speaks (2015).

1. **Alabama**: Requires a health benefit plan to offer coverage for the screening, diagnosis, and treatment of autism spectrum disorders for an insured child who is nine years of age or under in policies and contracts issues or delivered to employers with at least 51 employees for at least 50 percent of its working days during the preceding calendar year. Treatment is defined as treatment that is prescribed by the child's treating physician or psychologist in accordance with a treatment plan and may include behavioral health treatment (including applied behavior analysis), pharmacy care, psychiatric care, psychological care, and therapeutic care. The coverage required may not be subject to dollar limits, deductibles, or coinsurance provisions that are less favorable to an insured than the limits or deductibles that apply to illness generally under the health insurance plan, except for coverage for behavioral therapy which is subject to a $36,000 maximum benefit per year (2012 SB 283) (2012 Ala. Act 298).
2. **Alaska**: Requires health care insurers, except for a fraternal benefit society, to provide coverage for the costs of diagnosis and treatment of autism spectrum disorders. Covered treatment includes medically necessary pharmacy care, psychiatric care, psychological care, habilitative or rehabilitative care (including applied behavior analysis), and therapeutic care. Coverage is only required for individuals under 21 years of age and the number of visits to an autism service provider for treatment may not be limited. Coverage is subject to copayment, deductible, and coinsurance provisions included in a health insurance policy to the same extent as other health care services covered by the policy. An insurer providing insurance to a small employer in the group market with 20 or fewer employees is not required to provide this coverage, and the coverage requirement may be waived for an insurer providing insurance to a small employer with 21–25 employees if the small employer demonstrates that compliance with the requirement increased the premium cost of the small employer's health policy by three percent or more during a consecutive 12-month period (2011 SB 74). (2012 Alaska Sess. Laws. Chap. 63.)

3. **Arizona**: Require policies issued by certain health insurers, beginning July 1, 2009, to provide coverage for the diagnosis and treatment of autism spectrum disorders, with some limitations. Coverage for autism treatment may not be excluded or denied and dollar limits, deductibles and coinsurance cannot be imposed based solely on the diagnosis of an autism spectrum disorder. Coverage for medically necessary behavioral therapy services may not be excluded or denied and is subject to a $50,000 maximum benefit per year for an eligible person up to the age of 9 and a $25,000 maximum benefit per year for an eligible person who is between the ages of 9 and 16 years (Ariz. Rev. Stat. Ann. § 20-826-04, HB 2847 of 2008).
4. **Arkansas**: Requires health benefit plans to provide coverage for the diagnosis and treatment of autism spectrum disorders. Treatment is defined to include applied behavior analysis, pharmacy care, psychiatric care, psychological care, therapeutic care, necessary equipment to provide evidence-based treatment, and any care that is determined by a licensed physician to be medically necessary and evidence-based. Applied behavioral analysis is limited to $50,000 annually and to children under 18 years of age. Coverage is not subject to any limits on the number of visits an individual may make to an autism services provider. The law specifies that on or after January 1, 2014, to the extent that these provisions require benefits that exceed the essential health benefits specified under the federal Patient Protection and Affordable Care Act, the benefits that exceed the essential health benefits shall not be required of a health benefit plan when the plan is offered by a health care insurer in the state through the state medical exchange (2011 Ark. Acts. Act 196 (HB 1315 of 2011).
5. **California**: Requires every policy of disability insurance that covers hospital, medical, or surgical expenses in the state to provide coverage for the diagnosis and medically necessary treatment of severe mental illnesses, including pervasive developmental disorder or autism, for a person of any age under the same terms and conditions applied to other medical conditions (Cal. Insurance Code § 10144.5).
6. **Colorado**: Requires that all health benefit plans provide coverage for the assessment, diagnosis and treatment of autism spectrum disorders for a child. Treatment for autism spectrum disorders is defined to include treatments that are medically necessary, appropriate, effective or efficient and shall include evaluation and assessment services; behavior training and management and applied behavior analysis; habilitative or rehabilitative care, including occupational, physical or speech

therapy; pharmacy care and medication; psychiatric care; psychological care; and therapeutic care (Colo. Rev. Stat. § 10-16-104(1.3)(g); SB 244 of 2009).

7. **Connecticut**: Requires specified group health insurance policies to provide coverage for the diagnosis and treatment of autism spectrum disorder. Treatments must be medically necessary and identified and ordered by a licensed physician, psychologist or clinical social worker in accordance with a treatment plan. Treatments may include behavioral therapy, prescription drugs, psychiatric services, psychological services, physical therapy, speech and language pathology services and occupational therapy. Coverage for behavioral therapy may be limited to $50,000 per year for a child who is less than nine years of age, $35,000 for a child who is at least nine years of age and less than 13 years of age, and $25,000 for a child who is at least 13 years of age and less than 15 years of age. The policy may not impose limits on the number of visits to an autism services provider (Conn. Gen. Stat. § 38a-514b (SB 301 of 2009).
8. **District of Columbia**: Defines habilitative services as occupational, physical and speech therapy for the treatment of a child with a congenital or genetic birth defect to enhance the child's ability to function. Congenital or genetic birth defect is defined as a defect existing at or from birth, including a hereditary defect; includes autism or an autism spectrum disorder. Requires health insurers to provide habilitative services for children less than 21 years of age. The coverage shall not be more restrictive than coverage provided for any other illness, condition or disorder. A health insurer shall not be required to provide reimbursement for habilitative services delivered through early intervention or school services (D.C. Code Ann. § 31-3271 and § 31-3272 (2007 D.C. Stat., Act 16-0493).
9. **Florida**: Requires health insurance plans and health maintenance contracts to provide coverage to eligible individuals for well-baby and well-child screening for diagnosing the presence of autism spectrum disorders, treatment of autism spectrum disorders through speech, occupational and physical therapy and applied behavior analysis. Coverage is limited to treatment that is prescribed by the insured's treating physician in accordance with a treatment plan and is limited to $36,000 annual and may not exceed $200,000 in total lifetime benefits (Fla. Stat. § 627.6686).

10. **Georgia**: An insurer that provides benefits for neurological disorders shall not deny providing benefits for neurological disorders because of a diagnosis of autism (Ga. Code § 33-24-59.10 (HB 565 of 2001).
11. **Hawaii**: The purpose of this Act is to ensure the provision of quality health care by requiring insurance coverage for the diagnosis and treatment of autism. This Act shall be known and may be cited as "Luke's Law" (Haw. SB. 791).
12. **Illinois**: Requires all individual and group accident and health insurance or managed care plans to provide coverage for the diagnosis and treatment of autism spectrum disorders for individuals less than 21 years of age. Coverage is to include applied behavioral analysis and other treatments with a maximum benefit of $36,000 per year. Habilitative services includes occupational therapy, physical therapy, speech therapy and other services prescribed by the insured's treating physician pursuant to a treatment plan to enhance the ability of a child to function with a congenital, genetic or early acquired disorder (Ill. Rev. Stat. ch. 215, § 5/356z.14 et seq. (SB 101 of 2008).
13. **Indiana**: Requires an accident and sickness insurance policy that is issued on a group basis and a group contract with a health maintenance organization to provide coverage for the treatment of a pervasive developmental disorder. Coverage is limited to treatment that is prescribed by the insured's treating physician in accordance with a treatment plan. An insurer may not deny or refuse to issue coverage, or otherwise terminate or restrict coverage on an individual under an insurance policy solely because the individual is diagnosed with a pervasive developmental disorder. An insurer that issues an accident and sickness insurance policy on an individual basis or a health maintenance organization that enters into an individual contract that provides basic health care services must offer to provide coverage for the treatment of a pervasive developmental disorder of an enrollee (Ind. Code. § 27-8-14.2.1 (HB 1122 of 2001).
14. **Iowa**: Requires state employee health care plans to provide coverage for the diagnosis and treatment of autism spectrum disorders for individuals under 21 years of age. Treatment is defined as pharmacy care, psychiatric care, psychological care, rehabilitative care and therapeutic care. The law also establishes a $36,000 annual maximum benefit on coverage for children with autism spectrum disorder. The coverage plan cannot limit the number of visits to an autism service provider for treatment (Iowa House File 2531 of 2010).

15. **Kansas**: Requires state employee health insurance plans to provide coverage for the diagnosis and treatment of autism spectrum disorder for any covered individual up to 19 years old. Covered services are defined to include applied behavioral analysis and evidence-based services. The annual benefit cap for children up to age 7 is $36,000 and for children at least 7 years old and up to age 19, the annual cap is $27,000. The law also requires the state employees' health care commissioner to submit a report to the legislature that includes information on the impact of the mandated coverage for autism spectrum disorder on the state health care benefits program, data on the utilization of coverage and the cost of providing such coverage, and recommendations for whether such coverage should continue (Kan. Stat. Ann. § 75-6524 (2010 Kan Sess. Laws Chap. 120 (HB 2160 of 2010).
16. **Kentucky**: Requires large group health benefit plans to provide coverage for the diagnosis and treatment of autism spectrum disorders for individuals between the ages of one through 21 years of age. For individuals between the ages of one through their seventh birthday, the maximum annual benefit amount is $50,000, and the maximum benefit for individuals between the ages of seven through 21 is $1,000 per month. Coverage may not be subject to any limits on the number of visits an individual may make to an autism services provider. Treatment of autism spectrum disorders is defined to include medical care, pharmacy care (if covered by the plan), psychiatric care, psychological care, therapeutic care, applied behavior analysis, and rehabilitative and rehabilitative care. The law increases the maximum benefit per month from $500 to $1,000 (Ky. Rev. Stat. § 319C (2010 Ky. Acts. Chap. 150 (HB 159 of 2010).
17. **Louisiana**: Requires health insurance policies, including health maintenance organizations, to provide coverage for the diagnosis and treatment of autism spectrum disorders in individuals less than 21 years of age. Coverage is subject to a maximum benefit of $36,000. Treatment of autism spectrum disorders is defined to include habilitative or rehabilitative care (including applied behavior analysis), pharmacy, psychiatric, psychological and therapeutic care. (La. Rev. Stat. Ann. § 22.1050 (HB 958 of 2008).
18. **Maine**: Requires all individual health insurance policies and contracts, group health insurance policies, and all individual and group health maintenance organization contracts to provide coverage for the diagnosis and treatment of autism spectrum disorders for individuals five years of age and under. Treatment is defined as habilitative or

rehabilitative care, applied behavior analysis, counseling services and therapy services, including speech, occupational and physical therapy. The policy or contract may limit coverage for applied behavior analysis to $36,000 per year, and the insurance policy or contract may not include any limits on the number of visits. The law also requires the Department of Professional and Financial Regulation, Bureau of Insurance to review and evaluate the financial and social impact and medical efficacy of this mandated health insurance benefit, and submit a report to the Legislature by February 1, 2015 (Me. Rev. Stat. Ann. Tit. 24-A § 2768, 2010 Me. Laws, Chap. 635 (SB 446 of 2010).

19. **Maryland**: Requires insurers, nonprofit health service plans and health maintenance organizations to provide coverage of habilitative services for children less than 19 years of age. Habilitative services include occupational, physical and speech therapy for the treatment of a child with a congenital or genetic birth defect to enhance the child's ability to function. The definition of congenital or genetic birth defect includes autism spectrum disorder (Md. Insurance Code Ann. § 15-835 (2002 Md. Laws, Chap. 382 (HB 692).
20. **Massachusetts**: Requires specified individual, group and state employee health plans and health maintenance contracts to provide benefits on a nondiscriminatory basis for the diagnosis and treatment of autism spectrum disorder. Treatment is defined to include habilitative or rehabilitative, pharmacy, psychiatric, psychological and therapeutic care. The health plan may not contain an annual or lifetime dollar or unit of service limitation on coverage for autism which is less than the limitations imposed on coverage for physical conditions. The plan may not limit the number of visits an individual may make to an autism services provider. The law allows for exemptions from providing coverage under certain circumstances (Mass. Gen. Laws Ann. Ch. IV § 32A-25. (HB 4935 of 2010).
21. **Michigan**: Requires health maintenance organization group or individual contracts to provide coverage for the diagnosis and treatment of autism spectrum disorders. Coverage for treatment may be subject to a maximum annual benefit of $50,000 for children through age six, $40,000 for a child ages seven through 12, and $30,000 for a child ages 13 through 18. Treatment is defined to include behavioral health treatment (including applied behavior analysis), pharmacy care, psychiatric care, psychological care, and therapeutic care. As of January 1, 2014, to the extent that these required benefits exceed the essential health benefits specified under the federal Patient Protection and Affordable

Care Act, the specific benefits that exceed the essential health benefits are not required of qualified health plans that are offered in the state by a health carrier through a health benefit exchange (Mich. Pub. Acts, Act 100 (2011 SB 415).

22. **Mississippi**: A health insurance policy shall provide 6 coverage for the screening, diagnosis, and treatment of autism 7 spectrum disorder. To the extent that the screening, diagnosis, 8 and treatment of autism spectrum disorder are not already covered 9 by a health insurance policy, coverage under this section shall be 10 included in health insurance policies that are delivered, 11 executed, issued, amended, adjusted, or renewed in this state, or 12 outside this state if insuring residents of this state, on or 13 after January 1, 2016. (Miss. HB 885 of 2015).
23. **Missouri**: Requires all group health benefit plans to provide coverage for the diagnosis and treatment of autism spectrum disorders. Coverage is limited to medically necessary treatment that is ordered by the insured's treating physician or psychologist, in accordance with a treatment plan. Treatment for autism spectrum disorder is defined to include psychiatric, psychological, habilitative or rehabilitative care, applied behavior analysis, therapeutic care and pharmacy care. Coverage for applied behavior analysis is subject to a maximum benefit of $40,000 per year for individuals through 18 years of age. However, this limit may be exceeded, with approval by the health benefit plan, if the applied behavior analysis services are medically necessary for an individual. The health benefit plan may not place limits on the number of visits an individual makes to an autism service provider. The law requires the department of insurance and other institutions to submit a report to the legislature regarding the implementation of this coverage, including specified costs of this coverage (Mo. Rev. Stat. § 337.300 et seq. and §376.1224 (HB 1311 of 2010).
24. **Montana**: Requires specified disability policies, certificates of insurance and membership contracts to provide coverage for the diagnosis and treatment of autism spectrum disorders for a covered child 18 years of age or younger. Coverage must include habilitative or rehabilitative care, medications, psychiatric or psychological care, therapeutic care and other specified care. Coverage for treatment of autism spectrum disorders may be limited to a maximum benefit for $50,000 per year for a child 8 years of age and younger and to $20,000 per year for a child 9 years of age through 19 years of age (Mont. Code Ann. § 33-22-515, 2009 Mont. Laws, Chap. 359 (SB 234 of 2009).

25. **Nevada**: Requires an individual health benefit plan to provide the option of coverage for screening, diagnosis, and treatment of autism spectrum disorders for persons covered by the policy under the age of 18, or if enrolled in high school, until the person reaches the age of 22. Requires health insurance for small employers and group and blank health insurance benefit plans and health care plans issued by a health maintenance organization to provide coverage for screening, diagnosis and treatment of autism spectrum disorders to persons covered by the policy of group health insurance under the age of 18, or if enrolled in high school until the person reaches the age of 22. Treatment of autism spectrum disorders must be identified in a treatment plan and may include medically necessary habilitative or rehabilitative care, prescription care, psychiatric care, psychological care or behavior therapy (Nev. Rev. Stat. § 689A.0435, 2009 Nev. Stats., Chap. 331) (AB 162 of 2009).
26. **New Hampshire**: Clarifies and defines treatment of pervasive developmental disorder or autism, as required under N.H. Rev. Stat. Ann. § 417-E:1, to include professional services and treatment programs, including applied behavioral analysis, prescribed pharmaceuticals (subject to the terms and conditions of the policy), direct or consultative services provided by specified licensed professionals, and services provided by licensed speech, occupation or physical therapists. The policy, contract or certificate may limit coverage for applied behavior analysis to $36,000 per year for children 0 to 12 years of age, and $27,000 from ages 13 to 21 (N.H. Rev. Stat. Ann. § 417-E:2, 2010 N.H. Laws, Chap. 363 (HB 569 of 2010).
27. **New Jersey**: Require specified health insurance policies and health benefit plans to provide coverage for expenses incurred in screening and diagnosing autism or another developmental disability. When the covered person's primary diagnosis is autism or another developmental disability, coverage must be provided for expenses incurred for medically necessary occupational therapy, physical therapy, and speech therapy, as prescribed through a treatment plan. When the covered person is under 21 years of age and the person's primary diagnosis is autism, coverage must be provided for expenses incurred for medically necessary behavioral interventions based on the principles of applied behavioral analysis and related programs, as prescribed through a treatment plan. (2009 N.J. Laws, Chap. 115, AB 2238 of 2009)
28. **New Mexico**: Requires specified insurance policies, health care plans, certificates of health insurance or contracts to provide coverage to an

eligible individual who is 19 years of age or younger, or an individual who is 22 years of age or younger and is enrolled in high school for well-baby and well-child screening for diagnosing the presence of autism spectrum disorder and the treatment of autism spectrum disorder through speech therapy, occupational therapy, physical therapy and applied behavioral analysis. Coverage is limited to $36,000 annually and shall not exceed $200,000 in total lifetime benefits (N.M. Stat. Ann. § 59A-22-49, 2009 N.M. Laws, Chap. 74 (SB 39 of 2009).

29. **New York**: Require specified policies and contracts that provide coverage for hospital or surgical coverage to not exclude coverage for the screening, diagnosis and treatment of medical conditions otherwise covered by the policy solely because the treatment is provided to diagnose or treat autism spectrum disorder. Treatment of autism spectrum disorder is defined to include behavioral health treatments, psychiatric care, psychological care, medical care, therapeutic care and specified pharmacy care. These provisions specify that coverage for applied behavior analysis is subject to a maximum benefit of $45,000 per year (N.Y. Insurance Laws § 3216, § 3221 and § 4303).
30. **Oklahoma**: Requires all individual and group health insurance policies that provide medical and surgical benefits to provide the same coverage and benefits to any individual under the age of 18 years who has been diagnosed with an autistic disorder as it would provide coverage and benefits to an individual who has not been diagnosed with an autistic disorder (2010 Okla. Sess. Laws, Chap. 166 (SB 2045 of 2010).
31. **Oregon**: Requires specified health benefit plans to provide coverage for an enrolled child less than 18 years of age who is diagnosed with a pervasive developmental disorder or autism all medical services, including medical and rehabilitative services, that are medically necessary and are otherwise covered under the plan. Rehabilitative services include physical, occupational or speech therapy services to restore or improve function (Or. Rev. Stat. § 743A.190, 2007 Or. Laws, Chap. 872 (HB 2918).
32. **Pennsylvania**: Requires a health insurance policy or government program to provide coverage for individuals less than 21 years of age for the diagnostic assessment and treatment of autism spectrum disorders. Maximum benefit of $36,000 per year (Pa. Cons. Stat. tit. 40, § 764h, Pa. Laws, Act 2008-62 (HB 1150 of 2008).
33. **Rhode Island**: Requires specified contracts and policies to provide coverage for autism spectrum disorder. Benefits include coverage for applied behavior analysis, physical therapy, speech therapy,

occupational therapy, pharmaceutical, psychology, and psychiatrist services for the treatment of autism spectrum disorder and apply until the covered individual reaches age 15. Coverage for applied behavior analysis is limited to $32,000 per year (R.I. Gen. Laws § 27-20.11-1 et seq., 2011 R.I. Pub. Laws, Chap. 159 (HB 5275).

34. **South Carolina**: Requires a health insurance plan to provide coverage for the treatment of autism spectrum disorders. Coverage is limited to treatment that is prescribed by the insured's treating medical doctor in accordance with a treatment plan. To be eligible for coverage, an individual must be diagnosed with autism spectrum disorder at age eight or younger and be less than 16 years of age (S.C. Code Ann. § 38-71-280, 2007 S.C. Acts, Act 65 (SB 20 of 2007).
35. **South Dakota**: "Autism spectrum disorder," as defined in the American Psychiatric Association's 6 Diagnostic and Statistical Manual of Mental Disorders, edition DSM-V-TR (S.D. HB 1257).
36. **Tennessee**: Defines autism spectrum disorder as a neurological disorder. Requires that contracts and policies that provide benefits for neurological disorders to provide benefits and coverage for treatment of children less than 12 years of age with autism (Tenn. Code Ann. § 56-7-2367, 2006 Tenn. Pub. Acts, Chap. 894 (SB 2719).
37. **Texas**: Requires a health benefit plan to provide coverage for all generally recognized services prescribed in relation to autism spectrum disorder by the enrollee's primary care physician in the treatment plan recommended by the physician. The law defines "generally recognized services" to include applied behavior analysis; speech, occupational and physical therapy; medications or nutritional supplements; and other treatments. This coverage may be subject to annual deductibles, copayments and coinsurance that are consistent with annual deductibles, copayments and coinsurance required for other coverage under the health benefit plan (Tex. Insurance Code § 1355.015, 2007 Tex. Gen. Laws, Chap. 877, (HB 1919 of 2007).
38. **Vermont**: Requires health insurance plans to provide coverage for the evidence-based diagnosis and treatment of early childhood developmental disorders, including applied behavior analysis for children up to age 21. Early childhood developmental disorders is defined as a childhood mental or physical impairment or combination of mental and physical impairments that results in functional limitations in major life activities, accompanied by a diagnosis defined by the Diagnostic and Statistical Manual of Mental Disorders (DSM) or the International Classification of Disease (ICD). The term includes autism spectrum

disorders but does not include a learning disability. Treatment of early childhood developmental disorders is defined to include evidenced-based care and related equipment, behavioral health treatment, pharmacy care, psychiatric care, psychological care and therapeutic care. The law was also was amended to allow children to receive care from birth until 21 years of age. The act also added that as of January 1, 2014, to the extent that these required benefits exceed the essential health benefits specified under the federal Patient Protection and Affordable Care Act, the specific benefits that exceed the essential health benefits are not required of qualified health plans that are offered in the state by a health carrier through a health benefit exchange (Vt. Stat. Ann. Tit. 8 § 4088i, 2010 Vt. Acts, Act 127 (SB 262 of 2010).

39. **Virginia**: Requires health insurers, health care subscription plans and health maintenance organizations to provide coverage for the diagnosis and treatment of autism spectrum disorders in individuals from age two to six. The requirement applies to the state employees' health insurance plan and to the local choice health program and does not apply to an insurer, corporation, or health maintenance organization, or to government employee programs, if the costs associated with coverage exceed one percent of premiums charged over the experience period. Treatment is defined to include behavioral health treatment, pharmacy care, psychiatric care, psychological care, therapeutic care, and applied behavior analysis. Coverage is limited to an annual maximum benefit of $35,000 for applied behavior analysis unless the insurer elects to provide coverage in a greater amount. Coverage is not subject to any visit limits. As of January 1, 2014, to the extent that these required benefits exceed the essential health benefits specified under the federal Patient Protection and Affordable Care Act, the specific benefits that exceed the essential health benefits are not required of qualified health plans that are offered in the state by a health carrier through a health benefit exchange (2011 Va. Act. Chap. 876 and 2011 Va. Act. Chap. 878 (HB 2467 of 2011).
40. **West Virginia**: Requires specified health insurers, including the state's Children's Health Insurance Program (CHIP), to provide coverage for the diagnosis and treatment of autism spectrum disorders in individuals from the age of 18 months through 18 years. To be eligible for coverage, the individual must be diagnosed with autism spectrum disorder at age 8 or younger. Coverage includes treatments that are medically necessary and ordered or prescribed by a licensed physician or licensed

psychologist, including but not limited to, applied behavioral analysis. The annual maximum benefit for applied behavioral analysis is $30,000 per year for the first three years after treatment commences, and $2,000 per month after three years (2011 W. Va. Act. Chap. 13 (HB 2693 of 2011).

41. **Wisconsin**: Requires specified disability insurance policies and self-insured health plans to provide coverage for treatment for autism spectrum disorder if the treatment is prescribed by a physician, including specified therapies. The statute defines intensive-level and nonintensive-level services (Wis. Stat. § 632.895 and Wis. Stat. § 609.87 (Assembly Bill 75 of 2009).

# CHAPTER 8

# THE RELATIONSHIP BETWEEN COMMUNITY EDUCATIONAL ATTAINMENT AND THE DISCIPLINE IMPLEMENTATION OF FOURTH AMENDMENT LEGAL PRINCIPLES IN PUBLIC SCHOOLS

Jeffrey Burke and Mario Torres

## ABSTRACT

*This chapter examines the relationship between community educational attainment and Fourth Amendment legal principles being implemented in public schools. Using education attainment data obtained from the U.S. Census, this study examined the influence of educational attainment on how searches of students were conducted and the relative legal and judicial outcomes. The results of this study offer insight on issues related to forms of discipline in public schools and contribute to knowledge bases in the fields of economics, law, social theory, and educational leadership and administration.*

**Legal Frontiers in Education: Complex Law Issues for Leaders, Policymakers and Policy Implementers**
**Advances in Educational Administration, Volume 24, 147–163**

**ISSN: 1479-3660/doi:10.1108/S1479-366020150000024035**

*Prior studies regarding the Fourth Amendment in schools focused largely on administrative decisions, judgments, and practices, but the aspect of educational attainment has been minimally investigated. Findings suggest community educational attainment has little to no predictive influence on aspects related to student searches examined in the study, which include the intrusiveness level of the search and the number of searches occurring during a single search event. Implications for future research and leadership are discussed.*

## INTRODUCTION

This chapter examines the link between community educational attainment and the disciplinary actions of school officials in court cases involving student searches in public schools. In light of the highly uncertain nature of student searches and increasing attention given to school violence, students are faced with the possibility of having their Fourth Amendment rights violated on any given day. Stefkovich and Torres (2003) suggest "a student, not suspected of any violations whatsoever, might be required to: have his/her possessions searched by canines; be scanned by a metal detector ... or be subjected to highly invasive strip searches if suspected of wrongdoing" (p. 260). This is not to suggest school administrators intentionally violate the legal rights afforded to those in their stead. Rather, as suggested by Stefkovich and O'Brien (2001), administrators and teachers may be deficient in their knowledge of the basic principles of law, specifically facets of law related to search and seizure.

Given the risk inherent in this deficiency, and the position in which students are placed where this deficiency exists, it is important to analyze what factors might impact the treatment of student rights in a school. Therefore, researchers examined to what degree educational attainment (a minimally investigated construct as it relates to disciplinary outcomes) influences the actions of administrators when making disciplinary choices. If student rights are to be adequately protected, it is important to more fully understand the nexus between community knowledge and legal decisions in schools. At the very least, the findings of this study enhance school leaders' awareness of the interplay between community education attainment and decisions involving students' privacy rights. As such, this study contributes to a growing body of research investigating legal nuances of school leadership in varying demographic contexts. To begin, an explanation of the legal principles underlying student searches is provided followed by discussion of educational attainment as a form of legal capital. The method of analysis is explained in brief followed by discussion of the findings, implications, and conclusions.

# BACKGROUND

### *Legal Framework: The Scope of Students' Rights under the Fourth Amendment*

Student searches reflect one of the more common forms of disciplinary action in schools. The Fourth Amendment of the U.S. Constitution is the overarching touchstone for student searches and guarantees "the right of the people to be secure in their persons, houses, papers, and effects, against unreasonable searches and seizures ... shall not be violated" (U.S. Const., amend. IV, § 1). The principles currently guiding student searches stem largely from four U.S. Supreme Court rulings: *New Jersey v. T.L.O.* (1985), *Vernonia v. Acton* (1995), *Board of Education v. Earls* (2002), and *Safford Unified School District v. Redding* (2009).

Throughout these decisions, one principle appears consistently in the court's analyses and is often reintroduced amid varying contexts such as drug testing and strip-searching. Most are familiar with the concept of "probable cause" as the guiding standard in determining the decision of a police officer to search an individual, one's possessions, or premises. In U.S. criminal law, probable cause is the standard by which an officer or agent of the law has the grounds to make an arrest, to conduct a personal or property search, to obtain a warrant for arrest, etc. when criminal charges are being considered. However, many may be unfamiliar with the concept of "reasonableness," the standard by which school administrators operate in relation to searches of students in schools. The four cases discussed below have firmly established reasonableness as the primary core principle in deciding the legality of a search in public schools.

According to the U.S. Supreme Court in *New Jersey v. T.L.O.*, the reasonableness standard is defined as having two central parts relative to searches: (a) the search must be justified at the beginning, or inception and (b) the scope must be "reasonably" related to its objective (*New Jersey v. T.L.O.*, 1985). *T.L.O.* (1985) addressed the question of determining the proper and acceptable standard for student searches by officials in schools.

This particular case involved a student who was caught smoking in a restroom. The student was questioned by the assistant principal and denied the charge, upon which the administrator searched the student's bag for cigarettes. Instead of finding cigarettes, the administrator found marijuana paraphernalia and a list of students who owed money. When the school pressed for delinquency charges against the student, T.L.O. moved to suppress the evidence on grounds that the search violated the Fourth Amendment. The Supreme Court, in a majority opinion, ruled the standard of "reasonableness" in the context of a school environment in which teachers and administrators are charged with maintaining safety and order does not require a warrant, nor does it require "probable cause" (New *Jersey v. T.L.O.*, 1985).

The *T.L.O.* court established the two-pronged rule for searches. As long as the search is justified at its inception and the scope of the search was reasonable in its relation to "the circumstances which justified the interference in the first place," then the school has met the standard of reasonableness (*New Jersey v. T.L.O.*, 1985, p. 341). The outcome and subsequent applicability of the ruling in this case indicated that the standards established for reasonableness as it relates to searches by school officials "neither burden the efforts of administrators in maintaining order nor authorize ... intrusions upon the privacy of schoolchildren" (*New Jersey v. T.L.O.*, 1985, p. 341).

To be sure, the standard of reasonableness provided much needed guidance to school administrators and subsequent search and seizure court cases at the state and federal. However, for certain school administrative situations like drug testing, the T.L.O. two part test lacked enough information to know whether reasonableness was being achieved. Future High Court cases in *Vernonia v. Acton* in (1995) and *Board of Education v. Earls* in 2002, which examined the constitutionality of student drug testing among athletic participants and student participation in extracurricular activities, respectively, would elaborate on the prevailing standard. In *Vernonia v. Acton* (1995), the Court had to determine if the search constituted by the random drug testing policy "balanced the intrusion on Acton's Fourth Amendment rights 'against promotion of legitimate government interests'". *Vernonia v. Acton* (1995) clearly expanded the latitude of school officials in conducting searches.

Similarly in *Earls* (2002), the High Court reasoned that due to the "general regulation of extracurricular activity" by the School District, students' legitimate expectations of privacy were diminished, and that the confidential methods of both obtaining urine and maintenance of drug test results were "minimally intrusive" (*Board of Education v. Earls,* 2002). The Court found that Tecumseh's policy was a reasonable means of furthering the School District's interest in preventing and deterring drug use among its students.

In the final of the four cases, *Safford v. Redding* (2009) concerned the strip search of a female middle school student, Savana Redding, based on a tip from another student claiming that Ms. Redding had ibuprofen on her person, a violation of school policy. Redding sued the school district as well as the school official who conducted the search. Important to note in this case is the legitimacy of a strip search and the potential personal liability of school officials in a search case. The U.S. Supreme Court held, citing the standard established in *New Jersey v. T.L.O.* (1985), that the search was justified at its inception yet the search was unconstitutional because school officials did not have sufficient suspicion to extend the search to the student's underwear. Be that as it may, school administrators enjoyed immunity from personal liability because "clearly established law did not show that the search violated the Fourth Amendment" (*Safford v. Redding,* 2009).

The outcome in *Safford* (2009) does appear to reveal a willingness on the part of the Court to look more closely at discretionary power. Further study of extraneous factors, which may influence administrative decisions and discipline, seems prudent. In the four cases, the Court sided with the school district in three, finding fault in the actions of school officials in *Safford.* Therefore, it is reasonable to infer school officials are granted latitude to conduct student searches based on the justification and reasonableness of the search in question. Further, school officials enjoy a greater scope of power in conducting searches if the reason for the search is to keep the school and students safe from harm. This chapter now turns to a discussion on what if anything the collective knowledge of a community poses for carrying out the somewhat enigmatic reasonableness standard in schools.

### *The Nexus between Education Attainment and Students' Fourth Amendment Rights*

Educational attainment, as addressed by James Coleman (1988) and in economics by Becker (1964), is closely related to family background, including parents' education and parents' socio-economic status (Bjorklund & Salvanes, 2011). There is a wealth of extant research on maternal education levels and the "intergenerational transmission of human capital" (Antonovics & Goldberger, 2005) as well as the effect of family composition on children's outcomes (Black, Devereaux, & Salvanes, 2005). Additionally, existing literature has examined the equality of educational opportunity, most notably by Coleman et al. (1966) as well as the causal effect of a parent's schooling on children's schooling (Holmlund, Lindahl, & Plug, 2008). A study by Lindahl (2010) compared family and neighborhood effects on grades, test scores, educational attainment, and income. The majority of extant literature focuses on the effects of educational attainment on learning itself, not the application of the law in a public school setting. Thus far, no research to date has probed the relationship between educational attainment of a community and discipline implementation in schools. Burke and Torres collected data (1,347 valid cases) from the General Social Survey (GSS) between 1972 and 2012 and it revealed education as a considerable predictor of respondents' openness to stricter discipline. Data from the GSS revealed as the respondent completed more years in school, they were less likely to believe strict discipline was necessary or effective in improving a behavioral situation. Thus, a negative relationship seemed to be at play. The extent to which community educational attainment influences perceptions about a school administrator's authority and level of knowledge about discipline implementation under "reasonableness" is the core thesis for this inquiry.

Few if any studies have probed the nexus between education attainment and civil liberties. However, there are a number of studies that have explored the impact of educational attainment on other closely related social dimensions. Ream and Palardy (2008) examined how class-stratified social networks of parents perpetuated educational inequality among students in schools. The researchers investigated parent social capital and the idea of collective efficacy and its influence on school policies and practices and found levels of education and social class may influence collective action regarding practices in schools, which includes the protection of civil liberties. While Ream and Palardy's (2008) research focused on student achievement, the notion of collective efficacy based on social class and parental social capital as a result of common levels of educational attainment is especially relevant to the present study.

The research by Owens (2010), investigating different neighborhood and school contexts for educational attainment, found the absolute level of neighborhood resources positively predicted earning a bachelor's degree, a measure of educational attainment used in the present study. Referring to prior work by Hanushek (2003), the author asserted the importance of "social context" for educational achievement (p. 288). The findings by Owens suggest community educational attainment may serve as both a predictive measure of the creation of social norms and a simultaneous result of social norms in action. Little research examines this relationship, especially the shared norms aspect of educational attainment as a driver of school policy and practice change. While a number of studies have examined school composition as a predictor of educational attainment (Mayer, 2002; Orfield & Eaton, 1996), very few have investigated the predictive nature of educational attainment on school practices, outside of academic achievement.

Of particular interest to this study is education attainment research related to residential geography. A study by Byun, Meece, and Irvin (2012) on rural–non-rural disparities in post-secondary educational attainment found that rural students lagged behind non-rural students in attaining a bachelor's degree largely due to their lower socio-economic background. Given that previous studies on educational attainment and the rural, non-rural gap have focused largely on high school completion (Roscigno & Crowle, 2001) or college enrollment (Hu, 2003), this study examined the completion of a college degree as an indicator of educational attainment. The study further utilized data for the National Center for Educational Statistics and the American Community Survey to examine educational attainment as measured by the completion of a bachelor's degree or higher. Byun et al. (2012) acknowledged the identification of educational attainment as measured by completion of college degree is a relatively new foray into empirical research.

In a separate study, researchers investigated the potential role of family background, academic preparation, and community resources in explaining rural and non-rural differences in post-secondary educational attainment. The results of this study (Turley, 2009) suggest demographic and regional background are sources of differences in college degree attainment, thus lending credence to the use of school district type as a control variable in the present analysis. Expectations of children to obtain a bachelor's degree were higher in urban areas as well, as were instances of children in urban settings receiving more help with academic work, the study suggests.

Investigating related research on educational attainment in a broader social sense will lend insight into a more specific outcome of community education related to student search outcomes in schools. As discussed earlier, the existing research on educational attainment has focused heavily on academic achievement, or the effect of other causal factors on the development of educational attainment. No studies to date have investigated the causal effect of educational attainment on legal issues in schools regarding the searching of students. However, understanding how educational attainment is measured and analyzed across a variety of contexts of empirical research informs the present study.

A central tenet to this research is the idea that legal information can be a form of capital (part cultural, part social) and that communities whose members have more formal education may have a more advanced knowledge of the law. The intention of law is to provide a level of equality to those who may not be treated equally, and it is a vehicle by which people and communities can begin to coalesce and forge an identity. Wise and Schauer (2007) believe "the bonds that are created by shared legal status can be understood as a form of social capital, the mechanism of cooperation and coordination by which communities perform tasks that could not be performed ... by unconnected individuals" (p. 268). Understanding laws are written to be applicable over time and to be applied to different situations and a "multiplicity of people" (Wise & Schauer, 2007, p. 267), it is assumed law should apply equitably to all citizens. This applicability should, and is intended, to include students in schools, especially those students who are at risk of having their right to privacy violated in searches. This study aims to apply community awareness, through the construct of formal education attainment, to the applicability of the law. Thus the question becomes to what extent the level of education in a community bears upon how students are searched in schools.

If a shared understanding of the law can create communities and forge social capital through civic action, then it stands to reason that this extends to the treatment of children in community schools. Law can be a force that brings different people together in the pursuit of a common goal, thus creating the context for cooperation. Further, the specific contention that information about the law can create a platform for dialog and understanding that "makes it clear to all those who are discussing and debating that they are involved in a common enterprise" (Wise & Schauer, 2007, p. 271).

Central to the idea of legal information as social capital is the notion of shared information, which happens in communities virtually every day through civic and community organizations. Whether these community issues involve decisions regarding placement of roads, public safety, or business development, these civic functions involve shared purpose, resources, and information. As to the present inquiry, it is based largely on the assumption collective community knowledge, which the present authors concede may reflect varying understandings of law, may in some way relate to how students are treated in disciplinary situations. The researchers fully acknowledge that an aggregate level of "educational attainment" may not explain the aggregate level of "legal educational attainment." Be that as it may, the researchers approached the analysis and results with a fair amount of discretion.

By examining the nexus between community educational attainment and the manner in which students were searched under the standard of "reasonableness," the findings should provide valuable insights for future research, legislation, policy, and application regarding Fourth Amendment rights in schools. If as Stefkovich and O'Brien (2001) note, school administrators' knowledge of the law is somewhat lacking in the area of search and seizure, then how does one begin to estimate the level of legal understanding of the "average" community member? If a community's level of legal knowledge, again partially measured in this analysis, is low, then what may be the implications for administrative discretion and students' rights?

## METHOD

The construct of educational attainment has been largely examined within academic achievement (Bjorklund & Salvanes, 2011), legal information as social capital (Wise & Schauer, 2007), and the role of public education in a democracy (Goodman, 1996). However, no study has investigated the potential effect of educational attainment on school official decisions relating to student searches. The present research investigates the effect of community educational attainment, defined in this study as the percentage of bachelor's degrees and higher in a given community, on the intrusiveness of a student search. The question was examined using logistic regression analysis.

### *Sources of Data*

The researchers employed the Stefkovich and Torres Fourth Amendment database, a nonprobability sample comprised 263 cases beginning with the *New Jersey v. T.L.O.* ruling on January 15, 1985, which contains specific legal, demographic, and search information regarding each of the cases. The database provided information such as the school district in which the search occurred, the date of the search, and other variables utilized in this study. For the purposes of this study, two variables were employed as primary dependent variables reflecting the intrusiveness of the search: the type of search for which the student was subjected and the number of searches that were administered by school officials. Additionally, this database was useful in identifying the object of the search leading to the case, reported in this study as the seriousness of the offense.

Data from the 1990 and 2000 U.S. Census as well as the 2005–2010 American Community Survey were collected to calculate an estimate of educational attainment level of communities where these searches occurred. In both the U.S. Census and the American Community Survey databases, the level of educational attainment was identified by which level of school all members of the community had completed. These levels ranged from no high school completed to doctorate level. For this study, the level of educational attainment was identified as the percentage of the community holding a bachelor's degree or higher. However, because census data were not available yearly for all years, interpolation techniques were used to estimate yearly changes in community educational attainment. However, missing data resulted in cases being eliminated. In total, 114 cases contained adequate data to conduct the analysis.

### *Data Description and Coding*

To allow for logistic regression analysis, it was necessary to code or recode variables into binary variables. The independent variables included community educational attainment, the school district type, and the seriousness of the offense. Researchers opted to include the school district geographical location and the object initiating the search (i.e., seriousness of the offense) as variables to account for context influences on education attainment. The variable of greatest interest to this study, community educational attainment, was measured as the percentage of the population having a bachelor's degree or higher. To create a roughly equal distribution based on these categories, the median of 25% served as the dividing criteria. Communities where the percentage of bachelor's degrees was 25% or higher were coded as high educational attainment; less than 24% designated as low. The school district type was coded as rural or urban. Similar to coding used by Torres (2003), "all schools situated in a 'large central city' or 'urban fringe of large city' were classified as urban schools" (p. 98). The population of the urban areas was at least 250,000. If a community fell below that threshold, then they were identified in the study as rural. The seriousness of the offense was also recoded into binary form. Searches that were conducted because of the presence of illegal drugs or weapons, constituting a felony offense, were coded as more serious. All other offenses of a lesser nature were coded as less serious. The specific coding of the independent variables employed in this study is reflected in Table 1.

### *Dependent Variables*

Two independent variables were employed: the intrusiveness level of the search and the number of separate searches employed on the student by school officials. The variable, level of intrusiveness, was measured according to the type of search administered. More than 25 different types of searches were recorded in the Stefkovich and Torres database based largely on models of degrees of intrusiveness identified by Gluckman (1984) and O'Hara (1984). For example, Gluckman (1984) identified more intrusive searches as more individual in nature, while O'Hara (1984) treated the level of intrusive searches with degrees of danger or the goal of criminal prosecution. Thus, searches were coded as less intrusive or more intrusive. A second construct for search intrusiveness was the number of separate searches occurring during a single search event. As more searches were conducted, the level of intrusiveness of rose and was coded as more intrusive. Consequently, if only one search was conducted, it was coded as less intrusive (Table 2).

### *Data Technique*

For this study, binary logistic regression was employed to study the effects of community and school factors on disciplinary outcomes (i.e., search

***Table 1.*** Independent Variables.

| Variable | Level of Measurement |
|---|---|
| Educational attainment | Nominal: Binary variable<br>1: 25 bachelor's degree and above, 0: 24% below |
| School district type | Nominal: Binary variable<br>1: Urban, 0: Rural |
| Seriousness of the crime | Nominal: Binary variable<br>1: More serious, 0: Less serious |

***Table 2.*** Dependent Variables.

| Variable | Level of Measurement |
|---|---|
| Intrusiveness level of the search | Nominal: binary variable<br>1: more, 0: less |
| Number of searches | Nominal: binary variable<br>1: 2+, 0: 1 |

intrusiveness). The primary purpose of the study was to test the effect of a previously untested variable, community educational attainment, on the dependent variables used in the study. Given the categorical nature of the dependent variables, logistic regression was the most appropriate analysis. In logistic regression, the dependent variable is a logit, which centers on the natural logarithm of the odds (Agresti, 1996a, b). This link-function transformation is described below:

$$\text{Logit}\,(p) = \alpha + \beta x$$

where $\alpha$ is the intercept and $\beta x$ is the slope; change in units in logit at every unit change of $x$.

A backward stepwise logistic regression was employed to eliminate explanatory variables in succession by changes in −2 log likelihood in order to arrive at the most parsimonious model at $p < .05$. Goodness-of-fit models, including the Hosmer and Lemeshow test, were employed to determine how well the data fit the final model.

## FINDINGS

### *Intrusiveness of the Search (*N = *121/263)*

A binary logistic regression analysis was conducted to examine the influence of community educational attainment, the type of school district where the search occurred, and the seriousness of the student offense on the intrusiveness level of the search (see Table 3). From the 263 cases, full data could only be collected from 121 of these cases to conduct this analysis. The variable "seriousness of the crime" was the only predictor found to be statistically significant (Wald's $\chi^2 = 6.083$, df = 1, $p < .014$, Nagelkerke's $R^2 = .071$). As the findings suggest, for every unit increase in the

***Table 3.*** Binary Logistic Regression Analysis: Intrusiveness Level of the Search.

| | $\beta$ | Wald | df | Sig | Exp($\beta$) |
|---|---|---|---|---|---|
| Educational attainment | −0.222 | 0.048 | 1 | 0.827 | 0.801 |
| School district type | 0.154 | 0.163 | 1 | 0.686 | 1.167 |
| Seriousness of the crime | −1.173 | 6.083 | 1 | 0.014* | 0.31 |

*Note*: Number of searches ($N = 123/263$).
*Significant at the .05 level (two-tailed).

***Table 4.*** Binary Logistic Regression Analysis: Number of Searches.

| | $\beta$ | Wald | df | Sig | Exp($\beta$) |
|---|---|---|---|---|---|
| Educational attainment | 0.431 | 0.181 | 1 | 0.67 | 1.539 |
| School district type | 0.402 | 1.184 | 1 | 0.276 | 1.495 |
| Seriousness of the crime | 0.073 | 0.027 | 1 | 0.869 | 0.93 |

"seriousness of the crime," the odds of a highly intrusive search decreased by 1.173, meaning searches were more likely to be less intrusive as the crime calling for the search was more serious. There was no indication that the variables "school district type" or "educational attainment" had any statistical significance on the level of intrusiveness.

A second binary logistic regression analysis examined whether the same explanatory variables (i.e., community educational attainment, the type of school district where the search occurred, and the seriousness of the student offense) might predict the number of separate searches administered on the student by school officials (see Table 4). From the 263 cases, full data could only be collected from 123 of these cases to conduct this analysis. None of the predictor variables were statistically significant. Therefore, the variables did not statistically explain the number of searches performed on a student by school officials.

## DISCUSSION, IMPLICATIONS, AND CONCLUSIONS

The ideal of the "horizontal collective initiative of social capital" (Wise & Schauer, 2007, p. 267) reflected this study's core premise that shared knowledge influences how law is implemented within schools. Shared knowledge of a community, especially knowledge about the operations of governmental institutions like public schools, was a central to this study. It was used as the basis for exploring the influence of educational attainment. The idea that legal information can serve as a base for collective effort is especially relevant. However, the results suggest level of collective knowledge may only have a slight effect on how students are treated in the search process, at least according to the intrusiveness level. The findings according to the available case law suggest that students appear to be given equitable treatment during school searches and that the level of intrusiveness of the search does not fluctuate in a pattern depending on the educational attainment of the community.

It is uncertain whether such results offer reassurance administrators are conducting searches fairly and responsibly given the less than optimum sample size. These results, however, do not necessarily contradict research regarding educational attainment and knowledge of the law; rather, the results reveal a potential gap in research and again, suggest that regardless of the level of educational attainment, students' rights to privacy are not being unduly compromised with searches that are too highly intrusive. Because educational attainment research focused largely on the effect of parent's schooling on the schooling of their children (Holmlund et al., 2008), educational attainment as a measure of economic success (Becker, 1964), the socio-economic status of parents and family background (Bjorklund & Salvanes, 2011), maternal education levels (Black, Devereaux, & Salvanes, 2005), and race as a predictor of educational attainment (Branigan et al., 2013; Caldwell, 2008; Turley, 2009), the present research addressed a critical void in the literature. Investigating shared community norms and subsequent community action regarding issues in schools other than academic achievement would be a logical next step.

Interestingly, the predictor "seriousness of the offense" did significantly predict one construct for search intrusiveness. In cases where the seriousness of the offense increased, the intrusiveness level of the search decreased. This relationship could be attributed to the level of awareness of administrators or school personnel on the importance of conducting searches correctly and equitably, or due to the presence of the police, who have a stricter standard to meet. As discussed, police are required to use probable cause as the standard for searches, while school personnel employ the standard of reasonableness, meaning they can exercise more latitude. A possible implication here is that as the seriousness of the crime is elevated, administrators may feel more pressure to involve police, which triggers the stricter search standard, or at the very least, an understanding by school officials that searches need to be conducted thoughtfully and carefully, no matter the level of education of the community. These results seem to suggest a case-by-case legal sensitivity on the part of school officials as opposed to patterns of actions that are reckless or woefully lack reason.

Future research on the construct of the educational attainment of the community as a whole would be beneficial in informing many areas, including academic achievement and student civil liberties. Possibilities exist for future research in constructing other measures of educational attainment, not just the possession of college degrees. More investigation is needed to more fully understand the link between legal information and educational attainment. Understanding more fully the nature of the acquisition of legal knowledge and the subsequent application of that knowledge to student rights in schools would inform school administrators and policy makers (e.g., examining high school curricula, college and university programs).

The highly nuanced civic action ideal may also be avenue to explore further. It behooves researchers to investigate factors spurring community action and concern in regards to public school issues connected to discipline and civil liberties. For leaders, the potential violations of student's rights to privacy need to be recognized. As discussed in the review of literature, threats to student safety continue to be a pivotal factors in the manner in which administrators employ their discretion for the greater good (Torres & Chen, 2006). Similarly, Furlong, Kingery, and Bates (2001) suggest school shootings such as Columbine have initiated action on the part of public agencies and private institutions to combat the "perceived crisis in schools" (p. 221). Given these greater concerns, the potential exists for school officials to act, even with a thought to the protection of students, in a manner that undermines individual liberties.

In conclusion, community educational attainment fell considerably short of explaining the manner in which students were searched. The findings suggest school officials are signaling awareness of their responsibilities in upholding the reasonableness standard established by the U.S. Supreme Court in *New Jersey v. T.L.O.* (1985) and are conducting searches in an equitable manner, regardless of the level of education of students' community. While the results may instill confidence in the actions of school officials, it remains a goal of public school officials, families, communities, law enforcement, legislatures, and policy makers to ensure students are safe in schools. Safety does not just mean protection from drugs, violence, or the epidemic of bullying currently engulfing this nation. Student safety also means being free from unreasonable violations of privacy in the form of student searches and that school officials receive appropriate training and judgment to ensure student rights are protected. How does legal knowledge inform and potentially spur action? The answer may inform lawmakers and those sworn to uphold the law, and whose institutions rely on the generality of law to provide equitable treatment to different people at different times. School leaders who so often are the ultimate arbiters of law need the skills and encouragement to consider factors demographic and otherwise that may prove to be influential in how critical decisions are made.

## REFERENCES


Agresti, A. (1996a). Order-restricted tests for stratified comparisons of binomial proportions. *Biometrics*, *52*, 1103–1111.

Agresti, A. (1996b). *An introduction to categorical data analysis* (Vol. 135). New York, NY: Wiley.

Antonovics, K. L., & Goldberger, A. S. (2005). Does increasing women's schooling raise the schooling of the next generation? Comment. *American Economic Review*, *95*, 1738–1744.

Becker, G. S. (1964). *Human capital: A theoretical and empirical analysis with special reference to education*. Chicago, IL: University of Chicago Press.

Bjorklund, A., & Salvanes, K. (2011). Education and family background: Mechanisms and policies. *Handbook of the Economics of Education*, *3*, 201–247.

Black, S., Devereaux, P., & Salvanes, K. (2005). The more the merrier? The effect of family composition on children's outcomes. *Journal of Economics*, *120*, 669–700.

*Board of Education v. Earls*, 536 U.S. 822 (2002).

Branigan, A. R., Freese, J., Patir, A., McDade, T. W., Liu, K., & Kiefe, C. I. (2013). Skin color, sex, and educational attainment in the post-civil rights era. *Social Science Research*, *42*(6), 1659–1674.

Byun, S. Y., Meece, J. L., & Irvin, M. J. (2012). Rural-nonrural disparities in postsecondary educational attainment revisited. *American Educational Research Journal*, *49*(3), 412–437.

Caldwell, R., Jr. (2008). Erosion of affirmative action and its consequences for the black-white educational attainment gap. *The University Kansas Law Review*, *57*, 813.

Goodman, J. (1996). Finding common ground in an era of public support. *ASCD*, (7).

Coleman, J., Campbell, E., Hobson, C., McPartland, J., Mood, A., & Weinfield, F. (1966). Equality of educational opportunity. US Department of Health, Education & WelfareWashington, DC: U.S. Government Printing Office.

Coleman, J. S. (1988). Social capital in the creation of human capital. *American Journal of Sociology*, *94*, S95–S120.

Furlong, M. J., Kingery, P. M., & Bates, M. P. (2001). Introduction to the special issue on the appraisal and prediction of school violence. *Psychology in the Schools*, *38*(2), 89–91.

Gluckman, I. B. (1984). Schools searches and the 4th Amendment. *West's Education Law Reporter*, *13*(1), 199–299.

Hanushek, E. A. (2003). The failure of input-based schooling policies. *The Economic Journal*, *113*(485), F64–F98.

Holmlund, H., Lindahl, M., & Plug, E. (2008). *The causal effect of parent's schooling on children's schooling: A comparison of estimation methods* (IZA Working Paper 3630). Retrieved from http://nbn-resolving.de/urn:nbn:de:101:1-20080820153

Hu, S. (2003). Educational aspirations and postsecondary access and choice. *Education Policy Analysis Archives, 11*, 14.

Lindahl, L. (2010). A comparison of family and neighborhood effects on grades, test scores, educational attainment and income: Evidence from Sweden. *Journal of Inequality, 9*(2), 207–226. doi:10.1007/s10888-010-9144-1

Mayer, S. E. (2002). How economic segregation affects children's educational attainment. *Social Forces, 81*(1), 153–176.

*New Jersey v. T.L.O.*, 469 U.S. 325 (1985).

O'Hara, J. U. (1984). Search and seizure analysis in school settings. *West's Education Law Reporter, 13*(1), 1–7.

Orfield, G., & Eaton, S. E. (1996). *Dismantling desegregation: The quiet reversal of Brown v. Board of education*. Cambridge, MA: The New Press.

Owens, A. (2010). Neighborhoods and schools as competing and reinforcing contexts for educational attainment. *Sociology of Education, 83*(4), 287–311.

Ream, R. K., & Palardy, G. J. (2008). Reexamining social class differences in the availability and the educational utility of parental social capital. *American Educational Research Journal, 45*(2), 238–273.

Roscigno, V. J., & Crowle, M. L. (2001). Rurality, institutional disadvantage, and achievement/attainment. *Rural Sociology, 66*(2), 268–292.

*Safford Unified School District v. Redding*, 129 S.Ct. 2633 (2009).

*Vernonia* School District 47J v. Acton, 515 U.S. 646 (1995).

Stefkovich, J., & O'Brien, G. (2001). The fourth amendment and the quest for drug and weapon free schools. *Primer on Legal Affairs for the School Business*, 215–226.

Stefkovich, J. A., & Torres, M. S. (2003). The demographics of justice: Student searches, student rights, and administrator practices. *Educational Administration Quarterly, 39*(2), 259–282.

Torres, M. S. (2003). *The impact of demographics and the political environment on the implementation and interpretation of fourth amendment law in schools*. Doctoral dissertation, Pennsylvania State University.

Torres, M. S., & Chen, Y. (2006). Assessing Columbine's impact on students' fourth amendment case outcomes: Implications for administrative discretion and decision making. *NASSP Bulletin, 90*(3), 185–206.

Turley, R. N. L. (2009). College proximity: Mapping access to opportunity. *Sociology of Education, 82*(2), 126–146.

Wise, V. J., & Schauer, F. (2007). Legal information as social capital. *Law Library Journal, 99*, 267.

# CHAPTER 9

# EDUCATIONAL ADMINISTRATION IN INDIAN COUNTRY: THE PECULIAR POSITION OF INDIGENOUS LANGUAGES, TRIBAL SELF-DETERMINATION, AND FEDERAL POLICY

Hollie J. Mackey

## ABSTRACT

*Educational leaders in schools serving Native American students must understand, communicate, and apply state and federal education policies along with specific federal Indian policies relating to tribal self-determination and the education of these students. Tribal peoples residing in native communities typically view revitalization of indigenous language as a crucial first step in achieving the cross-cultural goal of school success for all tribal children. Inclusion of indigenous languages serves multiple purposes such as transmitting traditional cultural values, supporting overall academic achievement, and fostering self-determination and independence for native communities. Title III and Title VII of*

**Legal Frontiers in Education: Complex Law Issues for Leaders, Policymakers and Policy Implementers**
**Advances in Educational Administration, Volume 24, 165–180**

**ISSN: 1479-3660/doi:10.1108/S1479-366020150000024036**

*the No Child Left Behind Act are the designated policy "homes" for indigenous language inclusion and the Individuals with Disabilities in Education Act addresses indigenous language as an obstacle to overcome, giving the unintended impression that native languages are somehow situated within a deficit framework of poverty and special education. This chapter explores the foundations of the inclusion of native languages into current federal policy and argues that the placement might be better suited as stand-alone legislation in order to more effectively promote community development and self-determination for Native American peoples.*

Well over 200 years of federal Indian policy implementation and judicial interpretation intended to alleviate the "Indian problem" has resulted in an incoherent legal framework through which modern scholars and practitioners must navigate. Scholars often attribute this incoherence to the U.S. Congress' and Supreme Court's neglect in repealing or overturning previous law when new law is implemented (Anderson, Berger, Frickey, & Krakoff, 2008; Frickey, 1997). Others argue that federal Indian law is coherent if understood as "rooted in the fundamental contradiction between the historical fact and continuing realities of colonization ... and the constitutional themes of limited government, democracy, inclusion, and fairness ..." (Frickey, 1993, p. 384). In other words, the historical shifts in federal Indian law illustrate the ongoing tension between a nation established as a free and independent republic in territory requiring colonization of indigenous populations to achieve that freedom and independence.

Additional incoherence is found in the ways in which historians, scholars, and governmental documents refer to the indigenous people of North America, often grouping diverse tribal nations with distinct cultural values and identity under an umbrella term such as Native American or Indian. This chapter uses the terms "Native American," "American Indian," "Indian," and "Indigenous" interchangeably throughout the chapter. The appropriate ethnic title for indigenous tribal people of North America is not agreed upon and many tribal people reject the term "Native American," therefore no standard term is used. Tribal people typically refer to the specific tribe's name when speaking of others and use the term "Indians" when referring to the collective 567 federally recognized tribes.

Native American people have survived the United States government's intentional efforts to remove, assimilate, and terminate them in the name of westward expansion and Manifest Destiny. These same people have relied on federal support to reorganize and develop self-determination strategies for greater tribal control over "Indian Country," a basic jurisdictional concept found in 18 U.S.C. § 1151 (1948) denoting land areas where the federal government and tribal nations typically hold exclusive civil and criminal jurisdiction. In this chapter, the term is used colloquially to denote the regions of land across the United States thought of as belonging to American Indian people including lands within the boundaries of a reservation, dependent Indian communities, and Indian allotments to which titles have not been extinguished. Developing strong systems of education to include pre-school through post-secondary educational opportunities is essential for tribes to realize true self-determination.

Educational leaders in schools serving Native American students must understand, communicate, and apply state and federal education policies along with specific federal Indian policies relating to tribal self-determination and the education of these students. Similarly, policy-makers should understand and be mindful of the legislative history of federal involvement with Indian Education when crafting education policy. The degree to which educational leaders or policy-makers understand federal policy supporting tribal self-determination is unclear; however, native communities across the United States have earnestly sought to restore tribal customs and values through schools serving tribal children. Tribal peoples residing in native communities typically view revitalization of indigenous language as a crucial first step in achieving the cross-cultural goal of cultural restoration and school success for all tribal children (Lomawaima & McCarty, 2006). Inclusion of indigenous languages serves multiple purposes such as transmitting traditional cultural values, supporting overall academic achievement, and fostering self-determination and independence for native communities (Lomawaima & McCarty, 2006).

The abovementioned lack of understanding coupled with the momentum of self-determination goals in tribal communities places native languages in a peculiar position in American schools. Policy-makers have established Title III and Title VII of *Public Law 107-110*, the No Child Left Behind Act of 2001 (NCLB) (formerly named the Elementary and Secondary Education Act) as the designated policy "homes" for indigenous language inclusion and instruction. Similarly, indigenous languages are often addressed through *Public Law 101-476*, the Individuals with Disabilities Education Act (IDEA) (formerly named the *Education for All Handicapped Children Act of 1975*) as an obstacle to overcome. Combined, these policy placements give the unintended impression that native languages are situated within a deficit framework of poverty and special education.

Educational leaders and policy-makers pay scant attention to the far more important legal foundation for inclusion of indigenous languages in schools, as a function of self-determination, found in *Public Law 93-638*, the Indian Self-Determination and Education Assistance Act of 1975, which includes the following policy goal:

> Congress has recognized the obligation of the United States to respond to the strong expression of the Indian people for self-determination by assuring maximum Indian participation in the direction, planning, conduct and administration of educational as well as other Federal programs and services to Indian communities so as to render such programs and services more responsive to the needs and desires of those communities. (Sec. 900.3 (a)(1))

This chapter discusses the historical perspective of Indian education and inclusion of native languages into federal policy, examines these policies through a Tribal Critical Theory lens, introduces a proposition that promotes legally just processes and outcomes for native communities, and makes recommendations for improving educational leadership preparation and practice. It concludes by contending the placement, or policy "home," for native languages would be better suited as stand-alone legislation in order to more effectively promote community development and self-determination of Native American peoples.

## TOWARDS UNDERSTANDING FEDERAL INDIAN LAW

An understanding of federal Indian policy is imperative for understanding how federal Indian law has developed from various policy goal perspectives. According to Royster, Blumm, and Kronk (2013), "Like a perpetual wave machine, federal policy has flowed between two poles: the protection of tribal autonomy on the one hand, and the incorporation and assimilation of Indians into the majority society on the other" (p. 51). Similarly, the history of Indian education is complex and often difficult to understand. There is no single narrative or logical progression from first establishment to contemporary constructs with improvements along the way driven by the desire of ensuring the common good of the nation. Rather, education in Native American communities is only understandable as the manifestation of two centuries of Congressional uncertainty in addressing the socio-cultural, ethnic, and political construct of the American Indian.

This uncertainty is illustrated through distinct policy eras that emerged as "one of the competing norms [became] dominant over the other" (Royster et al., 2013, p. 51). Approaches to education were also uncertain and dependent on the stance towards Indians in any given era. The next section will establish the basic history of federal policy affecting Native American education beginning with an overview of foundational concepts of land titles, plenary authority, and jurisdiction followed by a closer examination of federal policy focusing on the Allotment and Assimilation Era (1871) to present.

### *Incoherent Doctrine and the Effects on Indian Education*

The federal government holds exclusive authority over Indian affairs through Art. 1, § 8, Cl. 3 of the United States Constitution that empowers Congress "[t]o regulate Commerce with foreign Nations, and among the several States, and with the Indian Tribes." The President, with consent from the Senate, is empowered to make treaties (Art. 2, § 2, Cl. 2) with treaty enforcement protected by the Supremacy Clause (Art. VI). The relationship between the federal government and tribes was further defined through the Trade and Intercourse Acts (1790–1834) that established a regulatory process for trade, a criminal and compensatory scheme for interracial crimes, and most importantly, prohibition of buying and selling Indian lands without federal consent (Prucha, 1986). The Trade and Intercourse Acts protected Indians from unscrupulous colonists, and while the Acts affected external relations, they recognized tribal autonomy by not interfering with the internal working affairs of tribes. Concurrently, the United States Supreme Court was interpreting the legal contours of these enumerated powers and statutes under the guidance of Chief Justice John Marshall. The Marshall Court heard three important cases between 1823 and 1832 that laid the foundations for federal Indian law that are present still today. These cases, known as the Marshall Trilogy, include *Johnson v. McIntosh* (1823) where the Court ruled Indian tribes had only occupancy rights on tribal land, *Cherokee Nation v. Georgia* that established Indian tribes were "domestic-dependent nations" whose relationship to the United States resembles that of a ward to his guardian (30 U.S. (5 Pet.) 1, 17, 1831), and *Worcester v. Georgia* that identified tribes as "distinct political communities" that had exclusive authority over the land within the defined territorial boundary of their individual nations (31 U.S. (6 Pet.) 515, 557, 1832). This meant States' laws did not apply in Indian territories. Despite the *Worcester* ruling, Georgia continued meeting with some members of the Cherokee nation to negotiate tribal relocation, triggering the Trail of Tears before the federal government could enforce the Supreme Court's decision.

The Reservation Era (1848–1886) marks a shift in policy from tribal autonomy to federal interference with the internal affairs of tribes. As the nation grew so did demand for land and the realization that maintaining an Indian Territory was not possible against the backdrop of Westward Expansion. Assimilation strategies included forcing Indians onto concentrated areas of land where federal Indian agents could begin the work of "civilizing" the tribes through Christianization and promotion of an agricultural lifestyle. The primary tool for this approach to civilization in the wake of colonization was Indian boarding schools designed to divest native people of all cultural ties and inculcate them into the dominant Western society (Churchill, 2004). This is the setting for the often-cited phrase: "Kill the Indian, save the man." The guiding principles and rationale behind federal policy from the Reservation Era through the beginning of the Reorganization Era (1928) included: "(1) the 'need' for inculcation of individualism among native people, (2) to achieve this end Indians should be universally 'educated' to hold eurowestern beliefs, and, (3) all Indians, duly educated and thus individualized, should be absorbed as citizens into the U.S. body politic" (Churchill, 2004, p. xvii). Indian boarding schools were devastating to tribal people who were inculcated into viewing their culture through the eyes of the colonizers once it had been fully stripped from their consciousness (Churchill, 2004). Many of these schools used torture and abuse to gain compliance along with sexual predation to the extent that the majority of children placed in these schools experienced occurrences of rape, often repeated for years (Churchill, 2004).

The Allotment and Assimilation Era ushered in "extreme judicial deference to Congress, even in the absence of a clear constitutional basis" (Royster et al., 2013, p. 55). In *United States v. Kagama*, 118 U.S. 375 (1986), the Supreme Court held federal interference in matters of "major crimes" was valid as an execution of general federal power in protecting the "dependent" Indian nations. Federal plenary authority was used as the basis for allowing the federal government to unilaterally abrogate treaties in *Lone Wolf v. Hitchcock*, 187 U.S. 553 (1903). While these examples demonstrate deference to Congress, the Supreme Court held, conversely, that tribes had reserved rights stemming from inherent sovereignty that pre-dated the establishment of the United States in *United States v. Winans*, 198 U.S. 371 (1905). This begs the question, how can federal policy interfere with the internal affairs of Indians when tribes hold inherent sovereignty over tribal members and tribal lands? *Cherokee Nation v. Georgia* held tribes were domestic-dependent nations while *Worcester* established tribal authority over internal working affairs within the boundaries of tribal land. How is it possible for Congress to work around these constitutional interpretations and have the Supreme Court reject precedence in favor of general federal power and the Supremacy Clause?

### *Reorganization and a Positive Shift in Policy*

The Reorganization Era ushered in another shift in federal policy resulting in laws intended to support tribal self-government, due in large part to the Meriam Report (1928), which "detailed the economic, social, and cultural devastation of the allotment policy" (Royster et al., 2013, p. 55). Unilaterally condemning allotment and assimilation policy due to governmental inaction, Anderson et al., 2008 state, "It almost seems as if the government assumed that some magic in individual ownership of property would in itself prove an educational civilizing factor, but unfortunately this policy has for the most part operated in the opposite direction" (2013, p. 131). In response, Congress passed the Indian Reorganization Act 1934, 25 U.S.C. § 461, that ended the practice of allotment, held existing allotments in trust, returned some reservation lands back to the tribes to be held in trust, and provided "a mechanism for tribes to organize as constitutional governments and to obtain business charters" (p. 55). The Meriam Report addressed education directly, stating "[t]he survey staff finds itself obliged to say frankly and unequivocally that the provisions for the care of the Indian children in boarding schools are grossly inadequate" (1928, p. 11). The report noted poor diet, disease, poor living conditions, overcrowded dormitories, lack of toilet facilities and soap, extreme child labor, and unsafe working conditions. The Meriam Report addresses the matter of academic achievement and language by stating:

> Some years ago in an effort to raise standards the Indian Service adopted a uniform curriculum for all Indian Schools. Modern experience has demonstrated that the effective device for raising standards is not curriculum control but the establishment of high minimum qualifications for the teaching staff. The uniform curriculum works badly because it does not permit of relating teaching to the needs of the particular Indian children being taught. It requires the same work for Indian children who are the first generation to attend school and who do not speak English as it does for those who are of the third generation of school children, who have long been in contact with the whites, and speak English in the home. (p. 13)

These criticisms are not unlike contemporary debates among policy-makers, educational leaders, and education scholars who all provide perspectives on high quality, relevant curriculum, highly qualified teachers, differentiated instruction, and language support. The problems revealed through the Meriam Report are still present and yet to be remedied through federal law.

The Meriam Report demonstrates the nexus between *American* education and *American Indian* education that becomes the catalyst for widespread Indian education reform founded on the philosophy of John Dewey and other progressive educators of the time. The American education system was under national scrutiny in general and Dr. W. Carson Ryan, Jr., another prominent scholar from the Progressive Education group, wrote the education section of the Meriam Report through the existing filter of widespread national educational reform (Reyhner & Eder, 2004). The Indian Reorganization Act prompted a shift in the approach to Indian education from boarding school to Indian day schools, however many of the boarding schools remained operational. In February 1932, the academic journal *Progressive Education* released a special issue dedicated to Indian education that advocated teachers should receive training in progressive approaches to teaching prior to returning to teach Native American students (Reyhner & Eder, 2004). Of particular note, John Collier, Indian advocate and primary author of the Indian Reorganization Act, envisioned tribal self-government inclusive of bilingual schools that would serve both adults and children in native communities.

The federal trust responsibility required Congress provide for the education of Native American students. As the number of schools and districts increased, management became difficult, leading to the Johnson O'Malley Act of 1934 that allowed the Secretary of the Interior to contract with States for the provision of educational services in public schools to Indian children. This allowed Indian students to attend public schools or Bureau of Indian Affairs (BIA) schools, prompting building construction on tribal lands and increased numbers of accredited schools across the nation (Reyhner & Eder, 2004). The number of BIA schools has decreased considerably since public schools were first opened to Native American children; however, this dual system of education has survived with both public and BIA schools operating in Indian Country.

Progressive education as a strategy for improving Indian education waned as Indian schools focused more on "life adjustment" classes rather than academic content. The primary issue hindering successful implementation of a progressive approach was that it required extremely creative and gifted instructors (Reyhner & Eder, 2004). In *A Century of Failed School Reform*, Diane Ravitch concludes, "When used by teachers who saw activities as a better way of teaching subject matter ... the activity program was valuable. But in the hands of teachers who lacked subject matter knowledge, the activities became ends in themselves" (2000, p. 244). World War II largely stalled all education improvements for Native American communities as funds were diverted to the war effort followed by another shift in federal policy post-war that returned to promoting assimilation of American Indians through the Termination and Relocation Era (1944–1969). This was short lived as Congress recognized the folly in the policy leading to the current Self-Determination Era (1961–present).

Congress passed several laws triggering the Self-Determination Era, particularly in the field of education. Multiple analyses of the history of Indian education cite the distinct assimilative approach either overtly or covertly evident in curriculums, structures, and processes of schools. Beginning with the Meriam Report (1928), echoed in the Kennedy Report (1969), restated in the Bureau of Indian Affairs Report on BIA Education (1988), and reinforced through annual reports in compliance with NCLB. In response, Congress has attempted to address matters of self-determination and cultural restoration, particularly for native languages, however whether out of convenience or oversight, bilingual education remains housed in laws intended to alleviate poverty and support individualized instructional programs for special needs students. Public Law 89-10, the Elementary and Secondary Education Act of 1965 (ESEA), one of President Johnson's War on Poverty bills, absorbed the Bilingual Education Act as Title VII to support bilingual education and teaching English as a second language, and Impact Aid provided crucial funding to support new school construction and funding to offset state revenue losses for un-taxable land. The Indian Self-Determination and Educational Assistance Act of 1975 (*Public Law 638*) provides greater control over federal programs in Indian Country, authority for tribes to enter into contracts with external entities, block grants for construction, and numerous categorical grant opportunities to support tribally controlled schools and public schools serving predominantly Native American students.

More recently, Congress passed the Tribally Controlled Schools Act (1988) that provides greater administrative flexibility for tribally controlled schools and the Public Law 101-477, Native American Languages Act (1990) that acknowledges the importance of preserving native languages. The 2001 reauthorization of ESEA, renamed the NCLB Act and the reauthorization of the Individuals with Disabilities in Education

Improvement Act (IDEIA) (2007) brought about sweeping shifts in attitudes about Native American education because the disaggregation of subgroup data mandated by NCLB illustrated the lack of gains in Indian education and the overrepresentation of native children in special education despite nearly 30 years of federal policy intended to reverse this dismal trend. The next section analyzes current federal law supporting tribal self-determination in education as it applies to cultural revitalization and native languages through the lens of Tribal Critical Theory (TribalCrit).

## NO PONIES, ONLY PIGS

The Reservation Era created one of the most restrictive environments found in the United States outside of penitentiary or detention facilities. Native Americans were not yet considered fully human, nor were they recognized as having any of the rights conferred to all other citizens of the United States at that time, even in the wake of the Civil War and the ratification of the Fifteenth Amendment (1870) prohibiting state and federal denial of voting rights because of race, color, or previous condition of servitude. American Indians were prohibited from leaving reservations without permission: federal policy aligned with the maxim "no ponies, only pigs." This and other "civilization" regulations intended to promote an agrarian lifestyle and deter renegade Indians from attempting to leave the reservation on horseback had no federal law underlying their promulgation or enforcement yet remained in place when challenged.

As discussed in earlier sections, understanding federal Indian law requires an understanding of the interplay of racial and colonial constructs as they apply to U.S. policy development that vacillates between assimilation on one hand and self-determination on the other hand. Critical Race Theory (CRT) has been used to analyze the phenomenon of race-based discrimination embedded within law and policy. However, CRT falls short of explaining the full spectrum of both overt and covert discrimination found in federal Indian law and judicial interpretations of these laws. Brayboy (2005) theorizes a more appropriate construct for understanding Indian education is through the lens of TribalCrit, stating "[t]he basic premise of CRT is that racism is endemic in society. In contrast, the basic tenet of TribalCrit is the notion that colonization is endemic to society. By colonization, I mean that European American thought, knowledge, and power structures dominate present-day society in the United States" (p. 429).

TribalCrit recognizes the role race plays in legal constructs affecting American Indians, yet, maintains race as a secondary premise behind colonization.

Federal Indian education policy has been used as a weapon to deconstruct indigenous knowledge and fracture the relationships of Native American people, a necessary element for successful colonization. Native inhabitants of North America were considered uncivilized by western European standards that placed value on individual wealth accumulation and the use of natural resources as a means of accumulating that wealth. It was unthinkable that American Indians would have access to the vast "wilderness" of the continent without actively seeking to tame and harvest all that was available. Battiste (2002) argues, "Eurocentric thinkers dismissed Indigenous knowledge in the same way they dismissed any socio-political cultural life they did not understand: they found it to be unsystematic and incapable of meeting the productivity needs of the modern world" (p. 5).

Even under the best of circumstances, Indian education marginalized Native American culture by painting broad foundational strokes of assimilation. For example, the Indian Self-Determination and Educational Assistance Act of 1975 provides greater tribal autonomy yet gives the federal government the final decision-making authority regarding the ways in which tribes utilize their autonomy. Understanding the importance of native languages for transmitting cultural values and supporting self-determination, the federal government included these languages into the Bilingual Education Act; however, this Act found its policy home as Title VII of the NCLB Act. NCLB is the result of multiple iterations of the Elementary and Secondary Education Act, a poverty bill meant to divert federal money to public education for increasing access and equity. Further, the IDEIA serves a disproportionate number of American Indian students, often mislabeled due to limited English skills presenting as learning or speech disability. TribalCrit explains the misplacement of native languages into poverty and disability legislation as a natural result of colonial thinking whereby everything falling outside the norm of western constructs of education are viewed as a deficit, therefore embedded in deficit theory legislation. It is unlikely native languages and other educational issues supporting tribal self-determination will find their way into mainstream State level legislation, however removing them from deficit theory legislation would serve to "decolonize" native language inclusion and instruction by recognizing the merit of including these languages independent of federal mandate.

## EDUCATIONAL ADMINISTRATION FOR LEGALLY JUST OUTCOMES

School administrators have significant influence on student achievement school culture. Administrators in schools serving American Indian children have access to a greater number of resources, both from the state and federal governments and the local community. Tribal values and the practices that stem from them provide an alternative approach to educational reform and improved academic achievement in schools serving native students. Native American culture is premised on the interconnectedness of all people and things. Similarly, scholars maintain the premise that successful schools rest on the interconnectedness of all facets of the school community. This shared understanding of community is central for facilitating legally just outcomes for Native American students and communities. TribalCrit is a community-oriented theoretical lens that views communities as complete only when all of the individuals within the community have contributed to the whole. If school administrators serving Indian students placed genuine value on indigenous knowledge, tribal languages would be centrally placed in the curriculum, not as a federal mandate but in recognition of their importance for tribal self-determination. Brayboy (2005) asserts:

> [T]he fact that the knowledge and skill sets [Native American students] acquired at the [school] institution, combined with their Indigenous ways of knowing, would help them better meet the educational and cultural needs of their communities .... [highlighting] the importance of making connections between different types and forms of knowledge in order to meet larger, community goals of self-education and sovereignty. (p. 426)

Elevating native languages is in contrast to the language native people have grown accustomed to, the language that continually reinforces the inferiority of a people whose history is largely invisible prior to 1776 through the eyes of colonizing education policy. Federal policy has used language to denigrate Native American people since the inception of the United States. School administrators are in a position to correct this by recognizing native languages and indigenous knowledge as valuable and central to developing school communities that support academic success and tribal self-determination.

School administrators have the ability to organize community efforts to place native language inclusion before State level legislators and lobby for policies that recognize the importance of language in transmitting cultural values. However, most administrators know very little about the struggle for native language and cultural revitalization against the backdrop of 200 years of assimilation policies. Rather than hope school administrators working in Native American communities will gain a deep understanding of these marginalizing policies through on-the-job training, these matters should be addressed through leadership preparation programs. The fundamental concepts found in Native American culture are not only relevant for these communities but also they are healing values that have the potential to profoundly transform education through a philosophical shift administration.

## INDIGENOUS VALUES AND LEADERSHIP PREPARATION

The values of American Indians and indigenous people around the globe should not be reduced to imply there is one static set of values; however, LaDonna Harris (Brannum, 2014) submits that despite the myriad of differenced found in and among indigenous people, there are undeniable commonalities. These commonalities inform the foundation for an Ethic of Indigeneity I have developed and introduced here as an applied ethical lens informing educational leadership for socially just and interconnected responses to an increasingly globalized society focused on acquiring resources and wealth. The Ethic of Indigeneity is the counter narrative to acquisition that instead focuses on how we are going to live with one another in a pluralistic society. The Ethic of Indigeneity asserts:

1. All matters can be reduced to relationships between people and in and among communities. Indigenous values are defined through the relational nature of all people.
2. Community is comprised of family and each family member has a responsibility to be an individual while remaining a part of the collective. Despite differences, all belief systems are valued and allowed without forcing those systems on others.
3. The political contours within schools are not reduced to an either/or, this or that reductionist point of reference. Multiple solutions can exist but these solutions are not predicated on the exclusion of all other possible solutions.
4. Indigenous knowledge requires the individual to continually strive to find someone to replace them to ensure the transmission of invaluable lessons to the next generation.

Leadership preparation programs already address issues of social justice, law, and ethical decision-making. Incorporating a formal applied ethical frame, the Ethic of Indigeneity, would provide legitimacy to historically marginalized indigenous knowledge while providing future educational leaders with another tool that might find utility in practice.

## CONCLUSION

This chapter identified federal Indian law and American Indian education policy that undermines the federal government's stated policy goal of tribal self-determination. The historic foundation of incoherent doctrine and judicial interpretation devoid of any actual legal standing has created an impossible framework that hinders tribal self-determination for education. The most recent policy era has included a number of laws intended to facilitate greater tribal control over education however, these policies inadvertently communicate the pervasive message that native languages and cultural revitalization are a deficit to overcome manifestations of poverty and disability.

School administrators in schools serving American Indian students are required to adhere to the same federal policy mandates as all other public schools in the nation, specifically NCLB and IDEA but this does not mean that they cannot reframe native language inclusion and instruction within their own schools outside these particular policies. Understanding the history of federal Indian education policy through a TribalCrit lens provides administrators with the ability to understand these policies as the lingering remnants of assimilation and colonization as they are currently conceptualized within contemporary education policy.

Leadership preparation that includes practice in ethical decision-making aligned with the premise of the developing Ethic of Indigeneity provides future leaders the opportunity to discuss the importance of indigenous knowledge and values and gives them an additional tool for ethical decision-making in the field. Indigenous knowledge and ways of understanding are not isolated as applicable only to indigenous people. They are founded on the interrelatedness of people, require responsibility of community members to both themselves and the collective, and do not make political value judgments between differing beliefs, instead respecting the multiple perspectives inherent to a pluralistic society. Finally, an indigenous knowledge requires that individuals must replace themselves to continue the transmission of cultural and epistemological understanding. Indigenous values serve to fill in the gaps of western values as applied to globalization and increasing interdependence between differing cultures. Western notions of globalization are founded on getting resources and acquiring wealth; Indigenous notions of globalization seek understanding in how to live with one another.

Native language inclusion and instruction would be better served as a vehicle for tribal educational self-determination if they were not embedded within deficit theory policies addressing poverty and special education. School administrators need not wait for an official policy shift to begin including native languages as a normative feature in schools serving Native American students.

## REFERENCES

18 U.S.C. § 1151. (1948). The Indian Country Statute.

Art. 1 U.S.C. § 8, Cl.3.

Art. 2 U.S.C. § 2, Cl.2.

Anderson, R. T., Berger, B., Frickey, P. P., & Krakoff, S. (2008). *American Indian law: Cases and commentary* (2nd ed.). St. Paul, MN: West Group.

Battiste, M. (2002). *Indigenous knowledge and pedagogy in First Nations education: A literature review with recommendations*. Ottawa: Apamuwek Institute.

Brannum, J. (2014). *Ladonna Harris: Indian 101*. Cleveland, OH: Nara Mui Films.

Brayboy, B. M. J. (2005). Toward a tribal critical race theory in education. *The Urban Review*, *37*(5), 425–446.

Cherokee Nation v. Georgia. (1831). 30 U.S. (5 Pet.) 1, 17, 1831.

Churchill, W. (2004). *Kill the Indian, save the man: The genocidal impact of American Indian residential schools*. San Francisco, CA: City Lights Books.

Frickey, P. P. (1993). Marshalling past and present: Colonialism, constitutionalism, and interpretation in federal Indian law. *Harvard Law Review*, *107*(384), 381–440. Retrieved from http://scholarship.law.berkeley.edu/facpubs/1841

Frickey, P. P. (1997). Adjudication and its discontents: Coherence and conciliation in federal Indian law. *Harvard Law Review*, *110*(1174), 1754–1784. Retrieved from http://scholarship.law.berkeley.edu/facpubs/1920

Indian Reorganization Act 1934 25 U.S.C. § 461.

Johnson v. McIntosh, 21 U.S. (8 Wheat.) 543 (1823).

Lomawaima, K. T., & McCarty, T. (2006). *To remain an Indian: Lessons in democracy from a century of Native American education*. New York, NY: Teachers College Press.

Lone Wolf v. Hitchcock, 187 U.S. 553 (1903).

Merriam, L. (1928). *The problem of Indian administration*. Report of a survey made at the request of Honorable Hubert Work, Secretary of the Interior, and Submitted to Him, February 21, 1928.

Prucha, F. P. (1986). *The great father: The United States Government and the American Indians* (abridged ed.). Lincoln, NE: University of Nebraska Press.

Public Law 89-10, the Elementary and Secondary Education Act of (1965).

Public Law 107-110, *the No Child Left Behind Act of 2001.*

Public Law 101-476, *the Individuals with Disabilities in Education Act of 1997 and 2004.*

Public Law 101-477, Native American Languages Act of (1990).

Public Law 93-638, *the Indian Self-Determination and Education Assistance Act of 1975.*

Ravitch, D. (2000). *A century of failed school reform.* New York, NY: Simon and Schuster.

Reyhner, J., & Eder, J. (2004). *American Indian education: A history.* Norman, OK: University of Oklahoma Press.

Royster, J., Blumm, M. C., & Kronk Warner, E. A. (2013). *Native American natural resources law: Cases and materials.* Durham, NC: Carolina Academic Press.

The Kennedy Report. (1969). *Indian education: A national tragedy, a national challenge.* Senate Special Subcommittee on Indian Education.

United States v. Kagama, 118 U.S. 375 (1986).

United States v. Winans, 198 U.S. 371 (1905).

United States (1988). *Report on BIA education: Excellence in Indian education through the effective schools process* [Final review draft]. Washington, DC: Office of Indian Education Programs, Bureau of Indian Affairs, U.S. Department of the Interior.

25 U.S.C. § 2501, Tribally Controlled Schools Act of (1988).

Worcester v. Georgia, 31 U.S. (6 Pet.) 515 (1832).

# CHAPTER 10

# HOPE FOR HOMELESS YOUTH: THE MCKINNEY-VENTO ACT AND THE PROMISE OF EDUCATIONAL ACCESS AND OPPORTUNITY

Susan C. Bon and Nicole D. Snyder

## ABSTRACT

*The McKinney-Vento Homeless Assistance Act (42 U.S.C. 11431 et seq.) establishes basic levels of service, support, and protection for homeless students and families in the United States and specifically prohibits discrimination while ensuring educational rights. According to the 2014 Annual Homeless Assessment Report, homelessness continues to be a pervasive concern, particularly for children under the age of 18 who account for nearly 25% (135,701) of homeless individuals, and youth between 18 and 24 who represent nearly 10% (58,601) of the homeless population. Despite the statutory protections afforded by McKinney-Vento, a number of barriers persist and prevent full enjoyment of the basic rights established by the Act. Overcoming these barriers in the courts has provided some relief, but is insufficient given the limits of McKinney-Vento. Thus, homeless students and families need school leaders who promote social justice and educational opportunities to prepare*

**Legal Frontiers in Education: Complex Law Issues for Leaders, Policymakers and Policy Implementers**
**Advances in Educational Administration, Volume 24, 181–200**

**ISSN: 1479-3660/doi:10.1108/S1479-366020150000024037**

*them for meaningful participation in democratic society. This chapter provides analysis regarding the legal rights of homeless youth, including an overview of significant cases and federal policy updates, and concludes with several recommendations for school leaders to establish clear guidelines and implement procedures to address the educational needs of homeless students.*

## INTRODUCTION

The number of homeless families and children is on the rise in the United States given recent economic struggles and the 2007 recession (National Alliance to End Homelessness, n.d.). According to the National Alliance to End Homelessness, 578,424 people experienced homelessness in January 2012 on any given night. The Department of Housing and Urban Development reported that 216,261 people in families were homeless on a single night in 2014 in the United States (HUD Exchange, n.d.). Families and students who are experiencing homelessness face especially harsh realities in educational systems that are poorly funded and inadequately prepared to respond to the growing numbers of homeless youth and families. In order to break the cycle of poverty and promote opportunity for this disadvantaged population of students, school systems must recognize both the moral and legal imperative to provide an education to students who are experiencing homelessness.

This chapter will focus on the educational needs and challenges facing children and youth who fall within this homeless population. In the United States, homeless children are struggling academically (National Center on Family Homelessness, 2009) with lower grades, higher suspension rates, and greater identification of emotional and learning disabilities than their peers (Wiik, 2009). Perhaps the most important reason for the low academic performance of homeless children is that they do not attend school on a regular basis. Although 87% of homeless youth are enrolled in school, only 77% attend school regularly (National Center for Homeless Education, 2014). The purpose of this chapter is multi-pronged: to provide an overview of local, state, and national laws of the United States that protect the rights of homeless students, to examine the moral and legal consequences of decision-making involving this protected population, and to consider future implications for a school leader working within a school district to address the needs of homeless students and their families.

Homeless children and those who work to help them must overcome a variety of serious and urgent problems. Many of these problems, such as obtaining food, shelter, and medical attention, often take precedence over educational concerns. In other words, the educational needs of homeless children may not be perceived as an immediate threat given the other pressing areas of need such as shelter and nutrition. However, adequate education for homeless children is perhaps the most important key to break the cycle of poverty and homelessness in which such children find themselves.

Schools may provide the only stable and safe environment that these students will experience in a day; thus, school systems must develop the capacity to ensure that homeless students not only receive the educational services to which they are entitled, but also the necessary nutritional as well as caring and competent staff who are dedicated to serving this disadvantaged student population. School administrators are in a critical position to lead a staff committed to knowing the community in order to identify students for whom homelessness may be an issue and be aware of the resources available in the community to provide necessary assistance.

Similarly, school leaders and educational communities must increase their awareness and preparedness to provide support for homeless students and families who are no longer isolated to urban settings (National Alliance to End Homelessness, 2010) and may also be immigrants from impoverished global communities who have fled to the United States and other nations to escape instabilities in their home countries (Toro, 2007). Such preparation includes identifying available resources in the community to provide necessary assistance and utilizing international, national, state, and local laws to protect the rights of homeless students and their families. Given the lack of a global term or definition for homeless individuals, we will rely on the statutory definition of homelessness provided by the McKinney-Vento Homeless Assistance Act (McKinney-Vento, 2002) as it is most directly applicable to our focus on the educational rights of students and youth in the United States.

## MCKINNEY-VENTO ACT

Early efforts to establish basic levels of service and support for homeless children and their families had originated in the McKinney Act 1987.

Subsequent reauthorizations have strengthened protections and the Act is currently titled McKinney-Vento Homeless Assistance Act (2002). McKinney-Vento seeks to remedy the numerous challenges and impediments to regular school attendance by children who are homeless. Specifically, McKinney-Vento prohibits educational discrimination and promotes the educational rights of homeless children and youth by requiring each local educational agency (LEAs) to make case-by-case determinations for individual children based on their best interests. Homeless children and youths are defined as individuals who lack a fixed, regular, and adequate nighttime residence. According to the Act, if a child's nighttime residence is shared with other persons due to loss of housing, economic hardship, or similar reason, the child is homeless. Likewise, if the child is sleeping in a motel or on a camping ground due to lack of alternative accommodation, or is sleeping in a "car, park, public space, abandoned building, substandard housing, bus or train station, or similar setting" (42 U.S.C.S. § 11302 (a)(2)), the child is homeless. Further, a child is to be considered homeless even if he or she is in an "emergency or transitional shelter, [or has been] abandoned in a hospital, [or is] awaiting foster care placement" (42 U.S.C.S. § 11434a (2)(B)(i)).

The Education for Homeless Children and Youth (EHCY) Program of McKinney-Vento was reauthorized under the No Child Left Behind Act of 2001 (2002), and is known as the McKinney-Vento Homeless Education Assistance Improvements Act. Among the most important provisions of the EHCY Program is the requirement that all states, whether the state is receiving funding from the Act or not, ensure that all homeless children receive the same free appropriate public education that is available to other, non-homeless children (McKinney-Vento, 2002). One goal is to ensure that students are able to remain in their current school, as this is expected to support academic success for students in homeless situations by providing stability and improved opportunities and services.

The EHCY Program also requires each state to create and submit a detailed plan for addressing the educational needs of children and youth who are homeless (McKinney-Vento, 2002). A state coordinator must also be identified and tasked with developing and carrying out the state plan. The state plan must clearly establish how the state will proactively identify homeless children, as well as how it will ensure that homeless children have access to the same programs and opportunities available to non-homeless children. In addition, a district level homeless education liaison must be identified to work collaboratively with the state coordinator to implement and oversee the state plan. Finally, the state plan must also identify and articulate strategies to address the key barriers to educational success for students who are homeless. These barriers include (a) lack of transportation, (b) bureaucratic enrollment requirements, and (c) stigma (McKinney-Vento, 2002).

### *Lack of Transportation*

The McKinney-Vento Act states "the State and its local educational agencies will adopt policies and practices to ensure that transportation is provided, at the request of the parent or guardian (or in the case of an unaccompanied youth, the liaison), to and from the school of origin" (2002, § 11432(g)(1)(J)(iii)). In addition to ensuring that homeless children are not prevented from attending school simply because they lack transportation, by specifically referring to the school of origin, this provision also provides homeless children with a sense of educational stability. Even if they are forced to move from shelter to shelter, the state is required to transport them to the school they have always attended. Practically speaking, this means that if a child once lived on the east side of town, but now lives in an emergency shelter on the west side of town, the Act requires that the state make a reasonable effort to transport the child to her original school located on the east side of town. This provision is not an affirmative guarantee of transportation for homeless children. Rather, the parent/guardian or liaison is required to request that the school district provide such transportation when/if needed, in order to trigger the transportation provision. Once the parent/guardian requests transportation, the school district is required to provide it; however, safety, travel time, and student well-being overall may also be considered when making the determination about transportation services. If it is in the student's best interest to continue his or her education in the school of origin, then the LEAs must provide or arrange transportation to and from the school of origin.

### *Bureaucratic Enrollment Requirements*

In addition to addressing the issue of transportation, the Act also requires that LEAs develop strategies to address "problems resulting from enrollment delays that are caused by – (i) immunization and medical records requirements; (ii) residency requirements; (iii) lack of birth certificates, school records, or other documentation; (iv) guardianship issues; or

(v) uniform or dress code requirements" (2002, § 11432(g)(1)(H)). Unlike the transportation provision, this is an affirmative responsibility placed on school districts to create educational policy that provides homeless children with reasonable and timely access to public education. McKinney-Vento establishes an immediate enrollment requirement for homeless children or youth, despite the inability to produce the required enrollment records (§ 11432(g)(2)(C)(i)).

### *Stigma*

Finally, the Act addresses the potentially debilitating stigma faced by homeless students. It requires state educational agency (SEAs) and LEAs to provide assurances that they "will adopt policies and practices to ensure that homeless children and youths are not stigmatized or segregated on the basis of their status as homeless" (2002, § 11432(g)(1)(H)). The language of this provision is broad; thus, it is not merely a recommendation that school districts avoid segregative practices and the stigmatizing of homeless children. Rather, this provision establishes a clear mandate to SEAs and LEAs to proactively determine ways to ensure that homeless children are not stigmatized by administrators, teachers, or students while pursuing a public education (§ 722(g)(3)(B)(i)).

## ADVOCACY GROUPS

Despite the statutory protections afforded to homeless children and youth by McKinney-Vento, a number of barriers persist and prevent full enjoyment of the basic rights established by the Act (2002). These barriers have been the focus of a number of lawsuits and include, for example, systemic violations of transportation mandates, failure to ensure educational access, inadequate identification of homeless youth (*Collier v. Board of Education of Prince George's County*, 2001), and misinterpretation of the statutory definition of homelessness (*Bullock v. Board of Education of Montgomery County*, 2002). Advocacy groups have intervened in an effort to protect the rights of homeless children. While efforts to enforce compliance with the McKinney-Vento provisions have led to a small number of class action as well as individual lawsuits, as discussed below, primary efforts have focused on education and awareness of the laws protecting the rights of homeless children. Thus, increasing awareness of the educational needs of homeless children is a central focus of many advocacy groups.

Advocacy groups such as the National Law Center on Homelessness and Poverty (NLCHP) are critical partners in the battle to overcome educational barriers posed by homelessness. As an advocacy group, the NLCHP has a clear focus on compliance with the legislative mandates, but also asserts that preventive strategies such as outreach and education are likewise effective means of promoting compliance. This organization includes primarily attorneys who are focused on ending homelessness. The National Association for the Education of Homeless Children and Youth (NAEHCY) has similar goals as the NLCHP, but focuses specifically on advocating for the education of children and youth experiencing homelessness. In addition to an advocacy role, NAEHCY seeks to build strong partnerships with schools and communities, and also focuses on increasing awareness through education (National Association for the Education of Homeless Children and Youth, n.d.).

## JUDICIAL INTERVENTION: CASES

Mechanisms within the McKinney-Vento Act (2002) offer an opportunity for SEAs and LEAs to address issues regarding homeless children and youths without the need to resort to costly and protracted litigation and judicial intervention, thus many legal disputes over McKinney-Vento services have been handled at the administrative level. The McKinney-Vento Act requires each state to submit a State Plan that includes a description of procedures for the state's prompt resolution of disputes regarding the educational placement of homeless children and youths (§ 11432(g)(1)(C), 2002). The State Plan must also describe how the state will ensure that LEAs comply with LEAs requirements set forth in the Act including: ensuring immediate enrollment, providing written notice of a school's decision, promptly resolving enrollment disputes, and providing pendency in the school of choice while a dispute is resolved (§§ 11432(g)(2)(A), (g)(3)–(7)). When disputes arise relative to LEAs actions, the State often intervenes to resolve disputes in an effort to avoid costly and time-consuming litigation.

There have been notable exceptions to the general rule regarding infrequent judicial interventions in matters involving homeless youths as explained more fully herein. In such cases, courts are typically called upon to enter declaratory judgment and injunctive relief to enforce LEAs compliance with the Act and to eliminate barriers to the education of homeless students. In a number of recent cases, courts have been called upon to certify class actions and/or to approve settlement agreements related to McKinney-Vento Act violations.

McKinney-Vento litigation has traditionally addressed the following areas: (1) the enrollment and attendance of students in schools; (2) the provision of comparable services to homeless youth (including but not limited to transportation); (3) issues surrounding the education of children awaiting foster placement; and (4) state level compliance issues. Under the Act, the LEAs is required to continue a homeless child's education in the school of origin for the duration of homelessness, or enroll the child in the appropriate public school within the attendance area of the student's temporary housing (§ 11432(g)(3)(A)). The school of origin is specifically identified as the school that the child or youth attended when permanently housed or the school in which the child or youth was last enrolled (§ 11432(g)(3)(G)). According to the best interest standard, a homeless child's education should be in the school of origin where feasible, except when doing so is contrary to the wishes of the parent or guardian (§ 11432(g)(3)(B)). In the case of an unaccompanied youth, the best interest standard requires involvement of the homeless liaison whose duty is to assist in placement or enrollment decisions, to consider the views of unaccompanied youth, and to provide notice to these youth of regarding their right to appeal (§ 11432 (g)(3)(B)).

The McKinney-Vento Act also requires the LEAs to provide each homeless child with services comparable to those offered to other students who attend the selected school, including transportation (§ 11432(g)(4)), and to assist the parent or guardian of a homeless child in accessing transportation to the selected school (§ 11432(g)(6)(A)(vii)). Finally, the Act requires the LEAs to "review and revise any policies that may act as barriers to the enrollment of homeless children and youths" in the selected school (§ 11432(g)(7)(A)).

Jacoby (2010) suggests that decreased funding, limited programs supporting homeless youths, and the economic and housing crisis are likely to result in an increase of litigation that focuses, in particular, on funding adequacy or equity issue impacting students who are homeless (Tanabe & Mobley, 2011). Litigation has commenced in some states regarding the constitutionality of school funding schemes generally. Judicial interventions may be limited to some extent, however, by statutory limitations on liability as well as the litigation costs and limited opportunities to recover attorneys' fees (Tanabe & Mobley, 2011). The following discussion of cases demonstrates the typical issues that arise and lead parents or guardians to litigate their claims pursuant to the McKinney-Vento Act.

### *Enrollment of Homeless Children and Youths*

In *Plyler v. Doe* (1982), the Supreme Court recognized that a Texas statute denying education to the children of illegal immigrants "imposes a lifetime hardship on a discrete class of children not accountable for their disabling status. The stigma of illiteracy will mark them for the rest of their lives. By denying these children a basic education, we deny them the ability to live within the structure of our civic institutions, and foreclose any realistic possibility that they will contribute in even the smallest way to the progress of our Nation" (p. 223). According to the Court, this 1975 Texas law violated the Equal Protection Clause of the Fourteenth Amendment by treating a class of children of illegal immigrants differently than children within Texas' borders for purposes of enforcing residency requirements related to the enrollment of students in the Texas public school system. The Court did not accept Texas' contention that the school districts could refuse to enroll children based upon their state residency status because they had been illegally admitted to the country. The Court found that these students were entitled to protection under the United States Constitution and extended equal protection to the student class, in part, based on the theory that the Equal Protection Clause protects all persons and that minors are not held responsible for the actions of their parents.

Following the Court's decision in *Plyler*, SEAs and LEAs are permitted to impose legitimate enrollment documentation or residency requirements on students prior to attendance in schools as part of state laws and regulations often promoting the health and safety of students (i.e., immunization requirements). However, courts have intervened on behalf of students when residency and enrollment requirements violate applicable federal laws such as the McKinney-Vento Act (*Doe v. Richardson*, 1998).

In *Lampkin v. District of Columbia* (1995), parents of homeless children residing in the District of Columbia sued under Section 1983 to enforce provisions of the McKinney-Vento Act pertaining to the education of homeless children. The United States Court of Appeals for the District of Columbia issued a temporary injunction requiring the District of Columbia to identify the homeless children in a timely fashion and determine the necessary educational services as well as transportation needs required by McKinney-Vento. Subsequent court proceedings in this case, however, reveal the inherent flaws in McKinney-Vento. Namely, the District of Columbia thereafter withdrew from the McKinney-Vento EHCY Program, given their budgetary shortfalls and appealed to the court for relief from the temporary injunction. The court concluded that the District of Columbia could voluntarily withdraw from participation in the EHCY Program due to the financial burden on taxpayers. In essence, these homeless children were provided a remedy by the court that would never be enforceable.

Parents of homeless children in New York and Maryland similarly sought and were granted class action certification in their efforts to secure enrollment, transportation, and educational services from school systems in these states. In *National Law Center on Homelessness and Poverty, R.I. v. New York* (2004), homeless children and their parents living in Suffolk County, New York sought declaratory and injunctive relief against the State of New York, New York State Education Department (NYSED), and other named individuals for alleged violations of McKinney-Vento and the Equal Protection Clause of the Fourteenth Amendment. They alleged that the school system violated McKinney-Vento Act by failing to (a) locate and ensure enrollment of homeless children, (b) provide transportation, (c) provide immediate enrollment, and (d) provide education services that are comparable to the services received by non-homeless children. The Court adopted the heightened scrutiny standard set forth in *Plyler*, asserting that the school system's actions penalized the homeless children because of the misfortunes or misdeeds of their parents.

In *Bullock v. Board of Education of Montgomery County* (2002), a federal district court in Maryland certified a class of parents of homeless children who alleged that the Board of Education and Superintendent had violated McKinney-Vento by (a) failing to identify homeless students using the established definition under the Act, using the families as homeless as defined by the Act; (b) failing to select schools that were in the best interest of the homeless child; (c) failing to consult the parent of a homeless child regarding the best interest of the child determination; (d) failing to ensure school of origin mandate; (e) failing to provide transportation; and (f) failing to remove barriers to enrollment. The court held that the numerosity and commonality and typicality elements for class certification in this matter were satisfied and that two parents living in transitional housing could serve as class representatives.

A federal district court in Pennsylvania issued a preliminary injunction requiring a school district to enroll a student who temporarily resided with an aunt in another school district after fire destroyed the home in which he previously resided within the district (*L.R. ex rel. G.R. v. Steelton-Highspire School District*, 2010). According to the court, the student was homeless, within the meaning of the McKinney-Vento Act, until he and his grandmother obtained a fixed, regular, and adequate nighttime residence. As such, McKinney-Vento required the district to continue educating the child in the school of origin for the duration of homelessness, in light of the McKinney-Vento requirement to immediately admit a child who is homeless to the school in which enrollment is sought, pending resolution of the dispute (2002, 42 U.S.C. § 11432(g)(3)(E)(i)). The *L.R.* court branded the foregoing McKinney-Vento requirement as the pendency provision, which is a significant reminder of the responsibility school systems have to ensure the protection of educational rights for students who are experiencing homelessness, in a timely fashion and even though homelessness may be for a temporary basis.

The decisions reported largely favor the parents and students with respect to enrollment disputes. These cases likewise signal a need for school systems to promote timely enrollment, evaluate transportation policies, and consistently address the best interests of the child standard with respect to the rights of children who are homeless. Recent cases such as *L.R.* highlight the responsibility of LEAs to supply student records and information to receiving LEAs timely and without delay. Similarly receiving LEAs must request and obtain student records and information from transferring LEAs necessary for promptly educating students (i.e., special education records/individualized education program, health and immunization records). Court decisions on enrollment serve as a caution to receiving LEAs that requesting and obtaining such records, however, should not serve to delay the enrollment of students or the provision of a free and appropriate public education to those students (2002, 42 U.S.C.A. § 11432(g)(1)(H)).

### *Comparable Services*

The McKinney-Vento Act requires that each homeless child be provided services comparable to services offered to other students in the school selected, including: transportation services; educational services for which the child or youth meets the eligibility criteria, such as services provided under Title I of the Elementary and Secondary Education Act of 1965 or similar state or local programs; educational programs for children with disabilities; educational programs for students with limited English proficiency; programs in vocational and technical education; programs for gifted and talented students; and school nutrition programs (2002, § 11432 (g)(4)).

In at least one case, the McKinney-Vento comparable service challenges were raised by the parent of a disabled student in combination with claims under other federal laws, including the Individuals with Disabilities Education and Improvement Act of 2004 (IDEA) and Section 504 of the Rehabilitation Act of 1973 (Section 504). Yet, in this case, the court failed to rule on the McKinney-Vento issue, in light the parent's insufficient factual allegations regarding the violation and instead focused solely on the IDEA and Section 504 claims (*Holmes-Ramsey v. District of Columbia*, 2010).

While it is typically parents of students and advocacy groups who commence litigation pursuant to the McKinney-Vento Act, a recent challenge has been filed by an activities association in an Oregon State Court alleging an improper interpretation of the Act by the State Board of Education (*Oregon School Activities Association v. State Board of Education*, 2011). A student who had experienced poverty and homelessness throughout his education, sought to continue participating in track and choir, even though he turned 19 at the beginning of his senior year. Participation in high school interscholastic activities was governed by the Oregon School Activities Association (OSAA); however, and an OSAA rule provided that no student 19 or older at the beginning of a school year could participate in those activities. The student requested a waiver of the age requirement and OSAA denied the request.

The Board concluded that applying the age restriction to the student violated McKinney-Vento. The Board concluded that there was no evidence presented that the student had a competitive advantage in any of his activities because of his age or size. There was also no evidence presented that his enrollment in high school was delayed for competitive advantage. Instead, there was ample evidence presented of the benefits to the student if he was allowed to participate. In addition, there was testimony that the student was at-risk of not completing high school when he was denied eligibility. Thus, the Board concluded that the student's rights to equitable educational services under McKinney-Vento, including participation in interscholastic activities, outweighed any perceived risk identified by OSAA as a result of permitting the student to participate. The state court dismissed OSAA's appeal, determining the case was moot because the student graduated (*Oregon School Activities Association v. State Board of Education*, 2011).

In light of the above cases and claims, school systems are encouraged to carefully examine the interplay among federal and state laws regarding students with disabilities in particular, and determine the implications of possible conflicts between federal and state mandates. School system obligations under the Act are susceptible to protract and costly litigation in which parents simultaneously raise issues regarding homelessness, pendency, placement, and compensatory education services denied to homeless students.

### *Children Awaiting Foster Placement*

Children and youths awaiting foster care placement are considered homeless children and youths under the McKinney-Vento Act (42 U.S.C. § 11434a(2)(B)(i)). The statute does not define the term "awaiting foster care placement" with any greater specificity. Thus, the phrase is subject to differing interpretations among states (Chambers & Palmer, 2011). According to the NAEHCY, ensuring access to equitable educational opportunities for youth in care depends to a great extent on child welfare and educational agencies working together and assuming responsibility for the benefit of children awaiting foster care placement (Julianelle, 2008).

Some states have elected to address foster children via regulatory and/or statutory guidance (Legal Center for Foster Care & Education, n.d.). For instance, the Pennsylvania Department of Education issued guidance (Education for Homeless Youth Basic Education Circular (BEC), 2011) expanding upon definitions in the McKinney-Vento Act as a result, in part, of class action litigation commenced against the Pennsylvania Department of Education and a LEAs (*A.E. v. Carlynton School District*, 2009). The BEC defines children and youths awaiting foster care placement, as "children who are placed in shelters, emergency foster care, transitional foster care or respite care" (*A.E. v. Carlynton School District*, 2009). The BEC further states "these placement settings are intended to be short term, and do not typically last longer than 30 days." However, individual circumstances may, at times, require a longer length of stay. If the placement exceeds 30 days, contact should be made with the child welfare worker and the local McKinney-Vento Coordinator to determine if there is any valid reason to conclude that the child's foster care placement is pending.

Additionally, the Fostering Connections to Success and Increasing Adoptions Act was adopted in 2008 to address school stability for children in foster care (Chambers & Palmer, 2011). Under the Act, child welfare agencies in states that accept federal child welfare dollars must ensure that a child who enters foster care remains in the school of origin. If remaining in the school of origin is not in the child's best interest, the child welfare agency should make every effort to ensure the child is provided with immediate and appropriate enrollment in a new school.

Recognizing the need to provide comparable services to children awaiting foster care placement is an essential mandate of the Act. Failure of LEAs to recognize their responsibilities in this area may lead to federal and/or state complaints or lawsuits. It is also important to consider the needs of these students when analyzing LEAs policies and procedures regarding Title I services; IDEA and Section 504 compliance; and attendance and truancy monitoring and elimination plans.

### *State Level Compliance Issues*

McKinney-Vento compliance issues do not only involve LEAs. Rather, statewide practices have been called into question in some cases. For instance, in 2007, the American Civil Liberties Union (ACLU) of Hawaii and a small team of other attorneys successfully sued the Hawaii State Department of Education (HDOE) for failing to comply with the McKinney-Vento Act (*Kaleuati v. Tonda*, 2007). In the original complaint for declaratory and injunctive relief, the ACLU opens by explaining that there are at least 5,000 homeless persons living on beaches and in parks, sleeping on benches, in cars, and in homeless shelters in Hawaii on any given night. And, that there are more than 100,000 "hidden homeless," or persons moving from one temporary living arrangement to another (2007, p. 2). The complaint goes on to show that the HDOE's own records revealed that only 908 homeless children had enrolled in school, and that the HDOE has publically admitted that its own statistics on homeless students vastly understated the problem.

In 2008, the United States District Court Chief Judge Helen Gillmor granted the plaintiff's motions for certification of classes and for preliminary injunction. Judge Gillmor found that the allegations of irreparable injury to a legal right and the strong likelihood that the plaintiffs would win on the merits provided ample ground for issuing the preliminary injunction. As one commenter noted, the Court justified the final ruling based on the public interest principle that failing to provide homeless children educational opportunities would harm society in general (Petersburg, 2008).

Among the HDOE's responses to the complaint are the claim that the actual number of homeless children who have been denied access to public education in Hawaii is very small and that even if the number is not small, the McKinney-Vento Act does not stipulate specific methods or activities that must be followed, rather these decisions are left to the discretion of the LEAs. Thus, the HDOE argues, it is not possible to reasonably claim that what they are doing is not actually in compliance. Moreover, the HDOE explains that it has recently placed posters identifying the rights of homeless families at all HDOE offices, schools, and homeless shelters in the state of Hawaii. And, finally, the HDOE asserts that it has been developing a plan to provide "more robust transportation services" to homeless children (Petersburg, 2008).

Following Judge Gillmor's decision at the hearing for preliminary injunction, the *Kaleuati* case was settled. Among the long list of stipulations that the HDOE agreed to in the settlement is a mandate that the school district hire additional homeless education support staff, immediately enroll any and all homeless students, identify personnel at each public school who may serve as a point of contact for homeless families, provide ongoing training for HDOE personnel regarding the McKinney-Vento requirements, and ensure greater supervision of school-level efforts to comply with McKinney-Vento. Additionally, the HDOE agreed to publish and distribute multilingual information regarding the rights of homeless children, improve their recordkeeping processes for homeless students, and revise all relevant forms to include information about McKinney-Vento rights (Petersburg, 2008).

Conflicts between McKinney-Vento provisions and state regulations may also arise with respect to residency issues. For example, in *N.J. v. New York* (2011), a New York federal district court asserted that the NYSED's refusal to issue a stay of disenrollment to children pending determination of their qualification as homeless, although permissible under a state regulation, likely conflicts with the McKinney-Vento pendency provision (2002, 42 U.S.C. § 11432(g)(3)(E)(i)). According to the court, Congress expressed a specific public interest in treating homeless students no differently than other students. Thus, the court issued a preliminary injunction to stay the disenrollment proceedings and to afford the plaintiffs an opportunity to show that the state regulation likely conflicts with the McKinney-Vento pendency provision.

## CONCLUSIONS AND RECOMMENDATIONS FOR POLICYMAKERS

A first step toward compliance with the Act is ensuring the adoption of Homeless Youth policies referencing the McKinney-Vento Act and its notice and procedural requirements so that all stakeholders are made aware of relevant and applicable requirements within the school, LEAs and/or SEAs. While this list is not exhaustive, schools should ensure that the following actions are taken:

- Provide contact information for the local liaison for homeless children and youths and the state coordinator for education of homeless children and youths.
- Provide assistance to the parent or guardian of each homeless child or youth (or, in the case of an unaccompanied youth, the youth) to exercise the right to attend the parent's or guardian's (or youth's) choice of schools.
- Coordinate with the LEAs with jurisdiction for the school selected by the parent or guardian (or youth), to provide transportation and other necessary services.
- Ensure that the parent or guardian (or, in the case of an unaccompanied youth, the youth) shall receive the information required in a manner and form understandable to such parent or guardian (or youth), including, if necessary and to the extent feasible, in the native language of such parent or guardian (or youth).
- Demonstrate in the school's application for funds under this part that such school is in compliance with the McKinney-Vento Act (2002, § 11432 (e)(3)(C)).

According to the reauthorized McKinney-Vento Act (2002, § 11432 (e)(3)(C)(IV)), all school districts are required to appoint a local liaison to ensure the law is implemented effectively at the local level. The local homeless liaison in many schools is also an administrator, such as a Principal or Assistant Principal. When the liaison role is assigned as an additional duty on top of an already full set of responsibilities, it may lead to insufficient support for the homeless youths and families. Given these challenges, school districts are encouraged to provide district-wide training and to create resource manuals for local liaisons to support their ability to respond to the needs of a diverse population of homeless children, youths, and families given increasing global economic and stability challenges (Toro, 2007).

For the state to be eligible to receive funds under the McKinney-Vento Act, LEAs must also implement a coordinated system for ensuring that homeless children and youths are advised of the choice of schools. The focus of such a system must be on immediate enrollment in the school selected and prompt provision of necessary services, including transportation, to allow homeless children and youths to exercise their choices of schools. In addition, the LEAs should document that written notice has been provided and prohibit schools within the LEA's jurisdiction from referring homeless children or youths or requiring homeless children and youths to enroll in or attend, a separate school. Finally, LEAs must identify and remove any barriers that exist in schools within the agency's jurisdiction that may have contributed to the creation or existence of separate schools and not use funds received under this part to establish new or additional separate schools or sites for homeless children or youths (2002, § 11432(e)(3)(E)). Homeless youth policies should reference all of the above requirements.

Additionally, LEAs should carefully adopt Enrollment policies that comply with applicable state and federal laws and regulations, recognizing the supremacy of federal laws, such as McKinney-Vento over state or local regulations or ordinances. Enrollment policies should take homeless children and youth into account when citing to required documentation. Homeless children and youth and their parents may not have ready access to birth certificates, immunization records, student records, or proof of residency (Valosky, 2014). Lack of proper documentation for homeless children and youth cannot be a basis for delay in enrollment. Moreover, enrollment policies should recognize the needs of homeless children and youth who may qualify as English learners (ELs) and who may require information provided in their native language. Additionally, the administration of a home language survey in accordance with federal laws regarding EL students should not be overlooked for homeless children and youths.

A number of standard school policies that present minimal negative impacts on students who live in permanent residential homes can serve as significant deterrents to enrollment, attendance, and access for students experiencing homelessness. For example, transportation policies must be adopted that eliminate barriers to student attendance at the school of choice as well as comply with the State's plan for transportation. Similarly, truancy efforts should be tailored to include a level of flexibility given the unique challenges of children who are homeless yet should also focus efforts on minimizing poor school attendance and reducing unexcused absences and tardies for students. Similarly, discipline policies should be non-discriminatory in nature, and account for the physical and emotional needs of students who are homeless. School-wide uniform and dress code policies, as well as Title I and Parent Involvement Policies should also be sensitive to the needs of homeless children and be monitored for assurance that the appropriate services and programs are provided to all students in an accessible and equitable manner.

Finally, in designating the liaison required under the Act, LEAs must take into account the vital role that the liaison plays in ensuring compliance. LEAs should consider procedures for liaisons to follow, trainings, opportunities for professional development on the issues impacting homeless students and the availability of resources to this individual so that the liaison is fully informed and performing his or her essential functions in a manner that will promote the policy statements of the Act and minimize the potential for McKinney-Vento litigation.

## CONCLUSION

Ensuring that homeless children have access to education has continued to be a crucial focus of many advocacy groups. Their efforts have been strengthened primarily by federal legislative mandates, but SEAs and LEAs may also enhance both awareness and implementation of homeless education policies. Although McKinney-Vento, the HEARTH act and provisions under NCLB are widely known by school officials, relying on federal funding and legislative mandates alone is insufficient. Other solutions include an increasing number of state legislative versions of McKinney-Vento. For example, Illinois and Colorado enacted statutes to protect the educational rights of unaccompanied youth (Vissing, 2012).

Additional recommendations for school systems include adopting procedures to identify and track homeless students and families, strengthening the role of homeless liaisons, establishing partnerships with social service agencies and homeless shelters, and engaging in outreach activities to educate homeless families about their rights. School systems are encouraged to hire and train key staff members to implement and monitor homeless education efforts.

It is important that educators, particularly those who are responsible for compliance with McKinney-Vento, recognize their critical role in protecting educational opportunities for homeless youth. Given the serious academic challenges facing homeless children, school systems are encouraged to build partnerships with families in need, community groups, and local agencies in order to seek ways to remove barriers to learning for homeless students. As revealed in the numerous cases and settlements, LEAs and SEAs must respond appropriately to the Act's mandatory provisions, whether it is through the provision of reasonable transportation efforts and timely enrollment decisions, or through the elimination of stigmatizing practices that hinder the free and appropriate public educational opportunities afforded to students.

## REFERENCES

A.E., B.E., S.E., and M.E. ex rel. C.E. and W.E. v. Carlynton Sch. Dist. No. 09-1345 (W.D. Pa. 2009).

Bullock v. Bd. of Educ. of Montgomery Cnty. 210 F.R.D. 556 (D. Md. 2002).

Chambers, C., & Palmer, E. (2011). Educational stability for children in foster care. *Touro Law Review*, *26*, 1103–1127.

Collier v. Bd. of Educ. of Prince George's Cnty. 01-cv-1179, No. 1 (D. Md. 2001). Retrieved from http://publicjustice.org/our-work/index.cfm?pageid=111

Doe v. Richardson. No. 98-1165-N (M.D. Ala., 1998).

Holmes-Ramsey v. District of Columbia. 747 F. Supp. 2d 32 (D.D.C. 2010).

HUD Exchange. (n.d.). *2014 AHAR: Part 1 – PIT estimates of homelessness*. Retrieved from https://www.hudexchange.info/resource/4074/2014-ahar-part-1-pit-estimates-of-homelessness/

Individuals with Disabilities Education and Improvement Act of 2004 (IDEA). 20 U.S.C.S. § 1400 et seq.

Jacoby, M. B. (2010). The value(s) of foreclosure law reform. *Pepperdine Law Review*, *37*, 511–562.

Julianelle, P. (2008). *Building futures through education: The McKinney-Vento Act and children and youth awaiting foster care placement, strategies for improving educational outcomes through school stability*. Retrieved from https://www.michigan.gov/documents/mde/M-V_and_Youth_Awaiting_Foster_Care_2008_-_NAEHCY_Book_311303_7.pdf

Kaleuati v. Tonda. CV07-00504 (D. Haw. 2007).

Lampkin v. District of Columbia. Civ. No. 92-0910, 1992 WL 151813 (D.D.C. 1992), *rev'd*, 27 F.3d 605 (D.C. Cir. 1994), enforced on remand, 879 F. Supp. 116 (D.D.C. 1995).

L.R. ex rel. G.R. v. Steelton-Highspire Sch. Dist. 54 IDELR 155 (M.D. Pa. 2010).

Legal Center for Foster Care & Education. (n.d.). *States at a glance: Awaiting foster care placement under the McKinney-Vento Act*. Retrieved from http://www.americanbar.org/content/dam/aba/migrated/child/education/publications/AFCPchart.authcheckdam.pdf

McKinney-Vento Homeless Assistance Act. 42 U.S.C. § 11431 et seq. (2002).

National Alliance to End Homelessness. (2010). *Geography of homelessness*. Retrieved from http://www.endhomelessness.org/library/entry/geography-of-homelessness

National Alliance to End Homelessness. (n.d.). *Snapshot of homelessness*. Retrieved from http://www.endhomelessness.org/pages/snapshot_of_homelessness

National Association for the Education of Homeless Children and Youth. (n.d.). *Mission*. Retrieved from http://www.naehcy.org/about-naehcy/mission

National Center for Homeless Education. (2014). *Education for homeless children and youths program data collection summary*. Retrieved from http://center.serve.org/nche/downloads/data-comp-0910-1112.pdf

National Center on Family Homelessness. (2009). *America's youngest outcasts: State report on child homelessness*. Retrieved from http://www.homelesschildrenamerica.org/media-docs/280.pdf

National Law Center on Homelessness and Poverty, R.I. v. New York. 224 F.R.D. 314 (E.D. N.Y. 2004).

N.J. ex rel. N.J. v. New York. 872 F.Supp.2d 204 (2011).

No Child Left Behind Act of 2001. Pub. L. No. 107-110, 115 Stat. 1425 (2002).

Oregon Sch. Activities Ass'n v. State Bd. of Educ. 260 P.3d 735 (Or. App. 2011).

Pennsylvania Department of Education. (2011). *Education for homeless youth*. Basic Education Circular. Retrieved from file:///C:/Users/susanb/Downloads/Education%20for%20Homeless%20Youth%20(42%20USCA%2011431)%20(1).pdf

Petersburg, B. (2008). Reconciling the McKinney-Vento Act with the vision of the Universal Declaration of Human Rights: Improving local educational agency liaisons' ability to serve America's homeless children. *Hamline Journal of Public Law & Policy*, *30*, 447–495.

Plyler v. Doe. 457 U.S. 202 (U.S. 1982).

Section 504 of the Rehabilitation Act of 1973. 29 U.S.C.S. § 794.

Tanabe, C. S., & Mobley, I. H. (2011). The forgotten students: The implications of federal homeless education policy for children in Hawaii. *Brigham Young University Education & Law Journal*, *51*, 59–61.

Toro, P. A. (2007). Toward an international understanding of homelessness. *Journal of Social Issues*, *63*(3), 461–481.

Valosky, K. (2014). Reform of McKinney-Vento Homeless Education Assistance Act dispute resolution procedures and federal oversight mechanisms. *Georgetown Journal on Poverty Law & Policy*, *22*(1), 189–210.

Vissing, Y. (2012). Homeless children and youth: An examination of legal challenges and directions. *Journal of Law in Society*, *13*, 455–501.

Wiik, K. B. (2009). Justice for America's homeless children: Cultivating a child's right to shelter in the United States. *William Mitchell Law Review*, *35*(3), 876–935. Retrieved from http://open.wmitchell.edu/wmlr/vol35/iss3/3

# CHAPTER 11

# TO PROTECT AND EDUCATE: LEGAL MANDATES AND COMPLEX LEADERSHIP OF SCHOOL RESOURCE (POLICE) OFFICERS

Anthony H. Normore, Darius Bone, Delaney Jones and Stacy Spell

## ABSTRACT

*School resource officers (SROs) are sworn law enforcement who are responsible for providing security and crime prevention services in the American school environment. SROs have become commonplace in American schools, but support for their continued work is meeting more resistance from those who feel that schools need to be focused on education and not police actions. The responsibilities of SROs are similar to regular police officers in that they have the ability to make arrests, respond to calls for service, and document incidents that occur within their jurisdiction. They are expected to be more than a law enforcement officer; they are expected to be leaders, educate students about*

**Legal Frontiers in Education: Complex Law Issues for Leaders, Policymakers and Policy Implementers**
**Advances in Educational Administration, Volume 24, 201–220**

**ISSN: 1479-3660/doi:10.1108/S1479-366020150000024038**

*law-related topics; be a role model to youth; and typically have additional duties to include mentoring and conducting presentations on youth-related issues. SRO programs receive valuable augmented training from a partner in school safety, the non-profit organization – National Association of School Resource Officers (NASRO). Towards this end, we will: (1) provide a historical context of SRO programs in the United States, (2) highlight concerns and challenges of school communities, (3) briefly present the case of SRO in Los Angeles, and (4) highlight implications for educational leadership. Conclusions and recommendations are presented.*

School resource officer (SRO) programs have been a topic of great debate in the United States during the past few years. SROs have become commonplace in American schools, but support for their continued work is meeting more resistance from those who feel that schools need to be focused on education and not police actions. The American education system, from kindergarten to 12th grade, has tried to offer schooling in a safe environment (Guerra, 2015a). One tool that school districts use to provide a safe educational environment is the SRO. Broadly, SROs are law enforcement personnel who focus on K-12 school campus duties, including preventing juvenile delinquency. An SRO is almost always a police officer or sheriff's deputy assigned to a particular school. SROs typically work for their parent police agencies, with schools being their assigned beat. In many schools, SROs partner with guidance counselors in an effort to improve student grades and attendance. Juvenile delinquency, or crime, and truancy are always concerns, and SROs work to help to reduce its occurrence through early intervention activities in the schools (Guerra, 2015b).

Police have been involved in American schools for more than 60 years in the role of SROs. SRO programs began in the United States in the early to mid-1950s; however, the program did not gain prominence until the 1990s in response to various school shootings. According to national data (National Association of School Resource Officers [NASRO], 2015), SROs can be found in 35% of schools across America, regardless of level (elementary, middle, or high school), urbanicity (rural, town, suburban, or city), or enrollment size. However, there is currently a dearth of meaningful research addressing the role and effectiveness of SROs (e.g., Benigni, 2004;

Brown, 2006; Brown & Benedict, 2005; Clark, 1994a, 1994b; Cray & Weiler, 2011; Finn, 2006; Finn, McDevitt, Lassiter, Shively, & Rich., 2005; Girouard, 2001; Hirschfield, 2008; Huffman, 1995; Jackson, 2002; Kupchik & Bracy, 2010; Lambert & McGinty, 2002; May, Cordner, & Fessel, 2004; Morimune, 2012; NASRO, 2015; Thurau & Wald, 2010; Travis & Coon, 2005). We will begin by providing the context in which SROs evolved in the United States.

## HISTORICAL OVERVIEW OF SROS

The origin of SROs in the United States dates back to the 1950s, when an officer was assigned to a school in Flint, Michigan, in 1953. In the 1960s and 1970s, various towns in Florida followed suit and assigned local police officers to some schools. The term "school resource officer" is credited to a Miami police chief (HARO, 2015). SROs also began in Tucson, Arizona, in the early 1960s. During the late 1960s, the Fresno Police Department in California also stationed seven officers in elementary and junior high schools to try to better relations between the police and the community (HSRO, 2015). The topic was not broadly discussed in the years to follow but then in 1968, the Fresno Police Department in California looked to the SRO program as a tool to revitalize its image in the eyes of its youth. This early adaptation of the program involved placing plain clothed officers in the middle schools and elementary schools to foster the relationship that the department had with the youth, which is still a goal of the program today. Although Fresno's program began with non-uniformed officers, it has progressed into what is seen in most communities today to include a uniformed officer, operating a marked police vehicle, and who is responsible for safety and security on the school property. In addition to these responsibilities, SROs must be able to communicate effectively with school officials and be able to address a variety of situations. They must also be willing to communicate with parents, assist with behavior issues and give presentations when necessary.

All 50 states have SROs and internationally, England, Canada, and Australia have SROs as well. For example, many secondary schools in Canada have not only installed security cameras and hired security personnel to enhance the safety of staff and students, but schools in Toronto, Ontario have also sought the assistance of armed police officers, who are present in the school throughout the day (Weiler & Cray, 2011). In

Toronto, SRO stands for student resource officer. In 2008, the Toronto District School Board and the Toronto Catholic District School Board, in collaboration with the Toronto Police Service, institutionalized the SRO program by permanently placing armed, uniformed police officers in secondary schools (Cray & Weiler, 2011). Like SROs in the United States, student resource officers in Toronto are responsible for providing security and crime prevention services in schooling environments.

SROs are becoming more commonplace in Canadian schools and, like the United States, many groups feel that their presence in secondary schools creates an atmosphere that leads to an increase of youth/adolescents being introduced to the criminal justice system (Weiler & Cray, 2011). School districts in collaboration with police agencies across the United States are implementing criminal justice system practices in order to achieve a safe schooling environment; however, this trade-off comes at the cost of exposing youth/adolescents to the criminal justice system and tarnishing their educational achievements. Table 1 provides a history of how SRO programs spread across America.

During the 1980s and early 1990s, the development of SROs lapsed (McDaniel, 1998). Local police departments, however, began utilizing officers to provide an educational role in the school. In 1983, the Los Angeles Police Department (LAPD) established the Drug Abuse Resistance Education (D.A.R.E., 2015) program for students. In D.A.R.E. programs, police officers originally presented a 15-hour curriculum to students in fifth and eighth grades. The program was intended to be presented during the final year of a student's time in a particular level of education, such as elementary school and middle school. As it evolved, D.A.R.E. expanded its curriculum to all grades from kindergarten to the senior year in high school (D.A.R.E., 2015).

***Table 1.*** Tracing School Resource Officer Program across America.

- 1950s – Flint MI. P.D.
- 1963 – Tucson AZ. P.D.
- 1966 – Saginaw MI. P.D.
- 1967 – Cincinnati OH. P.D.
- 1968 – Los Angeles CA. P.D. & S.O.
- 1969 – Miami FL. P.D.
- 1971 – Charlotte N.C.
- 1972 – Orlando P.D. (Leon, Sarasota, Seminole, and Pinellas Counties FL. followed)
- 1975 – Hillsborough County FL.

*Source*: http://scasro.org/HISTORY.htm

D.A.R.E. represented the first widespread formal and ongoing partnership between the police of a local community and the schools in that community. Much controversy exists as to the effectiveness of the D.A.R.E. curriculum in preventing future drug use and abuse by students. Interestingly though, D.A.R.E. has a previously unrecognized benefit – the development of positive relationships between D.A.R.E. officers and both students and school leaders who work in the schools. These relationships helped to dispel many myths about the negative consequences of having police officers on school grounds (Commons, 2005). Presently (2015), D.A.R.E. is now implemented in nearly 80% of American school districts and more than 54 countries around the world (D.A.R.E., 2015). Building off the D.A.R.E. curriculum, the Phoenix (Arizona) Police Department and the U.S. Bureau of Alcohol, Tobacco, Firearms, and Explosives began the Gang Resistance Education and Training program (G.R.E.A.T., 2015). This began as an eight-lesson program curriculum for middle school in 1992. Now, G.R.E.A.T. is a 13-lesson, 13-week program that is offered to elementary and middle school students. It is also offered in summer programs. While G.R.E.A.T. seems to have more success than D.A.R.E. (Finn, Peterson, Terrance, Taylor, & Osgood, 2012), both programs served as opportunities for police to interact with students in a school setting. These programs and many similar local programs that have developed during the past 20 years have brought police into schools in a crime prevention role. These programs used police to present a curriculum but not to play a broader role in school safety or student counseling. In these programs, the police officer would go into the school each week and present the next module of the curriculum and then leave. The officer would not have a formal role in the safety issues facing the school.

In the mid-1990s, SRO programs began to grow out of a national perception that school violence was increasing (May et al., 2004). In response to the public concern, in 1999, the Office of Community-Oriented Policing Services (n.d.) (COPS) initiated the Cops in Schools Program to fund police officers in schools across the country. To help schools continue to be safe so that children can learn and develop, the community policing philosophy engages law enforcement, school administrators, parents, and students in a problem-solving partnership. The central mission of this partnership is student success. When students succeed, the entire community succeeds: students who experience achievement and make positive contributions within their schools become productive citizens in the larger community. Officers are expected to take leadership roles and take the initiative to finalize school safety planning and build partnerships for future needs. An officer's primary responsibility is law enforcement; however, whenever possible, SROs should strive to employ non-punitive techniques when interacting with students, and an arrest should be used only as a last resort under specified circumstances. SROs play an integral role in the educational system and should positively impact the school environment (Guerra, 2015a, 2015b).

Officers generally volunteer for the SRO program. They are most frequently assigned full time to the local school or schools. Many SROs do not report to roll call at the police department but in fact spend their entire day within the school setting. Many SROs receive training – frequently they attend programs presented by National Association of School Resource Officers (NASROs) – but it is often the case that due to scheduling conflicts, this training comes after the officers have already begun their assignments as SROs. To conclude this section of the chapter, we provide accounts of school violence intended as a response to provide evidence for the need of SROs (Moskos, 2014) (Tables 2 and 3).

### *Leadership and SROs*

SROs are expected to work to reduce juvenile delinquency rates by establishing close contact with students and to build positive relationships with them. SROs also conduct security inspections, monitor crime statistics, and

***Table 2.*** Students and Violence Nationwide.

| Students and Violence Nationwide |
|---|
| • Nearly 3 million incidents occur each year on our nation's school campuses.<br>• Approximately 282,000 students are attacked in schools each month.<br>• Youth homicide has tripled in the last 20 years (since 1990).<br>• Fourteen children are killed every day by handguns suicides, homicides, or accidents.<br>• An estimated 100,000 children carry a gun to school each day.<br>• 98% could get a handgun if they wanted to.<br>• 75% have carried a weapon at school.<br>• 52% had not or did not remember receiving any instruction in school on ways to avoid a fight.<br>• 78.6% believe they should fight if someone hits them.<br>• 77.5% believe not passing on information that could cause a fight is the most effective way to avoid fighting.<br>• The average age of a cop killer is 30 years of age. |

*Source*: http://www.copinthehood.com/2014/12/police-killing-whites-and-blacks.html

***Table 3.*** Specific Incidents of Threats and Injuries from U.S. Department of Education.

| Threats and Injuries |
|---|
| • 9% of students threatened/injured with a weapon. |
| • 12% of those students were in the ninth grade. |
| • 7% of students age 12–18 reported being bullied. |
| • 14% of those students were in the sixth grade. |
| • From 1998 to 2002, male teachers were more likely than female teachers to be victims of violent crime. |
| • 21% of students reported that there were gangs in their schools. |

*Source*: http://scasro.org/HISTORY.htm

work with local police and students to design crime prevention strategies. The ability to work closely with school leaders is essential for any SRO, particularly the ability to train school personnel in handling crisis situations (Guerra, 2015a, 2015b). They must attend and participate in many school functions, including at night and on weekends. The literature (e.g., Huffman, 1995) indicates that local communities have tailored the function of SROs to fit their needs. SROs are sworn law enforcement officers who are responsible for providing security and crime prevention services in the American school environment. SROs are typically employed by a local police or sheriff's agency and work closely with administrators in an effort to create a safer environment for both students and staff. The responsibilities of SROs are similar to regular police officers in that they have the ability to make arrests, respond to calls for service, and document incidents that occur within their jurisdiction. SROs typically have additional duties to include mentoring and conducting presentations on youth-related issues (e.g., substance abuse, bullying).

Most SROs are police officers who serve in schools full time. The initial model of SROs has been described as the "triad" concept, where the SRO's job is divided into the roles of teacher, counselor, and law enforcement (McDaniel, 1998). It is important to note that this model is suggested by both the COPS office and the NASROs (NASRO, 2015). For point of clarification, NASRO was founded on the "triad" concept of school-based policing. The triad concept divides the SRO's responsibilities into three areas: law enforcement officer, teacher, and counselor. Each component of the triad model is briefly described below. Of critical importance to the SRO's success is being an active listener and being a positive role model.

*Law Enforcement Officer*
The model describes a police officer who is assigned full time to a school, or set of schools, who engages in a combination of activities that support, promote, and foster the maintaining of a safe and secure learning environment The officer is required to enforce the laws of the jurisdiction within the school setting by engaging in investigation of drug distribution networks, gambling operations, and thefts that occur in or around school settings. The law enforcer promotes safety in or around the school by addressing crime and fear of crime, while serving as a liaison between the school and outside agencies. Among the activities are using opportunities to define community policing, foster school-based partnerships, and address school-related crime and disorder such as vandalism, campus threats, bomb threats, and break-ins (Guerra, 2015b; NASRO, 2015).

*Law-Related Educator/Teacher*
SROs are aware they will make contact with students to make a difference. To do this, they need access to the classroom. They use structured lesson plans to teach on topics within the teacher's lesson plans. Some schools have officers who coach various sporting teams. In schools where the SROs teach, they may teach a legal issues course or a life skills course, but it appears to be much more common that SROs teach a day or a module of an existing course. These lectures or modules frequently include topics such as drug education, teenage victims of crime, underage drinking, drunk-driving prevention, legal rights, and bullying prevention. Teaching and demonstrating topics related to law enforcement geared toward positive student behavior and collaborating with stakeholder groups (Guerra, 2015b; NASRO, 2015).

*Law-Related Counselor*
In this capacity, officers work with individual student to deal with substance abuse problems and refer them to existing programs. The officers may also work with students who are having difficulty at home and help them get in touch with programs that can support them. The law-related counselor is also referred to as an advisor. SROs are available in schools if students, faculty members, and school staff need someone to come and talk to. They advise school staff on various topics, which may include law-related matters, crisis management, and crime prevention methods. Since the SROs are not professionally trained counselors, their role is to connect students experiencing difficulties in their lives with programs that can help them. SROs are expected to build relationships and reinforce positive

behaviors, while connecting youth with needed services. In this role, they help to address bullying in schools, foster student safety for breaking the code of silence (e.g., stop snitching phenomenon), and help to address child abuse and neglect in the home (Guerra, 2015b; NASRO, 2015). Thus, SROs do more than just law enforcement. In a 2002 NASRO survey, officers reported spending more than half their time in non-law enforcement tasks. It is worth noting however that the amount of law enforcement tasks an officer engages in may differ depending on whether the officer serves a middle school or high school. To enter into the various types of training programs, an officer must be an SRO for three years; must attend 40 hours of training and a 24-hour supervisor training course; and must complete 160 hours of additional in-service training pertaining to school issues (e.g., school counseling) (NASRO, 2015).

SROs have developed security plans for potential catastrophic events. An additional action taken by a large number of SROs have been to review or develop a school security plan in the event of incidents such as those which have occurred at various schools across America (e.g., Columbine High School, in Colorado, in 1999; Sandy Hook Elementary School, Newtown, Connecticut, in 2014; Amish school shooting at a one-room school in Nickel Mines, PA, in 2006) or even terrorist attacks. These plans spell out evacuation procedures and communication lines and also include an up-to-date functional layout of the building(s) so that emergency responders can quickly assess the situation and vulnerabilities.

## CHALLENGES OF SRO PROGRAMS

SRO programs do not come without challenges. The literature has identified several of these challenges including how to sustain the continuation of funding, administering the day-to-day function of the SROs, determining whether the SRO has the legal right to discipline within the school, and whether the SRO should wear a police uniform (Girouard, 2001; HSRO, 2015).

### *Continued Funding and Administration of Programs*

The COPS office originally provides three years of funding to communities to begin or expand their SRO programs. According to NASRO (2015), when communities reach the three-year sunset point, they are faced with the difficult decision of how to replace the federal funding with local funds.

In some communities, SRO programs have been eliminated since alternative funding could not be identified. However, due to the widespread popularity of these programs, in many communities, the costs of such programs were either absorbed into the overall police budget or the community voted on a tax increase or additional levy to continue the program. In a large number of communities, taxpayers have approved these requests. In many communities, a conflict has arisen around the ability of school administrators to set goals and provide direction to SROs about how they should function on a day-to-day basis.

### *Role of the SRO in Enforcing School Discipline*

Some conflicts have developed around the SRO's responsibility in enforcing school policies. Some school administrators believe that the SRO should support the mission of the school by enforcing school policies. The SROs also have to decide on whether they are serving as an assistant to the school administrator or as a police officer in the school (HSRO, 2015). The SRO has to contend with various constitutional issues in deciding whether to issue the Miranda warning and in matters involving search and seizure. The criteria in deciding whether to search a student vary for school staff and officers. Also, this can cause problems when a principal asks an officer to search a student: Is the officer searching the student as an officer (who makes decision based on the request of the principal) or as a subordinate of the principal who must do what the boss asks (HSRO, 2015). To provide clarity and understanding to these issues, it is critical that the law enforcement agency and the school board have clear rules and guidelines that are delineated in a memorandum of understanding (MOU) (NASRO, 2015). Likewise, the MOU must be routinely reviewed to ensure that its provisions are consistent with laws and the social/political climate. A final issue facing SROs regarding their role is deciding whether to wear a uniform on duty in the school (Girouard, 2001). Some argue that the police should wear uniforms to serve as an easily recognizable police deterrent. Others argue that SROs should wear either civilian clothes or a modified "soft uniform" (i.e., dress pants and polo type shirt with an official monogram). This position argues that the official police uniform might intimidate students and thwart police and community relations. Finally, some argue that police should wear their regular uniforms part of the week and their soft uniform or civilian clothes the other part of the week, allowing the students to see both sides of the officer (SRO, 2015).

*Effectiveness of SRO Programs*

Numerous key areas regarding the use of SROs are often mentioned during debates as to the effectiveness of the program. Those areas include crime prevention, the increasing number of juvenile arrests, and the cost of SRO programs compared to other services that could be provided to students.

*Crime Prevention.* The Center for Technology in Education from Johns Hopkins University (2004) provides a simple job description for SROs and contained within that document they note that the SRO shall develop crime prevention programs and conduct security inspections to deter criminal or delinquent activities. Some may be under the impression that SROs are in place to only protect the students from external matters but the SRO is also responsible for reducing the juvenile crimes that occur on school property. Johns Hopkins University considers this to be a basic requirement for SROs and indicate that SROs prevent crime. An article by the Justice Policy Institute shows that during the period from 2003 to 2007, there was an 8.9% decrease in the number of SROs in the United States and during that same period, no increase was noted in the number of reported offenses (Petteruti, 2011). Petteruti further asserted that incidents that occur in schools that employ SROs are under reported due to the fact that school administrators or teachers will simply contact the SRO when assistance is needed which reduces the number of calls that are received by 911 centers. In another article, Swift (2013) also refers to the report that was prepared by the Justice Policy Institute and similarly argues that the presence of SROs does not lead to a reduction in crime. The presence of SROs can deter crimes that would otherwise be committed on a school campus. However, there are also data that show that other administrative measures that are seen in schools that do not have SROs can still contribute to a lower crime rate.

*Increasing Arrests of Juveniles.* An area of concern for SRO programs is the rate of juvenile arrests. A 2011 article by Amanda Petteruti issued by the Justice Policy Institute reports that school referrals to the juvenile justice system have increased with the presence of SROs. A high percentage of those referrals were for minor offenses that may have been handled by the administration had an SRO not been present. This concern has attracted attention and some studies indicate that the use of the juvenile justice system for minor offenses aids in a phenomenon known as the "School to prison pipeline" (Morimune, 2012, p. 13). Morimune presented his *Differential Association Theory*, which asserts that criminal behavior is learned from peers and associates, and, therefore, "SRO programs are a rational method to preventing an increase in delinquency especially in schools that are more susceptible to crime and violence" (p. 28). Kim and Geronimo (2009) suggest SRO programs should be designed to provide a different response for disciplinary matters as opposed to criminal offenses that occur on school grounds. This recommendation was intended to ensure that juveniles were not receiving disparate treatment based upon the presence of a law enforcement officer within their school.

Although quantifiable data such as statistics are necessary to measure crime reduction, a factor that cannot be accurately measured is prevention or reduction in casualties for statistically improbable mass shootings involving an active shooter on the school. Anklam, Kirby, Sharevski, and Dietz (2014) found that the reduction of casualties was specifically linked to reduction in response times and in scenarios with an armed SRO, casualties dropped by 66.5% and response times were cut by 59.5%. Reynolds High School in Troutdale, Oregon involved an active shooter situation in which two SROs engaged the suspect before the suspect took his own life (Wright & Bain, 2014). Arapahoe High School, Centennial, Colorado also involved an active shooter situation. It ended within 80 seconds after a deputy who was assigned as the SRO intervened (Watkins & Cabrera, 2013). Granite Hills High School, El Cajon, California, in March 2001 was another example in which an SRO interrupted an active shooter situation. All three schools involved intervention by an SRO. Casualties were potentially reduced through quick response times and an SRO engaging the suspect. Although statistically rare, the aftermath of such publicized shootings reverberate throughout the community, both locally and nationally. The role of an SRO in those statistically improbable incidents can have broad implications to practices and policies that extend beyond the daily crime reduction by SROs.

*Cost.* One final area of concern is the expense that is associated with placing SROs in public schools. May, Hart, and Ruddell (2011) provided some background data from the American Association of School Administrators, which reported that "84% of school districts believed that they are inadequately funded" (p. 126). The authors further explained how a large number of districts were facing reductions in force issues and some had experienced five years of budget cuts. Many of the cuts were made to areas that were not academic in nature which only leaves a few areas where reductions could occur. One of those areas was school safety initiatives. In the SRO–school relationship, if the school is not able to supply the funding, then the costs of the officers typically falls to the local law enforcement agency (May et al., 2011). When the issue of cost is discussed, the controversy seems to split on a very specific line. Principals typically give great reports when surveyed about the importance of having an SRO present at their school (May et al., 2011).

Those on the other side of the discussion do not feel that the funding costs are justified by the service that is provided by the SROs. Petteruti (2011) also discusses the issues of budget reductions in her article but she goes on to include that for the price of one SRO, most districts could hire one teacher and have money left over. The concerns expressed by Petteruti regarding cost show that during times of budget cuts and financial shortfalls that school administrators should examine their operations and see if another service would benefit the school more than having a law enforcement officer on campus. In addition to the expense of the local officer, some look at the national reductions that have been seen in the COPS grants that are administered by the United States Department of Justice. Those grants made their first major impact in 2000 when the grants provided money to employee almost 600 SROs in 289 different communities.

The funding allocations peaked in 2002 and have decreased ever since. Some see this as a message that the issue is not a priority for the Department of Justice and those ideas are reinforced when you see large metropolitan school systems reduce the number of officers that they have on campuses. In addition, Petteruti (2011) argues that "School resource officers are a relatively new means of maintaining school safety, having only gained real traction in schools in the 1990s. Experienced faculty and staff have been in schools for much longer and are trained to work with students to keep everyone at school safe and to maintain a positive learning environment" (p. 24). This creates an entirely new debate as to the importance of SROs versus the importance of educators in a public school setting. As budget cuts and educational needs change, the SRO program may be affected in the future.

## PROMISING LEADERSHIP PRACTICES FOR SUCCESSFUL SRO PROGRAMS

A report published by the COPS Office notes that there is a lack of research on SRO programs, so it is not possible to identify a "one-size-fits-all" series of recommendations for implementing a maximally successful SRO program (Raymond, 2010). The report, however, identifies several promising practices for a successful SRO program. First, it emphasizes that all schools should develop a comprehensive school safety plan based on a thorough analysis of the problem(s) the school is facing and resources should be deployed accordingly. The report also notes that while SROs might be an important component of an overall safety plan, they should not be the only component. In some instances, school safety plans might not require the deployment of an SRO. If the school decides to use an SRO, there should be clear goals for the program, SROs should engage in activities that directly relate to school safety goals and address identified needs, and data should be collected to determine whether the program is achieving its goals. Finally, the report notes that effective SROs engage in problem-solving policing rather than simply responding to incidents as they occur (Raymond, 2010, p. 24).

Operational obstacles can threaten the success of an SRO program, including a lack of resources for the officer such as time constraints or lack of training, or turnover and reassignment (Raymond, 2010, p. 22). These challenges can be addressed with a proper framework, but it can require in-depth discussion and negotiations between school administrators and the law enforcement agency. The report also stresses that schools and law enforcement agencies should be aware of any pitfalls before agreeing to establish an SRO program (Raymond, 2010). There may be philosophical differences between school administrators and law enforcement agencies about the role of the SRO. Law enforcement agencies focus on public safety while schools focus on educating students. Establishing an operating protocol or MOU, according to the report, is a critical element of an effective school–police partnership (p. 30). The MOU should clearly state the roles and responsibilities of the actors involved in the program. Researchers who conducted an evaluation of 19 SRO programs note that "[w]hen SRO programs fail to define the SROs' roles and responsibilities in detail before, or even after, the officers take up the post in the schools, problem are often rampant, and the results could last for months and even years" (Finn & McDevitt, 2005, p. 43).

While it is possible to recruit officers with some of the skills necessary to be an effective SRO (e.g., who can effectively work with students, parents, and school administrators, have an understanding of child development and psychology, and who have public speaking and teaching skills), it is nonetheless important to provide training so officers can hone skills they already have or develop new skills that can make them more effective SROs. It might also be important for SROs to receive training before or shortly after starting their assignment. The study of 19 SRO programs concluded "any delay in training can be a serious problem because SROs then have to learn their jobs by 'sinking or swimming'" (Finn & McDevitt, 2005, p. 44).

### *An Exemplar: Area School Cars ("J-Car") with the LAPD*

Uniquely, the SRO assigned to the LAPD has a uniform policy for the deployment of SROs. In addition, their policy also defines the responsibilities of personnel assigned to area School Cars. In 1994, the LAPD established a uniform policy for the deployment of School Cars and defined the responsibilities of officer assigned to area. Additionally, the Department convened a short-term strategy committee on juvenile delinquency. The purpose of the committee was to develop a strategy to improve the effectiveness of the department's response to incidents, which involved juveniles. Through extensive interviews and studies, the committee identified several areas in which the department could improve its response to criminal activity involving juveniles. One specific item identified by the committee was the utilization of SROs, which are commonly referred to as "Juvenile-Cars" or "J-Cars." The committee found that in order to be effective, officers assigned to area school cars could not act independently and had to be deployed under the direct supervision of the area Juvenile Coordinator who would ensure the SROs are complying with their clearly defined responsibilities (LAPD, 1994).

Some of the responsibilities included SRO's handling juvenile-related matters on and around school campuses in their respective areas. This should include, but not limited to, the following:

- Providing visible patrol during school hours.
- Making arrests for offenses committed on campuses or in the vicinity of school grounds.
- Responding to calls for service for all school campuses from school personnel and taking appropriate action, i.e., child abuse investigations, missing juveniles.
- Handling any juvenile-related matter as directed by the juvenile coordinator, i.e., providing advice to youths and their families who seek assistance from the Department in juvenile-related matters such as incorrigibility, truancy, child abuse/neglect, and gang intervention.
- Providing expertise to other non-juvenile field units that may handle juvenile-related matters.
- Providing roll call training to patrol officer on juvenile-related matters.

On June 23, 2005, LAPD also established minimum training requirements for all school car officers due to the often complex nature of juvenile investigations that they may handle on a daily basis (LAPD, 2005). In addition to the standard juvenile training officers received at the Los Angeles Police Academy, all officers selected to the Juvenile School Car must also attend the four-day 32-hour Department Juvenile Procedures School, or an approved substitute with 60 days of their appointment to the position. This type of training along with policies and procedures ensured and reinforced that officers assigned as SROs were consistently and identically trained. Furthermore, the department would be able to hold the SRO's accountable for providing the school districts and the school communities with critical front-end intervention measures that will aid in reducing juvenile-related crime throughout the City of Los Angeles.

## CONCLUSIONS AND IMPLICATIONS FOR LEADERSHIP

School-based policing is one of the fastest growing areas of law enforcement. The time is ripe to reassess ways to improve the overall school climate and look beyond simply having more police officers in schools. SROs are members of the law enforcement community who teach, counsel, and protect the school community. When SROs are integrated into a school system, the benefits go beyond reduced violence in schools. The officers often build relationships with students while serving as a resource to students, teachers, and administrators helping to solve problems (Kerlikowske, 2013). We need to look beyond the law enforcement function of SROs and recognize their value in cultivating a safe, supportive environment for our young people with the help of educational leaders.

SROs are not armed guards standing sentry at school entrances. According to Kerlikowske (2013), they receive training in counseling and other skills that help them be effective in a school setting. Part of an SRO's job is building relationships with students and faculty, and the job often does not end at the close of the school day. They can be present at extracurricular activities and in school hallways, building trust with the students. SROs can get involved if they believe a young person may pose a danger to the school community. They can even visit students at home and speak with parents and family.

SRO programs across the nation are founded as collaborative efforts by police agencies, school and district leaders, students, parents, and communities. The goal of NASRO and SRO programs is to provide safe learning environments in our nation's schools, provide valuable resources to school staff, foster a positive relationship with our nation's youth, and develop strategies to resolve problems affecting our youth with the goal of protecting every child so they can reach their fullest potential.

From the selection process to the training, supervision, and evaluation of SROs, law enforcement agencies play an important role in the program's implementation. While SRO's broad and disparate roles and the program's flexibility are taken into consideration, agencies are required to apply high selection standards. However, the selection process of SROs can only be effective with the help of the school and district leaders, so the scope and role are clearly defined. School leaders should be open to communicating with and understanding resource officers' involvement in schools. Without neglecting their separate roles, school leaders and SROs should develop a mutual trust and understanding. Additionally, school authorities should provide integration of SROs in order to produce the best results and enhance the safety image of law enforcement as perceived by juveniles and staff.

The presence of resource officers in schools has proven to be more valuable than other safety precautions (Scheffer, 1987). Law enforcement agencies need to establish long-term plans to achieve program goals including the assignment of an adequate number of SROs and providing them with training that will better prepare them to respond to critical situations. Perhaps schools should at least share together with the agencies in funding the SRO program. In conclusion, it is possible to reduce violence in schools, prevent juveniles from engaging antisocial behaviors, and gain increased understanding of law enforcement. This can be accomplished through implementing the correct program, collective collaboration between school and district level leaders and law enforcement personnel, adequate funding, and support from the community.

## REFERENCES

Anklam, C., Kirby, A., Sharevski, F., & Dietz, J. E. (2014). Mitigating active shooter impact: Analysis for policy options based on agent/computer based modeling. *Journal of Emergency Management*, *13*(3), 201–216.

Benigni, M. D. (2004). The need for school resource officers. *FBI Law Enforcement Bulletin*, *73*, 22–24.

Brown, B. (2006). Understanding and assessing school police officers: A conceptual and methodological comment. *Journal of Criminal Justice*, *34*, 591–604.

Brown, B., & Benedict, W. R. (2005). Classroom cops, what do the students think? A case study of student perceptions of school police and security officers conducted in an Hispanic community. *International Journal of Police Science & Management*, *7*, 264–285.

Clark, J. (1994a). The crest of a new trend? *Law Enforcement News*, *20*(408), 1.

Clark, J. (1994b). Cops score as a school resource. *Law Enforcement News*, *20*(409), 1.

Commons, J. L. (2005). *Teachers or "real" police officers? A study of DARE officers in Northeast Tennessee*. Master's thesis. East Tennessee State University, Johnson City, Tennessee. Retrieved from http://dc.etsu.edu/etd/985/

Community Oriented Policing Services. (n.d.). *2013 CHP school resource officers list by state*. Retrieved from http://www.cops.usdoj.gov/Default.asp?Item=2367

Cray, M., & Weiler, S. C. (2011). Policy to practice: A look at national and state implementation of school resource officer programs. *The Clearing House: A Journal of Educational Strategies, Issues and Ideas*, *84*, 164–170.

Drug Abuse Resistance Education. (2015). *D.A.R.E.: Teaching students good decision-making skills to help them lead safe and healthy lives*. Retrieved from http://www.dare.com/

Finn, A. E., Peterson, D., Terrance, J., Taylor, T. J., & Osgood, D. W. (2012). *Is G.R.E.A.T. effective? Does the program prevent gang joining? Results from the National Evaluation of G.R.E.A.T.* St. Louis, MO: University of Missouri-St. Louis.

Finn, P. (2006). School resource officer programs. *FBI Law Enforcement Bulletin*, *75*(8), 1–7.

Finn, P., & McDevitt, J. (2005). *National Assessment of School Resource Officer Programs: Final Project Report*, Washington, DC, p. 43. Retrieved from https://www.ncjrs.gov/pdffiles1/nij/grants/209273.pdf. Accessed on February 28, 2005, hereinafter "*National Assessment of School Resource Officer Programs*".

Finn, P., McDevitt, J., Lassiter, W., Shively, M., & Rich, T. (2005). *Case studies of 19 school resource officer (SRO) programs* (NCJ 209271). Washington, DC: U.S. Department of Justice.

Gang Resistance Education and Training. (2015). *Has G.R.E.A.T. been proven effective?* Retrieved from http://www.great-online.org/

Girouard, C. (2001). *School resource officer training program* (FS 200105). Washington, DC: U.S. Department of Justice, Office of Justice Programs, Office of Juvenile and Delinquency Prevention.

Guerra, T. (2015a). *Community oriented policing services: Supporting safe schools*. Retrieved from http://www.cops.usdoj.gov/Default.asp?Item=2687

Guerra, T. (2015b). *Job description of school resource officers*. Retrieved from http://work.chron.com/job-description-school-resource-officer-19546.html

Hirschfield, P. J. (2008). Preparing for prison? The criminalization of school discipline in the USA. *Theoretical Criminology*, *12*, 79–101.

History of School Resource Officers (HSRO). (2015). Retrieved from http://what-when-how.com/police-science/school-resource-officers-police/

Huffman, D. (1995). School resource officer program. *TELEMASP Bulletin*, *7*(2), 1–7.

Jackson, A. (2002). Police-school resource officers' and students' perception of the police and offending. *Policing: An International Journal of Police Strategies & Management*, *25*(3), 631–650.

Kerlikowske, G. (2013). *School resource officers*. Retrieved from https://www.whitehouse.gov/blog/2013/03/28/school-resource-officers

Kim, C. Y., & Geronimo, I. (2009). Policing in schools: Developing a governance document for school resource officers in K-12 schools, an ACLU White Paper. New York, NY: American Civil Liberties Union.

Kupchik, A., & Bracy, N. L. (2010). To protect, serve, and mentor? Police officers in public schools. In T. Monahan & R. D. Torres (Eds.), *School under surveillance: Cultures of control in public education* (pp. 21–37). New Brunswick, NJ: Rutgers University Press.

Lambert, D. R., & McGinty, D. (2002). Law enforcement officers in schools: Setting priorities. *Journal of Educational Administration, 40*(3), 253–273.

Los Angeles Police Department, LAPD. (1994). *Office of Operations, Order No. 20, Deployment and Responsibilities of Area School Cars*, September 14, p. 1.

Los Angeles Police Department, LAPD. (2005). *Office of the Chief of Police, Administrative Order, No. 5, Training Requirements for Juvenile/School Car Officers*, June 23, p. 1.

May, D. C., Cordner, G., & Fessel, S. D. (2004). School resource officers as community police officers: Fact or fiction. *Law Enforcement Executive Forum, 4*, 173–189.

May, D. C., Hart, T. A., & Ruddell, R. (2011). School resource officers in financial crisis: Which programs get cut and why. *Journal of Police Crisis Negotiations, 11*, 125–140.

McDaniel, J. (1998). *School resource officers: Profiles in preventing school violence*. Raleigh, NC: Center for the Prevention of School Violence.

Morimune, R. J. (2012). *The school resource officer perspective: Examining crime, violence, law enforcement, and education on public high school campuses*. Retrieved from http://csus-dspace.calstate.edu/

Moskos, P. (2014). *Police killing whites and blacks*. Retrieved from http://www.copinthehood.com/2014/12/police-killing-whites-and-blacks.html

National Association of School Resource Officers (NASRO). (2015). *To Protect and Educate*. Retrieved from https://nasro.org/cms/wp-content/uploads/2013/11/NASRO-To-Protect-and-Educate-nosecurity.pdf

Petteruti, A. (2011). *Education under arrest: The case against police in schools*. Washington, DC: Justice Policy Institute.

Raymond, B. (2010). *Assigning police officers to schools*. Retrieved from http://www.cops.usdoj.gov/Publications/e041028272-assign-officers-to-schools.pdf, hereinafter "*Assigning Police Officers to Schools*".

Scheffer, M. W. (1987). *Policing from the schoolhouse: Police-liaison and resource officer programs*. Springfield, IL: Charles C. Thomas.

School Resource Officers (Police). (2015). *What? When? How?: School Resource Officers (Police)*. Retrieved from http://what-when-how.com/police-science/school-resource-officers-police/

Swift, J. (2013). *School resource Officers: A topic of hot debate, even prior to Sandy Hook*. Retrieved from http://jjie.org/school-resource-officers-topic-of-hot-debate-even-prior-sandy-hook/102868/

The Center for Technology in Education from Johns Hopkins University. (2004). *Role of the school resource officer*. Retrieved from http://cte.jhu.edu/courses/ssn/sro/ses1_act4_pag1.shtml

Thurau, L. H., & Wald, J. (2010). Controlling partners: When law enforcement meets discipline in public schools. *New York Law School Law Review, 54*, 977–1023.

Travis, L. F. III., & Coon, J. K. (2005). *The role of law enforcement in public school safety: A national survey*, Washington, DC: U.S. Department of Justice, National Institute of Justice.

Watkins, T., & Cabrera, A. (2013). *Colorado's school shooting over in 80 seconds*. Retrieved from http://www.cnn.com/2013/12/14/us/colorado-school-shooting/

Weiler, S., & Cray, M. (2011). Police at school: A brief history and current status of school resource officers. *Clearing House: A Journal of Educational Strategies, Issues and Ideas 84*(4), 160–163.

Wright, D., & Bain, J. (2014). *Male teen killed student in Oregon school and then himself*. Retrieved from abcnews.go.com/US/male-teen-kills-student-oregon-school-police/story?id=24080146

# CHAPTER 12

# FRASER AND THE CHEERLEADER: VALUES AND THE BOUNDARIES OF STUDENT SPEECH☆

Patricia A. L. Ehrensal

## ABSTRACT

*Student speech has and continues to be a contested issue in schools. While the Supreme Court ruled in* Tinker *that students do not shed their rights at the schoolhouse gate, in the* Kuhlmeier *and* Fraser *decisions the Court gave school officials greater latitude in regulating student speech, especially when it bears the imprimatur of the school. However, in its* Frederick *decision, the Court established school officials as the arbiters of the* meaning *of student speech. This chapter will explore the underlying values in schools that rejected the speech of Fraser while accepting the speech act of cheerleaders' dance routines. It will examine how the interpretation of these speech acts by school officials contributes to gender reproduction, with all the inequalities imposed.*

☆This chapter has been previously published in *Journal of School Leadership: Constructing a Bridge Between Law and Social Justice: An ethical journey, 22*(2), pp. 309–334, Rowman & Littlefield, Lanham, USA.

**Legal Frontiers in Education: Complex Law Issues for Leaders, Policymakers and Policy Implementers**
**Advances in Educational Administration, Volume 24, 221–246**

**ISSN: 1479-3660/doi:10.1108/S1479-366020150000024053**

Student "free speech" rights in public school settings have and continue to be a contested issue. In its landmark decision in *Tinker v DesMoines* (1969), the U.S. Supreme Court ruled that children do not shed their rights at the schoolhouse gate. However in the *Bethel School District v Fraser* (1986) and *Hazelwood v Kuhlmeier* (1988) decisions, the Court gave school officials greater latitude in regulating student speech, especially when it bears the imprimatur of the school. Further, in its more recent *Morse v Frederick* (2007) decision, the Court established school officials as the arbiters of the *meaning* of student speech. Thus, in the school context, teachers and administrators (adults) interpret the speech of students (children) and based on that interpretation determine if the speech is *inappropriate* and therefore, questioned or *appropriate* and therefore, left unquestioned.

The intention here is not to give a legal analysis of the U.S. Supreme Court decisions on student speech and applying it to cheerleader dance routines. Rather, I will examine the speech that got Fraser into trouble and the speech acts of cheerleaders' dance routines. While both "speeches" are *sexual*, Fraser's speech was constructed as inappropriate, therefore questionable and the speech acts of cheerleaders are constructed as appropriate thus left unquestioned. Consequently, Fraser was disciplined for giving his speech, while cheerleaders' speech is condoned and indeed rewarded. To understand this contradiction, I will interrogate the underlying values, particularly those concerning gender constructs, which led school officials to reject the speech of Fraser and accept, indeed encourage, the speech acts of cheerleaders' dance routines. This interrogation will be done through Critical Discourse Analysis (CDA).

## THEORETICAL PERSPECTIVE

This chapter is grounded in critical theory. It draws from critical law theory, particularly the work of Kairys (1982) and Conley and O'Barr (1998), cultural legal studies (Kahn, 1999), and feminist legal studies (MacKinnon, 1987, 1989, 2008). It will also draw on Bernstein's (1977, 1990) and Bourdieu and Passeron (1990) work on social reproduction, Foucault's (1979, 1980, 1991) work on disciplinary drills, discourse, power/knowledge, and governmentality, as well as on critical feminist education theory (Griffin, 1993, 1997; Thorne, 1993). By analyzing the two "speeches" of concern here through these theories, I will explore how both law and school organizations act in concert to legitimate and reproduce gender roles with all of the inequities and asymmetrical power relations embedded within them.

## *Critical Legal Theory*

Critical legal theory denies the separation of law from the political and social spheres. Thus it calls into question law's claims to neutrality and seeking the truth (Conley & O'Barr, 1998; Kairys, 1982; Kelman, 1987; Ward, 2002). Judges, Kairys (1982) argues, do not leave their preconceptions at their chamber door. Rather, not only their decisions, but also the very way they "read" the cases before them is influenced by these preconceptions. Consequently, they are political actors advancing a political agenda (Ward, 2002). This however is taken as unproblematic, both in the legal field and in society. "This is the great source of the law's power: it enforces, reflects, constitutes, and legitimizes dominant social and power relations without a need for or the appearance of control from outside and by the means of social actors who largely believe in their own neutrality and the myth of nonpolitical, legally determined results" (Kairys, 1982, p. 6).

Kelman (1987) further calls into question the separation of law from the social spheres by arguing that law defines the very actors and society that in turn influence law. Said another way, it is difficult for one to consider a person or group of people, without reference to the normalized legal attributes imposed on them. In this way then, law is defined "in terms of both state control over conduct and rhetorical understandings of the world" (p. 253).

For Conley and O'Barr (1998), the language of the law is extremely important. Drawing from Foucault's work, they argue that in law language *is* power. "The abstraction we call power is at once the cause and the effect of countless linguistic interactions taking place every day at every level of the legal system. Power is thus determinative of and determined by the linguistic details of legal practice ..." (Conley & O'Barr, 1998, p. 14). Thus, their research is concerned with seeking out the ways in which power is exercised through the dominant discourse, as well as the sources of such power.

MacKinnon (2005) is also concerned with *power* and law. She argues that, "[o]ne of law's main function is to organize social power among groups. Most legal conflicts ... involve social ranking and distribute social resources and treasure for the living of live, most have dimensions of, or effect on, 'who gets what, when and how'" (p. 3).

MacKinnon then is concerned with issues of equity and equality. Arguing that legal construction of *equality* is based on the Aristotelian concept, MacKinnon (2005) states "'formal equity' ... has become the familiar equality calculus of sameness and difference, of identity and distinction, requiring same treatment if one is the same, different treatment if one is different. Inequality means different treatment for likes, same treatment for unalikes" (p. 46). This construction of equability has particular consequences for women.

Gender, MacKinnon argues, is defined as difference. Thus, women are defined in terms of how they are *different* from men. Additionally, regardless of the (non)reality of these constructed differences, they work to disadvantage women. This, MacKinnon (2005) argues, poses a problem with the logic. If equality is constructed as sameness and women are defined as different from men, then women can never be equal to men until they no longer women. Thus, for MacKinnon, under such logic "[s]ex equality becomes something of an oxymoron, a contradiction in terms" (p. 50).

Salient to this study, the type of student speech that is questioned or remains unquestioned is not only a result of Court decisions, but also of the interpretation of these decisions. Further, these decisions and interpretations establish/reproduce boys as the advantaged and girls as the disadvantaged group.

Kahn (1999) argues that law is a cultural practice not a philosophical system. For him, law is a social practice, a way of *being* in the world. "To live under the rule of law is to maintain a set of beliefs about self and community, time and space, authority and representation. It is to understand the actions of others and the possible actions of the self as expressions of these beliefs" (Kahn, 1999, p. 36). In such a cultural practice, judges share the same values and beliefs of society. Thus, like Kairys, Kahn posits that judges do not approach a case *tabula rasa*. Rather, they bring to bear all of the norms, values, beliefs, and assumptions of the culture in which they live. For Kahn then, the rule of law is a means of organizing society "under a set of beliefs that are constitutive of the identity of the community and of its individual members. It is a way of understanding the unity of the community through time and of the self as the bearer of that history" (p. 6). Thus, the critical point for Kahn (1999) is "[t]he issue is not whether law makes us better off, but rather what is it that law makes us" (p. 6).

Critical legal theory then is concerned with uncovering the asymmetrical power relations that are codified and normalized within the rule of law. It seeks to uncover the false barriers between legal, political, and social spheres. Further, it is concerned with how the norms, values, and beliefs of a society simultaneously shape and are shaped by law. In doing so, it reveals how the language and logic of law obfuscates systems of domination and oppression by presenting them as normal and natural by "'trashing' the various mythologies of liberal legalism, particularly notions of adjudicative neutrality" (Ward, 2002, p. 156). Finally, critical legal theory is concerned with the "entire disciplinary process, part of which is certainly legalistic, but part also is governmental" (Ward, 2002, p. 150). Thus, Ward (2002) argues that we are ruled by law *and* by and whole governmental system.

Schools are an interregnal part of this governmental system. Like other social systems, I argue that these organizations simultaneously shape and are shaped by the laws concerning them. Consequently, in order to understand the social constructions that influence judges' decisions about school, it is important to understand the role of these organizations in the reproduction of systems of power and domination in society.

## *Power, Domination, and Social Reproduction*

Bernstein (1990) investigates *symbolic control*, which "translates power relations into discourse and discourse into power relations" (p. 134). Specialized agents within the field of symbolic control (re)produce these power relations. Two groups of agents are significant here. The first are *regulators* "whose function is to define, monitor, and maintain the limits of persons and activities. These would include legal systems and religious agencies" (p. 138). The second are the *reproducers*, which includes schools and educators, who *teach* the defined limits of persons and activities, thereby ensuring that the power relations are reinforced and reproduced.

Foucault (1979) describes schools as a place where societies send their children to be *disciplined* into acceptable thinking and behavior. Further, in these organizations, children are no longer individuals. As Foucault (1979) describes, "[g]radually ... the educational space unfolds; the class becomes homogeneous, it is no longer made up of individual elements ... 'rank' begins to define the great form of distribution of individuals in the educational order ..." (p. 146). Thus, "[b]y assigning individual places it made possible the supervision of each individual and the simultaneous work of all. It organized a new economy of the time of apprenticeship. It made the educational space function like a learning machine, but also as a machine for supervising, hierarchizing, and rewarding" (p. 147). Schools, then are what Foucault calls "learning machines" (p. 147). In such institutions, children are classified as students, and their activities are carefully monitored and controlled. Disciplinary technologies are employed to ensure that the students internalize dominant ideologies, as well as develop a correct view self (subjectivity) and behaviors (governmentality), which in turn reinforce power relations (Foucault, 1979, 1980, 1991).

Bourdieu and Passeron (1990) also look at the role of schools in the reproduction of power and domination in society. Schools they argue enact symbolic violence. That is it imposes systems of symbols and meanings on the students, which are experienced as legitimate. This is accomplished through "pedagogic work." This is "a process of inculcation which must last long enough to produce a durable training, i.e. a habitus, the product of internalization of the principles of a cultural arbitrary capable of perpetuation itself after [pedagogic action] has ceased and thereby of perpetuating in practices the principles of internalized arbitrary" (Bourdieu & Passeron, 1990, p. 31). Pedagogic work, then legitimates the power structure, thus obscures the objective truth of the habitus. The more extensive the pedagogic work, the greater the internalization of the cultural arbitrary.

School organizations are important institutions of social reproduction. In such institutions, children are "disciplined" to internalize the cultural arbitrary. Included in this are social constructions of gender, race, and social class, which are viewed as "normal" and "natural." That is, they *learn* to accept as normal and natural the asymmetrical power relations with the systems of domination and oppression embedded within them. Additionally, through governmentality children become self-limiting, and self-regulating, however not self-determining. As such, children learn to become the agents of their own hegemony. Through such *teaching* and *learning*, the asymmetrical power relations are reproduced in both school and society.

## METHODOLOGY

The "methodology" employed here is CDA. In every discourse, there are stories and many interpretations of the stories. Each story and interpretation privileges one set of views over others. When a particular set of views is dominant that set becomes a construct (Cherryholmes, 1988). When a set of constructs is dominant, voices and views that differ from them become marginalized and silenced (Morrow & Brown, 1994). Foucault (1972) argues that because speech is located within existing social institutions whose rules, interests, and power relations determine what can and cannot be said, power precedes speech. Habermas (1984) also argues that power structures are entangled in communication and meaning. Thus, to understand these constructs, one must reveal the obscured power relations that govern the discourse. One approach to interrogate and uncover such power relationships is CDA.

Fischer (2003) argues that unlike positivist methods of policy analysis, CDA does not view either policy making or the act of analyzing it as "value-neutral." As such "CDA researchers have to be aware that their own work is driven by social, economic, and political motives like any other academic work and that they are not in any privileged position" (Wodak & Meyer, 2009, p. 7).

CDA has two defining traits: "first, interpretations of meaning are sensitized to detecting forms of distorted communication linked to power and strategic (or manipulative) forms of interaction; second, discourses eventually are recontextualized with reference to the historical social relations through which they are constituted" (Morrow & Brown, 1994, p. 262). Thus, CDA is concerned with the uncovering of the power relationships and ideologies that are both constitute and are constituted by the discourse (Fairclough & Wodak, 1997).

The CDA applied here, then will seek to uncover why the nominating speech that Fraser gave at a school assembly was constructed as inappropriate and therefore questioned, while the dance acts of cheerleaders and dance teams performed at school sporting events are constructed as appropriate and therefore left unquestioned.

Boje and Dennehey (1993) offer a strategy or guidelines for story deconstruction, which can be applied to CDA. These guidelines include eight tactics. While these are offered in a linear way for ease of reading, these tactics are not necessarily utilize is a set sequence. First, do a *duality search*, which is listing any bipolar terms or dualities, even if only one side is mentioned. Second is to *reinterpret* the story, seeking other scenarios to find alternative interpretations than those offered by the dominant group. Third is to seek the *rebel voices*. Here one determines the privileged voices and seeks out the silenced voices and where they are in the hierarchy. Fourth is to tell the *other side of the story*. Here one turns the story around by putting the bottom on the top and the marginalized in control. Fifth is to *deny the plot*. Stories have plots, scripts, and scenarios which one needs to turn around to expose the underlying power relations. Sixth is to *find the exception* that breaks the rule. Additionally, the rules are overstated to make them seem absurd and extreme. Seventh is to *state what is in between the lines*. Here the interaction between speaker and listener/reader is scrutinized by attending to the nonverbal queues taken-for-granted meanings. In determining what is between the lines, one can expose how the storyteller is manipulating the listener/reader's experience to promote the teller's view. Eighth is to *resituate*, that is to "restory" removing the dualities, silenced voices, etc., to script new actions.

## DISCOURSE OF U.S. SUPREME COURT DECISIONS IN STUDENT SPEECH CASES

It is not the purpose or intention to do a traditional legal analysis here. Rather, I will present the "story" of student free speech rights in the school context as told by the U.S. Supreme Court. Afterwards, I will present the "restory," that is, retelling the story to include the social constructions and ideologies concerning children, children in schools, and school organizations that are taken for granted and thus influencing the Justices' understanding of the facts and ruling (Kahn, 1999; Kairys, 1982; Ward, 2002).

### *Story*

The U.S. Supreme Court has addressed the issue of student speech in four cases. *Tinker v DesMoines* (1969) was concerned with students wearing black armbands in protest of the Vietnam War. The second case was *Bethel School District v Fraser* (1986), which as stated earlier dealt with a student's "lewd" nomination speech at as school assembly. The third was *Hazelwood v Kuhlmeier* (1988) concerning a principal pulling two articles from the student newspaper. Finally, *Morse v Frederick* (2007) concerning a student's banner being interpreted as pro-drug speech by the principal.

The *Tinker* Court (1969) did state that children do not leave their rights at the schoolhouse gates, however it also stated that children do not have the full extent of rights as that of an adult. Further, the Court highlighted the important role schools played in preparing citizens. Understanding the need to balance student free speech rights with school officials' need to maintain an orderly environment, the Court ruled that speech could be retrained if it interfered materially and substantially with the school environment. In this particular case, the *Tinker* Court did not see the quiet wearing of an armband as materially and substantially interfering with school discipline, thus restricting such speech was unconstitutional. However, by stating that the nature of children's rights are not consistent with that of adults, and that the extent of these rights are to be balanced with school official's need to maintain an orderly school environment, the *Tinker* Court reaffirms and further legitimates the power of school officials to prescribe and control conduct in school.

The *Fraser* (1986) Court stressed the importance of public education to inculcate the habits and manners of civility, as well as shared values to prepare students for citizenship. Here the Court asserted that education takes place both inside and outside the confines of the classroom. All activities in school then, needs to instruct students in these habits, manners, and shared values of society. The lewd speech given by Fraser at a school assembly did not demonstrate these shared value or the habits and manners of society, therefore the school officials punishing him for the speech did not violate Fraser's First Amendment Speech rights. This speech and the Court's discourse concerning it will be examined in the next section.

In *Hazelwood* (1988) the Court ruled that schools may disassociate from speech that is inconsistent with its fundamental values. Further, school officials have authority over school-sponsored publications, and other expressive activities that are perceived to bear the imprimatur of the school. Thus here, the principal did have the authority to remove two articles from the student newspaper before publication, based on the principal's judgment that the subject matter was inappropriate and did not meet the school standards for journalism.

The *Morse* (2007) case involved a student unfurling a banner reading "Bong Hits for Jesus" while watching the Olympic Torch being carried in front of the school. The student claimed that the words were meaningless, and he did this to get the attention of the television cameras. The Court however, concluded that the principal's interpretation of this banner as promoting illegal drug use was reasonable. Consequently, the Court ruled, the principal may restrict such speech at a school event. In this ruling, the Court has determined that the principal's interpretation of student speech is paramount and final.

## *Restory*

Given that it is the (un)acceptable speech of children in school that is of concern here, one needs to understand the cultural and social "norms" that (un)consciously influenced the Justices' consideration of the facts before them.

Children and childhood are social constructions (Jenks, 1996). Further, this construction is made by adults through the filter of adult experiences and needs (Thorne, 1987). Given the biological fact that children *grow*, embedded in the social construction of children is "development." As such, children are constructed in terms of the future. They are judged not by who they are now, but what they will become in the future, or as Mayall (1994) states, they are "human *becomings*." Children then, need to be socialized to ensure that they *become* proper consumers and reproducers (Griffin, 1997). Outside of the family, schools are the primary institution charged with socializing children. Indeed, the U.S. Supreme Court in these and other cases highlights the importance of schools in inculcating the habits and manner of civility and therefore does not wish to interfere with school officials' authority in managing schools and teaching children.

In the cases presented here, U.S. Supreme Court has affirmed and legitimated the power and authority of principals to disallow student speech (s) he deems to be vulgar, too sexual in content, inconsistent with the values of the school organization, which may be perceived as bearing the imprimatur of the school. In doing so, the Court has extended the role of *regulator* (Bernstein, 1990) to school principals. That is, like that of legal and religious systems, principals are able to "define, monitor, and maintain the limits of [students] and activities" (p. 138). This, in conjunction with their role as *reproducers* (Bernstein, 1990; Bourdieu & Passeron, 1990), gives principals unique and unrestrained power to impose hegemonic constructs of gender and identity. Given the influence this allows in determining *governmentality* (Foucault, 1979, 1980, 1991), two questions emerge. What is the content and audience of student speech determined to be too vulgar and too sexually explicit in content, making it either unacceptable and questioned, or acceptable and unquestioned? Following from this then, what are the norms, values, beliefs, and assumptions that allow for the differing interpretations of such speech?

## (UN)ACCEPTABLE AND (UN)QUESTIONED SPEECH

### *Fraser's Unacceptable and Questioned Speech*

On April 26, 1983, Mathew Fraser gave a speech nominating his friend Jeff Kuhlman for student body vice president. He delivered this speech at a school assembly, which students were required to attend. This assembly was school-sponsored and was part of an educational program on self-government (*Bethel School District v Fraser*, 1986). Although warned by a teacher prior to giving it, told that he probably should not give the speech and there might be severe consequences of he did, Fraser gave the following speech:

> I know a man who is firm – he is firm in his pants, he's firm in his shirt, his character is firm – but most ... of all, his belief in you the students of Bethel, is firm. Jeff Kuhlman is a man who takes his point and pounds it in. If necessary, he'll take an issue and nail it to the wall. He doesn't attack things in spurts – he drives hard, pushing and pushing until finally – he succeeds. Jeff is a man who will go to the very end – even the climax, for each and every one of you. So please vote for Jeff Kuhlman A.S.B. Vice President – he'll never come between you and the best our school can be. (*Bethel School District v Fraser*)

The speech was considered inappropriately sexual in its content, especially as it was given during a required school assembly, and the audience included teenaged girls and 14-year-old students. Asserting that the process of instilling the habits and manners of civility necessary for citizens in a self-governing democracy extended beyond books and classrooms, the *Fraser* Court stated that a school could not convey these shared values if it tolerated lewd, indecent or offensive speech or conduct. Further, the glorifying of male sexuality in a school-sponsored setting was insulting to teenage girls and possibly harmful to the younger students in the audience. In short, a high school assembly, according to the Court, is no place for sexually explicit, vulgar or lewd speech and school officials do not violate the First Amendment by disallowing such speech.

Fraser's speech was censured by the officials of Bethel High School because its glorifying of male sexuality was inconsistent with the values that the school was duty bound to inculcate in its students. Further, as lessons in these values extend beyond the classroom and formal curriculum, but are also taught by example through all school activities, the school officials were within their authority to discipline Fraser by imposing a two-day suspension. This disciplinary action, I will argue not only distanced the school from this speech – that is it ensured that the speech did not bear the imprimatur of the school – but also served as a disciplinary drill (Foucault, 1979). The imposition of a two-day suspension emphasized the serious and offensive nature of the speech, as well as the school organization's intolerance of having its values compromised or disregarded, to not only Fraser, but also the entire student body. The U.S. Supreme Court, in ruling that the school officials acted within their authority and did not violate Fraser's First Amendment rights to free speech, legitimated not only the response of the school officials, but also the underlying values the actions were meant to uphold and reinforce.

Fraser's speech then was unacceptable and questioned because of its explicit and implicit sexual content. Such sexualize speech has no place in a public school organization as it does not conform to notions of decorum and civility, together with the underlying values and ideologies these organizations are required to impose on the students in their charge. While it can be argued that Fraser's speech was indeed lewd and indecent, and perhaps is unacceptable in a school setting, such arguments ring hollow when one considers the speech acts of school cheerleaders.

### *Cheerleaders Acceptable and Unquestioned Speech*

#### *Dance as Speech*

While the U.S. Supreme Court has not heard a case concerning cheerleaders dance routines, it and lower courts have heard cases concerning nude and exotic dance, and in doing so ruled that dance does merit First Amendment protection.

In re Giannini (1968), the California Supreme Court stated that the actual definition of dance describes it as a communication of ideas and emotions, thus it is afforded protection under the First Amendment.

In *California v LaRue* (1972), the U.S. Supreme Court in determining the regulation of the sale of alcohol in clubs with nude dancing stated that some of the performances are within Constitutional protection. The Court in *Doran v Salem Inn* (1975) again hinted that some nude dancing performances merits First Amendment protection. In *Scad v Borough of Mount Ephraim* (1981), the U.S. Supreme Court again stated that nude dancing was entitled to some degree of First Amendment protection, and it confirmed this again in *Barnes v Glen Theatre, Inc.* (1991) stating that nude dancing was an expressive performance and is subject to a degree of First Amendment protection.

Dancing, including nude dancing intended to express the erotic, then, is a form of expression, which the U.S. Supreme Court has stated merits protection under the First Amendment. While cheerleaders perform their dance routines clothed, they are no less a form of expression, and as will be discussed in the next section an expression that evocative of the erotic. Further, although these dance routines are performed by teams and not (necessarily) individuals, the material point is that they are a form of expression (speech) that is sanction, controlled, and indeed encouraged by school officials. Thus, unlike the "speech" of Fraser, the "speech acts" of cheerleaders are acceptable and unquestioned.

*Cheerleading Dance*

"Cheerleading, an American invention with its roots in the institutions of sport and education, has become a staple in American culture" (Hanson, 1995, p. 1). Cheerleaders are high status members of middle and high school student populations (Adams & Bettis, 2003, 2005, 2006; Barnett, 2006; Eder & Parker, 1987; Merten, 1996), who wear uniforms with the name of their school and perform their routines at *school-sponsored* events. These events include pep-rallies, which are school assemblies with required attendance, as well as games, which are open to the public.

The speech acts (routines) that cheerleaders perform at these events are often highly sexualized.

> Cheerleading allows the erotic to enter into school-sanctioned space: in fact, it is one of the only school spaces in which girls can play with or try on the identity of the All-American nice girl next door and sexually provocative woman simultaneously. In many schools, cheerleaders are allowed to wear short skirts and tight –fitting vests, which often violate school dress codes, while performing sexually provocative dance moves such as pelvic thrusts to popular music – neither of which is typically allowed in school elsewhere. (Adams & Bettis, 2005, p. 83)

Cheerleading, then "allows girls to try on womanly (i.e., sexualized) identity in a school-sanctioned place" (Adams & Betts, 2005, p. 83). In observing cheerleaders, Adams and Bettis (2003) "noted the giddy emotional responses of girls when they were learning dance or cheer movements that were overtly sexual in nature. Part of what they were learning as they practiced these routines was how to move their bodies in new ways in a new arena where they were explicitly being gazed upon" (p. 83).

Cheerleaders then perform their overtly sexualized routines at school-sponsored events, to audiences that include members of both the school organization and the community. Additionally, as many middle schools, as well as high schools, have cheerleading squads, the audience, and indeed the cheerleaders themselves, includes children 14-years-old and younger. Further, these girls while performing their routines have the imprimatur of the school organization, not only because they do so at school-sponsored events, but also have it blazed across their chests. Thus, their sexualized speech acts are performed in front of larger audiences than that of Fraser's. Why then, are cheerleading speech acts acceptable and unquestioned, while Fraser's speech was unacceptable and questioned?

## CHEERLEADERS AND SOCIAL REPRODUCTION

Cheerleading is a highly visible and therefore high status activity for girls in middle and high school (Adams & Bettis, 2003, 2005, 2006; Barnett, 2006; Eder & Parker, 1987; Merten, 1996). The construct of cheerleader, however, is composed of several conflicting attributes. Here I will examine cheerleaders as school leaders, athletes, and the aesthetically pleasing "ideal" of American girlhood. Interrogation of these attributes reveals that they indeed conflated; thus, I will argue that cheerleading, as a high-status and highly visible activity, plays an important role in gender reproduction in schools.

### *Cheerleader as School Leader*

"Cheerleading operates at the interesting intersection of small-town local pride and national patriotism, both of which promote civic rituals and public spectacles" (Adams & Bettis, 2005, p. 17). Adams and Bettis (2005) state that cheerleaders "[ensure] that school spirit, loyalty, and pride [transcend] difference" (p. 17). They "must galvanize group members to remain supportive and part of [the] larger whole .... Ultimately, the job of the cheerleaders is to rally all of the school citizens to support the team against the week's opponent. This is the heart of patriotism – to galvanize people to come together to support a common goal through the use of symbols, rituals, and traditions" (Adams & Bettis, 2005, p. 18). As representatives of their schools, cheerleaders are expected to exhibit good and appropriate behavior in public (e.g., not smoke, drink, use foul language). Additionally, they are to be optimistic, happy, and enthusiastic. In short, they are role models for both the members of the school and the general community. Cheerleaders, then "represent the model citizens whose values and actions ... reflect the ideals of the community" (Adams & Bettis, 2005, p. 17).

This "leading" role of cheerleaders however is centered on supporting boys' athletic endeavors, particularly football and basketball. As "leaders" then, their job is to stay out of harms way and cheer for the boys actively engaged in battle (the game) for the honor and reputation of the school. This construct of leadership consequently reproduces the secondary and passive role of women. That is, it is a supportive role and without boys' sports, the cheerleader girls would have no purpose. "From the feminization of cheerleading in the 1950s to the 1990s, cheerleaders have not challenged the well-established dichotomy between masculine and feminine spheres or male female roles in society. Men play sports; girl cheerleaders ... support them in their athletic endeavors by motivating the fans to root for their fearless warriors" (Adams & Bettis, 2005, p. 67). This "leadership" role of girls' then is constructed in terms of the needs of boys.

### *Cheerleader as Athlete*

Within the world of cheerleading, there is great debate over whether or not cheerleading is a sport (Adams & Bettis, 2005). While cheerleading routines have always involved jumps, splits, and cartwheels, the level and difficulty of tumbling routines now incorporate have increased. This, coupled with the cheerleading teams now enter competitions, one can make the argument that cheerleading has become more athletic. Proponents of making cheerleading a sport not only point to the changes in cheerleading, they also argue that as a sport it would be on the same level as football and basketball, increasing its ability to secure resources, use of facilities, and funding (Adams & Bettis, 2005; Hanson, 1995). Opponents "fear that categorizing cheerleading as a sport is but another way to subvert the intentions of Title IX" (Adams & Bettis, 2005, p. 59). They worry that those traditional women's sports, such as volleyball would be removed from school athletic rosters (Adams & Bettis, 2005; Hanson, 1995).

In July 2009, The U.S. District Court for the Connecticut ruled that Quinnipiac University was out of compliance under Title IX (*Beidiger, et al. v Quinnipiac University*). In doing so the Court stated that as competitive cheerleading is not a sport recognized by the NCAA, the competitive cheerleading team at Quinnipiac was not entitled to be considered a sport under Title IX. Consequently, to bring the University into compliance, the 30 members of the competitive cheerleading team had to be removed from the athletic roster. Additionally, The Women's Sports Foundation "cites a 1975 Office for Civil Rights Memorandum to School Superintendents, which explicitly states that cheerleading is to be considered an extracurricular activity rather than part of the school's athletic program" (Adams & Bettis, 2005). The Foundation however also stated that if "[the cheerleading squad] have a coach, practice as frequently as a regular varsity team and compete against other cheerleading teams on a regular basis and more frequently than they appear to cheer for other teams, they may meet the definition of a varsity team" (Adams & Bettis, 2005, p. 59).

Thus, despite the athleticism of their routines, cheerleaders are not considered athletes, unless they can *prove* that they compete more than they serve. This is consistent with Walkerdine's (1990) findings that even when girls perform, this performance is downgraded or dismissed. Adams and Bettis (2005) argue that this question of athleticism gets at the core of gender reproduction. They state that institutionalized sports "[b]egun as a way for males to demonstrate their masculinity and to socialize young boys into the proper way to be a man ..." (p. 64). Consequently, there has been a long history of resisting women's attempts to participate in sports. Cheerleaders, on the other hand, have not threatened the status quo; rather they have served to reproduce it (Adams & Bettis, 2005; Hanson, 1995; Merten, 1996). Indeed, as will be discussed in the next section, even while performing difficult routines, cheerleaders are expected to maintain a particular feminized look and demeanor. However,

> as cheerleaders have become more athletic and less interested in cheerleading because of its traditional role of spirit booster and supporter of the athletes, anxieties about the appropriate and normal role of men and women surface once again and can be found simmering in the undercurrents of the cheerleading-as-sport debate. If cheerleaders are one of the last bastions of traditional femininity, what does it mean when they want to leave their poms and megaphones behind to be tough athletes who are competitor themselves? (Adams & Bettis, 2005, p. 67)

Consequently, even when performing difficult routines that demand a great deal of athleticism, cheerleaders are not constructed as "athletes." Indeed, "many administrators do not like the athletic turn cheerleading has taken, seeing their emphasis on preparing for competition as either too dangerous or time away from their real duty as a supporter of athletics" (Adams & Bettis, 2005, p. 68). Thus, discouraging cheerleading as a sport is constructed as protecting girls from danger and distractions from their proper role, supporting boys.

### *Cheerleader as the Aesthetically Pleasing "Ideal" of American Girlhood*

Cheerleading is an American invention, and this "ubiquitous cheerleader icon reveals both conflict and consensus in cultural values concerning status, youth, competition, success, celebrity, gender, and sexuality" (Hanson, 1995, p. 99). In short, cheerleaders embody the "ideal" of American girlhood. This idealized space of cheerleading, however is a precarious one and one that needs to be navigated with great care. "[T]he cheerleader embodies positive and negative stereotypes, reflecting contradictions and ambiguities in the cultural construction of gender roles and social ideals" (Hanson, 1995, p. 100).

"Contemporary images of the cheerleader often invoke positive connotations: a young female who is physically attractive (cute), socially popular and influential – a wholesome, extroverted, enthusiastic Good Girl" (Hanson, 1995, p. 100). They represent "an admired elite to other students [and to] adults, this image continues to define youthful success and appeal" (Hanson, 1995, pp. 100–101).

In terms of appearance, the "ideal" cheerleader conforms to white middle-class standards of feminine beauty. They are not tall, have petite body type, and don't look athletic (i.e., appear muscular) (Adams & Bettis, 2003, 2005; Hanson, 1995). In their study, Adams and Bettis (2005) noted that

> [a]thleticism clearly counted, but just as important was being "the cheerleading type," which meant that one's peer group, race and physical appearance were still central to defining what the "cheerleader type" was. Consequently, even girls who could perform most of the athletic requirements were not considered cheerleading material if they did not convey a "cheerleader look".... (p. 106)

While there were African American and Latino students in the school they studied, the cheerleading squad was disproportionately represented by the "preps" – girls from white middle-class families. Furthermore, while the school instituted a policy to put cheerleading try-outs on an equal footing, as a result of an Office of Civil Rights (OCR) investigation, the squad at the time of their study was still predominately white "prep" girls. Indeed, during the discussions of the OCR findings and policy remedies, White parents' "comments during the school board meetings, letters to the editor, and newspaper advertisements all suggested that they understood equality of opportunity to mean denigrating hard work, salving minority self-esteem, and destroying the will to excellence" (Adams & Bettis, 2003, p. 134). This echoed concerns about newly formed cheerleading squad in schools during desegregation, when it was believed that including African American girls would materially change cheerleading. "One of the primary reasons why many whites objected so vehemently to the selection of African American girls on cheerleading squads during desegregation was based on their own notions of who could best represent ideal girlhood and womanhood" (Adams & Bettis, 2005, p. 109).

Another important characteristic of the cheerleader is the ability to smile, appear happy, and be nice to everyone (Adams & Bettis, 2003, 2005, 2006; Hanson, 1995). In other words, cheerleaders must develop "self-discipline, particularly in how to control their emotions and out-ward actions" (Adams & Bettis, 2005, p. 62). This especially important to ensure that girls who make the squad do not "flaunt their success nor ... think they are suddenly better than those who did not make it" (Adams & Bettis, 2005, p. 62), because "being labeled a snob is the second worst and feared label one can have attached to her. Only being labeled a slut is worse" (*ibid.*, p. 62).

### *Feminine Spaces and the Secreting of Sexual Desire*

In the male-dominated school organization, cheerleading is one of the two feminine spaces; the other is the prom (Best, 2000, 2004). Like cheerleading, the prom is an icon of American culture. Here too, girls take on "leadership" roles in planning and organizing the arrangements surrounding the prom. Salient to this chapter is that it is also a space where school dress codes are relaxed. As a coming-of-age ritual, prom is a space where girls can practice their sexualized adult feminine role. Thus, on prom night, school officials indulge girls' desire to wear "sexy" dresses and be heavily made-up. The goal of many girls is look so completely different on prom night that no one, not even friends recognize them (Best, 2000, 2004).

Gleeson and Firth (2004) explored girls' sartorial identities. While understanding these 15-year-old girls rejecting pink in favor of more "sexualized" clothes, they were perplexed that the girls did not admit that these clothes made them feel "sexy." Gleeson and Firth blamed themselves for this, thinking that either they had not gained enough of the girls' trust, or that this was a form of power that the girls preferred not to give over to them. I argue that this lack of admission is because to do so, the girls would jeopardize their reputation. To admit that the clothes made them *feel* sexy and that is why they wear them would be tantamount to admitting that they have sexual desires. In admitting thus, they risk being labeled "slut" – the worse label possible. Good girls suppress their sexual desires, and certainly do not admit them openly (Lamb, 2001; Tolman, 1994).

Thus, because the goal of clothes and make-up chosen for prom night is to ensure that girls do not *look* like themselves, they are essentially a costume, which establishes a space between girls' everyday self and the role they adopt for the night. In this space they are able to *look* sexy while denying that that was the desired goal. Consequently, they are able to *play* with their sexuality and avoid being labeled a "slut."

The feminine space of cheerleading also offers a place where girls can play with their sexuality while protected from the "slut" label. Their smiles are required as part of the "cheerleader look," to show that they are enthusiastic and enjoying supporting the boys in their pursuit of victory, not because they are enjoying moving their bodies in a sexualized way. Additionally, these sexualized routines are performed before an audience therefore; they are done for the pleasure of the audience, not the cheerleaders. Finally, "[o]ne of the primary reasons girls [want] to be a cheerleader [is] because they [believe] that cheerleading [is] a route to instant popularity, which increase[s] the likelihood of getting a boyfriend, a high-status marker for adolescent girls. Hence, cheerleading operate[s] as a discursive practice that [affirms] heterosexualized femininity" (Adams & Bettis, 2006, p. 127). Cheerleaders then, can be sexually appealing, but not sexually active or available, thus avoiding being labeled a "slut." In doing so, cheerleading reproduces and reinforces the virgin/mother/whore trichotomy. That is, cheerleaders are good girls (virgins) who are willing to perform sexualized routines, not for their own pleasure (like a whore), but as a means of getting a boyfriend, and to support boys in athletic endeavors (mother). Cheerleading then can be sexualized because cheerleaders are protected by a "bulletproof sugar-coating" of wholesome and nice good girl (Hanson, 1995). "The same sugar-coating enables beaming parents and [school officials] to encourage teams of little girls to grind their baby hips in the cause of school spirit" (Hanson, 1995, p. 100).

## FRASER AND THE CHEERLEADER

"Agencies which operate in the field of symbolic control have, in Foucault's term, *explicit normalizing functions*. That is, they produce general norms for law, health (physical, mental, and social), administration, education, and for the legitimate production and reproduction of discourse itself" (Bernstein, 1990, p. 138). The U.S. Supreme Court in its Fraser, Kuhlmeir, and Morse decisions legitimated school officials' authority to interpret student speech and prohibit any speech that contradicts the values of the school organization. That is, they are the arbiters of which speech is acceptable and unquestioned and which is unacceptable and questioned. Consequently, they are at once both regulators and reproducers, that is, they establish what is legitimate speech and behavior for students, thus producing and reproducing the discourse of normalcy of identity development, including that of gender.

Cheerleaders sexualized routines are performed in a bulletproof sugar-coated space, which allows them to give pleasure to their (male) audience and to support the boys' athletic endeavors, while denying their own pleasure. Even when boys are invited into this space, the gender roles are maintained. Boys on cheerleading teams do the "macho stuff" such as stunts and tumbling (Powers, 2010). "These roles are a way to highlight the differences between women and men on the squad ..." (Adams & Bettis, 2005, p. 87). Male cheerleaders then do not dance. "While the girls may shimmey across their shoulders and chests, the boys will not, and while girls may use some provocative hip sways, the boys will not" (*ibid.*, p. 87). "For most male cheerleaders ... cheerleading is about strength and power, while the girls provide the beauty, the 'art' of the activity" (Adams & Bettis, 2005, p. 88).

Adams and Bettis (2005) assert that this is to spare the boys on the squad from being harassed, and Powers (2010) claims that boys will not join a squad if the girl cheerleaders asked them to dance or do arm motions. While this is true, I would argue that even if the boys were willing to "dance," school officials would not allow it. If boys were to "shimmy" their shoulders and chest, and sway their hips in a provocative manner, it would be interpreted, like Fraser's speech, as "lewd" because it contradicts the construct of the heterosexual male. That is, they would be opened to the same sexual objectification as their female counterparts, which contradict the values of the school organization.

Adolescence is a period in which defiance is assumed and the desire for freedom expected (Griffin, 1997). Consequently, adults (here school officials) must employ surveillance and control, however "successful socialization into adulthood is characterized by the development of 'appropriate' techniques of *self*-surveillance and *self*-control" (Griffin, 1997, p. 9). This "socialization" ensures that adolescents transition "into the 'adult' cycle of production/reproduction/consumption" (Griffin, 1997, p. 6), and gender identity socialization is critical to this transaction.

In glorifying male sexuality in his speech, Fraser demonstrated that he was not "transitioning" properly, and therefore was unacceptable and questioned. In disciplining him, school officials reasserted the construct of heterosexual male and denigrated Fraser's attempt to objectify males, and the U.S. Supreme Court strengthened this lesson by legitimating the values that underpin it.

Cheerleaders' sexualized routines however demonstrate proper transition to the adult state. By being sexually appealing but not sexually active or available, they are internalizing the virgin/mother/whore trichotomy and the domination, which it imposes. Consequently, this speech act is acceptable and unquestioned. Further, because cheerleaders do their routines at school-sponsored events and have the imprimatur of the school organization literally on their chest, the school legitimates and reproduces this system of gender inequality and domination.

## BRIDGING LAW AND ETHICS

The "restory" of the U.S. Supreme Court decisions concerning student speech presented here reveals the power of principals to de-center students as the authors of their own speech. This is accomplished by the legitimated power of principals to determine the meaning of student speech, and to "shape" the speech to ensure that is consistent with the norms values and beliefs of the school organization. Additionally, through restorying cheerleaders' dance routines as speech acts (forms of expression), I have problematized this as school permitted and encouraged speech. That is, the sexualized expression (speech) of these dance routines are acceptable and unquestioned while the sexual nature of Fraser's speech was unacceptable and questioned. As I have argued, cheerleaders and their speech (dance) play an important role in reproduction of gender. They represent the "ideal" of girl-/womanhood.

As discussed here, the characteristics that qualify girls to be cheerleaders – being pretty enthusiastic, friendly, helpful, respectful toward teachers and other authority figures, happy, smiling, and being sexually desirable but not sexually available – have very little to do with the "skills" required for performing the routines. The boys on the teams that the girls cheer for are not expected to "present a saintly appearance or a popular personality" (Bennett, 1990, p. 5) their performance on the team is all that matters. "That cheerleaders must have unusually high standards of character and morality because they publicly represent their schools has little merit" (Bennett, 1990, p. 5). Rather, these are desirable characteristics for *all* girls, and because cheerleaders are able to demonstrate these traits so well, they are rewarded with popularity and having the best chance of dating the most desirable boys in the school. Indeed, a "cheerleader may wear her uniform in the classroom, flaunting her success in a way that no other girl may" (Bennett, 1990, p. 4).

Cheerleaders then, are "innovative messages" (Bernstein, 1990) not only to girls but to the entire student body. They play an important role in reproducing the virgin/mother/whore trichotomy that girls and women must negotiate. Consequently, cheerleaders' sexualized dancing goes unquestioned because woman as object of sexual desire is so normalized.

This questioning and forbidding speech that celebrates male sexuality while allowing and indeed encouraging speech that glorifies female as objects of sexual desire contradicts the principles of ethical educational leadership.

### *The Ethics of Fraser and the Cheerleader*

"A crucial area of the moral influence of the school on both pupils and teachers is the way it is run, the management. [It is] the most pervasive aspect of the hidden curriculum; how a school is managed will have profound effects upon the institution" (Bottery,1990, p. 126). Following from Bottery then, how principals *manage* student behavior, including student speech, significantly influences the moral development of the students. Indeed, in his dissenting opinion in *New Jersey v T.L.O.* (1985), Justice Stevens asserted that students learn as much from example as they do by exhibition.

Authenticity, Starratt (2004) argues, is the determining of one's *true self* that is the ability to choose and determine one's life. This however cannot be done in isolation. Rather *authenticity* is relational; it is a dialogue between the self and another, the community, and the culture. Schools are a primary arena for such dialogues. "[S]chools as organizations impose a disciplined process of learning and interdependent structure for producing and enacting knowledge" (Starratt, 2004, p. 78), which includes the hidden curriculum of policy and practice (Bottery, 1990). Authentic educators then, "exercise their authenticity in their relationships" (Starratt, 2004, p. 78) in this arena. The authentic educational leader will similarly exercise authenticity in her/his relations, despite the power and authority that is vested in his/her position. "The work of the authentic leader involves the leader's deep commitments as a human being, as an educator, as an educational administrator, and as a citizen-administrator" (p. 79). As such Starratt (2004) asserts that an educational leader must remain an authentic educator and not let administrative agendas divert her/him from being an authentic leader.

Given that cheerleaders are the "innovative message" continually exhibiting the *ideal* that girls should strive for, limits girls' ability to negotiate and determine their *authentic* selves. In the school arena, where their authenticity is being shaped, these girls are in dialogue with a pretty, perky, sexually desired yet unavailable ideal. Thus, there is a limited dialogue, and a limiting of the possibilities for girls (and boys) to determine their authentic (gendered) selves. Additionally, to be an authentic leader also requires continual dialogue within the school arena (Starratt, 2004). Given the limited dialogue in terms of gender roles, one has to question the possibility of authentic leadership in these organizations.

Shapiro and Stefkovich (2010) argue for a multiple paradigm approach to resolving ethical dilemmas. Particularly they present the *ethics* of justice, critique, and care for this multiple paradigm approach. The ethic of justice, which focuses on rights and law, is committed to human freedom. The ethic of critique is grounded in critical theory. As such it seeks to uncover the unquestioned values and seeks to "redefine and reframe other concepts such as privilege, power, culture, language, and even justice" (Shapiro & Stefkovich, 2010, p. 13), and reveals ways in which schools reproduce the inequities found in the broader society. The ethic of care is concerned with relationships. Drawing from Nodding's assertion that the care of children in the primary job of schools, Shapiro and Stefkovich note that in the ethic of care, "students are at the center of the educational process and need to be nurtured and encouraged ..." (2010, p. 16). Consequently, it is concerned with how decisions will affect relationships with and the nurturing of children.

While these paradigms are helpful in exploring many aspects of an ethical dilemma, Shapiro and Stefkovich offer the ethic of the profession to help negotiate the tensions that arise between these paradigms. In the ethic of the profession, educational leaders must be aware of their own personal codes of ethics, as well as how these codes effect the way they approach ethical decisions. The student however, is at the center of the ethic of the profession. That is, when facing an ethical dilemma, the educational leader should act in the best interest of the student (Shapiro & Stefkovich, 2010).

The *restory* of (un)questioned and (un)acceptable student speech presented here is grounded in critical theory and the ethic of critique. In it the cheerleader as lesson in the hidden curriculum is revealed. That is, cheerleaders are innovative messages, which help reproduce and reinforce gender roles and systems of patriarchy. Although sexual in nature, cheerleaders' dance routines are acceptable and unquestioned speech because it is part of the important *message*. Thus, this sexualized speech performed by girls, which emphasizes their sexuality, is treated differently than a speech given by a boy, which alluded to male sexuality.

In leaving these dance routines unquestioned, educational leaders treat girls differently from boys. Thus, in their court-legitimated role as *regulators* (Bernstein, 1990), they construct girls as *different*. Gender equality in schools then, continues to be an oxymoron (MacKinnon, 2005). Such fostering of inequality certainly runs afoul of the ethic of justice. Additionally, as cheerleaders are expected to be happy, always smiling, in control of their emotions, and sexually desirable but unavailable, by making them the *ideal* that all girls should strive for, educational leaders limit the nature of the relationships that girls can have with both themselves and others. By controlling their emotions and always displaying a *happy face*, regardless of how unhappy they may feel, girls cannot have an honest relationship with themselves or anyone else. Further, being sexually desirable but unavailable requires cheerleaders (and girls) to deny their sexuality (Adams & Bettis, 2006; Bennett, 1990; Gleeson & Firth, 2004; Walkerdine, 1990) transitioning them *correct* consumers and reproducers (Griffin, 1997). In doing so, the virgin/mother/whore trichotomy is reproduced informing girls that virginity and motherhood are the only two acceptable states for them. Nurturing girls (and boys) to accept such a system of oppression as natural and desirable is not consistent with the ethic of care. Finally, as the system of patriarchy, with all of the inequality, oppression, and domination it brings, can neither be just or caring, educational leaders that allow for its reproduction in schools cannot be acting in the best interests of *any* student.

If however we purport an authentic ethical leadership (Starratt, 2004) which acts in the best interest of the student (Shapiro & Stefkovich, 2010), we must question that sexualized speech which objectifies girls by putting them on display to be "consumed" by an audience as much as we question speech which glorifies male sexuality. To find one acceptable and the other not is to reproduce gender inequality and patriarchal systems of domination.

## REFERENCES

Adams, N. G., & Bettis, P. (2003). Power of the preps and cheerleading equity policy. *Sociology of Education*, *76*, 128–142.

Adams, N. G., & Bettis, P. (2005). *Cheerleader! An American icon*. New York, NY: Palgrave.

Adams, N. G., & Bettis, P. (2006). Short skirts and breast juts: Cheerleading, eroticism and schools. *Sex Education*, *6*(2), 121–133.

Barnes v Glen Theatre, Inc. 501 U.S. 560; 111 S. Ct. 2456; 115 L. Ed. 2d 504; 1991.

Barnett, L. A. (2006). Flying high or crashing down: Girls' accounts of trying out for cheerleading and dance. *Journal of Adolescent Research*, *21*(5), 514–541.

Bennett, J. C. (1990). The secondary school cheerleader as ritualized sexual exploitation. *The Clearing House*, *64*(1), 4–7.

Bernstein, B. (1977). Class, codes and control. In *Towards a theory of educational transmissions* (Vol. 3). London: Routledge & Kegan Paul.

Bernstein, B. (1990). *The structuring of pedagogic discourse: Class, codes and control* (Vol. 4). London: Routledge.

Best, A. L. (2000). *Prom night: Youth, schools, and popular culture.* New York, NY: Routledge.

Best, A. L. (2004). Girls, schooling, and the discourse of self-change: Negotiating meaning of the high school prom. In A. Harris (Ed.), *About the girl: Culture, power, and identity* (pp. 195–203). New York, NY: Routledge.

Bethel School District v Fraser. 478 U.S. 675; 106 S. Ct. 3159; 92L. Ed. 2d549; 1986.

Boje, D. M., & Dennehey, R. F. (1993). *Managing the postmodern world: Americana's revolution against exploitation.* Dubuque, IA: Kendall/Hunt Publishing.

Bottery, M. (1990). *The morality of schools.* London: Cassell.

Bourdieu, P., & Passeron, J. C. (1990). *Reproduction in education, society and culture* (2nd ed.). London: Sage.

*California v LaRue.* 409 U.S. 109; 93 S. Ct. 390; 34 L. Ed. 2d 342; 1972.

Cherryholmes, C. H. (1998). *Power and criticism: Poststructural investigations in education.* New York, NY: Teachers College Press.

Conley, J. M., & O'Barr, W. M. (1998). *Just words: Law, language and power.* Chicago, IL: University of Chicago Press.

Doran v Salem Inn. 422 U.S. 922; 95 S. Ct. 2561; 45 L. Ed. 2d 648; 1975.

Eder, D., & Parker, S. (1987). The cultural production and reproduction of gender: The effect of extracurricular actives on peer-group culture. *Sociology of Education, 60,* 200–213.

Fairclough, N., & Wodak, R. (1997). Critical discourse analysis. In T. A. von Dijk (Ed.), *Discourse as social interaction* (pp. 258–284). London: Sage.

Fischer, F. (2003). *Reframing public policy: Discursive politics and deliberative practices.* Oxford: Oxford University Press.

Foucault, M. (1972). *The archaeology of knowledge and the discourse on language* (A. M. Sheridan Smith, Trans.). New York, NY: Pantheon Books.

Foucault, M. (1979). Discipline and punish: The birth of the prison *(A. Sheridan, Trans.).* New York, NY: Vintage Books.

Foucault, M. (1980). *Power/knowledge: Selected interviews and other writings.* New York, NY: Pantheon Books.

Foucault, M. (1991). Governmentality. In G. Burchell, C. Gordon, & P. Miller (Eds.), *The foucault effect: Studies in governmentality* (pp. 87–104). Chicago, IL: University of Chicago Press.

Gleeson, K., & Firth, H. (2004). Pretty in pink: Young women presenting mature sexual identities. In A. Harris (Ed.), *All about the girl: Culture, power, and identity* (pp. 103–114). New York, NY: Routledge.

Griffin, C. (1993). *Representations of youth: The study of youth and adolescence in Britain and America.* Cambridge: Polity Press.

Griffin, C. (1997). Troubled teens: Managing disorders of transition and consumption. *Feminist Review, 55,* 4–21.

Hanson, M. E. (1995). *Go! Fight! Win! Cheerleading in American culture.* Bowling Green, OH: Bowling Green State University Popular Press.

*Hazelwood School District v Kuhlmeier.* 484 U.S. 260; 108 S. Ct. 562; 98 L. Ed. 2d 592; 1988.

Habermas, J. (1984). *The theory of communicative action* (T. McCarthy, Trans.). Boston, MA: Beacon Press.

In re Giannini. 69 Cal. 2d 563; 446 P.2d 535; 72 Cal. Rptr. 655; 1968.

Jenks, C. (1996). *Childhood.* London: Routledge.

Kahn, P. (1999). *The cultural studies of law: Reconstructing legal scholarship.* Chicago, IL: University of Chicago Press.

Kairys, D. (1982). Introduction. In D. Kairys (Ed.), *Politics of law: A progressive critique* (pp. 1–9). New York, NY: Pantheon Books.

Kelman, M. (1987). *A guide to critical legal studies.* Cambridge, MA: Harvard University Press.

Lamb, S. (2001). *The secret lives of girls: What good girls really do – Sex play, aggression, and their guilt.* New York, NY: The Free Press.

MacKinnon, C. (1987). *Feminism unmodified: Discourses on life and law.* Cambridge, MA: Harvard University Press.

MacKinnon, C. (1989). *Towards a feminist theory of the state.* Cambridge, MA: Harvard University Press.

MacKinnon, C. (2005). *Women's lives men's laws.* Cambridge, MA: Harvard University Press.

MacKinnon, C. (2008). *Women's lives men's laws.* Cambridge, MA: Harvard University Press.

Mayall, B. (1994). Children in action at home and school. In B. Mayall (Ed.), *Children's childhoods: Observed and experienced.* London: Falmer Press.

Merten, D. E. (1996). Burnout as cheerleader: The cultural basis for prestige and privilege in junior high school. *Anthropology & Education Quarterly*, *27*(1), 51–70.

Morrow, R. A., & Brown, D. D. (1994). *Critical theory and methodology.* Thousand Oaks, CA: Sage.

*Morse v Frederick*. 551 U.S. 393; 127 S. Ct. 2618; 168 L. Ed. 2d 290; 2007.

New Jersey v. T.L.O. 469 U.S. 325, 105 S.Ct. 1985.

Powers, S. (2010). *So you want to start a coed squad in our high school.* Retrieved from http://cheerleading.about.com/od/malecheerleaders/a/020903a.htm?p=1

Scad v. Borough of Mount Ephraim 452 U.S. 61. (1981).

Shapiro, J. P., & Stefkovich, J. A. (2010). *Ethical leadership and decision making in education: Applying theoretical perspectives to complex dilemmas* (3rd ed.). New York, NY: Routledge.

Starratt, R. J. (2004). *Ethical leadership.* San Francisco, CA: Jossey-Bass.

Thorne, B. (1987). Re-visioning women and social change: Where are the children? *Gender and Society*, *1*(1), 85–109.

Thorne, B. (1993). *Gender play: Girls and boys in school.* New Brunswick, NJ: Rutgers University Press.

*Tinker v Des Moines Independent School District*. 393 U.S. 503; 89 S. Ct. 733; 21 L. Ed. 2d 731; 1969.

Tolman, D. (1994). Doing desire: Adolescent girl's struggles for/with sexuality. *Gender and Society*, *8*(3), 324–342.

Walkerdine, V. (1990). *Schoolgirl fictions.* London: Verso.

Ward, I. (2002). *An introduction to critical legal theory.* London: Cavendish Publishing Limited.

Wodak, R., & Meyer, M. (2009). Critical discourse analysis: History, agenda, theory, and methodology. In R. Wodak & M. Meyer (Eds.), *Methods of critical discourse analysis* (2nd ed., pp. 1–33). Los Angeles, CA: Sage.

# CHAPTER 13

# WHEN EQUALITY IS NOT EQUITY: REGIONAL COST DIFFERENCES AND THE REAL ALLOCATION OF EDUCATIONAL RESOURCES

Lori L. Taylor


## ABSTRACT

*Differences in the cost of living and the general attractiveness of communities lead to significant, regional differences in the prices school districts must pay for their most important resource – people. According to the most recent data from the National Center for Education Statistics, labor costs differ by more than 50% from the lowest-cost district to the highest-cost district within California, Florida, New York, Texas, and West Virginia. Furthermore, all states but Hawaii and Rhode Island face at least a 7.7% internal differential in labor cost. Most states fail to account for such cost differences in their school finance formulas, leading to inequitable differences in school district purchasing power. This chapter compares and contrasts the various strategies states use to make geographic cost adjustments to their school funding formula, describes the implications of geographic adjustment for interstate and intrastate measures of school finance equity (and corresponding litigation), and*


**Legal Frontiers in Education: Complex Law Issues for Leaders, Policymakers and Policy Implementers**
**Advances in Educational Administration, Volume 24, 247–266**

**ISSN: 1479-3660/doi:10.1108/S1479-366020150000024040**

*discusses the impact that such adjustments could have on the distribution of federal aid for economically disadvantaged students under Title 1 of the Elementary and Secondary Education Act.*

In the four decades since the US Supreme Court ruled (in *Rodriguez v. San Antonio*) that education is not a fundamental right under the US constitution, litigants and legislatures have been battling in state courts over the equity and adequacy of school funding formulas. Plaintiffs have challenged the constitutionality of school funding formulas in all but four of the 50 states, and prevailed in 26.[1] Furthermore, the battles are likely to continue. As of March 2015, litigation was ongoing in 15 states, 11 of which were among the 26 states where the plaintiffs had previously prevailed at the highest level (National Education Access Network, 2015a, 2015b).

The first successful, state-court challenge on equity or adequacy grounds, California's *Serrano v. Priest* in 1971, illustrates the role of the state courts in defining school finance equity (Minorini & Sugarman, 1999). The plaintiffs in *Serrano* argued that the California school finance system violated the equal protection clauses of both the state and federal constitutions. The California Supreme Court agreed, finding that the school "funding scheme invidiously discriminated against the poor because it made the quality of a child's education a function of the wealth of his parents and neighbors" (*Serrano I*, 1971, p. 1244). In subsequent litigation, the Court specified exactly what it meant by equity, requiring the state of California to implement a school finance formula that limited wealth-related differences in expenditures to less than $100 per pupil (*Serrano II*, 1976, p. 940, note 21). Differences in categorical aid special programs were not considered wealth-related, so the ruling did not require equalization of all expenditures. Nevertheless, the implication was clear; equity in California required substantial equality of educational expenditures.

Although it can be hard to separate the effects of Serrano from the effects of California's Proposition 13, which imposed strict limits on the taxation of local property wealth, there is little doubt that expenditures per pupil in California became more equal after *Serrano*.[2] "Disparities that remained as of 1985–1986 were sufficiently small to justify the argument the state has eliminated much of the inequality in opportunity with respect to taxable wealth" (Downes, 1992, p. 405). Hill and Kiewiet (2014) examined cross-district inequality before and after school finance reforms in 25 states. They found that "no other equity based decision rendered by a state supreme court has come close to having the equalizing impact of Serrano" (Hill & Kiewiet, 2014, p. 18).

Unfortunately, equalizing expenditures is not the same thing as equalizing the purchasing power of school districts. School districts in high-cost environments must spend more than other school districts just to provide the same level of services. In states with large internal differences in the cost of education, an equal distribution of resources will imply a very unequal distribution of expenditures. Similarly, an equal distribution of expenditures can imply a very unequal distribution of resources.

Most states exhibit large internal differences in the cost of education's most important input – labor. According to the most recent data from the National Center for Education Statistics, labor costs differ by more than 50% from the lowest-cost school district to the highest-cost school district within California, Florida, New York, Texas, and West Virginia.[3] Labor costs differ by more than 20% in another 35 states. All states but Hawaii and Rhode Island face at least a 7.7% internal difference in labor cost.

Most states fail to account for such cost differences in their school finance formula, leading to inequitable differences in school district purchasing power. This chapter compares and contrasts the various strategies states use to make geographic cost adjustments to their school funding formula, describes the implications of geographic adjustment for interstate and intrastate measures of school finance equity, and discusses the impact that geographic cost adjustments could have on the distribution of federal aid for economically disadvantaged students under Title I of the Elementary and Secondary Education Act.

## GEOGRAPHIC COST ADJUSTMENTS IN THEORY

Ideally, geographic cost adjustments equalize the purchasing power of school districts. Thus, geographic cost adjustment would direct additional funds to school districts in urban areas that must pay more than other districts to compensate for the higher cost of living, and additional funds to school districts in isolated areas that need to pay a premium to compensate for the lack of local amenities. A geographic cost adjustment could also direct additional funds to compensate for locally higher costs for energy or educational materials. The goal is to ensure that all districts are able to purchase the same amount of real educational resources.

Geographic cost adjustments are operationalized using a geographic cost index. A geographic cost index is a weighted average of the prices districts must pay for various educational inputs, where the weights are the typical budget shares for each input. Thus

$$\text{Regional Cost Index} = P_1S_1 + P_2S_2 + P_3S_3 \ldots P_nS_n$$

where $P_1$ is the relative price a district must pay for its most important input and $S_1$ is the share of the budget devoted to that input, $P_2$ is the relative price for a second type of input, and $S_2$ is the share of the budget devoted to that second input, and so on.[4]

Labor is the most important input from a school district's point of view, and the price of labor is more likely to vary geographically than the price of other educational inputs. Therefore, all geographic cost adjustments in education focus on correcting for regional differences in the price of labor. Most geographic cost indices currently used in state funding formulas adjust exclusively for labor price variations, essentially assuming that the price of nonlabor inputs does not differ from one school district to the next.

Three basic strategies have been used to develop labor price indices – hedonic teacher cost indices (also known as Hedonic Wage Indices), Cost-of-Living Indices, and comparable wage indices (also known as competitive wage indices). No one approach dominates the others; all have advantages and disadvantages.

### *Hedonic Teacher Cost Indices*

The basic premise of a hedonic Teacher Cost Index (TCI) is that observed differences in teacher salary can arise from factors within school district control as well as factors outside of district control. Examples of factors within district control (at least in the long run) include teacher demographics, teaching assignments, and the length of the school year. Uncontrollable factors typically include some measure of the cost of living, the degree of geographic isolation, and student demographics.

Only factors outside of school district control represent cost differences that should be accounted for in funding formulas and equity calculations. Therefore, researchers use hedonic wage models and regression analysis to divide the observed variation in teacher salaries into the part that is explained by controllable factors and the part that is explained by uncontrollable factors.[5] A TCI is then constructed by predicting the full-time-equivalent salary in each school district, assuming there were no differences across districts in the controllable factors, and then dividing that prediction by some reference salary (such as the state average prediction).

The hedonic wage approach to geographic cost adjustment has a number of attractive features. Instead of using indirect measures of labor cost, TCIs are based directly on teacher salaries, making them clearly relevant to educational costs. The hedonic wage approach goes beyond the direct comparison of district salaries however, by using regression analysis to control for differences across districts in the mix of school district personnel. TCIs are constructed from data at the school or school district level, allowing the resulting index to pick up systematic differences in cost from one district to another within the same labor market.

There are also a number of potential disadvantages to the hedonic wage approach. TCIs rely on statistical technique and researcher judgment to distinguish between controllable and uncontrollable factors. Statistical models and professional judgment are inherently subject to criticism. Important aspects of teacher quality may not be captured by the available data, leading to errors of measurement (Goldhaber, 1999). TCIs have also been criticized as biased by the noncompetitive nature of teacher labor markets (Goldhaber, Destler, & Player, 2010; Hanushek, 1999), subject to school district manipulation (McMahon, 1996), and likely to misidentify high-spending districts as high-cost districts (Rothstein & Smith, 1997).

### *Cost-of-Living Indices*

The basic premise underlying the Cost-of-Living approach is that districts in areas with a high cost of living will need to pay higher salaries to attract school employees, and therefore will need more funding than other districts just to be able to provide the same level of services. Typically, Cost-of-Living Indices are constructed by tabulating the cost of a specified collection of consumer goods and services using a method called the "market basket" approach. Differences among communities in the cost of a basket of consumer goods and services capture differences in the cost of living. The US Bureau of Labor Statistics (BLS) uses a market basket approach to construct its ubiquitous Consumer Price Index (CPI).

There are a number of advantages to using a CLI to adjust for regional variations in labor cost. The clearest advantage is that CLIs measure cost factors that are clearly beyond the control of school administrators. There is no risk that this cost adjustment will confuse high-spending districts with high-cost districts. The Cost-of-Living approach is also straightforward. While there are many complex measurement issues involved in the development of price indices (Rothstein & Smith, 1997; Wynne & Sigalla, 1994), the approach produces cost measures that are familiar and can be easily understood.

There are also a number of disadvantages to the Cost-of-Living approach to geographic cost adjustment. The method requires a substantial and recurring investment in data collection (Duncombe, Nguyen-Hoang, & Yinger, 2015). Teachers may live outside the district in which they teach, so the CLI values for districts may not accurately reflect the actual cost of living for the teachers they employ (McMahon, 1996). If the market basket used in constructing the CLI does not reflect the spending patterns of the typical teacher, then again, the CLI would not accurately reflect regional differences in the cost of living. For example, Taylor (2011) criticizes the Wyoming Cost-of-Living Index for putting too great a weight on the cost of housing, thereby biasing the index in favor of school districts where housing costs are particularly high. Perhaps most importantly, education cost adjustments based on a market basket also tend to over-estimate labor cost in locations that have both a high cost of living and attractive amenities that make them a desirable place to live and work (Rothstein & Smith, 1997; Stoddard, 2005; Taylor, 2011).

### *Comparable Wage Indices*

The third approach to geographic cost adjustment is to recognize that teachers are not the only workers who are sensitive to the cost of living and the general attractiveness of the community. All types of workers demand a higher salary where the price of a home is high, the climate is inhospitable, or the closest movie theater is many miles away. Therefore, regional variations in the price that school districts must pay to attract high-quality teachers will be reflected in the salaries of comparable professionals who are not teachers (Guthrie & Rothstein, 1999; Rothstein & Smith, 1997; Taylor & Fowler, 2006). Intuitively, if accountants, nurses, and computer programmers all earn 10% more than the state average for their professions in Chicago, then a good estimate of the cost of hiring teachers in Chicago is also 10% higher than the state average.

Typically, a Comparable Wage Index (CWI) is constructed by estimating the prevailing wage for non-educators in each labor market, and then dividing that local estimate by a reference wage (like the state or national average predicted wage). The wage estimate is made comparable by restricting the analysis to individuals who are demographically similar to teachers, or by restricting the occupations included in the analysis to those requiring similar skills. In either case, researchers typically use statistical techniques to ensure that differences in the local mix of occupations do not lead to differences in the index values.

The principal advantage of a CWI is that it avoids the difficult problems associated with distinguishing variations in school district expenditures that are controllable from those that are uncontrollable. Like a Cost-of-Living Index, a CWI is completely outside of school district control. After all, it is unlikely that school districts will be able to manipulate the general labor market. Furthermore, a CWI reflects not only differences in the cost of purchased goods and services (like housing), but also differences in amenities (like the climate or access to health care). As such, it is a more complete price index than a CLI.

There are also disadvantages to using a CWI for geographic cost adjustment. Comparability is always a concern. If the non-educator population differs substantially from the educator population in terms of age, educational background, or tastes for local amenities, then a CWI may overstate (or understate) the wage differentials that teachers will require. Second, like a CLI, a CWI cannot pick up district-level variations in the price of labor. Every school district in a labor market receives the same index value as every other district in the market, regardless of any potential differences in working conditions (Duncombe et al., 2015). Because a CWI relies on existing data on occupations and earnings, it inherits the limitations of those data, including missing values and measurement errors. Finally, as discussed in Taylor and Fowler (2006), a CWI reflects labor cost differentials only when labor is mobile. If moving costs prevent workers from moving into (or out of) a particular location, then local wage levels may not reflect local labor costs, and any index based on those wage levels may be biased.

## GEOGRAPHIC COST ADJUSTMENTS IN PRACTICE

As Table 1 illustrates, only 12 states explicitly incorporate a geographic cost index into their school finance formulas. Despite the small number

*Table 1.* Geographic Cost Adjustment Strategies, by State in 2014–2015.

| State | Name of Index | Labor Cost Strategy |
|---|---|---|
| Alaska | District Cost Factor | Teacher Cost Index |
| Colorado | Cost-of-Living Factor | Cost-of-Living Index |
| Florida | District Cost Differential | Comparable Wage Index |
| Maine | Regional Labor Market Area Adjustment | Teacher Cost Index |
| Maryland | Geographic Cost of Education Index | Teacher Cost Index |
| Massachusetts | Wage Adjustment Factor | Comparable Wage Index |
| Missouri | Dollar Value Modifier | Comparable Wage Index |
| New Jersey | Geographic Cost Adjustment | Comparable Wage Index |
| New York | Regional Cost Index | Comparable Wage Index |
| Texas | Cost of Education Index | Teacher Cost Index |
| Virginia | Cost of Competing Adjustment | Comparable Wage Index |
| Wyoming | Regional Cost Adjustment | Cost-of-Living Index and Teacher Cost Index |

*Source*: Lofgren (2007), Education Law Center (2013), and author's calculations.

of potential cases, however, each of the three methodologies for labor cost adjustment is used in at least one state. Texas uses a TCI. Colorado uses a CLI. New York uses a CWI. Wyoming uses a hybrid that combines a TCI with a CLI. Brief case studies for each of these examples are as follows.

### *Texas*

The Texas Cost of Education Index (CEI) is based on a hedonic wage analysis of teacher salaries in 1989, and has not been updated since it was first adopted in 1991 (Taylor, 2004). It ranges from 1.02 to 1.20, reflecting differences in five uncontrollable factors as they were circa 1990: average daily attendance; the percentage of low income students; district type (independent town, rural district, or other); average beginning teacher salaries in the surrounding districts; and an indicator for whether or not the county population exceeded 40,000. Much has changed in the Texas economic landscape since 1990 and researchers have repeatedly updated the hedonic wage analysis (e.g., Taylor, 2004), but the legislature has been unwilling to revise the CEI. Because the updates indicate that the gap between urban and rural labor costs is widening, this legislative sclerosis has been particularly unfortunate for urban school districts in Texas.

Although not commonly discussed in these terms, the Texas CEI functions in the Texas school funding formula as if it were part of a geographic cost index in which the weight on labor inputs were 71% and the price of nonlabor inputs did not vary geographically. Payroll expenditures averaged 79% of current operating expenditures in 2013–2014 (the most recent data available) so the labor weight is arguably too low, which again shortchanges districts in areas with relatively high labor costs.

No district receives the full cost adjustment indicated by the Texas CEI. The Texas funding formula has two tiers – a foundation formula for basic education (Tier I) and a guaranteed yield formula for enrichment (Tier II). Funding for many programs treated as categorical in other states including special education, gifted education, vocational education, and bilingual education are included in Tier I of the Texas Foundation School Formula, and all Tier I funding is adjusted using the implicit geographic cost index. However, districts receive only half of the CEI adjustment in the Tier II. In other words, the state makes substantially less effort to equalize district purchasing power for enrichment.

All open enrollment charter schools are assigned the state average CEI for funding formula purposes, regardless of their actual geographic location. Since charter schools are disproportionately located in urban areas, this approach undercuts the purchasing power of charter schools relative to that of the surrounding traditional public school districts.

### *Colorado*

Colorado's school funding formula incorporates a Cost-of-Living Factor that is based on the price of a designated market basket. The factor ranges from 1.011 to 1.65 for budget year 2015 (Colorado Department of Education, 2014). The weight assigned to the Cost-of-Living Factor in the geographic cost index varies from 79.9% to 90.5% and increases with school district size. For funding formula purposes, the price of nonlabor inputs is presumed not to vary geographically.

Colorado's Cost-of-Living Factor is updated every two years, based on a consultant's analysis of the changing price of a market basket of consumer goods and services (Corona Insights, 2014). "Under state law, a district's factor from the prior two-year cycle is increased when the cost of living in the district increases by a greater percentage than the increase in the statewide average teacher salary used in the study. For instance, the 2009 study was based on an average teacher salary of $47,500, an increase of 6.7% from the $44,500 used in the study two years earlier. As a result, any district where the cost of living increased by more than 6.7% saw an increase in its Cost-of-Living Factor for FY 2010–11 and FY 2011–12" (Colorado Legislative Council Staff, 2011, p. 6). There is no comparable mechanism for decreasing the Cost-of-Living Factor if prices rise more slowly than the statewide average, creating a potential ratchet effect.

The geographic cost adjustment applies to all funding that each school district receives under the School Finance Act of 1994 (as amended). It does not apply to categorical programs such as English language proficiency programs, gifted and talented education, or special education (Colorado Department of Education, 2014).

In Colorado, the money follows the child, so charter schools receive the full geographic cost adjustment available to the traditional public schools the student would otherwise attend.

### *New York*

New York has adopted a Regional Cost Index (RCI) that is based on a comparable wage analysis of 61 professional, non-education occupations.[6] The RCI divides the state into nine regions and ranges from 1.00 to 1.425 for the 2014–2015 aid year (New York Office of State Aid, 2015). The RCI is constructed so that regional differences in occupational mix do not influence the index values. It is updated regularly using data from the BLS's Occupational Employment Statistics (OES) program, which is an annual survey of nonfarm establishments that is conducted nationwide.

The RCI is assigned a 100% weight in the implicit geographic cost adjustment for the State of New York, and applies to all funding school districts receive through the state's Foundation Aid formula. On average, Foundation Aid represents approximately 71% of the total state aid districts receive (New York Office of State Aid, 2015).

Charter school funding per pupil is based on a two-year lag of the average per-pupil operating expenditures in the traditional school district the student would have otherwise attended, adjusted by a statewide inflation factor (Bifulco & Buerger, 2015). As such, charter schools receive roughly the same geographic cost adjustment as traditional public school districts in New York.

### *Wyoming*

Wyoming's Regional Cost Adjustment (RCA) applies only to the salary components of the state's school funding model, which is equivalent to an implicit geographic cost adjustment where the weights differ by school district according to the local personnel shares. The RCA ranged from 1.00 to 1.32 for budget year 2015.

The Wyoming RCA is a composite of two alternative labor price indices – the Wyoming Cost-of-Living Index (which is updated annually) and the Wyoming Hedonic Wage Index (which was last updated in 2005).[7] Both indices are centered on 100, with an index value of 110 indicating that labor costs are 10% above the state average and an index value of 90 indicating that labor costs are 10% below the state average (Taylor, 2011).

Each district's RCA is the larger of the Wyoming CLI, the Wyoming HWI or 100. In other words, districts where labor costs are below the state average are treated as if their costs were equal to the state average. This Lake Woebegone approach, wherein no districts are below average, attenuates the impact of the geographic cost adjustment, greatly diminishing the ability of the RCA to equalize district purchasing power.

Furthermore, there are reasons to believe that the Wyoming CLI exaggerates the cost of living in counties with relatively high housing costs. As a general rule, the residents of Wyoming spend a smaller share of their budgets on housing than the residents of any other state except Iowa and North Dakota (Taylor, 2011), yet the Wyoming CLI is constructed assuming that consumers in Wyoming spend as large a share of their budget on housing as the typical urban consumer in the rest of the United States.[8] This assumption gives too much weight to housing costs in the construction of the Wyoming CLI, making the Wyoming CLI artificially high in areas where housing costs are high.

Wyoming does not have charter schools so there is no geographic cost adjustment for them.

## THE EQUITY IMPLICATIONS OF GEOGRAPHIC COST ADJUSTMENT

As the discussion above makes clear, few states even attempt to adjust for regional variations in the cost of education, and those that do make such adjustments frequently fail to fully equalize school district purchasing power. But so what? Does a failure to adjust for regional differences in purchasing power mean anything in the context of school finance?

To answer this question, consider two pieces of evidence. The first is an analysis of measured equity, by state. The second is an analysis of the impact of geographic cost adjustment on the distribution of expenditures under Title I of the Elementary and Secondary Education Act.

### *Geographic Cost Adjustments and State-Level Equity*

Nationally, the best available index for geographic cost adjustment is the National Center for Education Statistics' Comparable Wage Index (Taylor & Fowler, 2006). The NCES CWI was specifically designed to capture regional wage differences for college graduates who are not educators. The baseline estimates for the NCES CWI come from a regression analysis of the individual earnings data from the 2000 U.S. Census. Annual updates to that baseline come from regression analyses of the BLS's OES data. The NCES CWI is not available from NCES for the years after 2005, but I have updated it through 2011 using the methodology I used to construct the NCES CWI.[9] All US school districts have been matched to one of the 800 labor market areas in the NCES CWI based on their county of record. For analysis purposes, I have embedded the NCES CWI in a geographic cost index assuming that labor's share of school district purchases is 80% (the national average in 2010–2011). Fig. 1

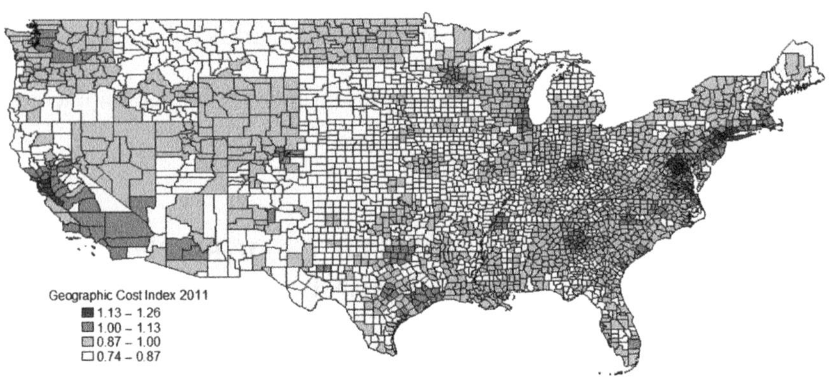


*Fig. 1.* The Geographic Cost Index, 2011.

illustrates that geographic cost index, with darker shades of gray indicating higher costs.

The most recent data on current expenditures for elementary and secondary education come from the NCES' School District Finance Survey and cover the 2010–2011 school year. As in Murray, Evans, and Schwab (1998), Taylor (2006), and Hill and Kiewiet (2014), I restrict attention to traditional public school districts that serve both elementary and secondary grades. I exclude districts that serve only elementary students, districts that serve only secondary students, and districts that serve fewer than 50 students because they are likely to have different resource needs than those of unified districts. Because they lack intrastate variation, I also exclude Hawaii and Washington, DC.

Table 2 presents three measures of distributional inequality for the 2010–2011 school year.[10] The first measure is the coefficient of variation. The second measure is the Gini coefficient and the third is the Theil Index. All three indicators are commonly used in school finance analyses (and school finance litigation). They each take on a value of zero under perfect equality and increase as inequality increases. They differ in the relative weight they put on inequality near the mean versus inequality in the extremes of the distribution.

As Table 2 illustrates, all three measures of inequality fall when differences in school district purchasing power are taken into account. Cost

***Table 2.*** The Impact of Geographic Cost Adjustment on Measured Inequality, 2010–2011.

| | Current Operating Expenditures | Cost-Adjusted Current Operating Expenditures |
|---|---|---|
| Gini coefficient | 15.65 | 14.63 |
| Coefficient of variation | 31.84 | 28.17 |
| Theil Index | 44.21 | 36.05 |
| Within states | 10.18 | 10.73 |
| Between states | 34.03 | 23.31 |

*Notes*: The expenditures data come from the NCES F-33 files for elementary and secondary school districts (NCES school code "03") with positive per pupil current expenditures and enrollments of at least 50. Because they lack intrastate variation, Hawaii and Washington, DC, are excluded. All descriptive statistics are weighted by the number of students in fall enrollment in each district. For notational convenience, the coefficient of variation and the Gini coefficient are multiplied by 100. The Theil Index and its components are multiplied by 1,000.

adjustment lowers the coefficient of variation for current expenditures per pupil in 2010–2011 from 31.84 to 28.17, lowers the Gini coefficient from 15.6 to 14.6, and lowers the Theil Index from 44.2 to 36.0.

The Theil Index can be decomposed into within-state and between-state components. As the table illustrates, cost adjustments reduce the measured inequality between states and increase the measured inequality within states. The share of inequality that comes from within-state variations increases from 23% to 46% when geographic cost adjustments are used.

The Theil Index of within-state inequality is a weighted average of the Theil Indexes for the individual states. It is higher with cost adjustments than it is without cost adjustments because the individual, state-level Theil Indexes are generally higher with cost adjustments than they are without (Fig. 2). In all but 10 states, geographic cost adjustment increases measured inequality. Those 10 states are Illinois, Louisiana, Massachusetts, Michigan, Missouri, New York, Ohio, Pennsylvania, Tennessee, and Virginia. It may be no coincidence that 5 of the 10 states where real resources were distributed more equitably than expenditures during 2010–11 were states that had explicit, geographic cost adjustments in their school funding formula.[11]

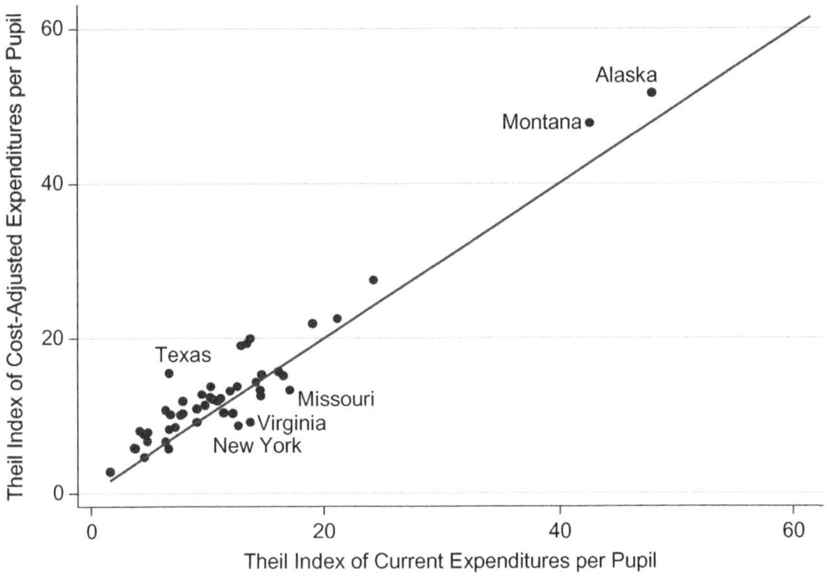


*Fig. 2.* The Theil Index of Within-State Inequality, with and without Cost Adjustment.

## *Geographic Cost Adjustments and Federal Equity*

In 2015, the U.S. Department of Education appropriated $14.4 billion in federal aid for disadvantaged students through Title I of the Elementary and Secondary Education Act (Title I), making Title I the largest educational grant program in the United States.[12] Given its structure, the Title I program is also particularly sensitive to geographic cost adjustment.

As discussed in Baker, Taylor, Levin, Chambers, and Blankenship (2013), there are four components to the Title I funding formula – basic grants, concentration grants, targeted grants, and education finance incentive grants. The first three components (basic, concentration, and targeted grants) allocate funding to each school district based (to varying degrees) on the number of children in poverty and the average per-pupil expenditure in the state. The higher the average per-pupil expenditure in the state, the larger is the Title I allocation. The fourth component (education finance incentive grants) allocates funding based not only on the number of children in poverty and average per-pupil spending, but also on state fiscal effort and state school funding equity.[13]

Geographic cost adjustment has the potential to impact all four components of the Title I funding formula. First, geographic cost adjustment could have a profound impact on the way we count the number of children in poverty. Under current law, children are identified as poor if they are living in households with annual incomes below the federal poverty threshold. But the federal poverty threshold is the same in rural Arkansas as it is in New York City, even though the cost of living in New York City is demonstrably higher. As a result, the current standard tends to undercount the number of children living in poverty in high cost-of-living areas, and overcount the number of children living in poverty in low cost-of-living areas. Geographic cost adjustments to the poverty thresholds would greatly increase the Title I funding for urban school districts and school districts in high-cost states like California (Baker et al., 2013). Conversely, our failure to use geographic cost adjustments in the construction of federal poverty rates shortchanges urban school districts that disproportionately serve minority students.[14]

In addition to impacting the poverty counts, geographic cost adjustment could also have a profound impact on the way that Title I distributes funds to districts. Currently, the formula directs additional resources to states with higher average per-pupil expenditures. Higher regional costs are associated with higher state spending, so this approach has the same effect on grant awards as a very rough and imprecise geographic cost adjustment. Arguably, scarce resources would be better targeted and compensatory education programs would do a better job of distributing real resources if Title I grants were cost adjusted so that every receiving district experienced the same increase in purchasing power (per eligible student). Cost-adjusting the Title I program would also redistribute compensatory education funds toward locations where labor cost is above the national average.

The previous two points have to do with cost adjustments implemented at the federal level. The final way in which cost adjustment could impact Title I funding arises from cost adjustments at the state and local level. Education finance incentive grants, which comprise 23% of all Title I programming, depend on a measure of state school finance equity. These grants are smaller and more progressively distributed in states with lower school finance equity (Baker et al., 2013). Unfortunately, the equity measure is remarkably unsophisticated. Title I measures equity using a weighted coefficient of variation in per-pupil expenditures (wherein children in poverty have a greater weight than other children). This measure does not take geographic cost differences into account, so states that equalize per-pupil expenditures despite large differences in purchasing power would receive larger grants than states that perfectly equalize the purchasing power of school districts, all other things being equal. In other words, under current law, states that implement geographic cost adjustments are disadvantaged when it comes to Title I funding.

## CONCLUSIONS AND RECOMMENDATIONS

In their influential analysis of school finance litigation, Murray, Evans, and Schwab concluded that most of the school finance inequality is between states and "thus school-reform litigation is able to attack only a small part of inequality" (Murray et al., 1998, p. 808). The evidence on cost-adjusted spending suggests otherwise; nearly half of the inequality in real educational resources occurs within states and is therefore amenable to state-level reform.

Real resource inequality stems, at least in part, from a lack of geographic cost adjustments in state funding formulas and federal grants programs. Try as they might, policymakers cannot rewrite the laws of supply and demand. If the price of labor in San Francisco, CA, is higher than the price of labor in Mendocino, CA (and it is), then one of two things must happen: either school districts in San Francisco must pay higher wages than school districts in Mendocino, or school districts in San Francisco will be unable to hire teachers of comparable quality to those hired in Mendocino. There can be real resource equality and spending inequality, or spending equality and real resource inequality. There can't be equality in both.

School leaders interested in educational equity or adequacy must recognize that those concepts start with real resources, so they require a foundation of purchasing power parity. Geographic cost adjustment is needed to provide that foundation, and school leaders – particularly those in urban areas and high-cost states – could be particularly effective advocates for geographic cost adjustment at the state and federal levels.

Fortunately, it isn't hard to explain why educational dollars can't stretch as far in some parts of the state as they can in others. Every business leader, legislator, and judge instinctively understands the argument because this is not an education issue; it is purely an economic one. The price of education is different from one place to the next, and those price differences cannot be ignored.

## NOTES

1. According to the National Education Access Network, as of March 2015, all US states except Delaware, Hawaii, Nevada, and Utah have had a lawsuit challenging the constitutionality of K-12 funding (National Education Access Network, 2015a).
2. Some researchers attribute the passage of Proposition 13 to *Serrano* because under *Serrano* local tax revenues could not be dedicated to local schools (e.g., Fischel, 1989, 2003). Other scholars aren't so sure (Martin, 2006; Stark & Zasloff, 2003).
3. These estimates are based on the NCES' Comparable Wage Index for 2005. Downloaded from https://nces.ed.gov/edfin/adjustments.asp
4. The relative price of an input is the price of that input divided by a state reference price – typically the state average or state minimum. For example, if the price of paper is $3.00 per ream in Bedford Falls, and the state average price of paper is $2.00 per ream then the relative price of paper in Bedford Falls is $3.00/$2.00 = 1.50.
5. For more on hedonic teacher cost indices, see Chambers (1996), Goldhaber (1999), or Taylor (2011).
6. The occupations used to construct the RCI typically require a bachelor's degree for employment at the entry level (New York State Department of Education, 2003).
7. The WCLI used in the school funding formula is a three-year moving average of the WCLI values generated by the state's Department of Administration & Information, Division of Economic Analysis.
8. Shelter also has a much larger share in the WCLI than is used in the construction of the Colorado Cost-of-Living Factor (Corona Insights, 2014).

9. The revised files are available at http://bush.tamu.edu/research/faculty/Taylor_CWI/

10. For more on these measures of inequality, see Berne and Stiefel (1984). For notational convenience, the Gini coefficient is multiplied by 100. The Theil index and its components are multiplied by 1,000.

11. Tennessee was in the process of phasing out its Cost Differential Factor during the 2010–2011 school year. The other four states are Massachusetts, Missouri, New York, and Virginia.

12. See U.S. Department of Education Fiscal Year 2016 President's Budget, downloaded from http://www2.ed.gov/about/overview/budget/budget16/16pbapt.pdf. Accessed on March 30, 2015.

13. State fiscal effort is measured by the percentage of per-capita income spent on elementary and secondary education, relative to the national average (Baker et al., 2013).

14. The same criticism can be leveled against the National School Lunch Program. Eligibility for the program is a function of the federal poverty level (Taylor & Dar, 2014). Adjusting the poverty-level-income thresholds for regional differences in the cost of living would increase the number of eligible students in high cost-of-living areas; thereby increasing the share of students identified as economically disadvantaged in those locations. Because school finance formulas in most states explicitly direct additional funding to districts with more economically disadvantaged students (Education Law Center, 2013), geographic cost adjustments to the poverty thresholds would also redistribute state-level funding for elementary and secondary education toward high cost-of-living areas.

## REFERENCES

Baker, B. D., Taylor, L., Levin, J., Chambers, J., & Blankenship, C. (2013). Adjusted poverty measures and the distribution of Title I aid: Does Title I really make the rich states richer? *Education Finance and Policy*, *8*(3), 394–417. doi:10.1162/EDFP_a_00103

Berne, R., & Stiefel, L. (1984). *The measurement of equity in school finance: Conceptual, methodological and empirical dimensions*. Baltimore, MD: Johns Hopkins University Press.

Bifulco, R., & Buerger, C. (2015). The influence of finance and accountability policies on location of New York state charter schools. *Journal of Education Finance*, *40*(3), 193–221.

Chambers, J. G. (1996). Public school teacher cost differences across the United States: Introduction to a Teacher Cost Index (TCI). In W. J. Fowler, Jr. (Ed.), *Developments in school finance: 1995* (NCES 96-344) (pp. 19–32). Washington, DC: U.S. Department of Education, National Center for Education Statistics.

Colorado Department of Education. (2014). *Understanding Colorado school finance and categorical program funding*. Retrieved from http://www.cde.state.co.us/cdefinance/fy2014-15brochure. Accessed on March 31, 2015.

Colorado Legislative Council Staff. (2011). *School finance in Colorado*. Retrieved from http://www.colorado.gov/cs/Satellite?blobcol=urldata&blobheader=application%2Fpdf&blobkey=id&blobtable=MungoBlobs&blobwhere=1251699592646&ssbinary=true. Accessed on March 31, 2015.

Corona Insights. (2014). *2013 Colorado school district cost of living study*. Retrieved from http://www.colorado.gov/cs/Satellite?blobcol=urldata&blobheader=application%2Fpdf&blobkey=id&blobtable=MungoBlobs&blobwhere=1251990492659&ssbinary=true. Accessed on March 31, 2015.

Downes, T. A. (1992). Evaluating the impact of school finance reform on the provision of public education: The California case. *National Tax Journal*, *45*, 405–419.

Duncombe, W., Nguyen-Hoang, P., & Yinger, J. (2015). Measurement of cost differentials. In H. Ladd & M. Goertz (Eds.), *Handbook of research in education finance and policy* (2nd ed., pp. 260–278). New York, NY: Routledge.

Education Law Center. (2013, February). *Funding, formulas and fairness: What Pennsylvania can learn from other states' education funding formulas*. Retrieved from http://www.elc-pa.org/wp-content/uploads/2013/02/ELC_schoolfundingreport.2013.pdf

Fischel, W. A. (1989). Did "Serrano" cause proposition 13? *National Tax Journal*, *42*, 465–473.

Fischel, W. A. (2003). Did John Serrano vote for proposition 13-A reply to Stark and Zasloff's Tiebout and tax revolts: Did Serrano really cause proposition 13. *UCLA Law Review*, *51*, 887–932.

Goldhaber, D., Destler, K., & Player, D. (2010). Teacher labor markets and the perils of using hedonics to estimate compensating differentials in the public sector. *Economics of Education Review*, *29*, 1–17.

Goldhaber, D. D. (1999). An alternative measure of inflation in teacher salaries. In W. J. Fowler, Jr. (Ed.), *Selected papers in school finance, 1997–99* (NCES 1999-334) (pp. 29–54). Washington, DC: U.S. Department of Education, National Center for Education Statistics.

Guthrie, J., & Rothstein, R. (1999). Enabling "adequacy" to achieve reality: Translating adequacy into state school finance distribution arrangements. In H. F. Ladd, R. Chalk, & J. S. Hansen (Eds.), *Equity and adequacy in education finance* (pp. 209–259). Washington, DC: National Academies Press.

Hanushek, E. A. (1999). Adjusting for differences in the costs of educational inputs. In W. J. Fowler, Jr. (Ed.), *Selected papers in school finance, 1997–99* (NCES 1999-334) (pp. 13–28). Washington, DC: U.S. Department of Education, National Center for Education Statistics.

Hill, S. A., & Kiewiet, D. R. (2014). The impact of state supreme court decisions on public school finance. *Journal of Law, Economics, and Organization*, *31*, 61–92. doi:10.1093/jleo/ewu001

Lofgren, J. L. (2007). Implementation and use of geographic cost indices in state school funding formulas: A Project for the Association of Metropolitan School Districts(Political Advocacy in the Public Interest Capstone Workshop, Hubert H. Humphrey Institute of Public Affairs). Retrieved from http://www.amsd.org/wp-content/uploads/2011/11/Geographic-Cost-Indices-_2007_-AMSD.pdf

Martin, I. (2006). Does school finance litigation cause taxpayer revolt? Serrano and proposition 13. *Law & Society Review*, *40*(3), 525–558.

McMahon, W. W. (1996). Intrastate cost adjustments. In W. J. Fowler, Jr. (Ed.), *Selected papers in school finance, 1994* (NCES 96-068) (pp. 93–114). Washington, DC: U.S. Department of Education, National Center for Education Statistics.

Minorini, P., & Sugarman, S. (1999). School finance litigation in the name of educational equity: Its evolution, impact and future. In H. F. Ladd, R. Chalk, & J. S. Hansen (Eds.), *Equity and adequacy in education finance: Issues and perspectives* (pp. 34–71). Washington, DC: National Academies Press.

Murray, S. E., Evans, W. N., & Schwab, R. M. (1998). Education-finance reform and the distribution of education resources. *American Economic Review*, *88*(4), 789–812.

National Education Access Network. (2015a). *Litigations challenging constitutionality of K-12 funding in the 50 states*. Retrieved from http://schoolfunding.info/wp-content/uploads/2015/01/Litigations-Challenging-Constitutionality-of-K-12-Funding-March2015-21.pdf. Accessed on June 18, 2015.

National Education Access Network. (2015b). *"Equity" and "adequacy" school funding liability court decisions*. Retrieved from http://schoolfunding.info/wp-content/uploads/2015/01/Equity-and-Adequacy-School-Funding-Liability-Court-Decisions_April-2015.pdf. Accessed on June 18, 2015.

New York Office of State Aid. (2015). *2014–2015 state aid handbook*. Retrieved from https://stateaid.nysed.gov/publications/handbooks/handbook_2014.pdf. Accessed on March 31, 2015.

New York State Department of Education. (2003). *Recognizing high cost factors in the financing of public education: The calculation of a regional cost index*. Retrieved from http://www.oms.nysed.gov/faru/new_york_state_education_departm.htm. Accessed on May 19, 2005.

Rothstein, R., & Smith, J. R. (1997). *Adjusting Oregon education expenditures for regional cost differences: A feasibility study*. Sacramento, CA: Management Analysis & Planning Associates, L.L.C.

Serrano v. Priest, 5 Cal.3d 584 (1971) (Serrano I).

Serrano v. Priest, 18 Cal.3d 728 (1976) (Serrano II).

Stark, K., & Zasloff, J. (2003). Tiebout and tax revolts: Did *Serrano* really cause proposition 13? *UCLA Law Review*, *50*, 801–858.

Stoddard, C. (2005). Adjusting teacher salaries for the cost of living: The effect on salary comparisons and policy conclusions. *Economics of Education Review*, *24*(3), 323–339. doi:10.1016/j.econedurev.2004.06.004

Taylor, L. L. (2004). *Adjusting for geographic variations in teacher compensation: Updating the Texas cost-of-education index*. Austin, TX: Joint Select Committee on Public School Finance.

Taylor, L. L. (2006). Comparable wages, inflation and school finance equity. *Education Finance and Policy*, *1*(3), 349–371.

Taylor, L. L. (2011). Updating the Wyoming Hedonic Wage Index. Submitted tothe WyomingJoint Appropriations Committee and Joint Education Committee. Retrieved from http://legisweb.state.wy.us/2011/Interim%20Studies/Taylor_UpdatingTheWyomingHedonicWageIndexFinal.pdf

Taylor, L. L., & Dar, J. (2014). The war on poverty needs a new map. *The Takeaway: Policy Briefs from the Mosbacher Institute for Trade, Economics, and Public Policy*, *5*(6), 1–4. Retrieved from http://bush.tamu.edu/mosbacher/takeaway/V5-6%20Takeaway%20Poverty%20Final.pdf. Accessed on June 4, 2015.

Taylor, L. L., & Fowler, W. J., Jr. (2006). *A comparable wage approach to geographic cost adjustment* (NCES 2006-321). Washington, DC: U.S. Department of Education, National Center for Education Statistics.

Wynne, M., & Sigalla, F. (1994). The consumer price index. In Economic review 2nd quarter. Federal Reserve Bank of Dallas. Retrieved from http://www.dallasfed.org/assets/documents/research/er/1994/er9402a.pdf

# CHAPTER 14

# COLLECTIVE BARGAINING: POLICY TENSIONS AND PRACTICAL OPTIONS FOR SCHOOL LEADERS

Mark Paige

## ABSTRACT

*Collective bargaining significantly impacts education policies, especially at the school district level. Its reach extends to consequential issues such as teacher evaluation and pay, to name a few. Because of this close link, education stakeholders disagree about the role of bargaining in education. On the one hand, some argue for the complete elimination of bargaining rights of teachers. This, according to some, will allow administrators the freedom to implement necessary reforms without the obligation to negotiate with unions. On the other hand, some note that collective bargaining provides a channel for teachers to voice their expertise in education. Under this view, bargaining is an essential component of advancing policy initiatives. Regardless, because collective bargaining is a creature of state statute, any modifications to those rights must occur by operation of law. Put another way, the law concerning collective bargaining plays a pivotal role in moderating the influence of unions and*

**Legal Frontiers in Education: Complex Law Issues for Leaders, Policymakers and Policy Implementers**
**Advances in Educational Administration, Volume 24, 267–282**

**ISSN: 1479-3660/doi:10.1108/S1479-366020150000024042**

*administrators regarding education policy. Given this interrelationship, a thorough exploration of the issue is warranted. Accordingly, this chapter will: (1) discuss the historical and legal framework of collective bargaining in public education; (2) highlight the ongoing debate regarding the appropriate role, if any, of it (and unions) in education policies; (3) identify significant changes to collective bargaining statutes that have occurred or have been proposed; (4) suggest recommendations to policymakers and leaders that will assist them in understanding both the potential and the limits of collective bargaining in improving schools.*

Over the past few years, many state legislatures have amended their respective collective bargaining statutes. For the most part, these changes have limited the rights of unions and teacher to bargain. In particular, legislatures have moved to exclude unions from negotiating contentious policy topics, such as teacher evaluation, pay plans, transfers, and dismissals, among other topics. These acts to restrict union involvement assume that if unions can be bypassed, policies that are in the best interests of students can readily be implemented. Recent events in Wisconsin illustrate this shift. Teachers can no longer bargain over *any* education policy topic, such as those listed above. Indeed, changes to that state's bargaining laws limit negotiations exclusively to "base wages" (Wisconsin State Statutes § 111.70 (4), 2013). Yet Wisconsin should not be seen as an isolated example; other states have passed similar laws (see Indiana State Code § 20-29-6-4.5, 2014).

However, as this chapter notes unions and collective bargaining can have a positive impact on seeking change in schools. It may be a mistake to view them as something to be bypassed. Instead, states should encourage *greater involvement of unions* in education policy, especially through collective bargaining (Malin, 2009; Paige, 2013a, 2013b). If this is the case, then recent amendments to collective bargaining statutes that restrict union involvement may just be steps in the wrong direction (Malin, 2009) in general and, in particular, as it relates to teacher evaluation (Paige, 2013a). The chapter highlights some local and state initiatives that, in contrast to the Wisconsin example, promote greater union involvement through collective bargaining, not less. The author provides guidance to school leaders regarding the potential use of collective bargaining, especially as it relates to designing teacher evaluation systems, and for meeting their local needs.

It distinguishes bargaining approaches that may, practically speaking, assist school leaders in this regard. It pays particular attention to the application of one bargaining method (interest-based bargaining) as uniquely suited to address the issue of creating fair teacher evaluation systems at the district level. Unfortunately, with few exceptions (see DeMitchell, 2010; Paige, 2013b), scholars have yet to give practical advice to school leaders to prepare for when they bargain especially regarding some of the most contentious topics of the day. This is a significant omission.

The chapter is organized as follows. First, the author discusses the legal framework of collective bargaining. Then, a summary of arguments is presented in relation to education research and how it is related to the appropriate role of unions and bargaining in education policy. Next, various approaches to bargaining for consideration of school leaders are articulated. This is followed by ways in which bargaining in a collaborative fashion can be – and has been – employed to design teacher evaluation systems. The chapter concludes with recommendations for practitioners and policymakers.

## THE LAW OF COLLECTIVE BARGAINING

### *The Legal Framework*

A thorough discussion of collective bargaining necessarily begins with its governing legal framework. Collective bargaining is a creature of state statute. State legislatures can enact – or choose not to enact – laws that allow teachers (and other public sector employees) the right to organize and bargain collectively. At the moment, 45 states in the United States allow teachers to bargain collectively (Sanes & Schmitt, 2014). In five states, collective bargaining is illegal (see North Carolina General Statutes §§ 95–98, 2014). It should be noted that in some states the scope of bargaining is restricted even though bargaining is technically permitted. As discussed above, in Wisconsin, unions may bargain only over the "base wage" of teachers and, moreover, any increase in the base wage cannot exceed the consumer price index (see Wisconsin Statutes Annotated § 111.70 (4)(mb), 2014).

What is collective bargaining? Generally speaking, collective bargaining is a process by which management and employees negotiate an agreement to govern the employment relationship. Toward this end, statutes require school officials and unions to negotiate "in good faith" over proposals related to "wages, hours and terms and conditions" of employment (see Massachusetts General Laws, c.150E-6, 2014; New Hampshire Revised Statutes Annotated § 273-A:3, 2014). At the outset, it is important to recall that bargaining is a negotiating process; no party is compelled to accept the proposal of the other side (see New Hampshire Revised Statutes Annotated, § 273-A:3, 2014).

What qualifies as "wages, hours, and conditions of employment" and therefore triggers the obligation to bargain? In other words, what is the scope of subjects that *must* be bargained by statute? Some topics are easy to classify. Take for instance, a union proposal to increase the pay of teachers by 5% annually. Clearly that is a "wage." Therefore, in states where bargaining is permissible, the proposal *must* be negotiated. Sometimes a proposal does not neatly qualify as a "wage, hour, and condition of employment." At the bargaining table, this raises some uncertainty with respect to whether school officials must negotiate a proposal. For instance, a union may propose that class sizes do not exceed 20 students per class and demand that proposal be negotiated. Certainly, it is not an "hour" which would trigger the duty to bargain in good faith. On the other hand, it *could* be considered a condition of employment. A class of 40 students creates different demands on a teacher than a class of 25 and impacting the "conditions" of employment. Yet school administrators would consider the topic more of an education policy matter – something that they should be able to determine outside of negotiations – that is relatively unrelated to the employee's working conditions.

Courts and legislatures must resolve these issues, like class size, that do not neatly fit into the category of "wages, hours, and conditions of employment." In other words, they must determine what the law refers to as the appropriate *scope of bargaining* (see *Appeal of State of New Hampshire*, 1994). Generally speaking, there are three categories under which a legislature or court can classify a particular subject for purposes of negotiations (DeMitchell, 2010; Malin, 2009). First, a subject can be considered a *mandatory* subject of bargaining. Proposals on mandatory subjects *must* be negotiated. Legislatures, by statute, can create mandatory subjects of bargaining. For example, in Massachusetts, teacher evaluation is a mandatory subject of bargaining (Massachusetts General Laws, c. 150-6E). Other legislatures are silent on these issues. In these instances, courts must determine if the subject is mandatory for bargaining purposes (see *Appeal of State*, 1994). They typically employ a balancing test to make this determination that asks whether a proposal *primarily* relates to wages, hours, and conditions of employment (DeMitchell, 2010; Malin, 2009; Paige, 2013a).

Second, a subject could be classified as *permissive*. In this case, the subject does not primarily relate to the wages, hours, or conditions of employment. However, management and unions may bargain the subject if they choose to do so. Yet there is no requirement that management to bargain a permissive subject; it is at the discretion of the parties. Many issues touching on "education policy" are permissive subjects of bargaining. For instance, some courts have determined that teacher evaluation is a permissive subject of bargaining (see *Appeal of White Mountain Regional School District*, 2006).

Third, a subject could be classified as *prohibited*. As the name suggests, a prohibited subject cannot be bargained. A subject is prohibited because the legislature or constitution has addressed the issue and therefore it is unsuitable to be negotiated. The topic of days in a school year provides a good example. In most states, the legislature determines how many days its children must attend school (e.g., 180 days). Thus, management and union officials could not subvert that statute at the bargaining table (e.g., propose a contract that had 160 days of school).

### *Policy Arguments regarding Collective Bargaining in Education*

In addition to the legal framework discussed above, school leaders must also understand the various policy debates related to bargaining in public education. Indeed, scholars and education stakeholders disagree regarding what role, if any, collective bargaining should play in our public education system. Thus, toward this end, the following section presents the predominant themes that education stakeholders have raised with respect to the relative role of bargaining in education. Research has noted that the debate over unions in education has fallen along two lines – those who oppose unions and collective bargaining in education and those who are in favor of it (DeMitchell, 2010; Lindy, 2011; Loveless, 2000; Malin, 2009; Paige, 2013a).

#### *Unions and Collective Bargaining as Obstacles*

Some argue that collective bargaining is anti-democratic (Hess & Kelly, 2006; Summers, 1980). In this view, many note that unions influence education policy over elected school boards through the collective bargaining process. Indeed, elected officials must negotiate with unions' education policies before they can be exercise their authority as elected representatives. This seems counterintuitive to our democratic impulses. In theory, we elect school officials to exert their wisdom to run public schools on behalf of the people.

School districts, like Boston (Boston Public Schools, 2015), have extended the school day because research suggests benefits to such policy changes (ECONorthwest, 2008). This is the sort of decision we expect our elected officials to make – we delegate to them the direction of our schools. However, a school board cannot unilaterally implement a proposal, such as the one related to extending the school day. Because an extended school day would extend the hours of teachers, it is mandatory subject of bargaining; the proposal must be negotiated with the union. Thus, because unions can interject their interests through collective bargaining, this is inherently undemocratic (Summers, 1980).

Others contend that collective bargaining agreements (CBAs) sap resources from the classroom (Moe, 2009; Moskowitz, 2006). Unions use CBA as a means to maximize the economic gain for their teachers through expensive benefit and salary arrangements (McDonnell & Pascal, 1988). They are costly impediments that prevent resources from being directed to student needs; they serve adult economic needs (teachers') instead, according to at least one think tank report (Edwards, 2010).

Third, some argue that CBAs perpetuate social injustice. The critics of CBAs in this regard suggest that CBAs are impediments to improving teacher quality, especially in high-need school districts. CBAs can require that seniority be the primary factor in determining reductions in force, or layoffs. Critics contend this prevents school management from making performance-based decisions and, accordingly, allows ineffective teachers to remain in the classroom (Steelman, Powell, & Carini, 2000). Likewise, processes and procedures in CBAs, such as "just cause" provisions related to discipline and termination of poor performing employees, can make termination a difficult process (see Paige & DeMitchell, 2013). In the eyes of many, the CBA embeds cumbersome restrictive processes that serve the interests of unions and not students (see Moskowitz, 2006).

### *Unions Improve Education with Bargaining*

Unions have been seen as positive forces in education because of collective bargaining. Some view the interests of teachers and students as mutually reinforcing (see Lindy, 2011). When teachers bargain to improve their working conditions, there is a natural benefit to the quality of education. If teachers bargain for reduced class sizes, extend teacher preparation periods, or improve the quality of air in a classroom, the learning culture is enhanced for students. In other words, collective bargaining improves the overall educational environment and benefits secured through the CBA extend to both teachers and students (Rowan, Chiang, & Miller, 1997).

Collective bargaining and unions can stimulate education innovation. Proponents of bargaining suggest that collective bargaining is a catalyst – rather than an inhibitor – to policy change. Unions and school leaders have used bargaining agreements to implement successful mentor programs, peer evaluation, and longer school years (Steelman et al., 2000). Because these reforms bind both sides contractually, they have the force of law, certainly an added benefit of the bargaining process.

Third, greater union involvement in bargaining promotes democracy (Malin, 2009). It has been argued (Malin, 2009) that when school districts include unions in their efforts to govern through the collective bargaining process, reforms stand a greater chance of success. At first, this seems counterintuitive. If we want to strengthen the link between the voters and their elected officials, a logical course of action would be to *restrict* unions in influencing school district direction through the collective bargaining process.

If unions are excluded from the important policy discussions, they will focus energy and resources on frustrating the implementation of the policy. Unions effectuate this when they demand to bargain over the *impact* of a proposed policy to their wages, hours, and conditions of employment (Malin, 2009). For instance, the decision to adopt an evaluation system may unilaterally rest with the school leadership because the matter is an education policy. However, how that evaluation system is implemented would certainly impact the "wages, hours, and condition of employment" for teachers. Accordingly that impact would be subject to mandatory bargaining.

Yet, if unions are actively engaged in crafting a proposal, they have a vested interest in its success. Embracing more union involvement improves the chances of success of a board proposal. In this way, democratic principles are advanced.

## OPTIONS AT THE TABLE: PROCESSES AND PRACTICES

School leaders should grasp the underlying policy debates about the role of bargaining in education. But, perhaps more significantly, school leaders must be prepared *to negotiate* a CBA. Negotiating a contract is perhaps one of the most essential functions of school boards and leaders. From a leadership perspective, a CBA can play a pivotal role in advancing a district's initiatives or changes.

School leaders, such as superintendents and principals (Ingram, 2004), play a pivotal role in this process. They assist the school board in preparing for negotiations by analyzing data related to compensation and benefits. They need to know what reform proposals they may seek to implement that have implications for bargaining (e.g., merit pay, or reassignment of teachers). In sum, they must determine how the resulting CBA and negotiation process can support the educational mission of the district. In the current context – where education policy is rapidly changing – negotiating a CBA is a skill that school leadership must develop. There are two approaches to bargaining: traditional and interest-based bargaining.

### *One Approach to Negotiations: Traditional Bargaining*

Under traditional bargaining, each side views negotiations as a vehicle to maximize the gains for its constituents (Smart, 2012). Benefits that accrue to one side of the table come at the expense of the other side. The parties see bargaining as a oppositional, rather than collaborative (Kerchner & Mitchell, 1986). Moreover, in traditional bargaining, parties cannot easily maneuver from a position; once a party publicly declares during bargaining, they feel obliged to maintain that public stance. Backing down would appear weak.

From a practical perspective, a number of points are worth noting as they relate to traditional bargaining. To begin with, each side develops proposals with their respective negotiations committee or teams (DeMitchell, 2010). If done well, this requires a great deal of preparation. Typically, each side will seek to understand what issues are most important to their membership. These are divided into economic (e.g., pay raises, health insurance) and non-economic topics (duty free lunch, preparation periods, professional development opportunities, etc.) (see DeMitchell, 2010; Smart, 2012).

Once the parties have developed their proposals, they are able to sit down to begin negotiations. At this beginning phase, sides typically exchange proposals with the other side. Of course, both sides realistically understand that they will not be able to obtain all of their goals through negotiations. However, from a positional standpoint, neither side gives away their "bottom line." A union may develop a proposal for a wage increase that is unrealistic. Yet, the union recognizes that there may be an appropriate time to concede to a more realistic wage increase (if any is appropriate) in exchange for management concession on another point. Through this process – with neither side revealing their bottom lines – an agreement is cobbled together.

Traditional bargaining has benefits. It can inspire faith from the party's constituents, empowering unions (Grimshaw, 1979). If a union bargains "hard" (i.e., unrelenting) on an issue, teachers see their union "fighting" for their interest. In this light, union dues look like money well spent to members of a union.

Traditional bargaining has significant drawbacks. To begin with, it leaves little room for reaching an agreement. During negotiations the parties take a position and attempt to convince the other side of the wisdom of that position. As they make the case, they become further fused to that position, making it difficult to alter course without looking hypocritical or weak. Oftentimes, positions can be associated with people. When this occurs negotiations can devolve into personality conflicts that last beyond contract negotiations and spill into the operation of schools (Kerchner & Mitchell, 1986). Communication lines between teachers and administrators become fractured and tense (Grimshaw, 1979; Kerchner & Mitchell,1986). Others have detailed the significant issues related to positional bargaining that occurs both during and after the process (DeMitchell, 2010; Fisher & Ury, 1981; Hess & West, 2006; Mitchell, Kerchner, Erck, & Pryor,1986; Moe, 2009; Smart, 2012).

### *An Alternative Approach to Negotiations: Interest-Based Bargaining*

Another method of negotiations – interest-based bargaining (IBB) – is available for purposes of contract negotiations. The process is also known as "problem-based" bargaining. For our purposes, the terms interest-based and problem-based are used synonymously. This process addresses perceived shortcomings associated with traditional bargaining, such as those discussed immediately above. IBB is distinguishable from traditional or positional bargaining.

To begin with, IBB approaches bargaining from a different premise. At its core, the parties must review problems or issues on the merits, rather than attempting to maximize their gain for a constituency (Ury & Fisher, 1981). In this way, bargaining is viewed as a shared problem-solving exercise. The parties measure proposed solutions against, if possible, objective criteria. In practice, IBB operates quite differently from traditional bargaining (Bluestone & Kochan, 2011). Parties meet together to identify the issues or problems that they want to address through negotiations. Once identified, they generate proposed solutions to the issues. In the school setting, the proposals are measured against one question: is the proposal good for children? Representatives from both parties – unions and management – discuss and determine the fate of proposals generally in the same room against this question. The objective is for a proposal to be a "win–win" for all involved (Fisher & Ury, 1981).

There are benefits for using IBB. The process focuses on larger policy issues. The touchstone of any proposal under IBB is whether it benefits children. Reasonable minds may disagree about a proposal's relative ability to address this question. However, the IBB process forces the focus on this inquiry and not on maximizing each side's relative gain. Likewise, the focus is on issues, not on personalities. In addition, IBB promotes shared ownership of a problem and trust, an important element in negotiations (Kerchner & Mitchell, 1986). Under IBB, sides develop solutions together, usually in real-time. Too often in education, the parties point fingers at one another. We see that today where many education stakeholders blame unions for education inequity (see Hess & Kelly, 2006; Hoxby, 1996; Moe, 2006; Moskowitz, 2006). Of course, the reality is much more complicated than simple finger pointing. Under IBB, with both management and union agreeing on a proposed solution, the likelihood of playing the blame game is reduced.

## CHOOSING A BARGAINING PROCESS TO RESOLVE POLICY DISAGREEMENTS AT THE LOCAL LEVEL

IBB may be a particularly well-suited method for school leaders and unions to resolve difficult policy questions, such as how to evaluate teachers. The distinguishing feature of IBB – its joint problem-solving approach – is exactly what may be needed for unions and school administrators to reach consensus on important issues. In the case of teacher evaluation, unions and management have clashed over recent policy proposals, especially those that involve the use of value-added measures for evaluation (Harris, 2011). Both sides have passionate – and very different – positions regarding the topic. Because of this, traditional bargaining may not be an advisable method for school leaders, especially with respect to negotiating contested education policy matters. In fact, IBB may be an appropriate choice, given its goal of reaching consensus through bargaining.

It is generally understood that teacher evaluation is viewed as one of the most important components of improving teacher quality (Hinchey, 2010). Of course, processes and purposes of evaluations have been a source of great contention. In particular, considerable dispute exists with respect to the use of student test scores (through the use of value-added models, "VAMs") in evaluating teachers. Some contend that VAMs should be used to make "high-stakes" employment decisions (e.g., termination) for our teachers (Hanushek, 2009). In this way, underperforming teachers leave the profession and are replaced by high-performing teachers. Yet, others hold that the use of test scores should be avoided in making such decisions (Paige, 2013b, 2014) because VAMs are unreliable.

The greater policy debates about VAMs and the appropriate evaluation systems are largely academic to practitioners debating the merits of such policies (Ballou & Springer, 2015; Harris, 2011). However, school leaders and districts must adopt evaluation systems in this context policy confusion. They make significant decisions based on conflicting information. In these situations, collective bargaining can play an important role: the negotiation process offers local school leaders an opportunity to resolve policy tensions through collaborative solutions appropriate for their local needs. To the extent permitted under state statute, the parties can craft CBAs that reflect a local position about the role of VAMs in teacher evaluation.

To be sure, management and unions would have to negotiate agreements that accord with requirements under state statutes. Depending on the state, some statutes require certain elements, including student test scores, to be included in personnel decisions and evaluation. In Florida, student test scores must account for at least 50% of a teacher's evaluation, and those evaluations must be used in making decisions about continued employment (Florida Statutes Annotated, § 1012.34, 2014). In contrast, New Hampshire imposes no statutory requirement with respect to the specifics of district's evaluation system. It simply requires each district to evaluate its teachers (New Hampshire Revised Statutes Annotated, 2014), and the state department of education gives recommendations on this point. In any event, the point is that collective bargaining is an effective means for union and management to come to terms about controversial policy topics, like teacher evaluation.

However, traditional bargaining, as described above, may not be a suitable method at the local level. It is inherently divisive and may prevent compromise. Parties can be locked into differing positions and without incentive to meet in the middle on a particular topic, especially one as contentious as teacher evaluation. Given the high-stakes of teacher evaluation (e.g., potential termination) parties may be less compromising in a traditional bargaining format.

IBB, in comparison, may be particularly well suited to address teacher evaluation and other divisive topics. In the context of teacher evaluation, IBB would require that the parties seek a joint resolution to a shared problem (U.S. Department of Education, 2012). In this case, the shared problem is ensuring that teachers are evaluated in a fair manner that accurately assesses their contributions. From this starting point, management and union can – together – craft proposals to address the larger issue. Within this space, they can determine the appropriate use, if any, of student test scores in teacher evaluation. Thus, in this way, IBB allows management and unions an organized opportunity to resolve the lingering tensions that filter to the local level (Paige, 2013b).

Several promising examples already existing in the field demonstrate the potential of IBB, especially with respect to creating agreement around teacher evaluation. In New Haven, Connecticut, for instance, union and management agreed on terms of a teacher evaluation system (American Federation of Teachers, 2014b). A hallmark of this system was the use of peer assisted review (PAR). In brief, PAR allows the opportunity for multiple opinions (from teachers and administrators) regarding the performance of a teacher.

Similar collaborative efforts have resulted in meaningful change that has improved teacher evaluation. For example, in Toledo, Ohio union officials and school leaders engaged in a collaborative process that, like the New Haven evaluation system, employed PAR (see Malin, 2014). Union leaders has been behind these efforts and, generally, seems willing to engage in a collaborative process that is geared to improving the profession (American Federation of Teachers, 2014a, 2014b).

State policy and lawmakers have encouraged the use of collaborative labor-management initiatives similar to IBB. In Massachusetts, policymakers have encouraged the use of IBB as a means to comply with the state's Race to Top obligations, especially those related to teacher evaluation (Bluestone & Kochan, 2011). In addition, the Illinois state legislature requires the formation of a joint committee of labor and management to reach agreement on evaluation systems (see Illinois Compiled Statutes, 5-24A-4(b), 2014). Thus, taken together, it appears that there may be opportunities for school leaders to leverage IBB to adopt teacher evaluation policies that are particularly suited for their local needs.

## CONCLUSION AND RECOMMENDATIONS

In the final analysis, school leaders must negotiate and work under CBAs. Accordingly, this chapter lends valuable insight that may help school officials leverage collective bargaining to improve their respective schools or districts. First, recent trends to exclude union involvement by restricting teacher collective bargaining rights may be a step in the wrong direction. Exclusion of unions may actually inhibit reforms. Examples cited here teacher–union collaboration through the bargaining process can advance reforms. Collective bargaining can be an important tool to address some of the most contested areas of policy dispute, like teacher evaluation.

Second, almost the entire landscape on collective bargaining depicts bargaining as an isolated event: respective sides sit at the table, hash out an agreement, or "dig in heels" when appropriate. Once a CBA is reached, each party goes back to work; management to their corner, teachers to theirs. But that view is shortsighted and can be misleading to school leaders who negotiate and then work under CBAs.

Collective bargaining does not simply end when the ink dries on a contract. Rather, collective bargaining does at least two things that all school leaders must keep in mind. First, the agreement itself establishes the working conditions – the parameters under which both sides must work – going forward for a defined period (usually a few years). As one state supreme court found: "[t]he essence of the collective bargaining process is that the employer and employees should work together in resolving problems related to employment" (*Timberlane Regional Education Association v. Timberlane Regional School District*, 1974, p. 251). Promoting a stable, transparent working environment is in everyone's interest, including students.

Second, and in a related point, collective bargaining must be seen from its human relations perspective. In other words, CBAs are the "footings" for continued relationships between the stakeholders. This is an essential point for school leaders. While collective bargaining results in "an agreement" it can build trust. Similarly, bargaining can undercut faith between management and teachers. In other words, bargaining should also be viewed as a process that sets the tone going forward. Negotiations are complicated. They can tire each side and bring people to various points of contention in the heat of the moment. But school leaders would be wise to recognize that bargaining is the function of a human process between school officials and teachers.

## REFERENCES


American Federation of Teachers. (2014a). *AFT president joins 400 educators and labor leaders at labor-management conference on collaborative school reforms.* Retrieved from http://www.aft.org/press-release/aft-president-randi-weingarten-join-400-educators-administrators-leaders

American Federation of Teachers. (2014b). *New haven teachers really behind contract.* Retrieved from http://www.aft.org/news/new-haven-teachers-rally-behind-landmark-contract

Appeal of State. 138 N.H. 716 (1994).

Appeal of White Mountain Regional School District. 908 A. 2d 790 (2006).

Ballou, D., & Springer, M. (2015). Using student test scores to measure teacher performance: Some problems in the design and implementation of evaluation systems. *Educational Researcher*, *44*(2), 77–86.

Bluestone, B., & Kochan, T. (2011). *Toward a grand new bargain: Collaborative approaches to labor-management reform in Massachusetts.* Boston, MA: Dukakis Center Publications.

Boston Public Schools. (2015). *Website, Mayor Walsh negotiates plan to extend school day by 40 Minutes.* Retrieved from http://www.bostonpublicschools.org/site/default.aspx?PageType=3&DomainID=4&ModuleInstanceID=14&ViewID=047E6BE3-6D87-4130-8424-D8E4E9ED6C2A&RenderLoc=0&FlexDataID=6524&PageID=1

DeMitchell, T. (2010). *Labor relations in education: Policies, politics, and practices.* New York, NY: Rowman & Littlefield Education.

ECONorthwest. (2008). *A review of research on extended learning time in K-12 schools.* The Chalkboard Project. Retrieved from http://chalkboardproject.org/images/PDF/Extended%20Learning%20final%20rev.pdf

Edwards, C. (2010). Public sector unions and the rising cost of employee compensation. *Cato Journal*, *30*(1), 87–115.

Fisher, R., & Ury, W. (1981). *Getting to yes: Negotiating an agreement without giving in.* London: Penguin Press.

Florida State Statutes. § 1012.34 *et seq* (2014).

Grimshaw, W. (1979). *Union rules in the schools.* Lexington, MA: Lexington Books.

Hanushek, E. (2009). Teacher deselection. In D. H. Goldhaber & J. Hannaway (Eds.), *Creating a new teacher profession* (pp. 165–180). Washington, DC: Urban Institute Press.

Harris, D. (2011). *Value added measures in education: What every educator needs to know.* Cambridge, MA: Harvard University Press.

Hess, R., & Kelly, A. (2006). Scapegoat, albatross, or what? The status quo in teacher collective bargaining. In J. Hannaway & A. Rothertham (Eds.), *Collective bargaining in education: Negotiating change in today's schools* (pp. 53–88). Cambridge, MA: Harvard Education Press.

Hess, R., & West, M. (2006). *A better bargain: Overhauling teacher collective bargaining for the 21st century*. Cambridge, MA: Harvard University Program on Education and Governance.

Hinchey, P. (2010). *Getting teacher assessment right: What policymakers can learn from research*. Boulder, CO: National Education Policy Center. Retrieved from http://nepc.colorado.edu/files/PB-TEval-Hinchey_0.pdf

Hoxby, C. (1996). How teachers unions affect production. *Quarterly Journal of Economics, 111*, 671–718.

Illinois Compiled Statutes. § 5-24A-4(b). (2014).

Indiana State Code § 20-29-6-4.5. (2014).

Ingram, R. L. (2004). Negotiating away barriers to educational opportunity. *Leadership, 33*(3), 28–38.

Kerchner, C., & Mitchell, D. (1986). Teaching reform and union reform. *The Elementary School Journal, 86*(4), 448–470.

Lindy, B. (2011). The impact of teacher collective bargaining laws on student achievement: Evidence from a New Mexico natural experiment. *Yale Law Journal, 120*, 1130–1191.

Loveless, T. (2000). *Conflicting missions: Teachers unions and educational reform* Washington, DC: The Brookings Institute.

Malin, M. (2009). The paradox of public sector labor law. *Indiana Law Journal, 84*, 1369–1399.

Malin, M. (2014). Education reform and labor management collaboration: What role for the law? *University of Toledo Law Journal, 45*, 527–543.

Massachusetts General Laws. c. 150 *et seq* (2014).

McDonnell, L., & Pascal, A. (1988). *Teacher unions and education reform*. Santa Monica, CA: RAND Corporation. Retrieved from http://eric.ed.gov/?id=ED293837

Mitchell, D., Kerchner, C., Erck, W., & Pryor, G. (1986). The impact of collective bargaining on school management and policy. *American Journal of Education, 89*, 147–188.

Moe, T. (2006). Union power and the education of children. In J. Hannaway & A. Rotherham (Eds.), *Collective bargaining in education* (pp. 229–256). Cambridge, MA: Harvard Education Press.

Moe, T. (2009). Collective bargaining and the performance of public schools. *American Journal of Political Science, 53*(1),156–174.

Moskowitz, E. (2006). Breakdown. *Education Next, 6*(Summer), 24–27. Retrieved from http://educationnext.org/files/ednext20063_24.pdf

New Hampshire Revised Statutes Annotated § 273-A:3. (2014).

North Carolina General Statutes §§ 95-98. (2014).

Paige, M. A. (2013a). Applying the 'paradox' theory: A law and policy analysis of collective bargaining rights and teacher evaluation reform from selected states. *Brigham Young Journal of Law and Education, 1*, 21–43.

Paige, M. A. (2013b). Teacher evaluation and collective bargaining: Resolving policy at the local level. *Journal of Cases in Educational Leadership, 16*(4), 45–57.

Paige, M. A. (2014). Commentary: A legal argument against the use of value added models in teacher evaluation. *Teachers College Record*. Retrieved from http://www.tcrecord.org/Content.asp?ContentId=17796

Paige, M. A., & DeMitchell, T. A., (2013). Arbitration litigation concerning teacher discipline for misuse of technology: A preliminary assessment. *West's Education Law Reporter*, *296*, 22–41.

Rowan, B., Chiang, F.-S., & Miller, R. J. (1997). Using research on employees' performance to study effect of teachers on students' achievement. *Sociology of Education*, *70*(4), 256–284.

Sanes, M., & Schmitt, J. (2014). *Regulation of public sector collective bargaining by state*. Center for Economic and Policy Research. Retrieved from http://www.cepr.net/documents/state-public-cb-2014-03.pdf

Smart, W. (2012). *Winning at collective bargaining: Strategies everyone can live with*. New York, NY: Rowman Littlefield Education.

Steelman, L., Powell, B., & Carini, R. (2000). Do teacher unions hinder educational performance? Lessons learned from state SAT and ACT Scores. *Harvard Educational Review*, *70*(4), 437–466.

Summers, R. (1980). Public sector bargaining substantially diminishes democracy. *Government Union Review*, *1*, 5–22.

Timberlane Regional Education Association v. Timberlane Regional School District. 114 N. H. 245 (1974).

U.S. Department of Education. (2012). Shared responsibility: A U.S. Department of Education white paper on labor-management collaboration.

Wisconsin State Statutes § 111.70(4)(mb). (2013).

Wisconsin Statutes Annotated § 111. 70 (4)(mb) (2014).

# EPILOGUE

It is a pleasure to write the epilogue to this amazing book. Normore, Ehrensal, First, and Torres have assembled some of the very best minds in our field in this compendium which explores the boundaries of complex legal thinking and policymaking as they relate to schools. In the past 25 years that I have been active in the field of education law, I have had the pleasure of working collaboratively with this publication's editors and meeting many of the chapter contributors. I have seen careers grow, new ideas formulate, and scholarship ripen, mature, and sometimes change direction.

Similarly, I have witnessed legal issues emerge, shift focus, take a hiatus, and often remerge in a different form years later. Throughout the 1960s and 1970s and well into the 1990s (when I started my career in academia), courts often addressed what I would characterize as "big picture" issues. Indeed, during this period the United States Supreme Court rendered a dozen decisions on school desegregation followed quickly by *Brown v. Board of Education*'s (1954) progeny, that is, a second tier of decisions based on the Constitution's Fourteenth Amendment, Equal Protection Clause, and applied to discrimination against groups such as such as women, linguistic minorities, and persons with disabilities.

A similar trend emerged with regard to the religion clauses of the First Amendment to the U.S. Constitution. Here, the Court regularly issued opinions on establishment clause cases ranging from bible reading and school prayer to use of school facilities for religious groups to various forms of federal aid for religious schools. The 1969 *Tinker v. Des Moines* decision, which allowed peaceful student protests of the Viet-Nam war, spawned a series of students' rights decisions related to free speech, school newspapers, search and seizure, and drug testing.

Indeed, *Safford v. Redding*, a 2009 case involving the strip search of 13-year-old girl for prescription-strength aspirin, was the last school case that the Supreme Court decided. Citing earlier High Court decisions as well as public comments from Justices Roberts and Justice Breyer, Walsh (2014) surmises that the Court has realized its limitations and does not want to become involved in the decision making of schools. During this time, the Court refused to hear cases centered on corporal punishment, special education, bullying, student religious speech, and student speech on the Internet (Walsh, 2014).

In this publication, Normore, Ehrensal, First, and Torres have chartered new territory by examining themes that are highly relevant today, many of which portend an ever-increasing litigious environment, but are not reliant on the Supreme Court to provide remedies. Instead, most of the authors focus on state laws and lower court decisions. If there is a call for a national response, it takes the form of an executive decision or a revamping of federal laws.

Not surprisingly, the chapters in this book are unique in several other ways. First, the authors are obviously knowledgeable as to the law and explain it in clear terms, but they are just as adept at identifying and analyzing policy implications and at providing suggestions for practice. Second, rather than concentrating merely on the letter of the law, they focus on social justice issues and practical solutions to complex issues. Consequently, many of the contributors are concerned about disenfranchised groups that the law has largely ignored or nuances that the law has missed. Finally, much of what is presented puts a new twist on law that many of us thought was resolved long ago. In other words, what is old is new again. The reader may want to keep these themes in mind as I turn to the content and interrelationship of these chapters.

Shariff (2009), a scholar who has written extensively on cyberbullying reminds us that bullying has always been with us but that the cyber element has exacerbated this behavior – made it public, possibly more hurtful, and less easy to control. In Chapter 1, James Vines details the legal complications that emerge when these incidents occur off campus. He articulates various states' cyberbullying laws and policies and calls for a unified way of handling this disruption. Kathleen Conn connects cyberbullying with free speech rights under the First Amendment and observes that many of these cases involve harassment. In addition to legal cases, she discusses in some depth the social and psychological effects of bullying. Her final conclusion is that the law cannot alone remedy this situation and that individuals must accept personal responsibility for their actions.

Janet R. Decker and Suzanne E. Eckes address legal issues related to bullying students with disabilities. Providing an historical context to this problem, these authors note that the current state of harassing students with disabilities has raised sufficient concern as to prompt the United States Department of Education (USDoE) to provide guidance on this matter. These authors believe that school leaders have the power to make great social change within schools but, among other things, they must be aware of the bullying that occurs with students who have disabilities, must ensure that their staff receive training, and must understand the legal protections given to these students under the special education laws as well as laws related to bullying and harassment.

Later, in their chapter on children with Autism Spectrum Disorder (ASD), Kevin P. Brady and Cynthia A. Dieterich devote a sizable portion of their article to bullying, this time aimed at students with ASD. Overall, they strongly suggest that school leaders become more literate in special education laws. Regarding bullying specifically, they caution educators to act when bullying occurs. While this behavior is harmful in itself, from a legal perspective, it may also be connected with harassment and discrimination against students with disabilities. Other suggestions center around teaching the child how to avoid situations that may encourage bullying and how to react to those who may potentially bully them.

Commensurate with this idea of old being new again, educating children of undocumented immigrants and providing instruction to second language learners have been with us for decades, presumably settled by the U.S. Supreme Court decisions in *Plyler v. Doe* (1982) and *Lau v. Nichols* (1974). Yet, in this current climate and with an unprecedented rise in both the number and diversity of immigrant populations (Zong & Batlova, 2015) and the politicization of immigration reform, a renewed interest in these groups has emerged. Examining what they characterize as a failure on the part of the federal government to provide meaningful immigration reform, Chinasa A. Elue and Patricia F. First contend that states have arbitrarily denied these students their right to an education.

Accordingly, the authors in two subsequent chapters discuss second language learners, but from very different perspectives. Caron Mellblom-Nishioka considers laws that drive classroom practices, but at the same time, emphasizes how legal mandates oppose what the field and pertinent research determine as effective ways of educating these students. Racines then applies quantitative and policy research methodologies to analyze case law and identify litigation trends in this field over the past 40 years in an effort to improve what she sees as a dysfunctional system that fails to provide EL students with an equitable education.

Hollie J. Mackey focuses on language and education, but with a group that has been long neglected, tribal peoples living in Native communities. Here she emphasizes the importance of indigenous languages in transmitting culture, supporting academic achievement, and fostering independence.

Mackey sees the current system as one which connects these students with deficit models. She advocates for standalone federal legislation that would promote community development and foster self-determination.

Homeless students comprise another population that seems to get lost in our educational system despite federal legislation. While the McKinney-Vento Homeless Assistance Act protects the educational rights of these students and prohibits discrimination against them, Susan C. Bon and Nicole D. Snyder note that there is not always a unified system to identify and provide support for these students. These authors encourage school personnel to receive training on the law and its implementation and to work closely with various community agencies to ensure that students receive appropriate services.

While Mackey, Bon, and Snyder explore the concept of community as related to achievement and disenfranchised populations, Jeffrey Burke and Mario Torres consider community educational attainment and how levels of education may be related to the privacy rights of students. Using data from the United States Census and the American Community survey, these scholars compare this information with the levels of intrusiveness of student searches that make it to court.

Other chapters involve students more indirectly, but the influence is still profound. For example, Anthony H. Normore, Darius Bone, Delaney Jones and Stacy Spell address some of the same school discipline issues as Burke and Torres, but from the perspective of School Resource Officers (SROs). Major functions of SROs include providing security and preventing crime. These professionals, however, also have an obligation to serve as role models, mentor students, and educate these youth on the law. In this chapter, Normore and his colleagues tackle the difficult issues of funding costs for SROs as well as those who believe schools should focus on education as opposed to law enforcement.

Not your typical article on school finance, Lori L. Taylor applies a social justice perspective to the allocation of resources, concluding that equality is not equity. Discussing the construction of school funding formulae and allocation of federal resources under Title 1 of the Elementary and Secondary Education Act, she concludes that there is a great deal of difference as to the cost of education and labor market forces within each state as well as among different states. Therefore, the actual price of education varies from place to place – a factor that is vitally important, often overlooked, and cannot be ignored if equity is to be achieved.

In their respective chapters, Patricia A. L. Ehrensal and Mark Paige turn to teachers and students. Ehrensal reviews student speech and how it continues to be a contested issue in schools. She examines the underlying values in schools that rejected the speech of *Fraser* while accepting the speech act of cheerleaders' dance routines. In contrast to Ehrensal's critical theory approach, Paige uses a more traditional legal and policy analysis to summarize the history of collective bargaining and discuss its current status. Paige iterates both the potential and the limitations of collective bargaining, but like his colleague, is concerned with giving teachers a chance to voice their expertise. For Paige, collective bargaining has the potential to allow school leaders and teachers to work together to build trust, mutually solve problems, and create a stable and transparent working environment that benefits everyone, including students.

In sum, when the Supreme Court backed away from rendering opinions on K-12 public school cases, it left a great deal of power to the lower courts in interpreting laws, to the states and federal government in making better, possibly more effective, laws, and to school districts and school boards in developing and implementing policies. Perhaps, even more importantly, this development left school districts with less guidance on legal issues but also much more discretion as to how to handle school matters. Paige speaks of school personnel working together to solve problems through collective bargaining. Eckes mentions ethics and the power that school leaders have to make great social change. Mackey stresses self-determination. Conn articulates a need for personal responsibility. Many of the authors ask that school leaders better support marginalized populations and that they collaborate and engage in community efforts. All suggest training and/or a greater understanding of the law. Power, discretion, potential, student advocacy. This may well be the rallying call for a newly-empowered profession. It is a decision for all of us.

Jacqueline A. Stefkovich

# REFERENCES

Brown v. Board of Education of Topeka, 347 U.S. 483 (1954).
Lau v. Nichols, 414 U.S. 563 (1974).
Plyler v. Doe, 457 U.S. 202 (1982).
Safford v. Redding, 557 U.S. 364 (2009).
Shariff, S. (2009). *Confronting cyber-bullying: What schools need to know to control misconduct and avoid legal consequences*. London: Cambridge University Press.

Tinker v. Des Moines Independent Community School District, 393 U.S. 503 (1969).

Walsh, M. (2014). After decades of action, Supreme Court cools on school cases. *Education Week*, *34*(6), 20–21.

Zong, J., & Batlova, J. (2015, February 26). Frequently requested statistics on immigrants and immigration in the United States. *Migration Information Source*. On-line journal of the Migration Policy Institute, Washington, D.C. Retrieved from http://www.migrationpolicy.org/article/frequently-requested-statistics-immigrants-and-immigration-united-states

Printed and bound by CPI Group (UK) Ltd, Croydon, CR0 4YY

15/09/2026

14962364-0001

# ABOUT THE AUTHORS

**Susan C. Bon**, J.D., Ph.D. is the Higher Education Program Coordinator and an Associate Professor in the Department of Educational Leadership and Policies at the University of South Carolina. Dr. Bon teaches the education law, higher education law, policy, and disability courses. She also holds an affiliate appointment in the University of South Carolina's School of Law. Her scholarship focuses on the impact of law and ethics on leadership and special education leadership in K-12 schools and higher education programs. She has authored and co-authored nearly 40 articles and book chapters addressing the legal and ethical principles that inform administrative practice and impact leadership. Dr. Bon is an active leader in national law-related organizations focusing on education law and special education law. Prior to her university faculty service, she worked as the ombudsman in the State Superintendent's Division of the Ohio Department of Education. She spent one year as a part-time Intern at the United States Education Department working on Title I, Part D (Neglected or Delinquent Youth), McKinney-Vento (EHCY), and Homeless Education Disaster Assistance (HEDA) Grant Programs. Dr. Bon received her J.D. law degree and Ph.D. from The Ohio State University.

**Darius Bone** is a Lieutenant with 30 years of professional experience that spans a wide range of disciplines. For the past 23 years, he has worked with the Los Angeles Police Department (LAPD). Woven throughout his careers are homeland security, public safety and service, risk management, liability mitigation, human factors analysis, and aviation safety. His professional career in public service began as an electrical engineer for a prominent government contracted aerospace corporation, Hughes Aircraft (eight years). Lt. Bone holds a Master's Degree in Negotiation and Conflict Management from California State University Dominguez Hills. Darius has published in *Law Enforcement Today*, and currently has an article "in press" with *FBI Law Enforcement Bulletin* titled "Human Factors: Leaders Improving Safety while Developing Meaningful Public Trust."

**Kevin P. Brady**, Ph.D., is an Associate Professor in the Department of Curriculum and Instruction at the University of Arkansas. He has published more than 60 articles and book chapters involving educational law and policy issues. His primary advocacy, research, and scholarly interests include special education law, school disciplinary issues, school funding fairness, and increasing legal literacy for today's school leaders. He is a former member of the Board of Directors of the Education Law Association (ELA). His research and scholarship appears in a wide range of leading educational law, policy, and technology journals. Dr. Brady currently serves on a number of editorial boards for peer-reviewed journals, including *Education and Urban Society*, *Education Law & Policy Review*, *Journal of Disability Policy Studies*, and *West's Education Law Reporter*. Along with coauthors, Gina Umpstead, Janet Decker, David Schimmel, and Matthew Militello, his most recent book, How to Prevent Special Education Litigation: Eight Legal Lesson Plans (2015) is to be published by Teachers College Press. He earned his Master's Degree in educational policy from Teachers College, Columbia University and his Ph.D. in educational policy analysis from the University of Illinois at Urbana-Champaign.

**Jeffrey Burke**, Ed.D., holds a doctoral degree from Texas A&M, College Station. He currently serves as the Assistant Superintendent of Academics for Georgetown Independent School District in Georgetown, Texas. Dr. Burke has previously served in Alvin ISD as Executive Director of Professional Learning and Director of Human Resources. Prior to his service in Alvin, he was the High School Principal in Anderson-Shiro CISD near College Station and taught High School English and History for seven years in the classroom. In his 19 years in public education, Dr. Burke has worked at all school levels and has served in a variety of roles, but in each role his passion has been to ensure that students are treated equitably and fairly, and that each student realizes his or her potential. School law has always been an interest for Dr. Burke, and his work at the campus and district leadership level exposed him to numerous situations and scenarios in which equitable and appropriate application of legal principles, policies, and practices were in play. It is his belief that public education serves to further our democracy and that we have a responsibility to ensure that students are given every opportunity to succeed, that it is our calling as educators to allow them to flourish, and that we are charged with protecting their best interests.

**Kathleen Conn**, Ph.D., J.D., LL.M, is a scientist, educator, consultant, and attorney. Dr. Conn is currently Of Counsel with the Education Law Group of King, Spry, Herman, Freund & Faul, LLC in Bethlehem, Pennsylvania.

She earned her B.S. in Physics from St. John's University, New York, an M.S. in Medical Physics/Radiation Biology at the University of California at Los Angeles (UCLA), and a dual Ph.D. in Physics/Biology at Bryn Mawr College Graduate School of Arts and Sciences in Pennsylvania. Dr. Conn's educational experience includes college/university teaching and 18 years of service in public school districts in Pennsylvania, as a teacher, K-12 curriculum supervisor, and elementary school principal. She has also been a consultant to schools and school districts on issues of school safety, bullying, cyberbullying, and sexual harassment. Kathleen also teaches as an Adjunct Professor at her alma mater, Widener University School Law in Wilmington, Delaware, where she earned her J.D. and LL.M. degrees. She is a member of the Pennsylvania bar and is admitted to the bar of the United States Supreme Court. Dr. Conn has published numerous commentaries in peer-reviewed law journals and authored three books and numerous book chapters. She is an annual presenter at the national Education Law Association (ELA) Conference, and has served on the Executive Board of ELA. She has presented internationally in Europe, China, New Zealand, and Australia.

**Janet R. Decker**, J.D., Ph.D., began her career as a special education teacher teaching students with autism. With a desire to affect policy change for students with disabilities, she received both her law degree and Ph.D. in Education Policy Studies from Indiana University. In 2011, the Education Law Association awarded her the Joseph C. Beckham Dissertation of the Year Award. Currently, Dr. Decker is an Assistant Professor at Indiana University's School of Education where she teaches school law courses to undergraduate and graduate students. Her research focuses on legal issues related to special education and charter schools.

**Cynthia A. Dieterich**, Ph.D., recently completed a position as a Visiting Faculty member in the Department of Teacher Education at Cleveland State University (CSU), Cleveland, Ohio. Previously, she held a position as a tenured, Associate Professor in special education for 14 years; also at CSU. Following her tenured position, she worked as a Research Consultant in the Washington, DC, area. She completed her Doctoral Degree at Kent State University, Kent, Ohio, in special education and psychometrics. Her experience as a researcher and practitioner is in both regular and special education within both private and public settings. Her publications appear in medical, legal, and educational journals, and include topics such as bullying, functional behavioral assessment, response to intervention, young children with hearing impairments, young children with hemangiomas, and health related services in special education. She has been actively involved in the Education Law Association (ELA) for 27 years and currently a member of the Board of Directors.

**Suzanne E. Eckes**, Ph.D., J.D., is a Professor in the Educational Leadership and Policy Studies Department at Indiana University. Dr. Eckes has published over 100 school-law articles and book chapters, is a co-editor of the *Principal's Legal Handbook and School Discipline and Safety*, and is a co-author of the leading school law books *Legal Rights of Teachers and Students and Legal Rights of Teachers and Students and Principals Teaching the Law*. Much of her research focuses on issues of equity for marginalized groups in public schools. She served on the board of directors for the Education Law Association and is currently the co-chair of the publications committee. She is the recipient of the Jack A. Culbertson Award for outstanding achievements in education from the University Council of Educational Administration. Prior to joining the faculty at Indiana University, Dr. Eckes was a high school French teacher in the Mississippi Delta region and an attorney at a Chicago law firm. She earned her Master's in Education from Harvard University and both her law degree and Ph.D. from the University of Wisconsin-Madison.

**Patricia A. L. Ehrensal**, Ed.D., is a Faculty Member at The College of New Jersey in the Educational Administration program. Her research focuses on discourses in and around school organizations. Particularly it examines how social construction of these organizations and the actors therein shape and are shaped by these discourses. The research is conducted from a critical theory perspective, drawing from the works of Foucault, Habermas, Bourdieu, and Berstien. Multi-disciplinary, this research draws from critical legal, policy, organizational and cultural studies, politics and governance, as well as critical children and youth studies. The research examines policy and legal documents, as well as the depiction of schools in the popular media. In addition to her numerous presentations at national and international conferences, Ehrensal has authored articles and book chapters examining ethics, law, the social construction of children in, and organizational arrangements of schools, and was the guest editor of the special edition of *The Journal of School Leadership* on law and ethics. Dr. Ehrensal earned her doctoral degree from Temple University in Philadelphia.

**Chinasa A. Elue**, Ph.D., is an Assistant Professor in Education Administration at Kent State University. Her lines of inquiry focus on issues of educational access and equity for underserved student populations across the P-20 continuum. The first strand of her research agenda explores the college choice decisions of marginalized students, specifically, rural student populations, and the different factors that impact their college choice decisions. Her second line of inquiry explores issues of educational access for immigrant student populations. Lastly, her third line of inquiry examines how law and policy, research, and practice connect to explore issues that impact the educational opportunities for marginalized student populations. Dr. Elue earned her Ph.D. in Educational Leadership from Clemson University, her M.Ed. from Valdosta State University in Educational Leadership, and her Bachelor's of Science degree in Psychology from the University of Georgia. Dr. Elue also serves as a Research Associate with the UCEA Center for Leadership in Law and Education for Law in Leadership and Education at Clemson University.

**Patricia F. First**, J.D., Ed.D., is Eugene T. Moore Distinguished Professor of Educational Leadership at Clemson University and Founding Director of the UCEA Center for Leadership in Law and Education. Dr. First's research and teaching are focused on the legal and policy issues of the education system, particularly those issues intersecting with ethical leadership furthering justice for children, the role of school boards and the financing of education. She is the author of *Education Policy for School Administrators*, and editor of *School Boards: Changing Local Control.* She has written numerous legal monographs, book chapters, and articles in scholarly and practitioner journals and presented education law topics nationally and internationally. Dr. First has served as Dean of the School of Education of the University of Dayton and Chairperson of the Faculties of Educational Leadership at the University of Arizona, Western Michigan University, and Northern Illinois University. She has been a teacher and administrator in K-12 education, a policy analyst with both state and federal government and a National Education Policy Fellow. Dr. First earned the Ed.D. and M.S. degrees at Illinois State University, the B.S. at the University of Massachusetts, and the J.D. at the University of Dayton School of Law. Among her national service roles, Dr. First has served on the Board of Directors of the Education Law Association and the Leadership Advisory Council of the American Association of School Administrators. Her current roles include service on the Board of the National Education Finance Conference, as Legislation Editor of *The Journal of Law and Education*, and participation in Educators Without Borders. Her current research focuses upon the legal and ethical rights of immigrant children, the interpretation of free and public in education policy dialog and the use of policy studies methodologies in legal research.

**Delaney Jones** is a police sergeant with 32 years of total Law Enforcement experience, which includes the U.S. Air Force Special Weapons and Tactics Team. For the past 29 years, he has worked for the Los Angeles Police Department. Some of his assignments include Patrol, Vice, Undercover Major Narcotics, Special Enforcement Unit, Bike Unit, OMBUDSMAN, Adjutant to the Commanding Officer, various Detective assignments and he is currently assigned to the Department's Employee Relations Group, where he is the Department's primary instructor for teaching Leadership Values, Conflict Resolution and Encouraging Effective Performance. Delaney completed his graduate education in Negotiation & Conflict Management, and his Bachelor's degree in Public Administration at California State University of Dominguez Hills. Delaney continues to strive to obtain his life goal as he is currently attending Concord University Law School.

**Hollie J. Mackey**, Ph.D. (Northern Cheyenne), is an Assistant Professor of Education at the University of Oklahoma. Her research includes K-12 educational leadership for equitable schools, American Indian education, education law and ethics, indigenous research paradigms, and leadership for social justice. She currently serves on the advisory board for the South Central Comprehensive Center (SC3) that focuses on American Indian education in the southwestern U.S. in partnership with the multiple state education agencies and the White House Initiative for Indian Education, and is a current nominee for the National Advisory Council for Indian Education (NACIE). Awards include the 2009 Harold F. Martin Outstanding Graduate Teaching Award, the 2013 International Willower Award for Excellence, and the 2014 Jack A. Culbertson Award for outstanding accomplishments as a junior professor of educational leadership. Dr. Mackey's publications can be found in Information Age, Emerald, Rowman and Littlefield, and Routledge Publishers and in the *International Journal for Qualitative Studies in Education*, *Mentoring and Tutoring*, the *Journal of Educational Administration*, and the *Journal for Critical Thought and Praxis*. Dr. Mackey works closely with school administrators, policymakers, and fellow scholars both in the United States and abroad as an advocate and activist for systemic educational improvement and reform.

**Caron Mellblom-Nishioka**, Ed.D., is a Professor of Special Education in the Department of Teacher Education at California State University,

Dominguez Hills. She is also a Speech Language Pathologist. Her research interests include alternative language development, assistive technology and communication development among individuals with disabilities, inclusive supported bilingual language development. Dr. Mellblom-Nishioka has authored numerous grant projects designed to provide supported learning to students and to improve the transition of students from one educational setting to the next. She has a strong background in program and school assessment, having served on more than 20 evaluation teams for Western Association of Schools and Colleges, (WASC), National Association of Colleges of Teacher Education, NCATE – now called the Council for the Accreditation of Educator Preparation, (CAEP), and The California Commission on Teacher Credentialing, (CCTC). She has over 20 published articles, books chapters, reports and book reviews. Dr. Mellblom-Nishioka has worked in the greater Los Angeles basin for 20 years and has developed awareness of the unresolved issues facing second language learners today. She brings this experience to her University seminars and graduate students.

**Anthony H. Normore (Tony)**, Ph.D., earned his Doctorate Degree from University of Toronto. He is Department Chair of Graduate Education, and Professor of Educational Leadership at California State University Dominguez Hills. Tony has served in various university administrative roles including Department Chair of Special Needs, Department Chair of Educational Leadership, Co-Chair of Teacher Education, and Director of Doctoral Programs. Tony has been a visiting professor of ethics and leadership at Seoul National University, a visiting professor in the Department of Criminal Justice Studies at University of Guelph/Humber and a regular graduate professor of law, ethics, and leadership for the Summer Leadership Academy at Teachers College-Columbia University. His 33 years of professional education experiences has taken him throughout North America, South Central Asia, Eastern Asia, United Kingdom, Continental Europe, and South Pacific. Tony's research focusses on urban leadership growth and development in the context of ethics and social justice. He is the author of several edited books including *What the Social Sciences Tell us about Leadership for Social Justice and Ethics* (2014, Information Age Publishing), *Moral Compass for Law Enforcement Professional* (2014, International Academy of Public Safety), and *Collective Efficacy: An Interdisciplinary Approach to International Leadership Development* (2013, Emerald Group Publishing Limited), and a contributor of numerous scholarly book chapters and peer-reviewed journal articles. He is the Chief Leadership and Ethics Officer, and the Chairman of the

Criminal Justice Commission for Credible Leadership Development with the International Academy of Public Safety (IAPS).

**Mark Paige**, J.D., Ph.D., is a Professor of public policy at the University of Massachusetts-Dartmouth. At UMASS, he researches legal issues in education and their educational policy dimensions. In particular, he focuses on the law relates to teacher evaluation, collective bargaining, public school finance, as well as special education law. He has an extensive background in the field of education law. He has been invited to present his research before academic and professional audiences. Before entering academia, he represented school districts before a variety of courts and tribunals. In this capacity, he also counseled school districts on employment and collective bargaining matters and authored the winning brief in a leading case regarding management rights before the New Hampshire Supreme Court. He received both his J.D., with honors, and Ph.D. from the University of Wisconsin-Madison.

**Delia E. Racines**, Ph.D., earned her Doctorate in Teacher Education and Educational Leadership from George Mason University in Fairfax, Virginia. Delia most recently worked as a Faculty member teaching English Learners at the University of Southern California's (USC) Language Academy (now International Academy) and also taught American Legal English with the Gould School of Law in the yearly Law & English program. Delia is currently an Educational Consultant for Teacher Created Materials in Huntington Beach, California, and also supports teachers in Orange County as a Title I Instructional Coach. Her dissertation was nominated for the Joseph C. Beckham Dissertation of the Year Award with the Education Law Association. Delia recently authored introductory chapters in *Teaching to Complexity* and *TIME For Kids: Practicing for Today's Tests*, and proudly serves as an Advisory Board member representing Southern California for English Language Development with Teacher Created Materials.

**Nicole D. Snyder**, J.D., is a Shareholder at Latsha Davis & McKenna, P.C. She represents numerous schools in special education law, education law and charter school law matters. She routinely advises and defends charter schools in cases arising under IDEA and Section 504, regularly conducts trainings for school personnel and school boards, and annually presents papers at various seminars on special education law, education law and ethics. Nicole is a member of PBI's Legal Services for Exceptional Children's Committee, the Education Law Association, National Alliance for Public Charter Schools, American Educational Research Association, and the Pennsylvania Bar Association. She has been admitted to practice before the Supreme Courts of Pennsylvania, Ohio and New Jersey, as well as numerous district courts. She received her J.D. from Villanova University School of Law and her B.A. in English magna cum laude from Villanova University. Prior to joining private practice, she served as a judicial law clerk for the Honorable Bonnie Brigance Leadbetter of the Commonwealth Court and served as a judicial intern for the Honorable Juan R. Sánchez when he presided over matters for the Chester County Court of Common Pleas.

**Stacy Spell** is a Lieutenant with 25 years of leadership experience, beginning with his service in the United States Army Infantry. Lieutenant Spell has been with the Los Angeles Police Department (LAPD) for 21 years, where he worked a variety of assignments in operations, investigations, and training. He completed his Master's Degree in Emergency Services Administration through California State University Long Beach. Stacy is a volunteer and staunch advocate for people with Autism and developmental disabilities.

**Jacqueline A. Stefkovich**, Ed.D., J.D., is Professor of Educational Leadership at The Pennsylvania State University. Previously, she served as Associate Dean for Graduate Programs, Research, and Faculty Development and also as Head of the Department of Education Policy Studies. Before Penn State, Dr. Stefkovich was a professor and coordinator of the Educational Administration program at Temple University in Philadelphia, Pennsylvania. Dr. Stefkovich holds a doctoral degree in Administration, Planning, and Social Policy from Harvard University's Graduate School of Education and a J.D. from the University of Pennsylvania Law School. She is licensed to practice law in Pennsylvania, New Jersey, and the District of Columbia. Earlier in her career, she worked as a teacher, school counselor, state-level administrator, and educational consultant. Dr. Stefkovich's research interests focus on school law, primarily students' constitutional rights, and on issues of ethics related to school leadership. She has authored or co-authored one monograph and four books as well as some 80 book chapters and articles in law reviews and refereed journals. She has presented workshops and papers at conferences in the United States, Canada, Colombia, S.A., South Africa, Australia, and New Zealand. She has taught summer courses at Columbia University and at Temple University's campus in Tokyo, Japan.

**Lori L. Taylor**, Ph.D., is Associate Professor and Director of the Mosbacher Institute for Trade, Economics and Public Policy at Texas A&M University. She holds the Verlin and Howard Kruse '52 Founders Professorship in the Bush School of Government and Public Service and is an adjunct associate professor in Texas A&M's Department of Economics. She is a member of the Policy Advisory Board for the Texas Institute for Education Reform (TIER) and a member of the Children At Risk Institute. Dr. Taylor holds a BA in economics and a BS in business administration from the University of Kansas, and a Master's and Ph.D. in economics from the University of Rochester. Prior to joining the Bush School, Dr. Taylor spent 14 years in the Research Department of the Federal Reserve Bank of Dallas. Dr. Taylor has written extensively on variations in the cost of education and has served as a consultant on school finance issues for a variety of legislative committees and state and federal agencies. She recently served as an expert consultant for the Texas Comptroller's Financial Allocation Study for Texas (FAST), and developed the Comparable Wage Index for the National Center for Education Statistics (NCES).

**Mario S. Torres, Jr.**, Ph.D., is an Associate Professor in the Educational Administration program at Texas A&M University, College Station. Dr. Torres earned his Ph.D. in Educational Administration from Penn State University, University Park in 2003. His research interests include school law, policy, ethics, and organizational inclusion. Dr. Torres has published in the field's premier journals including *the Educational Administration Quarterly*, *Journal of Educational Administration*, the *Journal of School Leadership*, and *Education and Urban Society* and recently co-authored a book with John Hoyle entitled *Six Steps to Preparing Exemplary Principals and Superintendents: Leadership at its Best* through Rowman and Littlefield Education Press. He recently co-edited a book entitled *The Principal's Legal Handbook* through the Education Law Association. He served on summer faculty at Teachers College, Columbia University and is a research fellow with the Mexican American and U.S. Latino Research Center.

**James Vines** recently earned his Ph.D. in Educational Leadership, with a focus on Higher Education, from Clemson University. As part of his Ph.D. studies he earned a Policy Studies Certificate from the Strom Thurmond Institute of Government and Public Affairs. His dissertation titled "An Explanatory Embedded Case Study of the Proposed Megan Meier Cyberbullying Prevention & Tyler Clementi Higher Education Anti-Harassment Statutes" examined policymaking, agenda setting, and the role of advocacy coalitions in the policy process. His ongoing research agenda covers cyberbullying and the creation of federal and state statutes. James is a Frederick Douglass Teaching Scholar at Bloomsburg University. At Bloomsburg he serves as an Academic Advisor for first-year students, and teaches graduate courses in college student affairs and undergraduate courses college readiness. Dr. Vines has served as a Guest Lecturer for several doctoral seminars regarding school policies and bullying. He has represented his colleagues as a former member of the University Council for Educational Administration (UCEA) Graduate Student Council.

# INDEX